WHAT THE
THE JOB

"... A superior series of job hunt directories."

-Cornell University
Career Center
WHERE TO START

"A timely book for Chicago job hunters follows books from the same publisher that were well received in New York and Boston...A fine tool for job hunters..."

-Clarence Petersen
THE CHICAGO TRIBUNE

"Job hunting is never fun, but this book can ease the ordeal...The Southern California Job Bank will help allay fears, build confidence and avoid wheel-spinning."

-Robert W. Ross
THE LOS ANGELES TIMES

"This well-researched, well-edited job hunter's aid includes most major businesses and institutional entities in the New York metropolitan area...Highly recommended."

-Cheryl Gregory-Pindell
LIBRARY JOURNAL

"Here's the book for your job hunt...Trying to get a job in New York? I would recommend a good look through the Metropolitan New York Job Bank..."

-Maxwell Norton
NEW YORK POST

"Help on the job hunt...Anyone who is job-hunting in the New York area can find a lot of useful ideas in a new paperback called The Metropolitan New York Job Bank..."

-Angela Taylor
THE NEW YORK TIMES

"If you are looking for a job...before you go to the newspapers and the help-wanted ads, listen to Bob Adams, editor of The Metropolitan New York Job Bank."

-Tom Brokaw
NBC TELEVISION

"No longer can job seekers feel secure about finding employment just through want ads. With the tough competition in the job market, particularly in the Boston area, they need much more help. For this reason, The Boston Job Bank will have a wide and appreciative audience of new graduates, job changers, and people relocating to Boston. It provides a good place to start a search for entry-level professional positions."

-from a review in
THE JOURNAL OF COLLEGE PLACEMENT

What makes the JOB BANK SERIES the nation's premier line of employment guides:

With vital employment information on thousands of the nation's largest companies, the **JOB BANK SERIES** is the most comprehensive and authoritative set of career directories available today.

Each of the entries provides contact information, telephone numbers, addresses and a thumbnail sketch of the firm's business. Many entries also include a listing of the firm's typical professional job categories, the principal educational backgrounds sought, and the fringe benefits offered.

All of the reference information in the **JOB BANK SERIES** is as up-to-date and accurate as possible. Every year, the entire database is thoroughly researched and verified, first by mail and then by telephone. More local **JOB BANK** books come out more often than any other comparable publications.

In addition, the **JOB BANK SERIES** features important information about the local job scene--forecasts on which industries are the hottest, overviews of local economic trends, and even lists of regional professional associations, so you can get your job hunt started off right!

Looking for a particular kind of employer? Each **JOB BANK** Book features a comprehensive cross-index, which lists entries both by industry and, in multi-state job markets, by state. This means a person seeking a job in, say, finance, can identify major employers quickly and accurately.

Hundreds of discussions with job-hunters show they prefer information organized geographically, because most people look for jobs in specific areas. The **JOB BANK SERIES** offers sixteen regional titles, from Minneapolis to Houston, and from Washington, D.C., to San Francisco. The future employee moving to a particular area can review the local employment data and get a feel not only for the type of industry most common to that region, but also for major employers.

A condensed, but thorough, review of the entire job search process is presented in the chapter, 'The Basics of Job Winning', a feature that has received many compliments from career counselors. In addition, each **JOB BANK** directory is completed by a section on resumes and cover letters **The New York Times** has acclaimed as "excellent".

The **JOB BANK SERIES** gives job-hunters the most comprehensive, most timely, and most accurate career information, organized and indexed to facilitate the job search. An entire career reference library, **JOB BANK** books are the consummate employment guides.

Cover photograph courtesy of the Chicago Convention and Visitors Bureau.

Published by Bob Adams, Inc.
260 Center Street, Holbrook MA 02343

Copyright © 1982, 1985, 1986, 1987, 1989, 1990, 1991 by Bob Adams, Inc. All rights reserved. No part of the material printed may be reproduced or utilized in any form or by any means, electronic or mechanical, including photo-copying, recording, or by any information storage retrieval system without written permission from the publisher.

The Chicago Job Bank and its cover design are trademarks of Bob Adams, Inc.

Brand name products mentioned in the employer listings are proprietary property of the applicable firm, subject to trademark protection, and registered with government offices.

While the publisher has made every reasonable attempt to obtain accurate information and verify same, occasional errors are inevitable due to the magnitude of data base. Should you discover an error, please write the publisher so that corrections may be made in future editions.

The appearance of a listing anywhere in this book does not constitute an endorsement from the publisher.

Cover design by Peter Weiss.

Manufactured in the United States of America.

ISBN: 1-55850-878-3

The Chicago Job Bank
1991

Managing Editor: Carter Smith
Associate Editors: Sharon C. Cook, Peter Weiss
Editorial Assistant: Elizabeth Gale

Top career publications from Bob Adams, Inc.:

THE JOB BANK SERIES:

The Atlanta Job Bank ($12.95)
The Boston Job Bank($12.95)
The Chicago Job Bank ($12.95)
The Dallas Job Bank ($12.95)
The Denver Job Bank ($12.95)
The Detroit Job Bank ($12.95)
The Florida Job Bank ($12.95)
The Houston Job Bank ($12.95)
The Los Angeles Job Bank ($12.95)
The Minneapolis Job Bank ($12.95)
The New York Job Bank ($12.95)
The Ohio Job Bank ($12.95)
The Philadelphia Job Bank ($12.95)
The Phoenix Job Bank ($12.95)
The San Fransisco Job Bank ($12.95)
The Seattle Job Bank ($12.95)
The St. Louis Job Bank ($12.95)
The Washington D.C. Job Bank ($12.95)

The Job Bank Guide to Employment Services (covers 50 states: $129.95)
The National Job Bank ($199.95)

CAREERS

Campus-Free College Degrees ($9.95)
Careers and the College Grad ($12.95)
Careers and the Engineer ($12.95)
Careers and the MBA ($14.95)

The Complete Guide to Washington Internships ($12.95)
Harvard Guide to Careers in Mass Media ($7.95)
How to Get a Job in Education ($6.95)
International Careers ($12.95)
Job Search Handbook ($6.95)
Knock 'em Dead with Great Answers to Tough Interview Questions ($6.95)
Over 40 and Looking for Work ($7.95)
Resume Handbook ($5.95)
Resumes that Knock 'em Dead ($7.95)
Which Niche? (Answers to the Most Common Questions About Careers and Job Hunting) ($4.95)

To obtain a copy of any of these books, please check your local bookstore. If unavailable, please call 1-800-USA-JOBS toll free. (In Massachusetts call 617-767-8100).

HOW TO USE THIS BOOK

A copy of *The Chicago Job Bank* is one of the most effective tools you can find for your professional job hunt. Use this guide for the most up-to-date information on most major businesses in the greater Chicago area. It will supply you with specific addresses, phone numbers, and personnel contact information.

Separate yourself from the flock of candidates who answer the help-wanted advertisements "looking for a job." The method this book offers, direct employer contact, boasts twice the success rate of any other. Exploit it.

Read and use *The Chicago Job Bank* to uncover new opportunities. Here's how:

Read the introductory economic overview section in order to gain insight on what the overall trends are for the state's economy.

Map out your job-seeking strategy by reading the "Basics of Job Winning" section. It's a condensed review of the most effective job search methods.

Write a winning resume and learn how to sell yourself most effectively on paper, by using the "Resumes and Cover Letters" section.

Focus your career goals by reading the "Jobs in Each Industry" section. This chapter lists salary ranges, educational background requirements, and forecasts for future growth of many of today's most common professional positions.

Formulate a target list of potential employers in your field. Consult the company listings in the "Primary Chicago Employers" section. Use that information to supplement your own research, so that you'll be knowledgeable about the firm - before the interview.

Increase your knowledge of your field, as well as your connections within it, by using our listings of some of Chicago's major professional and trade associations.

Whether you are just out of college starting your first job search, looking for a new position in your current field, or entering an entirely new sector of the job market, *The Chicago Job Bank* will give you an idea of the incredible diversity of employment possibilities in one of the country's most dynamic employment centers. Your ultimate success will largely depend upon how rigorously you use the information provided herein. This one-of-a-kind employment guide can lead you to a company, and a job, that would otherwise have remained undiscovered. With a willingness to apply yourself, a positive attitude, and the research within these covers, you can attain your career objective.

TABLE OF CONTENTS

INTRODUCTION/11

A complete and informative economic overview designed to help you understand all of the forces shaping Chicago's job market.

PART ONE: THE JOB SEARCH

The Basics of Job Winning/17

A condensed review of the basic elements of a successful job search campaign. Includes advice on developing an effective strategy, time planning, preparing for interviews, interview techniques, etc.

Resumes and Cover Letters/33

Advice on creating a strong resume. Includes sample resumes and cover letters.

PART TWO: OCCUPATION PROFILES

Jobs In Each Industry/51

Descriptions of many of the most common professional positions, with forecasts of their growth potential for the 1990's. Also includes current salary ranges for each position.

PART THREE: WHERE JOBS ARE

Primary Greater Chicago Employers/109

Greater Chicago organized according to industry. Includes the address, phone number, description of the company's basic product lines and services, and for most firms, the name of the contact person for professional positions.

Accounting/Auditing/111
Advertising/Marketing/Public Relations/112
Amusement, Arts, and Recreation/116
Apparel & Textile Manufacturing/117
Banking/Savings & Loan/119

Book & Magazine Publishing/123
Broadcasting/126
Charitable/Non-profit/Humanitarian/127
Chemicals & Related: Production, Processing & Disposal/129
Colleges and Universities/133
Communications/134
Computer-Related: Hardware, Software, and Services/136
Construction: Services, Materials & Related/138
Electrical & Electronic: Manufacturing & Distribution/143
Engineering/Architecture/152
Fabricated & Primary Metal/155
Financial Services/Management Consulting/163
Food & Beverage Related: Processing & Distribution/168
General Merchandise: Retail/176
Health Care & Pharmaceuticals: Products & Services/180
Highly Diversified/186
Hotels & Restaurants/187
Insurance/190
Legal Services/196
Manufacturing: Miscellaneous Consumer/198
Manufacturing: Miscellaneous Industrial/208
Miscellaneous Services/225
Newspaper Publishing/226
Paper, Packaging & Forest Products/Containers & Glass Products/227
Petroleum & Energy Related/Mining & Drilling/236
Printing & Graphic Arts/239
Real Estate: Services, Management, And Development/241
Research & Development/242
Rubber & Plastics/243
Transportation: Equipment & Services/245
Utilities/252

Professional Employment Services/255

Includes the address, phone number, description of each company's services, contact name, and a list of positions commonly filled.

Professional & Trade Associations/295

Includes both local and national addresses and phone numbers for professional and trade associations in each field.

Index/333

INTRODUCTION

CHICAGO: AN ECONOMIC OVERVIEW

When Chicago -- long-known as America's "Second City", with a population historically second only to New York City's -- fell to number three behind Los Angeles, some saw it as an inevitable sign of things to come. Traditionally, Chicago has served as the heart of the Midwest's economy, producing more fabricated metal and food products than any other metropolis in America.

Unfortunately, the shifting U.S. economy has turned these strengths into one of Chicago's greatest potential weaknesses. Since 1970, Chicago has lost more manufacturing jobs than any other city in the nation. Today, manufacturing accounts for only 22% of the jobs in the area, down from over 30%. The steel industry alone has lost over 13,000 workers during the 1980's.

Perhaps Chicago's biggest dilemma has been attracting big business to settle in the city and then convincing them to stay. Some analysts have argued that Chicago is hampered by an unfavorable labor relations climate. Some corporations have shied away from Chicago because the city has no "right to work" laws, and because the city's laborers are so heavily unionized. Over 40 percent of the city's manufacturing employment is unionized; the national figure is about half that.

For all the despair in the manufacturing sector, Chicago's employment picture is really not all that gloomy. For instance, one recent study indicates that metropolitan Chicago actually created more jobs between 1983 and 1987 than any other area except Los Angeles. The key behind this encouraging news is that Chicago is beginning slowly but surely to adjust to the economic realities of the service-intensive 1990s. To those who view reliance on the larger players as more of a link to the past than to the future, there are encouraging developments on the small-business front. According to Dun and Bradstreet, new business incorporations climbed 40 percent in Chicago between 1980 and 1985. In 1985 alone, 34,691 new companies were started in Illinois, making the state the fifth best place for beginning businesses.

In 1986, the Chicago Capital Fund was started with the aim of granting smaller investments for firms passed over by the traditional investment community. While "seed" money is still perhaps a bit too difficult to come by for many entrepreneurs, the Capital Fund represents a new step welcomed by many business observers.

In addition, Chicago has been and will remain the financial powerhouse of the nation's midsection. In addition to a number of major banking institutions, the city is also home to the Midwest Stock Exchange (second largest securities exchange in the U.S. after the NYSE), the 7th Federal Reserve Bank, and the Chicago Board of Trade (CBT). The CBT, founded in 1848, is the oldest exchange in the United States. The Chicago Mercantile Exchange is the busiest market for perishable goods. Between the CBT and the Mercantile Exchange, over 70% of all futures are traded through Chicago.

Cook County, located to the city's northwest, has benefitted greatly from corporate relocations out of Chicago. Lured by low property taxes and extensive land, a number of large companies have relocated to Chicago's suburbs. In fact, suburbs now account for 60 percent of the metro area's population, and 60 percent of its jobs. Shopping centers, restaurants and recreational facilities have enabled the surrounding area to become more or less independent of downtown Chicago's facilities.

Lake and DuPage counties are taking advantage of local booms in the high tech area. In recent years, a number of small to mid-size companies specializing in software, pharmaceuticals and telecommunications are building a solid technological foundation. According to one area specialist, however, "The biggest impediment is that there's no technology-based institution of higher learning that serves the area the way MIT, Stanford, or even the University of Minnesota does."

Just as the Boston and Silicon Valley areas look to area schools as breeding grounds for innovation in high tech, Chicago must do the same. The city houses twelve major colleges and universities, among them the University of Chicago, Northwestern, and DePaul.

The health care sector is another in which area economists see hope for the future. At present, Chicago is third in numbers of health care facilities, maintaining 226 doctors for every 100,000 residents.

For those seeking to work in the city of Chicago, the next five to ten years should prove to be an interesting period. As reliance on the traditional companies and industries has been reassessed, the foundation for some innovative economic development has been laid. Particularly at the community level, Chicago has introduced a number of programs that have revealed promising results thus far. The increase in service sector and high technology employment have initiated a definitive transition in Chicago's economy. Although many of the area's most promising new companies operate away from the central metropolitan area, there remain avenues of very high potential for the resourceful job seeker.

PART ONE: THE JOB SEARCH

The Basics of Job Winning

THE BASICS OF JOB WINNING: A CONDENSED REVIEW

The best way to obtain a better professional job is to contact the employer directly. Broad-based statistical studies by the Department of Labor show that job seekers have found employment more successfully by contacting employers directly, than by using any other method.

However, given the current diversity, and increased specialization of both industry and job tasks it is possible that in some situations other job seeking methods may prove at least equally successful. Three of the other most commonly used methods are: relying on personal contacts, using employment services, and following up help wanted advertisements. Many professionals have been successful in finding better jobs using one of these methods. However, the Direct Contact method has an overall success rate twice that of any other method and it has been successfully used by many more professionals. So unless you have specific reasons to believe that another method would work best for you, the Direct Contact method should form the foundation of your job search effort.

The Objective

With any business task, you must develop a strategy for meeting a goal. This is especially true when it comes to obtaining a better job. First you need to clearly define your objectives.

Setting you job objectives is better known as career planning (or life planning for those who wish to emphasize the importance of combining the two). Career planning has become a field of study in and of itself. Since most of our readers are probably well-entrenched in their career path, we will touch on career planning just briefly.

If you are thinking of choosing or switching careers, we particularly emphasize two things. First choose a career where you will enjoy most of the day-to-day tasks. Sure, this sounds obvious, but most of us have at one point or another been attracted by a glamour industry or a prestigious sounding job without thinking of the most important consideration: Would we enjoy performing the everyday tasks the position entailed?

The second key consideration is that you are not merely choosing a career, but also a lifestyle. Career conselors indicate that one of the most common problems people encounter in job seeking is a lack of consideration for how well-suited they are for a particular position or career. For example, some people, attracted to management consulting by good salaries, early responsibility and high level corporate exposure, do not adapt well to the long hours, heavy travel demands, and the constant pressure to produce. So be sure to determine both for your career as a whole and for each position that you apply for, if you will easily adapt to both the day-to-day duties that the position entails and the working environment.

The Strategy

Assuming that you have now established your career objectives, the next step of the job search is to develop a strategy. If you don't take the time to develop a strategy and lay out a plan you will probably find yourself going in circles after several weeks making a random search for opportunities that always seem just beyond your reach.

Your strategy can be thought as having three simple elements:

1. Choosing a method of contacting employers.

2. Allocating your scarce resources (in most job searches the key scarce resource will be time, but financial considerations will become important in some searches too.)

3. Evaluating how the selected contact method is working and then considering adopting other methods.

We suggest you give serious consideration to using the Direct Contact method exclusively. However, we realize it is human nature to avoid putting all your eggs in one basket. So, if you prefer to use other methods as well, try to expend at least half your effort on the Direct Contact method, spending the rest on all of the other methods combined. Millions of other job seekers have already proven that Direct Contact has been twice as effective in obtaining employment, so why not benefit from their effort?
With your strategy in mind, the next step is to develop the details of the plan, or scheduling. Of course, job searches are not something that most people do regularly so it is difficult to estimate how long each step will take. Nonetheless, it is important to have a plan so that your effort can be allocated the way you have cosen, so that you can see yourself progressing, and to facilitate reconsideration of your chosen strategy.
It is important to have a realistic time frame in mind. If you will be job searching full-time, your search will probably take at least two months and very likely, substantially longer. If you can only devote part-time effort, it will probably take four months.
You probably know a few people who seem to spend their whole lives searching for a better job in their part time. Don't be one of them. Once you begin your job search on a part-time basis, give it your whole-hearted effort. If you don't really feel like devoting a lot of energy to job seeking right now, then wait. Focus on enjoying your present position, performing your best on the job, and storing up energy for when you are really ready to begin your job search.
Those of you currently unemployed should remember that job hunting is tough work physically and emotionally. It is also intellectually demanding -- requiring your best. So don't tire yourself out by working on

your job campaign around the clock. It would by be counter-productive. At the same time be sure to discipline yourself. The most logical approach to time management is to keep your regular working hours.

For those of you who are still employed, job searching will be particularly tiring because it must be done in addition to your regular duties. So don't work yourself to the point where you show up to interviews appearing exhausted and slip behind at your current job. But don't be tempted to quit! The long hours are worth it - it is much easier to sell your skills from a position of strength (as someone currently employed).

If you are searching full-time and have decided to choose a mixture of contact methods, we recommend that you divide up each week allowing some time for each method. For instance, you might devote Mondays to following up newspaper ads because most of them appear in Sunday papers. Then you might devote Tuesdays, and Wednesday mornings to working and developing the personal contacts you have, in addition to trying a few employment services. Then you could devote the rest of the week to the Direct Contact method. This is just one plan that may succeed for you.

By trying several methods at once, job-searching will be more interesting for you, and you will be able to evaluate how promising each of the methods seems, altering your time allocation accordingly. Be very careful in your evaluation, however, and don't judge the success of a particular method just by the sheer number of interviews you obtain. Positions advertised in the newspaper, for instance, are likely to generate many more interviews per opening than positions that are filled without being advertised.

If you are searching part-time and decide to try several different contact methods, we recommend that you try them sequentially. You simply won't have enough time to put a meaningful amount of effort into more than one method at once. So decide how long your job search might take. (Only a guess, of course.) And then allocate so many weeks or months for each contact method you choose to use. (We suggest that you try Direct Contact first.)

If you are expected to be in your office during the business day then you have an additional time problem to deal with. How can you work interviews into the business day? And if you work in an open office, how can you even call to set up interviews? As much as possible you should keep up the effort and the appearances on your present job. So maximize your use of the lunch hour, early in the morning and late in the afternoon for calling. If you really keep trying you will be surprised how often you will be able to reach the executive you are trying to contact during your out-of-office hours. The lunch hour for different executives will vary between 12 and 3. Also you can catch people as early as 8 AM and as late as 6 PM on frequent occasions. Jot out a plan each night on how you will be using each minute of your precious lunch break.

Your inability to interview at any time other than lunch just might work to your advantage. If you can, try to set up as many interviews as possible for your lunch hour. This will go a long way to creating a relaxed rapport. (Who isn't happy when eating?) But be sure the interviews don't stray too far from the agenda on hand.

Lunchtime interviews will be much easier for the person with substantial career experience to obtain. People with less experience will often find that they have no alternative other than taking time off for interviewing. If you have to take time off, you have to take time off. But try to do this as little as possible, Usually you should take the whole day off so that it is not blatantly obvious that you are job searching. Try to schedule in at least two, or at the most three, interviews for the same day. (It is very difficult to maintain an optimum level of energy at more than three interviews in one day.) Explain to the interviewer why you might have to juggle your interview schedule -- he/she should honor the respect you are showing your current employer by minimizing you days off and will probably appreciate the fact that another prospective employer is showing an interest in you.

Once again we need to emphasize if you are searching for a job, especially part-time, get out there and do the necessary tasks to the best of your ability and get it over with. Don't let your job search drag on endlessly.

Remember that all schedules are meant to be broken. The purpose of a schedule in your job search is not to rush you to your goal, its purpose is to map out the road ahead of you and evaluate the progress of your chosen strategy to date.

The Direct Contact Method

Once you have scheduled a time you are ready to begin using the job search method that you have chosen. In the text we will restrict discussion to use of the Direct Contact method. Sideboards will comment briefly on developing your personal contacts and using newspaper advertisements.

The first step in preparing for Direct Contact is to develop a check list for categorizing the types of firms for which you would prefer working. You might categorize firms by their product line, their size, their customer-type (such as industrial or consumer), their growth prospects, or, of course by their geographical locations. Your list of important considerations might be very short. If it is, good! The shorter it is, the easier it will be to find appropriate firms.

Then try to decide at which firms you are most likely to be able to obtain employment. You might wish to consider to what degree your particular skills might be in demand, the degree of competition for employment, and the employment outlook at the firm.

Now you are ready to assemble your list of prospective employers. Build up your list to at least 100 prospects. Then separate your prospect list into three groups. The first tier of maybe 25 firms will be your primary target market, the second group of another 25 firms will be your secondary market, and remaining names you will keep in reserve.

DEVELOPING YOUR CONTACTS

Some career counselors feel that the best route to a better job is through somebody you already know or through somebody to whom you can be introduced. The counselors recommend you build your contact base beyond your current aquaintances by asking each one to introduce you, or refer you, to additional people in your field of interest.

The theory goes like this: You might start with 15 personal contacts, each of whom introduces you to 3 additional people, for a total 45 additional contacts. Then each of these people introduces you to three additional people which adds 135 additional contacts. Theoretically, you will soon know every person in the industry.

Of course, developing your personal contacts does not usually work quite as smoothly as the theory suggests because some people will not be able to introduce you to several relevant contacts. The further you stray from your initial contact base, the weaker your references may be. So, if you do try developing your own contacts, try to begin with as large an ititial group of people you personally know as possible. Dig into your personal phone book and your holiday greeting card list and locate old classmates from school. Be particularly sure to approach people who perform your personal business such as your lawyer, accountant, banker, doctor, stockbroker, and insurance agent. These people develop a very broad contact base due to the nature of their professions.

This book will help you greatly in developing your prospect list. Refer to the primary employers section of this book. You will notice that employer listings are arranged according to industry, beginning with Accounting, followed by Advertising, and so on through to Utilities. If you know of a firm, but you're unsure of what industry it would be classified under, then refer to the alphabetically ordered employer index at the rear of the book to find the page number that the firm's listing appears on.

At this stage, once you have gotten your prospect list together and have an idea of the firms for which you might wish to work, it is best to get to work on your resume. Refer to formats of the sample resumes included in the Resumes and Cover Letters section that follows this chapter.

Once your resume is at the printer, begin research for the first batch of 25 prospective employers. You will want to determine whether you would be happy working at the firms you are researching and also get a better idea of what their employment needs might be. You also need to obtain enough information to sound highly informed about the company during phone conversations and in mail correspondence. But don't go all out on your research yet! At some of these firms you probably will not be able to arrange interviews, so save your big research effort until you start to arrange interviews. Nevertheless, you should plan to spend about 3 or 4 hours, on average, researching each firm. Do your research in batches to save time and energy. Go into one resource at a time and find out what you can about each of the 25 firms in the batch. Start with the easiest resources to use (such as this book.) Keep organized. Maintain a folder on each firm.

If you discover something that really disturbs you about the firm (i.e. perhaps they are about to close their only local office) or if you discover that your chances of getting a job there are practically nil (i.e. perhaps they just instituted a hiring freeze) then cross them off your prospect list.

If possible, supplement your research efforts with contacts to individuals who know the firm well. Ideally you should make an informal contact with someone at the particular firm, but often a contact at a direct competitor, or a major supplier or customer will be able to supply you with just as much information. At the very least try to obtain whatever printed information that the company has available, not just annual reports, but product brochures and anything else. The company might very well have printed information about career opportunities.

Getting The Interview

Now it is time to arrange an interview, time to make the Direct Contact. If you have read many books on job searching you have probably noticed that virtually all tell you to avoid the personnel office like the plague. It is said that the personnel office never hires people, they just screen out candidates. In some cases you may be able to identify and contact the appropriate manager with the authority to hire you. However, this will take a lot of time and effort in each case. Often you'll be bounced back to personnel. So we suggest that you begin your Direct Contact campaign through personnel offices. If it seems that in the firms on your prospect list that little hiring is done through personnel, you might consider an alternative course of action.

The three obvious means of initiating Direct Contact are:

-Showing up unannounced
-Phone calls
-Mail

Cross out the first one right away. You should never show up to seek a professional position without an appointment. Even if you are somehow lucky enough to obtain an interview, you will appear so unprofessional that you will not even be seriously considered.

Mail contact seems to be a good choice if you have not been in the job market for a while. You can take your time to prepare a careful letter, say exactly what you want, tuck your resume in, and then the addressee can read the material at leisure. But employers receive many resumes every day. Don't be surprised if you do not get a response to your inquiry. So don't spend weeks waiting for responses that never come. If you do send a cover letter, follow it up (or precede it) with a phone call. This will increase your impact, and underscore both your interest in the firm and the fact that you are familiar with it (because of the initial research you did.)

Another alternative is to make a "Cover Call." Your Cover Call should be just like your cover letter: concise. Your first sentence should interest the employer in you. Then try to subtly mention your familiarity with the firm. Don't be overbearing; keep your introduction to three sentences or less. Be pleasant, self confident and relaxed. This will greatly increase the chances of the person at the other end of the line developing the conversation. But don't press. When you are asked to follow up "with something in the mail" don't try to prolong the conversation once it has ended. Don't ask what they want to receive in the mail. Always send your resume and a highly personalized follow-up letter, reminding the addressee of the phone conversation. Always include a cover letter even if you are requested to send a resume. (It is assumed that you will send a cover letter too.)

Unless you are in telephone sales, making smooth and relaxed cover calls will probably not come easily. Practice them on your own and then with your friends or relatives (friends are likely to be more objective and hence, better participants.)

If you obtain an interview over the telephone, be sure to send a thank you note reiterating the points you made during the conversation. You will appear more professional and increase your impact. However, don't mail your resume once an interview has been arranged unless it is specifically requested. Take it with you to the interview instead.

DON'T BOTHER WITH MASS MAILING OR BARRAGES OF PHONE CALLS

Direct Contact does not mean burying every firm within a hundred miles with mail and phone calls. Mass mailings rarely work in the job hunt. This also applies to those letters that are personalized -- but dehumanized -- on an automatic typewriter. Don't waste your time or money on such a project; you will fool no one but yourself.

The worst part of sending out mass mailings or making unplanned phone calls is that you are likely to be remembered as someone with little genuine interest in the firm, as someone who lacks sincerity, and as somebody that nobody wants to hire.

HELP WANTED ADVERTISEMENTS

Only a small fraction of professional job openings are advertised. Yet a majority of job seekers -- and a lot of people not in the job market -- spend a lot of time studying the help wanted ads. As a result, the comptetition for advertised openings is often much more severe.

A moderate-sized Manhattan employer told us about an experience advertising in the help wanted section of a major Sunday newspaper:

It was a disaster. We had over 500 responses from this relatively small ad in just one week. We have only two phone lines in this office and one was totally knocked out. We'll never advertise for professional help again.

If you insist on following up on help wanted ads, then research a firm before you reply to an ad so that you can ascertain if you would be a suitable candidate and that you would enjoy working at a particular firm. Also such preliminary research might help to separate you from all of the other professionals responding to that ad, many of whom will only have a passing interest in the opportunity. That said, your chances of obtaining a job through the want-ads are still much smaller than they are if you use the Direct Contact method.

Preparing For The Interview

Once the interview has been arranged, begin your in-depth research. You have got to arrive at the interview knowing the company upside down and inside out. You need to know their products, their types of customers, their subsidiaries, their parent, their principle locations, their rank in the industry, their sales and profit trends, their type of ownership, their size, their current plans and much more. By this time you have probably narrowed your job search to one industry, but if you haven't then you need to be familiar with the trends in this firm's industry, the firm's principle competitors and their relative performance, and the direction that the industry leaders are headed. Dig into every resource you can! Read the company literature, the trade press, the business press, and if the company is public, call your stockbroker and ask for still additional information. If possible, speak to someone at the firm before the interview, or if not, speak to someone at a competing firm. Clearly the more time you spend, the better. Even if you feel extremely pressed for time, you should set aside at least 12 hours for pre-interview research.

If you have been out of the job market for some time, don't be surprised if you find yourself tense during your first few interviews. It will probably happen every time you re-enter the market, not just when you seek your first job after getting out of school.

Tension is natural during an interview, but if you can be relaxed you will have an advantage over the competition. Knowing you have done a thorough research job should help you relax for an interview. Also make a list of questions that you think might be asked in an interview. Think out your answers carefully. Then practice reviewing them with a friend. Tape record your responses to the questions he/she raises in the role as interviewer. If you feel particularly unsure of your interviewing skills, arrange your first interviews at firms in which you are not very interested. (But remember it is common courtesy to seem excited about the possiblity of working for any firm at which you interview.) Then practice again on your own after these first few interviews. Go over each of the questions that you were asked.

How important is the proper dress for a job interview? Buying a complete wardrobe of Brooks Brothers pinstripes, donning new wing tip shoes and having your hair trimmed every morning is not enough to guarantee your obtaining a career position as an investment banker. But on the other hand, if you can't find a clean, conservative suit and a narrow tie, or won't take the time to polish your shoes and trim and wash your hair -- then you are just wasting your time by interviewing at all.

Very rarely will the final selection of candidates for a job opening be determined by dress. So don't spend a fortune on a new wardrobe. But be sure that your clothes are adequate. Men applying for any professional position should wear a suit; women should either wear a dress or a suit (not a pant suit.) Your clothes should be at least as formal or slightly more formal and more conservative than the position would suggest.

Top personal grooming is more important than finding the perfect clothes for a job interview. Careful grooming indicates both a sense of thoroughness and self-confidence.

Be sure that your clothes fit well and that they are immaculate. Hair must be neat and clean. Shoes should be newly polished. Women need to avoid excessive jewelry and excessive makeup. Men should be freshly shaven, even if the interview is late in the day.

Be complete. Everyone needs a watch and a pen and pad of paper (for taking notes.) Finally a briefcase or folder (containing extra copies of your resume) will help complete the look of professionalism.

Sometimes the interviewer will be running behind schedule. Don't be upset, be sympathetic. He might be under pressure to interview a lot of candidates and to quickly fill a demanding position. So be sure to come to your interview with good reading material to keep yourself occupied. This will help increase your patience and ease your tenseness.

The Interview

The very beginning of the interview is the most important part because it determines the rapport for the rest of it. Those first few moments are especially crucial. Do you smile when you meet? Do you establish enough eye contact, but not too much? Do you walk into the office with a self-assured and confident stride? Do you shake hands firmly? Do you make small talk easily without being garrulous? It is human nature to judge people by that first impression, so make sure it is a good one. But most of all, try to be yourself.

Often the interviewer will begin, after the small talk, by proceeding to tell you about the company, the division, the department, or perhaps, the position. Because of your detailed research, the information about the company will be repetitive for you and the interviewer would probably like nothing better than to avoid this regurgitation of the company biography. So if you can do so tactfully, indicate to the interviewer that you are very familiar with the firm. If he/she seems intent on providing you with background information, despite your hints, then acquiesce. But be sure to remain attentive. If you can manage to generate a brief discussion of the company or the industry at this point, without being forceful, great. It will help to further build rapport, underscore your interests and increase your impact.

Soon (if it didn't begin that way) the interviewer will begin the questions. This period of the interview falls into one of two categories (or somewhere in between): either a structured interview, where the interviewer has a prescribed set of questions to ask; or an unstructured interview, where the interviewer will ask only leading questions to get you to talk about yourself, your experiences and your goals. Try to sense as quickly as possible which direction the interviewer wishes to proceed and follow along in the direction he/she seems to be leading. This will make the interviewer feel more relaxed and in control of the situation.

SOME FAVORITE INTERVIEW QUESTIONS

Tell me about yourself...

Why did you leave you last job?

What excites you in your current job?

What are your career goals?

Where would you like to be in 5 years?

What are your greatest strengths?

What are your greatest weaknesses?

Why do you wish to work for this firm?

Where else are you seeking employment?

Why should we hire you?

Many of the questions will be similar to the ones that you were expecting and you will have prepared answers. Remember to keep attuned to the interviewer and make the length of your answers appropriate to the situation. If you are really unsure as to how detailed a response the interviewer is seeking, then ask. Query if he/she would prefer more details of a particular aspect.

As the interview progresses, the interviewer will probably mention what he/she considers to be the most important responsibilities of the position. If applicable, draw parallels between your experience and the demands of the position as seen by the interviewer. Describe your past experience in the same manner that you did on your resume: emphasizing results and achievements and not merely describing activities. If you listen carefully (listening is a very important part of the interviewing process) the interviewer might very well mention or imply the skills in terms of what he/she is seeking. But don't exaggerate. Be on the level.

Try not to cover too much ground during the first interview. This interview is often the toughest, with many candidates being screened out. If you are interviewing for a very competitive position, you will have to make an impression that will last. Focus on a few of your greatest strengths that are relevant to the position. Develop these points carefully, state them again in other words, and then try to summarize them briefly at the end of the interview.

Often the interviewer will pause towards the end and ask if you have any questions. Particularly in a structured interview, this might be the one chance to really show your knowledge of and interest in the firm. Have prepared a list of specific questions that are of real interest to you. Let your questions subtly show your research and your knowledge of the firm's activities. It is wise to have an extensive list of questions, as several of them may have already been answered during the interview.

Do not allow your opportunity to ask questions to become an interrogation. Avoid bringing your list of questions to the interview. And ask questions that you are fairly certain the interviewer can answer (remember how you feel when you cannot answer a question during an interview.)

Even if you are unable to determine the salary range beforehand, do not ask about it during the first interview. You can always ask about it later. Above all, don't ask about fringe benefits until you have been offered a position. (Then be sure to get all the details.) You should be able to determine the company's policy on fringe benefits relatively easily before the interview.

Try not to be negative about anything during the interview. (Particularly any past employer or any previous job.) Be cheerful. Everyone likes to work with someone who seems to be happy.

Don't let a tough question throw you off base. If you don't know the answer to a question, say so simply -- do not apologize. Just smile. Nobody can answer every question -- particularly some of the questions that are asked in job interviews.

Before your first interview, you may have been able to determine how many interviews the employer usually has for positions at your level. (Of

YOU'RE FIRED!!

You are not the first and will not be the last to go through this traumatic experience. Thousands of professionals are fired every week. Remember, being fired is not a reflection on you as a person. It is usually a reflection of your company's staffing needs and its perception of your recent job performance. Share the fact with your relatives and friends. Being fired is not something of which to be ashamed.

Don't start your job search with a flurry of unplanned activity. Start by choosing a strategy and working out a plan. Now is not the time for major changes in your life. If possible, remain in the same career and in the same geographical location, at least until you have been working again for a while. On the other hand, if the only industry for which you are trained is leaving, or is severely depressed in your area, then you should give prompt consideration to moving or switching careers.

Register for unemployment compensation immediately. A thorough job search could take months. After all, your employers have been contributing to unemployment insurance specifically for you ever since your first job. Don't be surprised to find other professionals collecting unemployment compensation as well. Unemployment compensation is for everybody who is between jobs.

Be prepared for the question, "Why were you fired?", during job interviews. Avoid mentioning you were fired while arranging interviews. Try especially hard not to speak negatively of your past employer and not to sound particularly worried about your status of being temporarily unemployed. But don't spend much time reflecting on why you were fired or how you might have avoided it. Look ahead. Think positively. And be sure to follow a careful plan during your job search.

course it may differ quite a bit within one firm.) Usually you can count on at least three or four interviews, although some firms, such as some of the professional partnerships, are well-known to give a minimum of six interviews for all professional postions.

Depending on what information you are able to obtain you might want to vary your strategy quite a bit from interview to interview. For instance if the first interview is a screening interview then try to have a few of your strengths really stand out. On the other hand, if later interviews are primarily with people who are in a position to veto your hiring, but not to push it forward (and few people are weeded out at these stages), then you should primarily focus on building rapport as opposed to reiterating and developing your key strengths.

If it looks as though your skills and background do not match the position your interviewer was hoping to fill, ask him or her if there is another division or subsidiary that perhaps could profit from your talents.

After The Interview

Write a follow-up letter immediately after the interview, while it is still fresh in the interviewer's mind. Then, if you have not heard from the interviewer within seven days, call him/her to stress your continued interest in the firm and the position and to request a second interview.

A parting word of advice. Again and again during your job search you will be rejected. You will be rejected when you apply for interviews. You will be rejected after interviews. For every job you finally receive you will probably have received a multitude of rejections. Don't let these rejections slow you down. Keep reminding yourself that the sooner you go out and get started on your job search and get those rejections flowing in, the closer you will be to obtaining the better job.

Resumes and Cover Letters

RESUMES AND COVER LETTERS

THIS SECTION CONTAINS:

1. Resume Preparation

2. Resume Format

3. Resume Content

4. Should You Hire A Resume Writer?

5. Cover Letters

6. Sample Resumes

7. General Model For A Cover Letter

8. Sample Cover Letters

9. General Model For A Follow-up Letter

RESUMES/OVERVIEW

When filling a position, a recruiter will often have 100 plus applicants, but time to interview only the 5 or 10 most promising ones. So he or she will have to reject most applicants after a brief skimming of their resume.

Unless you have phoned and talked to the recruiter -- which you should do whenever you can -- you will be chosen or rejected for an interview entirely on the basis of your resume and cover letter. So your resume must be outstanding. (But remember -- a resume is no substitute for a job search campaign. YOU must seek a job. Your resume is only one tool.)

RESUME PREPARATION

One page, usually.

Unless you have an unusually strong background with many years of experience and a large diversity of outstanding achievements, prepare a one page resume. Recruiters dislike long resumes.

8 1/2 x 11 Size

Recruiters often get resumes in batches of hundreds. If your resume is on small sized paper it is likely to get lost in the pile. If oversized, it is likely to get crumpled at the edges, and won't fit in their files.

Typesetting

Modern photocomposition typesetting gives you the clearest, sharpest image, a wide variety of type styles and effects such as italics, bold facing, and book-like justified margins. Typesetting is the best resume preparation process, but is also the most expensive.

Word Processing

The most flexible way to get your resume typed is on a good quality word processor. With word processing, you can make changes almost instantly because your resume will be stored on a magnetic disk and the computer will do all the re-typing automatically. A word processing service will usually offer you a variety of type styles in both regular and proportional spacing. You can have bold facing for emphasis, justified margins, and clear, sharp copies.

Typing

Household typewriters and office typewriters with nylon or other cloth ribbons are NOT good for typing the resume you will have printed. If you can't get word processing or typesetting, hire a professional with a high quality office typewriter with a plastic ribbon (usually called a "carbon ribbon.")

Printing

Find the best quality offset printing process available. DO NOT make your copies on an office photocopier. Only the personnel office may see the resume you mail. Everyone else may see only a copy of it. Copies of copies quickly become unreadable. Some professionally maintained, extra-high-quality photocopiers are of adequate quality, if you are in a rush. But top quality offset printing is best.

Proofread your resume

Whether you typed it yourself or had it written, typed, or typeset, mistakes on resumes can be embarrassing, particularly when something obvious such as you name is misspelled. No matter how much you paid someone else to type or write or typeset your resume, YOU lose if there is a mistake. So proofread it as carefully as possible. Get a friend to help you. Read your draft aloud as your friend checks the proof copy. Then have your friend read aloud while you check. Next, read it letter by letter to check spelling and punctuation.

If you are having it typed or typeset by a resume service or a printer, and you can't bring a friend or take the time during the day to proof it, pay for it and take it home. Proof it there and bring it back later to get it corrected and printed.

RESUME FORMAT

(See samples)

Basic data

Your name, phone number, and a complete address should be at the top of your resume. (If you are a university student, you should also show your home address and phone number.)

Separate your education and work experience

In general, list your experience first. If you have recently graduated, list your education first, unless your experience is more important than your education. (For example, if you have just graduated from a teaching school, have some business experience and are applying for a job in business you would list your business experience first.) If you have two or more years of college, you don't need to list high schools.

Reverse chronological order

To a recruiter your last job and your latest schooling are the most important. So put the last first and list the rest going back in time.

Show dates and locations

Put the dates of your employment and education on the left of the page. Put the names of the companies you worked for and the schools you attended a few spaces to the right of the dates. Put the city and state or city and country where you studied or worked to the right of the page.

Avoid sentences and large blocks of type

Your resume will be scanned, not read. Short, concise phrases are much more effective than long winded sentences. Keep everything easy to find. Avoid paragraphs longer than six lines. Never go ten or more lines in a paragraph. If you have more than six line of information about one job or school, put it in two or more paragraphs.

RESUME CONTENT

Be factual

In many companies inaccurate information on a resume or other application material will get you fired as soon as the inaccuracy is discovered. Protect yourself.

Be positive

You are selling your skills and accomplishments in your resume. If you achieved something, say so. Put it in the best possible light. Don't hold back or be modest, no one else will. But don't exaggerate to the point of misrepresentation.

Be brief

Write down the important (and pertinent) things you have done, but do it in as few words as possible. The shorter your resume is, the more carefully it will be examined.

Work experience

Emphasize continued experience in a particular type of function or continued interest in a particular industry. De-emphasize irrelevant positions. Delete positions that you held for less than four months. (Unless you are a very recent college grad or still in school.)

Stress your results

Elaborate on how you contributed to your past employers. Did you increase sales, reduce costs, improve a product, implement a new program? Were you promoted?

Mention relevant skills and responsibilities

Be specific. Slant your past accomplishments toward the type of position that you hope to obtain. Example: Do you hope to supervise people? Then state how many people, performing what function, you have supervised.

Education

Keep it brief if you have more than two years of career experience. Elaborate more if you have less experience. Mention degrees received and any honors or special awards. Note individual courses or research projects that might be relevant for employers. For instance if you are a liberal arts major, be sure to mention courses in such areas as: accounting, statistics, computer programming, or mathematics.

Job objective?

Leave it out. Even if you are certain of exactly the type of job that you desire, the inclusion of a job objective might eliminate you from consideration for other positions that a recruiter feels are a better match for your qualifications.

Personal data

Keep it very brief. Two lines maximum. A one-word mention of commonly practiced activities such as golf, skiing, sailing, chess, bridge, tennis, etc. can prove to be good way to open up a conversation during an interview. Do not include your age, weight, height, etc.

SHOULD YOU HIRE A RESUME WRITER?

Advantages to writing it yourself: If you write reasonably well, there are some advantages to writing your resume yourself. To write it well you will have to review your experience and figure out how to explain your accomplishments in clear, brief phrases. This will help you when you explain your work to interviewers.

If your write your resume, everything in it will be in your own words -- it will sound like you. I will say what you want it to say. And you will be much more familiar with the contents. If you are a good writer, know yourself well and have a good idea of what parts of your background employers are looking for, you may be able to write your own resume better than anyone else can. If you write your resume yourself you should have someone who can be objective (preferably not a close relative) review it with you.

When should you have your resume professionally written?

If you have difficulty writing in Resume Style (which is quite unlike normal written language.) If you are unsure of which parts of your background you should emphasize, or if you think your resume would make your case better if it did not follow the standard form outlined here or in a book on resumes.

There are two reasons even some professional resume writers we know have had their resumes written with the help of fellow professionals. First, when they need the help of someone who can be objective about their background, and second, when they want an experienced sounding board to help focus their thoughts.

If you decide to hire a resume writer

The best way to choose a writer is by reputation -- the recommendation of a friend, a personnel director, your school placement officer or someone else knowledgeable in the field.

You should ask, "If I'm not satisfied with what you write, will you go over it with me and change it?"

You should ask, "How long has the person who will write my resume been writing resumes?"

There is no sure relation between price and quality, except that you are unlikely to get a good writer for less than $50 for an uncomplicated resume and you shouldn't have to pay more than $300 unless your experience is very extensive or complicated. There will be additional charges for printing.

Few resume services will give you a firm price over the phone, simply because some people's resumes are too complicated and take too long to do at any predetermined price. Some services will quote you a price that applies to almost all of their customers. Be sure to do some comparative shopping. Obtain a firm price before you engage their services and find out how expensive minor changes will be.

COVER LETTERS

Always mail a cover letter with your resume. In a cover letter you can show an interest in the company that you can't show in a resume. You can point out one or two skills or accomplishments the company can put to good use.

Make it personal

The more personal you can get, the better. If someone known to the person you are writing has recommended you contact the company, get permission to include that name in the letter. If you have the name of a person to send the letter to, make sure you have the name spelled correctly and address it directly to that person. Be sure to put the person's name and title on both the letter and envelope. This will ensure that your letter will get through to the proper person, even if a new person now occupies this position. But even if you are addressing it to the "Personnel Director" or the "Hiring Partner," send a letter.

Type cover letters in full. Don't try the cheap and easy ways like photocopying the body of your letter and typing in the inside address and salutation. You will give the impression that you are mailing to a multitude of companies and have no particular interest in any one. Have your letters fully typed and signed with a pen.

Phone

Precede or follow your mailing with a phone call.

Bring extra copies of your resume to the interview

If the person interviewing you doesn't have your resume, be prepared. Carry copies of your own. Even if you have already forwarded your resume, be sure to take extra copies to the interview, as someone other that the interviewer(s) might now have the first copy you sent.

GENERAL MODEL
FOR A COVER LETTER

>Your Address
>
>Date

Contact Person Name
Title
Company
Address

Dear Mr.(Ms.) _____:

    Immediately explain why your background makes you the best candidate for the position that you are applying for. Keep the first paragraph short and hard-hitting.

    Detail what you could contribute to this company. Show how your qualifications will benefit this firm. Remember to keep this letter short; few recruiters will read a cover letter longer than a half-a-page.

    Describe your interest in the corporation. Subtly emphasize your knowledge about this firm (the result of your research effort) and your familiarity with the industry. It is common courtesy to act extremely eager to work for any company that you interview.

    In the closing paragraph you should specifically request an interview. Include your phone number and the hours when you can best be reached. Alternatively, you might prefer to mention that you will follow-up with a phone call (to arrange an interview at a mutually convenient time) within the next several days.

>Sincerely yours,
>
>(signature)
>
>Full Name (typed)

Enc. Resume

COVER LETTER

1012 Winding Hill Road
Newark, New Jersey 07101

December 10, 19__

Mr. Daniel Wentworth
Personnel Manager
Mitchell & Brothers Engineering Services, Inc.
Central Park Square Building
New York, New York 10019

Dear Mr. Wentworth:

My diversity as well as my depth of engineering experience in the wastewater treatment field could prove to be a particularly strong asset for Mitchell & Brothers given the firm's current and continued commitment to being a pioneering innovator in the engineering and construction of wastewater treatment facilities.

I offer an extensive background in investigating, reporting and designing multimillion dollar wastewater treatment facilities, pumping facilities and sewer lines in New Jersey and in Puerto Rico. In addition I have experience in coordinating engineering services during construction of sewers and pumping facilities in Hawaii.

One of my basic strengths is my ability to act as liason for diverse engineering and non-engineering individuals and groups to keep a project on schedule and in line with funding constraints.

I have come to a point in my career where I desire to expand into areas where I might utilize over 8 years of solid engineering experience. These areas include hazardous waste treatment, industrial wastewater and water treatment, and water supply.

I will be glad to furnish any additional information you desire. You may reach me during the day at 201/576-1100. I look forward to hearing from you.

Sincerely,

John T. Lent

Enc. Resume

COVER LETTER

311 East Wind Lake Towers
8355 Western Avenue
Minneapolis, Minnesota 55431

July 10, 19__

Mr. Jorge Melendez
President
Thompson Associates, Inc.
411 Longview Parkway
Chicago, Illinois 60611

Dear Mr. Melendez:

Can you utilize the talents of a competent, motivated, and well-organized Management Generalist who is thoroughly accomplished in accounting procedures, systems analysis, office administration, and personnel evaluation?

Thompson Associates' rapid growth in addition to the fast-paced environment of the software industry may have created general business needs best handled by a Management Generalist familiar with the software industry. A Management Generalist could perform tasks that would allow senior engineers to focus exclusively on creating the innovative software packages that have brought Thompson Associates the success it enjoys today.

I can offer a strong, multifaceted business background in which I have achieved notable success in communication, financial management, procedures analysis, and personnel development.

Can we meet to discuss what I might be able to contribute to Thompson Associates? You may reach me by calling 612/395-5847 or by sending a note to the above address. I look forward to hearing from you. Thank you for your consideration.

Sincerely,

Nancy L. Mellon

Enc. Resume

COVER LETTER

411 Lookout Avenue
Apartment 48c
Boston, Massachusetts 02131

March 15, 19__

Ms. Andrea Larson
Sales Manager
Northern Products Corporation
412 Elm River Expressway
Denver, Colorado 80201

Dear Ms. Larson:

I seek a position as a sales representative with Northern Products and I offer, in return, thorough industry experience and more than eleven years of solid practical background in sales.

As a sample of sales achievement, I increased my personal monthly gross sales volume to a point where it tripled the combined sales of three other full-time representatives for one ski manufacturer. Also, I have won numerous international and domestic sales awards.

As an experienced sales representative, I have succeeded in improving area or regional sales by utilizing a combination of aggressiveness, enthusiasm, and persistence. I have been able to bring out these traits in those whom I have hired and trained in my capacity as National Sales Instructor for two companies.

I feel that your new line of fiberglass competition skis offer an unbeatable price/performance combination for the serious skier. I am firmly convinced that I can improve your market penetration in the lucrative Upstate New York Area at least to a top five position.

I am an avid skier. As such, I am familiar with not only the technical terms involved, but with the types of equipment available and the extent to which it is marketed.

I look forward to hearing from you.

Sincerely,

Wayne L. Swanson

Enc. Resume

CHRONOLOGICAL RESUME

(Prepared on word processor.)

JOAN M. MORRISON
43 Hilltop Drive
Chicago, Illinois 60614
(312) 312-3123 (home)
(312) 423-4234 (work)

RELATED EXPERIENCE

1972-Present GREAT LAKES PUBLISHING CO., CHICAGO, ILLINOIS
Operations Supervisor (1976-Present) in the Engineering Division of this major trade publishing house, responsible for maintaining on line computerized customer files, title files, accounts receivable, inventory and sales files.

Organize department activities, establish priorities and train personnel. Provide corporate accounting with monthly reports of sales, earned income from journals, samples, inventory levels/value and sales tax data. Divisional sales average $3 Million annually.

Senior Customer Service Representative (1974-1976) in the Construction Division, answered customer service inquiries regarding orders and accounts receivable, issued return and shortage credits and expedited special sales orders for direct mail and sales to trade schools.

Customer Service Representative (1972-1973), International Division. Same duties as for Construction Division except sales were to retail stores and universities in Europe.

1970-1972 B. DALTON, BOOKSELLER, SALT LAKE CITY, UTAH
Assistant Manager of this retail branch of a major domestic book seller, maintained all paperback inventories at necessary levels, deposited receipts daily and created window displays.

EDUCATION

1966-1970 UNIVERSITY OF MAINE, ORONO, MAINE
Awarded a degree of Bachelor of Arts in French Literature.

LANGUAGES Fluent in French. Able to write in French, German and Spanish.

PERSONAL Willing to travel and relocate, particularly in Europe.

References available upon request.

CHRONOLOGICAL RESUME

(Prepared on word processor.)

JAMES WASHINGTON WHITE, JR.

U.S. Address:
486 East 77th Street
New York, New York 10021
(212) 212-2121

Jamaican Address:
Room 1234·
Playboy, Jamaica
Doctor's Beach, Jamaica
(809) 326-1312

experience
1974-present   PLAYBOY, JAMAICA LTD.   DOCTOR'S BEACH, JAMAICA
Resident Engineer for this publicly owned resort with main offices in Chicago, Illinois responsibilities include:

Maintain electrical generating and distribution equipment.

Supervise an eight-member staff in maintenance of refrigeration equipment, power and light generators, water purification plant, and general construction machinery.

1972-1974   NIGRIL BEACH HOTEL   NIGRIL BEACH, JAMAICA
Resident Engineer for a privately-held resort, assigned total responsibility for facility generating equipment.

Directed maintenance, operation and repair of diesel generating equipment.

1970-1972   Directed overhaul of turbo generating equipment in two Mid-Western localities and assisted in overhaul of a turbo generating unit in Mexico.

1965-1970   CAPITAL CITY ELECTRIC   WASHINGTON, D.C.
Service Engineer for the power generation service division of this regional power company, supervised the overhaul, maintenance and repair of large generators and associated auxiliary equipment.

other experience   A Night File Supervisor for Columbia Mutual Life Insurance Company (1963-1965) and an Apprentice Welder at the Potomac Naval Shipyard from 1961-1962.

Volunteer Co-ordinator Washington D.C. NAACP 1969; Activities Co-chairman 1968

education
1962-1965   FRANKLIN INSTITUTE   BALTIMORE, MARYLAND
Awarded a degree of Associate of Engineering. Concentration in Mechanical Power Engineering Technology.

personal   Willing to travel and relocate.
Interested in sailing, scuba diving, deep sea fishing.

References available upon request.

CHRONOLOGICAL RESUME

(Prepared on office quality typewriter.)

STEVEN M. PHILLIPS

1015 Commonwealth Avenue
Apartment 16
Boston, Massachusetts 02145
Phone: 617/277-1483

Home Address:
507 North 6th Street
Houston, Texas 77024
Phone: 713/461-2341

education
1977-1981 BOSTON UNIVERSITY   BOSTON, MASSACHUSETTS

Candidate for the degree of Bachelor of Arts in June 1981, majoring in Mathematics. Courses include Statistics and Computer Programming. Thesis topic: "New Applications of Co-Linear Coordinates." 3.4 grade point average. Awarded the Elliot Smith Scholarship in 1978.

Treasurer of The Mathematics Club. Responsible for $7,000.00 annual budget. Co-chairperson of Boston University's semi-annual symposium on The Future of Mathematics. Assistant Photography Editor of The Free Press. Exhibitor and prize-winner at local photography shows. Helped to establish university darkroom.

1973-1977 HOUSTON PUBLIC HIGH SCHOOL   HOUSTON, TEXAS

Received High School Diploma in June 1977. Achieved Advance Placement Standing in Calculus and Physics. Academic Honors all terms. Assistant Editor of Year-Book.

experience
summer
1980 DATA PUNCH ASSOCIATES, INC.   NEW YORK, NEW YORK

Mail Clerk and Courier for the Accounting Department. Reorganized mail distribution and sorting system in the department. Delivered sensitive documents to the executive branch.

summers
1978, 1979 HARVEY'S BEEFBURGERS, INC.   HOUSTON, TEXAS

Began work as a dishwasher. Was promoted to short-order cook.

part-time BOSTON UNIVERSITY   BOSTON, MASSACHUSETTS

One of six students invited to tutor for The Department of Mathematics. Also graded student papers and worked as a Research Assistant in Theoretical Calculus.

part-time
1977-1978 BOSTON UNIVERSITY BOOKSTORE   BOSTON, MASSACHUSETTS

Floor and Stockroom Clerk. Responsibilities included arranging merchandise displays, customer service and checking invoices against shipments.

personal
background Enjoy photography, reading science fiction, and playing bridge. Published two articles in mathematics journals.

references Personal references available upon request.

FUNCTIONAL RESUME

(Prepared on photo typesetter.)

JOHN SINGLETON COPLEY
420 Boylston Street
Pittsburgh, Pennsylvania 15234
412/323-3491

Solid background in plate making, separations, color matching, background definition, printing, mechanicals, color corrections, and supervision of personnel. A highly motivated manager, adept problem-solver and effective communicator. Proven ability to:

- Create Commercial Graphics
- Produce Embossing Drawings
- Color Separate
- Analyze Consumer Acceptance
- Meet Graphic Deadlines
- Control Quality
- Resolve Printing Problems
- Expedite Printing Operations

Qualifications

Printing—Black and white and color. Can judge acceptability of color reproduction by comparing it with original. Can make four or five color corrections on all media. Have long developed ability to restyle already reproduced four-color art work. Can create perfect tone for black and white match fill-ins for resume cover letters.

Customer Relations—Work well with customers to assure specifications are met and customers are satisfied. Can guide work through entire production process and strike a balance between technical printing capabilities and need for customer approval.

Management—Schedule work to meet deadlines. Direct staff in production procedures. Control budgets, maintain quality control from inception of project through final approval for printing.

Specialties Make silk screen overlays and overlays for a multitude of processes. Velo bind, GBC bind, perfect bind. Gold leaf embossing, silver inlay stamping. Have knowledge to prepare posters, flyers, business cards and personalized stationery.

Personnel Supervision – Foster an atmosphere that encourages highly talented artists to balance high level creativity with a maximum of production. Have managed a group of over 20 photographers, developers, plate etchers, checkers and artists. Met or beat production deadlines. Am continually instructing new employees, apprentices and students in both artistry and technical operations.

Experience

Assistant Production Manager, Artsign Digraphics, Erie, PA (1952-Present) Part time.
Professor of Graphic Arts, Pennsylvania College of Fine Arts, Pittsburgh, PA (1950-Present)

Education

Massachusetts Conservatory of Art PhD 1950

GENERAL MODEL
FOR A FOLLOW-UP LETTER

```
                                        Your
                                        Address
                                        Date

Contact Person Name
Title
Company
Address

Dear Mr.(Ms.) _____:

     Remind the interviewer of the position for
which you were interviewed, as well as the date.
Thank him (her) for the interview.

     Confirm your interest in the opening and the
organization.  Use specifics to emphasize both
that you have researched the firm in detail and
considered how you would fit into the company and
the position.

     Like in your cover letter, emphasize one or
two of your strongest qualifications and slant
them toward the various points that the inter-
viewer considered the most important for the posi-
tion.  Keep the letter brief, a half-page is
plenty.

     If appropriate, close with a suggestion for
further action, such as a desire to have addi-
tional interviews.  Mention your phone number and
the hours that you can best be reached.  Alter-
natively, you may prefer to mention that you will
follow-up with a phone call in several days.

                              Sincerely yours,

                              (signature)

                              Your Full Name (typed)
                              Phone number (if not in text)
```

PART TWO: OCCUPATION PROFILES

Jobs In Each Industry

JOBS IN EACH INDUSTRY

The following chapter includes descriptions of many of the most common occupations, with an emphasis on those that have especially strong growth outlooks for the 1990's. For each position, you will find a brief description of what the position entails, the background or qualifications you would need for entering and advancing in that occupation, the salary expectations for various levels within the occupational category, and a forecast of the job's growth potential for the 1990's.

The occupations listed are as follows:

> *Accountant/Auditor*
> *Actuary*
> *Administrator*
> *Advertising Worker*
> *Architect*
> *Attorney*
> *Bank Officer/Manager*
> *Biochemist*
> *Blue-Collar Worker Supervisor*
> *Buyer/Merchandise Manager*
> *Chemist*
> *Claim Representative*
> *Commercial Artist*
> *Data Processing Specialist*
> *Dietician/Nutritionist*
> *Draftsperson*
> *Economist*
> *Engineer*
> *Financial Analyst*
> *Food Technologist*
> *Forester*
> *Geographer*
> *Geologist/Geophysicist*
> *Hotel Manager/Assistant Manager*
> *Industrial Designer*
> *Insurance Agent/Broker*
> *Manager*
> *Manaufacturer's Sales Worker*
> *Personnel and*
>   *Labor Relations Specialist*

Physicist
Public Relations Worker
Purchasing Agent
Quality Control Supervisor
Reporter/Editor
Securities and Financial
  Services Sales Representative
Statistician
Systems Analyst
Technical Writer/Editor
Underwriter

ACCOUNTANT/AUDITOR

DESCRIPTION:

Accountants prepare and analyze financial reports that furnish important financial information. Four major fields are public, management, government accounting, and internal auditing. Public accountants have their own businesses or work for accounting firms. Management accountants, also called industrial or private accountants, handle the financial records of their company. Government accountants examine the records of government agencies and audit private businesses and individuals whose dealings are subject to government regulation. Accountants often concentrate on one phase of accounting. For example, many public accountants may specialize in auditing, tax, or estate planning. Others specialize in management consulting and give advice on a variety of matters. Management accountants provide the financial information executives need to make sound business decisions. They may work in areas such as taxation, budgeting, costs, or investments. Internal auditing, a specialization within management accounting, is rapidly growing in importance. Internal auditors examine and ensure efficient and economical operation. Government accountants are often Internal Revenue Service agents or are involved in financial management and budget administration.

About 60 percent of all accountants do management accounting. An additional 25 percent are engaged in public accounting through independent firms. Other accountants work for government, and some teach in colleges and universities. Accountants and auditors are found in all business, industrial, and governmental organizations.

BACKGROUND AND QUALIFICATIONS:

Although many graduates of business schools are successful, most public accounting and business firms require applicants for accountant and internal auditor positions to have at least a BA in Accounting or a closely related field. Many employers prefer those with a Master's degree in

Accounting. Most large employers prefer applicants who are familiar with computers and their applications in accounting and internal auditing.

Previous experience in accounting can help an applicant get a job. Many colleges offer students an opportunity to gain experience through summer or part-time internship programs conducted by public accounting firms. Such training is invaluable in gaining permanent employment in the field.

Professional recognition through certification or licensing also is extremely valuable. Anyone working as a certified public accountant (CPA) must hold a certificate issued by a state board of accountancy. All states use the four-part Uniform CPA Exam, prepared by the American Institute of Certified Public Accountants, to establish certification. The CPA exam is very rigorous, and candidates are not required to pass all four parts at once. Most states require applicants to have some public accounting experience for a CPA certificate, and those with BA's often need two years of experience. New trends require the candidate to have a BA plus 30 additional semester hours.

The Institute of Internal Auditors confers the Certified Internal Auditor (CIA) certificate upon graduates from accredited colleges and universities who have completed three years internal auditing and who have passed a four-part exam. The National Association of Accountants (NAA) confers the Certificate in Management Accounting (CMA) upon candidates who pass a series of uniform exams and meet specific educational and professional standards. A growing number of states require both CPA's and licensed public accountants to complete a certain number of hours of continuing education before licenses can be renewed. Increasingly, accountants are studying computer programming so they can adapt accounting procedures to data processing.

Junior public accountants usually start by assisting with auditing work for several clients. They may advance to intermediate positions with greater responsibility in one or two years, and to senior positions within another few years. Those who deal successfully with top industry executives often become supervisors, managers, or partners, or transfer to executive positions in private firms. Beginning management accountants often start as ledger accountants, junior internal auditors, or as trainees for technical accounting positions. They may advance to chief plant accountant, chief cost accountant, budget director, or manager of internal auditing. Some become controllers, treasurers, financial vice-presidents, or corporation presidents.

EARNINGS:

Starting: with BA, average $21,200; with MA, average $25,600. Entire career: Range is roughly $20,000 to $70,000.

OUTLOOK:

Employment of accountants and auditors is expected to grow much faster than the average for all occupations through the year 2000 due to the key role these workers play in the management of all types of businesses. Although increased demand will generate many new jobs, most openings will result from the need to replace workers who leave the occupation or retire. While accountants and auditors tend to leave the profession at a lower rate than members of most other occupations, replacement needs will be substantial because the occupation is large.

Accountants rarely lose their jobs when other workers are laid off during hard economic times. Financial information must be developed and tax reports prepared regardless of the state of the economy.

ACTUARY

DESCRIPTION:

Actuaries design insurance and pension plans that can be maintained on a sound financial basis. They assemble and analyze statistics to calculate probabilities of death, sickness, injury, disability, unemployment, retirement, and property loss from accident, theft, fire, and other hazards. Actuaries use this information to determine the expected insured loss. The actuary calculates premium rates and determines policy contract provision for each type of insurance offered. Most actuaries specialize in either life and health insurance, or property and liability (casualty) insurance; a growing number specialize in pension plans. About two-thirds of all actuaries work for private insurance companies, the majority in life insurance. Consulting firms and rating bureaus employ about one-fifth of all actuaries. Other actuaries work for private organizations administering independent pension and welfare plans.

BACKGROUND AND EXPERIENCE:

A good educational background for a beginning job in a large life or casualty insurance company is a Bachelor's degree in Mathematics or Statistics; a degree in Actuarial Science is preferred. Courses in accounting, computer science, economics, and insurance also are useful. Of equal importance, however, is the need to pass one or more of the exams offered by professional actuarial societies. Three societies sponsor programs leading to full professional status in the specialty. The Society of Actuaries gives nine actuarial exams for the life and health insurance, and pension fields; The Casualty Actuarial Society gives 10 exams for the property and liability fields; and the American Society of Pension Actuaries gives nine exams covering the pension field.

Actuaries are encouraged to complete the entire series of exams as soon as possible; completion generally takes from five to ten years. Actuaries who complete five exams in either the life insurance segment of the pension series, or seven exams in the casualty series are awarded "associate" membership in their society. Those who have passed an entire series receive full membership and the title "Fellow".

Beginning actuaries often rotate among different jobs to learn various actuarial operations and to become familiar with different phases of insurance work. At first, their work may be routine, such as preparing tabulations for actuarial tables or reports. As they gain experience, they may supervise clerks, prepare correspondence and reports, and do research. Advancement to more responsible positions such as assistant, associate, or chief actuary depends largely on job performance and the number of actuarial exams passed. Many actuaries, because of their broad knowledge of insurance and related fields, are selected for administrative positions in other company activities, particularly in underwriting, accounting, or data processing. Many advance to top executive positions.

EARNINGS:

New college graduates entering the life insurance field without having passed any exams average $19,000 to $24,000. After the completion of the first exam, the average is $21,000 to $25,000, and with two exams passed, the average is $23,000 to $26,000. Each exam passed usually earns an approximate $1,000 increase. Associates average $32,000 to $45,000. Beginning fellows average $44,000 to $55,000 and fellows with several years experience average more than $60,000.

OUTLOOK:

Employment of actuaries is expected to grow much faster than the average for all occupations through the year 2000. Most job openings, however, are expected to arise each year to replace actuaries who transfer to other occupations, or retire. Job opportunities should be favorable for college graduates who have passed at least two actuarial exams while still in school and have a strong mathematical and statistical background.

ADMINISTRATOR

DESCRIPTION:

Administrators perform a wide variety of office paperwork tasks. These tasks might range from preparing a summary of sales activity to filing and retrieving information. A lower-level administrator might serve primarily as a typist, office machine operator, or secretary, being closely supervised by an office superior. An upper-level administrator might supervise the work of many office workers and be responsible for a broad range of office duties that support an organization's activities.

BACKGROUND AND QUALIFICATIONS:

Because of the broad range of duties and responsibilities of administrators at different levels or within different organizations, the actual job and its requisite background and experience may vary greatly from one firm to the next, and from one position to the next. However, all but the highest managerial levels of administrative work require strong office skills such as fast and accurate typing and the ability to prepare business correspondence. In larger organizations with more complex office tasks, a college background is becoming an increasingly valuable asset. Also, experience or familiarity with computers, word processors, or data processing equipment greatly improves an applicant's employability and chances for promotion.

EARNINGS:

Pay varies widely depending upon the company and position. A position requiring only a high school diploma and no typing skills may pay $12,000 per year, while an entry-level position requiring a college degree, fast typing skills, and the ability to take shorthand may pay $18,000 per year.

OUTLOOK:

Despite the nearly universal use of computer and word processing automation in the office, administrative positions are still expected to offer above average growth. Also, with many new entrants to the job market trying to obtain junior managerial jobs and similar posts, Administrative positions are likely to be less competitive than many other types of jobs. Administrators are found in all industries, but especially in banking, insurance, utilities, and other companies with a high volume of paperwork.

ADVERTISING WORKER

DESCRIPTION:

There are several different occupations commonly associated with the field of advertising. Advertising managers direct the advertising program of the business for which they work. They determine the size of the advertising budget, the type of ad and the media to use, and what advertising agency, if any, to employ. Managers who decide to employ an agency work closely with the advertising agencies to develop advertising programs for client firms and individuals. Copywriters develop the text and headlines to be used in the ads. Media directors negotiate contracts for advertising for advertising space or air time. Production managers and their assistants arrange to have the ad printed for publication, filmed for television, or recorded for radio.

BACKGROUND AND QUALIFICATIONS:

Most employers prefer college graduates. Some employers seek persons with degrees in advertising with heavy emphasis on marketing, business, and journalism; others prefer graduates with a liberal arts background; some employers place little emphasis on the type of degree. Opportunities for advancement in this field generally are excellent for creative, talented, and hard-working people. For example, copywriters and account executives may advance to more responsible work in their specialties, or to managerial jobs if they demonstrate ability in dealing with clients. Some especially capable employees may become partners in an existing agency, or they may establish their own agency.

EARNINGS:

In 1986, the lowest 10 percent of advertising workers earned $17,700 or less, while the top 10 percent earned over $52,500. Salaries between $75,000 and $100,000 are not uncommon. Many earn bonuses equal to 10 percent or more of their regular salaries. Salary levels vary substantially depending upon the level of managerial responsibility, length of service, and size and location of the firm.

OUTLOOK:

Employment of advertising managers is expected to increase faster than the average for all occupations through the year 2000 as increasingly intense domestic and foreign competition in products and services offered consumers requires greater marketing and promotional efforts. In addition to rapid growth, many job openings will occur each year to replace managers who move into the top positions or retire. However, the ample supply of experienced professional and technical personnel and recent college graduates seeking these management positions may result in substantial job competition.

ARCHITECT

DESCRIPTION:

Architects provide a wide variety of professional services to individuals, organizations, corporations, or government agencies planning a building project. Architects are involved in all phases of development of a building or project, from the initial discussion of general ideas through completion of construction. Their duties require a variety of skills, including design, engineering, managerial, and supervisory.

The architect and client first discuss the purposes, requirements, and cost of a project. The architect then prepares schematic drawings that show the scale and the mechanical and structural relationships of the building. If the schematic drawings are accepted, the architect develops a final design showing the floor plans and the structural details of the project.

Architects also specify the building materials and, in some cases, the interior furnishings. In all cases, the architect must ensure that the structure's design and specifications conform to local and state building codes, zoning laws, fire regulations, and other ordinances. After all drawings are completed, the architect assists the client in selecting a contractor and negotiating the construction contract. As construction proceeds, the architect visits the building site from time to time to ensure that the contractor is following the design using the specified materials.

Besides designing structures, architects may also help in selecting building sites, preparing cost and land-use studies, and long-range planning for site development. When working on large projects or for large architectural firms, architects often specialize in one phase of work, such as designing or administering construction contracts. This often requires working with engineers, urban planners, landscape architects, and others.

Most architects work for architectural firms or for builders, real estate firms, or other businesses that have large construction programs. Some work for governmental agencies. Although found in many areas, a large proportion of architects are employed in seven cities: Boston, Chicago, Los Angeles, New York, Philadelphia, San Francisco, and Washington, DC.

BACKGROUND AND QUALIFICATIONS:

Every state requires individuals to be licensed before they may call themselves architects or contract for providing architectural services. To qualify for the licensing exam, a person must have either a Bachelor of Architecture degree followed by three years of acceptable practical experience in an architect's office, or a Master of Architecture degree followed by two years of experience. As a substitute for formal training, most states accept additional experience (usually 12 years) and successful completion of a qualifying test for admission to the licensing examination. Many architectural school graduates work in the field although they are not licensed. However, a registered architect is required to take legal responsibility for all work. New graduates usually begin as drafters for architectural firms, where they prepare architectural drawings and make models of structures under the direction of a registered architect. After several years of experience, they may advance to Chief or Senior Drafter responsible for all major details of a set of working drawings, and for supervising other drafters. Others may work as designers, construction contract administrators, or specification writers who prepare documents that specify the building materials, their method of installation, the quality of finishes, required tests, and many other related details.

EARNINGS:

The median annual earnings for salaried architects who worked full time were about $30,000 in 1986. The middle 50 percent earned between $21,700 and $37,600. The top 10 percent earned more than $51,000 and the lowest 10 percent, less than $16,200.

Architects who are partners in well-established architectural firms or solo practitioners generally earn much more than their salaried employees, but their income may fluctuate due to changing business conditions. Architects may have difficulty getting established in their own practices and may go through a period when their expenses are greater than their income.

OUTLOOK:

Employment of architects is expected to rise faster than the average for all occupations through the year 2000, although growth in employment will be slower than in recent years. However, demand for architects is highly dependent upon the level of construction, particularly of non-residential structures such as office buildings and shopping centers. Although rapid growth in this area is expected, construction is sensitive to cyclical changes in the economy. During recessions or slow periods for construction, architects will face competition for job openings or clients, and layoffs may occur.

ATTORNEY

DESCRIPTION:

Certain activities are common to nearly every attorney's work. Probably the most fundamental is interpretation of the law. Every attorney, whether representing the defendant in a murder trial, or the plaintiff in a lawsuit, combines an understanding of the relevant laws with knowledge of the facts in the case, to determine how the first affects the second. Based on this determination, the attorney decides what action would best serve the interests of the client.

A significant number specialize in one branch of law, such as corporate, criminal, labor, patent, real estate, tax, admiralty, probate, or international law. Communications lawyers, for example, may represent radio and television stations in their dealings with the Federal Communications Commission in such matters as preparing and filing license renewal applications, employment reports, and other documents required by the FCC on a regular basis. Lawyers representing public utilities before state and federal regulatory agencies handle matters involving utility rates. They develop strategy, arguments, and testimony; prepare cases for presentation;

and argue the case. These attorneys also inform clients about changes in regulations and give advice about the legality of certain actions.

A single client may employ a lawyer full time. Known as House Counsel, this lawyer usually advises a company about legal questions that arise from business activities. Such questions might involve patents, governments regulations, a business contract with another company, or a collective bargaining agreement with a union.

Some attorneys use their legal background in administrative or managerial positions in various departments of large corporations. A transfer from a corporation's legal department to another department is often viewed as a way to gain administrative experience and rise in the ranks of management. People may also use their legal background as journalists, management consultants, financial analysts, insurance claim adjusters, real estate appraisers, lobbyists, tax collectors, probation officers, and credit investigators.

BACKGROUND AND QUALIFICATIONS:

To practice law in the courts of any state, a person must be admitted to its bar. Applicants for admission to the bar must pass a written examination; however, a few states drop this requirement for graduates from its own law schools. Lawyers who have been admitted to the bar in one state may be admitted in another without taking an examination if they meet the state's standard of good moral character and have a specified period of legal experience. Federal courts and agencies set their own qualifications for those practicing before them. To qualify for the bar examination in most states, an applicant must complete at least three years of college, and graduate from a law school approved by the American Bar Association

EARNINGS:

Beginning attorneys in private industry averaged nearly $31,000 in 1986. In the Federal Government, annual starting salaries for attorneys in 1987 were about $22,500 or $27,200, depending upon academic and personal qualifications. Factors affecting the salaries offered to new graduates include: Academic record; type, size, and location of employers; and the desired specialized educational background. The field of law makes a difference, too. Patent lawyers, for example, generally are among the highest paid attorneys.

Salaries of experienced attorneys also vary widely according to the type, size, and location of the employers. The average salary of the most experienced lawyers in private industry in 1986 was over $101,000. General attorneys in the Federal Government averaged around $46,000 a year in 1986; the relatively small number of patent attorneys in the Federal Government averaged around $55,400.

OUTLOOK:

Rapid growth in the nation's requirements for lawyers is expected to bring job openings into rough balance with the relatively stable number of law school graduates each year and result in an easing of competition for jobs through the year 2000. During the 1970's, the annual number of law school graduates more than doubled, even outpacing the rapid growth of jobs. Although graduates with superior academic records from well-regarded law schools continued to enjoy excellent opportunities, most graduates encountered increasingly keen competition for jobs. Growth in the yearly number of law school graduates has tapered off during the 1980's, but, nevertheless, the number remains at a level high enough to tax the economy's capacity to absorb them. The number of law school graduates is expected to continue to remain near its present level through the year 2000, allowing employment growth to bring the job market for lawyers back into balance.

Employment of lawyers has grown very rapidly since the early 1970's, and is expected to continue to grow much faster than the average for all occupations through the year 2000. Increased population and growing business activity help sustain the strong growth in demand for attorneys. This demand also will be spurred by growth of legal action in such areas as employee benefits, consumer protection, the environment, and safety, and an anticipated increase in the use of legal services by middle-income groups through legal clinics and prepaid legal service programs.

Turnover of jobs in this occupation is low because its members are well paid and enjoy considerable social status, and a substantial educational investment is required for entry. Nevertheless, most job openings will stem from the need to replace lawyers who transfer to other occupations or retire.

BANK OFFICER/MANAGER

DESCRIPTION:

Because banks offer a broad range of services, a wide choice of careers is available. Loan officers may handle installment, commercial, real estate, or agricultural loans. To evaluate loan applications properly, officers need to be familiar with economics, production, distribution, merchandising, and commercial law, as well as having a knowledge of business operations and financial analysis. Bank officers in trust management must have knowledge of financial planning and investment for investment research for estate and trust administration. Operations officers plan, coordinate, and control the work flow, update systems, and strive for administrative efficiency. Careers in bank operations include electronic data processing manager and other positions involving internal and customer services. A correspondent bank officer is responsible for relations with other banks; a branch manager, for all functions of a branch office; and an international officer, for advising customers with financial dealings abroad. A working knowledge of a foreign country's financial system, trade relations, and economic conditions is beneficial to those interested in international banking. Other career fields for bank officers are auditing, economics, personnel administration, public relations, and operations research.

BACKGROUND AND QUALIFICATIONS:

Bank officers and management positions generally are filled by management trainees, and occasionally by promoting outstanding bank clerks and tellers. A Business Administration degree with concentrations in finance or a liberal arts curriculum, including accounting, economics, commercial law, political science, or statistics, serves as excellent preparation for officer trainee positions. In large banks that have special training programs, promotions may occur more quickly. For a senior officer position, however, an employee usually needs many years of experience. Although experience, ability, and leadership are emphasized for promotion, advancement may be accelerated by special study. The American Bankers Association (ABA) offers courses, publications, and other training aids to officers in every phase of banking. The American Institute of Banking, an arm of the ABA, has long filled the same educational need among bank support personnel.

EARNINGS:

The median salary of financial manager was $30,400 in 1986. The lowest 10 percent earned $17,100 or less, while the top 10 percent earned over $52,000. The salary level depends upon the size and location of the firm, and is likely to be higher in large institutions and cities. Many financial managers in private industry receive additional compensation in the form of bonuses, which also vary substantially by size of firm.

OUTLOOK:

Employment of financial managers is expected to increase about as fast as the average for all occupations through the year 2000. Expanding automation - such as use of computers for electronic funds transmission and for data and information processing - may make financial managers more productive. However, the growing need for skilled financial management in the face of increasing domestic and foreign competition, changing laws regarding taxes and other financial matters, and greater emphasis on accurate reporting of financial data should spur demand for financial managers. New jobs will also be created by the increasing variety and complexity of services - including financial planning - offered by financial institutions. However, most job openings will result from the need to replace those who transfer to other fields or retire.

BIOCHEMIST

DESCRIPTION:

Biochemists study the chemical composition and behavior of living things. They often study the effects of food, hormones, or drugs on various organisms. The methods and techniques of biochemists are applied in areas such as medicine and agriculture. More than three out of four biochemists work in basic and applied research activities. Some biochemists combine research with teaching in colleges and universities. A few work in industrial production and testing activities. About one-half of all biochemists work for colleges or universities, and about one-fourth for private industry, primarily in companies manufacturing drugs, insecticides, and cosmetics. Some biochemists work for non-profit research institutes and foundations; others for federal, state, and local government agencies. A few self-employed biochemists are consultants to industry and government.

BACKGROUND AND QUALIFICATIONS:

The minimum educational requirement for many beginning jobs as a biochemist, especially in research and teaching, is an advanced degree. A PhD is a virtual necessity for persons who hope to contribute significantly to biochemical research and advance to many management or administrative jobs. A BS in Biochemistry, Biology, or Chemistry may qualify some persons for entry jobs as research assistants or technicians. Graduates with advanced degrees may begin their careers as teachers or researchers in colleges or universities. In private industry, most begin in research jobs, and with experience may advance to positions in which they plan and supervise research. New graduates with a BA or BS often start work as research assistants or technicians. These jobs in private industry often involve testing and analysis.

EARNINGS:

According to the College Placement Council, beginning salary offers in private industry in 1986 averaged $19,000 a year for bachelor's degree recipients in biochemistry.
In the Federal Government in 1987, biological scientists having a BS could begin at $14,822 to $22,458, depending on their college records. Those having an MS could start at $18,358 to $22,458. Those with a PhD could begin at between $27,172 and $32,567 a year. Biological scientists in the Federal Government averaged $37,200 a year in 1986.

OUTLOOK:

Employment of biochemists is expected to increase about as fast as the average for all occupations through the year 2000. Most growth will be in private industry, primarily in genetic and biotechnical research and in production - using newly developed biological methods. Efforts to preserve the environment should also result in growth.

Biochemists are less likely to lose their jobs during recessions than those in many other occupations since most are employed on long-term research projects or in agriculture, activities which are not much affected by economic fluctuations.

BLUE-COLLAR WORKER SUPERVISOR

DESCRIPTION:

Supervisors direct the activities of other employees and frequently ensure that millions of dollars worth of equipment and materials are used properly and efficiently. While blue-collar worker supervisors are most commonly known as foremen or forewomen, they also have many other titles. In the textile industry, they are referred to as second hands; on ships, they are known as boatswains, and in the construction industry, they are often called overseers, strawbosses, or gang leaders. Supervisors make work schedules and keep production and employee records. They must use judgement in planning and must allow for unforeseen problems such as absent workers, or machine breakdowns. Teaching employees safe work habits and enforcing safety rules and regulations are among other supervisory responsibilities. Supervisors also may demonstrate timesaving or laborsaving techniques to workers, and train new employees. Worker supervisors tell their subordinates about company plans and policies; recommend good workers for wage increases, awards, or promotions; and deal with poor workers by issuing warnings or recommending that they be fired. In companies where employees belong to labor unions, supervisors meet with union representatives to discuss work problems and grievances. They must know the provisions of labor-management contracts and run their operations according to these agreements.

BACKGROUND AND QUALIFICATIONS:

When choosing supervisors, employers generally look for experience, skill, and leadership qualities. Most supervisors rise through the ranks; however, a growing number of employers are hiring trainees with a college background. This practice is most prevalent in industries with highly technical production processes, such as the chemical, oil, and electronics industries. Employers generally prefer backgrounds in business administration, industrial relations, mathematics, engineering, or science. The trainees undergo on-the-job training until they are able to accept supervisory responsibilities.

Outstanding supervisors may move up to higher management positions. In manufacturing, for example, they may advance to jobs such as department head or plant manager. Some supervisors, particularly in the construction industry, use the experience and skills they gain to go into business for themselves.

EARNINGS:

Median weekly earnings for blue-collar worker supervisors were about $485 in 1986. The middle 50 percent earned between $350 and $630. The lowest 10 percent earned less than $210, and the highest 10 percent earned over $790. Supervisors receive a salary determined by the wage rates of the highest paid workers they supervise. For example, most companies keep wages of supervisors about 10 to 30 percent higher than those of their subordinates. Some supervisors receive overtime pay.

OUTLOOK:

Employment of blue-collar worker supervisors is expected to increase more slowly than the average for all occupation through the year 2000. Although rising incomes will stimulate demand for goods such as air-conditioners, home entertainment equipment, personal computers, and automobiles, employment in manufacturing industries will decline, due in part to increasing foreign competition. The production-related occupations in manufacturing, including blue-collar worker supervisors, will be the ones most adversely affected. Offsetting the decline in the number of supervisors in manufacturing, however, will be an increase in jobs in non-manufacturing industries, especially in the trade and service sectors.

In addition to the jobs resulting in increased demand for supervisors, many openings will arise from the need to replace workers who leave the occupation. Supervisors have a relatively strong attachment to the occupation, but because the occupation is so large, turnover results in a large number of openings. Because blue-collar worker supervisors are so important to the successful operation of a firm, they are often protected from layoffs during a recession. Supervisors in the construction industry, however, may experience periodic layoffs when construction activity declines.

BUYER/MERCHANDISE MANAGER

DESCRIPTION:

All merchandise sold in a retail store appears in that store on the decision of a buyer. Although all buyers seek to satisfy their stores' customers and sell at a profit, the type and variety of goods they purchase depends on the store where they work. A buyer for a small clothing store, for example, may purchase its complete stock of merchandise. Buyers who work for larger retail businesses often handle a few related lines of goods, such as men's wear, ladies' sportswear, or children's toys, among many others. Some, known as foreign buyers, purchase merchandise outside the United States. Buyers must be familiar with the manufacturers and distributors who handle the merchandise they need. They also must keep informed about changes in existing products and the development of new ones. Merchandise Managers plan and coordinate buying and selling activities for large and medium-sized stores. They divide the budget among buyers, decide how much merchandise to stock, and assign each buyer to purchase certain goods. Merchandise Managers may review buying decisions to ensure that needed categories of goods are in stock, and help buyers to set general pricing guidelines.

Some buyers represent large stores or chains in cities where many manufacturers are located. The duties of these "market representatives" vary by employer; some purchase goods, while others supply information and arrange for store buyers to meet with manufacturer's representatives when they are in the area. New technology has altered the buyers' role in retail chain stores. Cash registers connected to a computer, known as point-of-sale terminals, allow retail chains to maintain centralized, up-to-the-minute inventory records. With these records, a single garden furniture buyer, for example, can purchase lawn chairs and picnic tables for the entire chain.

BACKGROUND AND QUALIFICATIONS:

Because familiarity with the merchandise and with the retailing business itself is such a central element in the buyer's job, prior retailing experience sometimes provides sufficient preparation. More and more, however, employers prefer applicants who have a college degree. Most employers accept college grads in any field of study and train them on the job. In many stores, beginners who are candidates for buying jobs start out in executive training programs. These programs last from six to eight months, and combine classroom instruction in merchandising and purchasing with short rotations in various store jobs. This training introduces the new worker to store operations and policies, and provides the fundamentals of merchandising and management. The trainee's first job is likely to be that of assistant buyer. The duties include supervising sales workers, checking invoices on material received, and keeping account of stock on hand. Assistant buyers gradually assume purchasing responsibilities, depending upon their individual abilities and the size of the department where they work. Training as an assistant buyer usually lasts at least one year. After years of working as a buyer, those who show exceptional ability may advance to merchandise manager. A few find promotion to top executive jobs such as general merchandise manager for a retail store or chain.

EARNINGS:

Median annual earnings of buyers were $20,700 in 1986. Most buyers earned between $14,600 and $29,000 a year. The lowest 10 percent averaged less than $11,400, while the top 10 percent earned more than $41,300. A buyer's income depends upon the amount and type of product purchased, the employer's sales volume and, to some extent, the buyer's seniority. Buyers for large wholesale distributors and for mass merchandisers such as discount or large chain department stores ar among the most highly paid.

Buyers often earn cash bonuses based on their performance and may receive discounts on merchandise bought from the employer. In addition, many firms have incentive plans, such as profit sharing and stock options.

OUTLOOK:

Employment of buyers is expected to grow more slowly than the average for all occupations though the year 2000 as more wholesale and retail trade establishments automate and centralize their purchasing departments. Productivity gains resulting from the increased use of computers to control inventory, maintain records, and reorder merchandise will be the principal factor restraining employment growth. Most job openings, therefore, will result from replacement needs, which occur as experienced buyers transfer to other occupations in sales or management, change careers, or stop working altogether.

The number of qualified jobseekers will continue to exceed the number of openings because merchandising attracts many college graduates. Prospects are likely to be best for qualified applicants who enjoy the competitive, fast-paced nature of merchandising.

CHEMIST

DESCRIPTION:

Chemists search for and put into practical use new knowledge about substances. Their research has resulted in the development of a tremendous variety of synthetic materials, such as nylon and polyester fabrics. Nearly one-half of all chemists work in research and development. In basic research, chemists investigate the properties and composition of matter and the laws that govern the combination of elements. Basic research often has practical uses. In research and development, new products are created or improved. Nearly one-eighth of all chemists work in production and inspection. In production, chemists prepare instructions (batch sheets) for plant workers that specify the kind and amount of ingredients to use and the exact mixing time for each stage in the process. At each step, samples are tested for quality control to meet industry and government standards. Other chemists work as marketing or sales representatives because of their technical knowledge of the products sold. A number of chemists teach in colleges and universities. Some chemists are consultants to private industry and government agencies. Chemists often specialize in one of several subfields of chemistry; analytical chemists determine the structure, composition, and nature of substances, and develop new techniques; organic chemists at one time studied only the chemistry of living things, but their area has been broadened to include all carbon compounds; inorganic chemists study non-carbon compounds; physical chemists study energy transformations to find new and better energy sources.

BACKGROUND AND QUALIFICATIONS:

A BA with a major in Chemistry or a related discipline is sufficient for many entry-level jobs as a chemist. However, graduate training is required for many research jobs and most college teaching jobs require a PhD. Beginning chemists with a Master's Degree can usually go into applied research. The PhD is generally required for basic research, for teaching in colleges and universities, and for advancement to many administrative positions.

EARNINGS:

According to the College Placement Council, chemists with a bachelor's degree were offered starting salaries averaging $23,400 a year in 1986; those with a master's degree, $28,000; and those with a PhD, $36,400.

According to the American Chemical Society, median salaries of their members with a bachelor's degree were $33,000 a year in 1986; with a master's degree, $37,900; with a PhD, $47,800.

In a Bureau of Labor Statistics survey, chemists in private industry averaged $22,500 a year in 1986 at the most junior level, and $74,600 at senior supervisory levels. Experienced midlevel chemists with no supervisory responsibilities averaged $41,500.

Depending on a person's college record, the annual starting salary in the Federal Government in early 1987 for an inexperienced chemist with a bachelor's degree was between $14,800 and $18,350. Those who had two years of graduate study began at $22,450 a year, and with a PhD, $27,170 to $32,570. The average salary for all chemists in the Federal Government in 1986 was $38,600 a year.

OUTLOOK:

Employment of chemists is expected to grow more slowly than the average for all occupations through the year 2000

CLAIM REPRESENTATIVE

DESCRIPTION:

The people who investigate insurance claims, negotiate settlements with policy holders, and authorize payments are known as claim representatives - a group that includes claim adjusters and claim examiners. When a casualty insurance company receives a claim, the claim adjuster determines whether the policy covers it and the amount of the loss. Adjusters use reports, physical evidence, and testimony of witnesses in investigating a claim. When their company is liable, they negotiate with the claimant and settle the case. Some adjusters work with all lines of insurance. Others specialize in claims from fire, marine loss, automobile damage, workers' compensation loss, or product liability. A growing number of casualty companies employ special adjusters to settle small claims. These workers, generally called inside adjusters or telephone adjusters, contact claimants by telephone or mail and have the policy holder send repair costs, medical bills, and other statements to the company. In life insurance companies, the counterpart of the claim adjuster is the claim examiner, who investigates questionable claims or those exceeding a specified amount. They may check claim applications for completeness and accuracy, interview medical specialists, consult policy files to verify information on a claim, or calculate benefit payments. Generally, examiners are authorized to investigate and approve payment on all claims up to a certain limit; larger claims are referred to a senior examiner.

BACKGROUND AND QUALIFICATIONS:

No specific field of college study is recommended. Although courses in insurance, economics, or other business subjects are helpful, a major in most college fields is adequate preparation. Most large insurance companies provide beginning claim adjusters and examiners with on-the-job training and home study courses. Claim representatives are encouraged to take courses designed to enhance their professional skills. For example, the Insurance Institute of America offers a six semester study program leading to an Associate's Degree in Claims Adjusting, upon successful completion of six exams. A professional Certificate in Insurance Adjusting also is available from the College of Insurance in New York City. The Life Office Management Association (LOMA), in cooperation with the International Claim Association, offers a claims education program for life and health examiners. The program is part of the LOMA Institute Insurance Education Program leading to the professional designation FLMI (Fellow, Life Management Institute) upon successful completion of eight written exams. Beginning adjusters and examiners work on small claims under the supervision of an experienced employee. As they learn more about claim investigation and settlement, they are assigned claims that are either higher in loss value or more complex. Trainees are promoted as they demonstrate competence in handling assignments and as they progress in their course work. Employees who show unusual competence in claims work or outstanding administrative skills may be promoted to department supervisor in a field office, or to a managerial position in the home office. Qualified adjusters and examiners sometimes transfer to other departments, such as underwriting or sales.

EARNINGS:

According to a survey of property and liability insurance companies, claim examiners earned a median annual salary of $29,100 in 1986; claim supervisors, $32,300; and claim managers, $41,300.

OUTLOOK:

Employment of claim representatives is expected to grow faster than the average for all occupations as the increasing volume of insurance sales results in more insurance claims. Shifts in the age distribution of the population will result in a large increase in the number of people who assume career and family responsibilities. People in this group have the greatest need for life and health insurance, and protection for homes, automobiles, and other possessions. A growing demand for insurance coverage for working women is also expected. New or expanding businesses will need protection for new plants and equipment and for insurance covering their employees' health and safety. Opportunities should be particularly good for claim representatives who specialize in complex business insurance such as marine cargo, workers' compensation, and product and pollution liability insurance.

COMMERCIAL ARTIST

DESCRIPTION:

A team of commercial artists with varying skills and specializations often creates the artwork in newspapers and magazines, and on billboards, brochures, and catalogs. This team is supervised by an art director, whose main function is to develop a theme or idea for an ad or advertising campaign. After the art director has determined the main elements of an ad or design, he or she will turn the project over to two specialists for further refinement. The sketch artist, also called a renderer, does a rough drawing of any pictures required. The layout artist, who is concerned with graphics rather than art work, constructs or arranges the illustrations or photographs, plans the typography, and picks colors for the ad.

Other commercial artists, usually with less experience, are needed to turn out the finished products. Letterers put together headlines and other words on the ad. Mechanical artists paste up an engraver's guide of the ad.

Paste-up artists and other less experienced employees do more routine work such as cutting mats, assembling booklets, or running errands.

Advertising artists create the concepts and artwork for a wide variety of items. These include direct mail advertising, catalogs, counter displays, slides, and filmstrips. They also design or lay out newspapers, magazines, and advertising circulars. Some commercial artists specialize in producing fashion illustrations, greeting cards, or book illustrations, or in making technical drawings for industry.

BACKGROUND AND QUALIFICATIONS:

Persons can prepare for a career in commercial art by attending either a 2- or 4-year trade school, community college, college, or university offering a program in commercial art.

EARNINGS:

Median earnings for salaried commercial graphic artists who usually work full time were about $20,000 a year in 1986. The middle 50 percent earned between $15,200 and $26,000 a year.

Earnings for self-employed visual artists vary widely. Those struggling to gain experience and a reputation may be forced to charge what amounts to less than the minimum wage for their work. Well-established freelancers and fine artists are able to make a very comfortable living. Self-employed artists do not receive fringe benefits such as paid holidays, sick leave, health insurance, or pension benefits.

OUTLOOK:

The graphic arts fields have a glamorous and exciting image. Because formal entry qualifications are few, many people with a love for drawing and creative ability qualify for entry. As a result, competition for both salaried jobs and freelance work is keen. Freelance work may be hard to come by, especially at first, and many freelancers earn very little until they acquire experience and establish a good reputation.

DATA PROCESSING SPECIALIST

DESCRIPTION:

The main function of a data processing specialist is to type data from documents such as checks, bills, and invoices quickly and accurately, and enter this information into a computer system. This is done with a variety of typewriter-like equipment. Many specialists use a machine that converts the information they type to magnetic impulses on tapes or disks. The information is then read into the computer from the tape or disk. Some specialists operate on-line terminals of the main computer system that transmit and receive data. Although brands and models of computer terminals and data entry equipment differ somewhat, their operation and keyboards are similar.

Some specialists working from terminals use data from the computer to produce business, scientific, and technical reports. In some offices, specialists also operate computer peripheral equipment such as printers and tape readers, and act as tape librarians.

BACKGROUND AND QUALIFICATIONS:

Employers usually require a high school education and the ability to key data in at a certain speed. Applicants are often tested for speed and accuracy. Some employers prefer applicants with experience or training in the operation of data entry equipment, and console operators are often required to have a college education. In some firms, other clerical workers such as tabulating and bookkeeping machine operators may be transferred to jobs as data processing specialists. Training in the use of data entry and similar keyboard equipment is available in high schools or private business schools.

EARNINGS:

In 1986, median annual earnings of full-time data processing specialists were $14,400. The middle 50 percent earned between $11,600 and $18,300. The bottom 10 percent earned less than $9,700, while the top 10 percent earned more than $23,100 a year. Specialists in the transportation and utilities industries and manufacturing had higher average earnings than those in trade and the financial and service industries.

OUTLOOK:

The employment of data processing specialists is expected to decline through the year 2000. Despite this decline, many openings, including part-time ones, will occur each year, due to the need to replace workers who transfer to other occupations or leave the labor force. Related occupations include secretaries, typists, receptionists, and typesetters and compositors.

DIETITIAN/NUTRITIONIST

DESCRIPTION:

Dietitians, sometimes called nutritionists, are professionals trained in applying the principles of nutrition to food selection and meal preparation. They counsel individuals and groups; set up and supervise food service systems for institutions such as hospitals, prisons, and schools; and promote sound eating habits through education and administration. Dietitians also work on education and research.

Clinical dietitians provide nutritional services for patients in hospitals, nursing homes, clinics, or doctors' offices. They assess patients' nutritional needs, develop and implement nutrition programs, and evaluate and report the results. Clinical dietitians, sometimes called therapeutic dietitians, confer with doctors and nurses about each patient in order to coordinate nutritional intake with other treatments-medications in particular.

Community dietitians counsel individuals and groups on sound nutrition practices to prevent disease and to promote good health. Employed in such places as home health agencies, health maintenance organizations, and human service agencies that provide group and home-delivered meals, their job is to establish nutritional care plans, and communicate the principles of good nutrition in a way individuals and their families can understand.

Research dietitians are usually employed in academic medical centers or educational institutions, although some work in community programs. Using established research methods and analytical techniques, they conduct studies in areas that range from basic science to practical applications. Research dietitians may examine changes in the way the body uses food over the course of a lifetime, for example, or study the interaction of drugs and diet. They may investigate nutritional needs of persons with particular diseases, behavior modification, as it relates to diet and nutrition, or applied topics such as food service systems and equipment.

BACKGROUND/QUALIFICATIONS

The basic educational requirement for this field is a bachelor's degree with a major in foods and nutrition or institution management. To qualify for professional credentials as a registered dietitian, the American Dietetic Association (ADA) recommends one of the following educational paths: Completion of a four-year coordinated undergraduate program which includes 900 to 1,000 hours of clinical experience; completion of a bachelor's degree from an approved program plus an accredited dietetic internship; completion of a bachelor's or master's degree from an approved program and six month's approved work experience.

EARNINGS:

Entry-level salaries of dietitians in hospitals averaged $20,400 a year in 1986. Outlook: Employment of dietitians is expected to grow faster than the average for all occupations through the year 2000.

DRAFTSPERSON

DESCRIPTION:

Drafters prepare detailed drawings based on rough sketches, specifications, and calculations made by scientists, engineers, architects, and designers. Final drawings contain a detailed view of the object from all sides as well as specifications for materials to be used, procedures to be followed, and other information needed to carry out the job. There are two methods by which these drawings are prepared. In the traditional method, drafters sit at drawing boards and use compasses, dividers, protractors, triangles, and other drafting devices to prepare the drawing manually. In the new method, drafters use computer-aided drafting (CAD) systems. They sit at computer work stations and may make the drawing on a videoscreen. In some cases, the design may never be placed on paper. It may be stored electronically and, in some factories, may be used to guide automatic machinery. These systems free drafters from much routine drafting work and permit many variations of a design to be prepared easily. CAD systems allow a design to be viewed from various angles and perspectives not usually available with more traditional drafting methods so that design work can be better, faster, and more thorough. In addition to drafting equipment and CAD systems, drafters use technical handbooks, tables, and calculators in preparing drawings and related specifications.

BACKGROUND/REQUIREMENTS

It is preferred that applicants have two years of post-high school training in technical institutes, junior and community colleges, or extension divisions of universities. Some persons receive training in the Armed Forces. Training for a career in drafting should include courses in mathematics, physical science, mechanical drawing, and drafting. Courses in shop practices and shop skills are also helpful, since most higher level drafting jobs require knowledge of manufacturing or construction methods. Many technical schools offer courses in structural design, architectural drawing, and engineering or industrial technology. Beginners usually start as junior drafters doing routine work under close supervision. After gaining experience, they do more difficult work with less supervision and may advance to senior drafter or supervisor. With appropriate college, they may become engineers, designers, or architects.

EARNINGS:

Median annual earnings of drafters who work year round, full time were about $21,400 in 1986; the middle 50 percent earned between $16,500 and $29,000 annually.

OUTLOOK:

Little change in employment of drafters is expected to occur through the year 2000. Related occupations include architects, engineering technicians, engineers, landscape architects, photogrammetrists, and surveyors.

ECONOMIST

DESCRIPTION:

Economists study the way a society uses scarce resources such as land, labor, raw materials, and machinery to produce goods and services. They analyze the costs and benefits of distributing and using resources in a particular way. Their research might focus on such topics as energy costs, inflation, business cycles, unemployment, tax policy, farm prices, and many other areas.

Being able to present economic and statistical concepts in a meaningful way is particularly important for economists whose research is policy directed. Economists who work for business firms may be asked to provide management with information on which decisions such as the marketing or pricing of company products are made; to look at the advisability of adding new lines of merchandise, opening new branches, or diversifying the company's operations; to analyze the effects of changes in the tax laws; or to prepare economic or business forecasts. Business economists working for firms that carry on operations abroad may be asked to prepare forecasts of foreign economic conditions. About three of every four economists work in private industry, including manufacturing firms, banks, insurance companies, securities and investment companies, economic research firms and management consulting firms. Some run their own consulting businesses. A number of economists combine a full-time job in government, business or an academic institution with part-time or consulting work in another setting.

BACKGROUND AND QUALIFICATIONS:

A Bachelors degree in Economics is sufficient for many beginning research, administrative, management trainee, and business sales jobs. However, graduate training is increasingly necessary for advancement to more responsible positions as economists. In government research organizations and consulting firms, economists who have Master's degrees can usually qualify for more responsible research and administrative positions. A PhD may be necessary of top positions in some organizations. Experienced business economists may advance to managerial or executive positions in banks, industrial concerns, trade associations, and other organizations where they formulate practical business and administrative policy.

EARNINGS:

According to a 1986 salary survey by the College Placement Council, persons with a bachelor's degree in economics received an average starting salary of about $22,400 a year; in marketing and distribution, about $19,300.

Median annual earnings of full-time economists were about $36,000 in 1986. According to a survey by the National Association of Business Economists, however, median base salary for business economists was $54,000. Economists in general administration and international economics commanded the highest salaries, while those in market research and econometrics received the lowest. The highest paid business economists were in the securities and investment, retail and wholesale trade and insurance industries; the lowest paid were in the education, non-profit research organizations and real estate industries.

OUTLOOK:

Employment of economists is expected to grow faster than the average for all occupations through the year 2000. Most job openings, however, will result from the need to replace experienced economists who transfer to other occupations, retire, or leave the labor force for other reasons.

ENGINEER

DESCRIPTION:

Engineers apply the theories and principles of science and mathematics to practical technical problems. Often, their work is the link between a scientific discovery and its useful application. Engineers design machinery, products, systems, and processes for efficient and economical performance. Engineering is a highly specialized field and the work an engineer does depends greatly upon the industry in which he/she is employed. The following descriptions outline the basic specialties and their respective employment outlooks.

Aerospace Engineer

Aerospace engineers design, develop, test, and help produce commercial and military aircraft, missiles, spacecraft, and related systems. They play an important role in advancing the state of the technology in commercial aviation, defense and space exploration. Aerospace engineers often specialize in an area of work like structural design, navigational guidance and control, instrumentation and communication, or production methods. They also may specialize in one type of aerospace product, such as passenger planes, helicopters, satellites, or rockets. **Outlook:** Employment of aerospace engineers is expected to grow more slowly than average for all occupations through the year 2000. During the 1980's, their employment grew very rapidly. However, because of Defense Department expenditures for military aircraft, missiles and other aerospace systems are not expected to grow much.

Chemical Engineer

Chemical engineers are involved in many phases of the production of chemicals and chemical products; They design equipment and chemical plants as well as determining methods of manufacturing these products. Often, they design and develop chemical processes such as those used to remove chemical contaminants from waste materials. Because the duties of the chemical engineer cuts across many fields, these professionals must have knowledge of chemistry, physics, and mechanical and electrical engineering. This branch of engineering is so diversified and complex that chemical engineers frequently specialize in a particular operation such as oxidation or polymerization. Others specialize in a particular area such as pollution control or the production of a specific product like plastics or rubber. **Outlook:** Employment of chemical engineers is expected to grow about as fast as the average for all occupations through the year 2000.

Civil Engineer

Civil engineers, who work in the oldest branch of the engineering profession, design and supervise the construction of roads, harbors, airports, tunnels, bridges, water supply and sewage systems, and buildings. Major specialties within civil engineering are structural, hydraulic, environmental/sanitary, transportation, urban planning, and soil mechanics. Many civil engineers are in supervisory or administrative positions ranging from supervisor of a construction site, to city engineer, to top level executive. Others teach in colleges and universities, or work as consultants. **Outlook:** Employment of civil engineers is expected to increase faster than the average for all occupations through the year 2000.

Electrical Engineer

Electrical engineers design, develop, test and supervise the manufacture of electrical and electronic equipment. Electrical equipment includes power-generating and transmission equipment used by electrical utilities, electric motors, machinery controls, and lighting and wiring in buildings, automobiles, and aircraft. Electronic equipment includes radar, computers, communications equipment, and consumer goods such as television sets and stereos. Electrical engineers also design and operate facilities for generating and distributing electrical power. Electrical engineers generally specialize in a major area, such as integrated circuits, computers, electrical equipment manufacturing, communications, or power distributing equipment, or in a subdivision of these areas, microwave communication or aviation electronic systems, for example. Electrical engineers design new products, specify their uses, and write performance requirements and maintenance schedules. **Outlook:** The outlook for electrical engineers is estimated to be good through the year 2000.

Industrial Engineer

Industrial engineers determine the most effective ways for an organization to use the basic factors of production--people, machines and materials. They are more concerned with people and methods of business organization than are engineers in other specialties, who generally are concerned more with particular products or processes, such as metals, power or mechanics. To solve organizational, production, and related problems most efficiently, industrial engineers design data processing systems and apply mathematical concepts. They also develop management control systems to aid in financial planning and cost analysis, design production planning and control systems to coordinate activities and control product quality, and design or improve systems for the physical distribution of goods and services. Industrial engineers also conduct plant location surveys, where they look for the best combination of sources of raw materials, transportation, and taxes, and develop wage and salary administration positions and job evaluation programs. Many industrial engineers move into managerial positions because the work is closely related. **Outlook:** Employment opportunities for industrial engineers are expected to be good; their employment is expected to grow faster than the average for all occupations through the year 2000. Most job openings, however, will result from the need to replace industrial engineers who transfer to other occupations or leave the labor force.

Metallurgical Engineer

Metallurgical engineers develop new types of metals with characteristics that are tailored for specific requirements, such as heat resistance, lightweight strength, or high malleability. They also develop methods to process and convert metals into useful products. Most of these engineers generally work in one of three major branches of metallurgy: extractive or chemical, physical, or mechanical. Extractive metallurgists are concerned with extracting metals from ores, and refining and alloying them to obtain useful materials. Physical metallurgists deal with the nature, structure, and physical properties of metals and their alloys, and with the methods of converting refined metals into final products. Mechanical metallurgists develop methods to work and shape materials, such as casting, forging, rolling, and drawing. **Outlook:** Employment of metallurgical, ceramic, and materials engineers is expected to grow more rapidly than the average for all occupations through the year 2000.

Mining Engineer

Mining engineers find, extract, and prepare minerals for manufacturing industries to use. They design open pit and underground mines, supervise the construction of mine shafts and tunnels in underground operations, and devise methods for transporting minerals to processing plants. Mining engineers are responsible for the economical and efficient operation of mines and mine safety, including ventilation, water supply, power, communications, and equipment maintenance. Some mining engineers work with geologists and metallurgical engineers to locate and appraise new ore deposits. Others develop new mining equipment or direct mineral processing operations, which involve separating minerals from the dirt, rock, and other materials they are mixed with. Mining engineers frequently specialize in the mining of one specific mineral such as coal or copper. With increased emphasis on protecting the environment, many mining engineers have been working to solve problems related to mined land reclamation, and water and air pollution. **Outlook:** The employment outlook for mining engineers is expected to remain constant through the year 2000, due to expected low growth in demand for coal, metals, and other minerals.

Petroleum Engineer

Petroleum engineers are mainly involved in exploring and drilling for oil and gas. They work to achieve the maximum profitable recovery of oil and gas from a petroleum reservoir by determining and developing the best and most efficient methods. Since only a small proportion of the oil and gas in a reservoir will flow out under natural forces, petroleum engineers develop and use various artificial recovery methods, such as flooding the oil field with water to force the oil to the surface. Even when using the best recovery methods, about half the oil is still left in the ground. Petroleum engineers' research and development efforts to increase the proportion of oil recovered in each reservoir can make a significant contribution to increasing available energy resources. **Outlook:** Employment of petroleum engineers is expected to grow more slowly than the average for all occupations through the year 2000. With the drop in oil prices, domestic petroleum companies have curtailed exploration, resulting in poor employment opportunities.

BACKGROUND AND QUALIFICATIONS:

A bachelor's degree in engineering from an accredited engineering program is generally acceptable for beginning engineering jobs. College graduates trained in one of the natural sciences or mathematics also may qualify for some beginning jobs. Most engineering degrees may be obtained in branches such as electrical, mechanical, or civil engineering. College graduates with a degree in science or mathematics and experienced engineering technicians may also qualify for some engineering jobs, especially in engineering specialties in high demand. Graduate training is essential for engineering faculty positions but is not required for the majority of entry level engineering jobs. All 50 states require licensing for engineers whose work may affect life, health, or property, or who offer their services to the public. Beginning engineering graduates usually work under the supervision of experienced engineers, and in larger companies, may receive seminar or classroom training. As engineers advance in knowledge, they may become technical specialists, supervisors, or managers or administrators within the field of engineering. Some engineers obtain advanced degrees in business administration to improve their growth opportunities, while others obtain law degrees and become patent attorneys.

EARNINGS:

Average starting salaries for engineers by category are: petroleum engineer, $33,000; chemical engineer, $29,256; electrical engineer, $28,368; mechanical engineer, $27,864; metallurgical engineer, $27,864; aeronautical engineer, $27,780; industrial engineer, $27,048; mining engineer, $25,956; civil engineer, $24,132. Those engineers in the private industry in 1986 averaged $27,866 at the most junior level, while those at senior managerial levels averaged $79,021.

FINANCIAL ANALYST

DESCRIPTION:

A financial analyst prepares the financial reports required by the firm to conduct its operations and satisfy tax and regulatory requirements. Financial analysts also oversee the flow of cash and financial instruments and develop information to assess the present and future financial status of the firm.

BACKGROUND AND QUALIFICATIONS:

A bachelor's degree in accounting or finance is suitable academic preparation for a financial manager. An MBA degree in addition to a bachelor's degree in any field is acceptable to many employers.

EARNINGS:

The median annual salary of financial managers was $30,400 in 1986. The lowest 10% earned $17,000 or less, while the top 10% earned over $52,000. The salary level depends upon the size and location of the firm, and is likely to be higher in large institutions and cities. Many financial analysts in private industry receive additional compensation in the form of bonuses, which also vary substantially by size of firm.

OUTLOOK:

Employment of financial managers is expected to increase about as fast as the average for all occupations through the year 2000.

FOOD TECHNOLOGIST

DESCRIPTION:

A food technologist studies the chemical, physical and biological nature of food to learn how to safely process, preserve, package, distribute, and store it. Some develop new products, while others insure quality standards. They are, like animal scientists, dairy scientists, horticulturists, soil scientists, animal and plant breeders, entomologists, and agriculturalists, classified generally as agricultural scientists by the U.S. Department of Labor.

BACKGROUND AND QUALIFICATIONS:

Educational requirements for the agricultural scientist depend a great deal upon the area and type of work performed. A PhD degree in agricultural science is usually required for college teaching, independent research, and for advancement to many administrative and management jobs. A bachelor's degree is sufficient for some sales, production management, inspection, and other nonresearch jobs, but, in some cases, promotions may be limited. Degrees in some related sciences such as biology, chemistry, or physics or in related engineering specialties also may be acceptable for some agricultural science jobs.

EARNINGS:

According to the College Placement Council, starting salary offers for agricultural scientists with a bachelor's degree averaged $19,200 a year in 1986. In the Federal Government in 1987, an agricultural scientist with a bachelor's degree started at $14,822 or $18,358 a year, depending on their college records.

OUTLOOK:

Employment of agricultural scientists is expected to grow about as fast as the average for all occupations through the year 2000.

FORESTER

DESCRIPTION:

Foresters plan and supervise the growing, protection and harvesting of trees. They plot forest areas, approximate the amount of standing timber and future growth, and manage timber sales. Some foresters also protect the trees from fire, harmful insects, and disease. Some foresters also protect wildlife and manage watersheds; develop and supervise campgrounds, parks, and grazing lands; and do research. Foresters in extension work provide information to forest owners and to the general public.

BACKGROUND AND QUALIFICATIONS:

A bachelor's degree in forestry is the minimum educational requirement for professional careers in forestry. In 1986, 55 colleges and universities offered bachelor's or higher degrees in forestry; 47 of these were accredited by the Society of American Foresters.

EARNINGS:

Most graduates entering the Federal Government as foresters, range managers, or soil conservationists in 1987 with a bachelor's degree started at $14,800 a year. Those with a master's degree could start at $22,500. Holders of doctorates could begin at $27,500, or, in research positions, at $32,600.

OUTLOOK:

Employment of foresters and conservation scientists is expected to grow more slowly than the average for all occupations through the year 2000.

GEOGRAPHER

DESCRIPTION:

Geographers study the interrelationship of humans and the environment. Economic geographers deal with the geographic distribution of an area's economic activities. Political geographers are concerned with the relationship of geography to political phenomena. Physical geographers study physical processes in the earth and its atmosphere. Urban geographers study cities and metropolitan areas, while regional geographers specialize in the physical, climatic, economic, political and cultural characteristics of a particular region or area. Medical geographers study the effect of the environment on health.

BACKGROUND AND QUALIFICATIONS:

The minimum educational requirement for entry-level positions is a BA or BS degree in Geography. However, a Masters degree is increasingly required for many entry level positions. Applicants for entry level jobs would find it helpful to have training in a specialty such as cartography, photogrammerty, remote sensing data interpretation, statistical analysis including computer science, or environmental analysis. To advance to a senior research position in private industry and perhaps gain a spot in management, a geographer would probably be required to have an advanced degree.

EARNINGS:

Starting salaries in government and industry average $16,000 to $20,000. Those with a Master's degree start at about $22,500, and while many of those with a PhD start at about $27,200, some can start as high as $32,600.

OUTLOOK:

Average growth is predicted throughout the 1990's.

GEOLOGISTS AND GEOPHYSISICTS

DESCRIPTION:

Geologists study the structure, composition and history of the earth's crust. By examining surface rocks and drilling to recover rock cores, they determine the types and distribution of rocks beneath the earth's surface. They also identify rocks and minerals, conduct geological surveys, draw maps, take measurements, and record data. Geological research helps to determine the structure and history of the earth, and may result in significant advances, such as in the ability to predict earthquakes. An important application of geologists' work is locating oil and other natural and mineral resources. Geologists usually specialize in one or a combination of general areas: earth materials, earth processes, and earth history.

Geophysicists study the composition and physical aspects of the earth and its electric, magnetic and gravitational fields. Geophysicists usually specialize in one of three general phases of the science -- solid earth, fluid earth, and upper atmosphere. Some may also study other planets.

BACKGROUND AND QUALIFICATIONS:

A Bachelor's degree in geology or geophysics is adequate for entry into some lower level geology jobs, but better jobs with good advancement potential usually require at least a master's degree in geology or geophysics. Persons with strong backgrounds in physics, mathematics, or computer science also may qualify for some geophysics jobs. A PhD is essential for most research positions.

EARNINGS:

Surveys by the College Placement Council indicate that graduates with bachelor's degrees in physical and earth sciences received an average starting offer of $19,200 a year in 1986.

In the Federal Government in early 1987, geologists and geophysicists having a bachelor's degree could begin at between $14,822 and $18,358 a year, depending on college records; those having a master's degree, between $27,172 and $32,567. In 1986, the average salary for geologists in the federal government was about $37,500, and for geophysicists, $40,900.

OUTLOOK:

Employment of geologists and geophysicists is expected to grow more slowly than the average for all occupations through the year 2000, mainly due to the reduction in energy exploration by oil companies.

HOTEL MANAGER/ASSISTANT MANAGER

DESCRIPTION:

Hotel managers are responsible for operating their establishments profitably and satisfying guests. They determine room rates and credit policy, direct the operation of the food service operation, and manage the housekeeping, accounting, security, and maintenance departments of the hotel. Handling problems and coping with the unexpected are important parts of the job. A small hotel or motel requires only a limited staff, and the manager may have to fill various front office duties, such as taking reservations or assigning rooms. When management is combined with ownership, these activities may expand to include all aspects of the business.

General managers of large hotels usually have several assistants or department heads who manage various parts of the operation. Because hotel restaurant and cocktail lounges are important to the success of the entire establishment, they are almost always operated by managers with experience in the restaurant field. Other areas that are usually handled separately include advertising, rental of banquet and meeting facilities, marketing and sales, personnel and accounting. Large hotel and motel chains often centralize some activities, such as purchasing and advertising, so that individual hotels in the chain may not need managers for these departments. Managers who work for chains may be assigned to organize a newly-built or purchased hotel, or to reorganize an existing hotel or motel that is not operating successfully.

BACKGROUND AND QUALIFICATIONS:

Experience is the most important consideration in selecting hotel managers. However, employers are increasingly emphasizing college education. A BA in Hotel/Restaurant Administration provides particularly strong preparation for a career in hotel management. Most hotels promote employees who have proven their ability, usually front office clerks, to assistant manager, and eventually to general manager. Hotel and motel chains may offer better employment opportunities because employees can transfer to another hotel or motel in the chain, or to the central office if an opening occurs.

EARNINGS:

In 1986, annual salaries of assistant hotel managers averaged an estimated $34,500, according to a survey conducted by the American Hotel and Motel Association. Assistants employed by large hotels, with 600 or more rooms, averaged an estimated $45,500 that year, while those in small hotels of 200 or fewer, averaged $21,100. Salaries of assistant managers also vary according to responsibilities. For example, food and beverage managers averaged $42,000, whereas front office managers averaged $24,700. The manager's level of experience is also an important factor.

In 1986, salaries of general managers averaged an estimated $63,900, ranging from an average of about $38,400 in hotels and motels with less than 200 rooms to more than $87,000 in hotels with 600 rooms or more.

OUTLOOK:

Employment of salaried hotel managers is expected to grow much faster than the average for all occupations through the year 2000 as more large hotels and motels are built.

INDUSTRIAL DESIGNER

DESCRIPTION:

Industrial designers combine artistic talent with a knowledge of marketing, materials, and methods of production to improve the appearance and functional design of products so that they compete favorably with similar goods on the market. Although most industrial designers are engaged in product design, others are involved in different facets of design. To create favorable public images for companies and for government service, some designers develop trademarks or symbols that appear on the firm's products, advertising, brochures, and stationery. Some design containers and packages that both protect and promote their contents. Others prepare small display exhibits or the entire layout for industrial fairs. Some design the interior layout of special purpose commercial buildings such as restaurants and supermarkets.

Corporate designers usually work only on products made by their employer. This may involve filling day-to-day design needs of the company, or long-range planning of new products. Independent consultants who serve more than one industrial firm often plan and design a great variety of products. Most designers work for large manufacturing companies designing either consumer or industrial products, or for design consulting firms. Others do freelance work, or are on the staffs of architectural and interior design firms.

BACKGROUND AND QUALIFICATIONS:

The normal requirement for entering this field of work involves completing a course of study in industrial design at an art school, university, or technical college. Most large manufacturing firms hire only industrial designers who have a Bachelor's degree in the field. Beginning industrial designers frequently do simple assignments. As they gain experience, they may work on their own, and many become supervisors with major responsibility for the design of a product or group of products. Those who have an established reputation and the necessary funds may start their own consulting firms.

EARNINGS:

Median annual earnings of experienced full-time designers were almost $25,000 in 1986. The middle 50 percent earned between $16,800 and $34,400 a year. The bottom 10 percent earned less than $15,200, and the top percent earned more than $46,500. Earnings of self-employed designers vary greatly, depending on their talent and business ability, but generally are higher than those of salaried designers.

OUTLOOK:

Employment in design occupations is expected to grow faster than the average for all occupations through the year 2000. Continued emphasis on product quality and safety, on design of new products for businesses and offices, and on high-technology products in medicine and transportation should expand the demand for industrial designers.

INSURANCE AGENT/BROKER

DESCRIPTION:

Agents and brokers usually sell one or more of the three basic types of insurance: life, casualty, and health. Underwriters offer various policies that, besides providing health benefits, may also provide retirement income, funds for education, or other benefits. Casualty insurance agents sell policies that protect individual policyholders from financial losses resulting from automobile accidents, fire, or theft. They also sell industrial or commercial lines, such as workers' compensation, products liability, or medical malpractice insurance. Health insurance policies offer protection against the high costs of hospital and medical care, or loss of income due to illness or injury. Many agents also offer securities, such as mutual fund shares or variable annuities.

An insurance agent may be either an insurance company employee or an independent who is authorized to represent one or more insurance companies. Brokers are not under exclusive contract with any single company; instead, they place policies directly with the company that best meets a company's needs.

Insurance agents spend most of their time discussing insurance needs with prospective and existing clients. Some time must be spent in office work to prepare reports, maintain records, plan insurance programs that are tailored to prospects' needs, and draw up lists of prospective customers. Specialists in group policies may help an employer's accountant set up a system of payroll deductions for employees covered by the policy.

BACKGROUND AND QUALIFICATIONS:

All insurance agents and most insurance brokers must obtain a license in the state where they plan to sell insurance. In most states, licenses are issued only to applicants who pass written examinations covering insurance fundamentals and the state insurance laws. Agents who plan to sell mutual fund shares and other securities also must be licensed by the state. New agents usually receive training at the agencies where they will work, and frequently at the insurance company's home office. Beginners sometimes attend company-sponsored classes to prepare for the examination. Others study on their own and accompany experienced sales workers when they call on prospective clients.

EARNINGS:

Beginners in this field are often guaranteed a moderate salary while they learn the business and build a clientele. In 1986, many large companies paid new agents a median salary of about $1,400 a month during this training period, which usually lasts about six months. Life insurance agents with about five to nine years of experience had a median income of about $47,000 in 1986; those with ten years or more of experience had a median income of $70,000. The size of the commission depends on the types and amount of insurance sold, and whether the transaction is a new policy or a renewal.

OUTLOOK:

Employment of insurance agents and brokers is expected to grow about as fast as the average for all occupations through the year 2000. Turnover is high because many beginners are able to establish a sufficiently large clientele in this highly competitive business. Most individuals and businesses consider insurance a necessity, regardless of economic conditions. Therefore, agents are not likely to face unemployment because of a recession.

MANAGER

DESCRIPTION:

Managers supervise employees and are accountable for the overall success of the operation which they direct. The scope and nature of a manager's responsibilities depend greatly upon the position and the size of his or her organization.

A department manager at a retail store, for example, may actually spend most of his or her time waiting on customers, and his or her managerial duties may be limited to scheduling employees' work shifts to properly staff the department, or to training new employees in such simple tasks as operating the check-out terminal, processing credit card purchases, and displaying merchandise.

A branch manager, even in a small store or service operation, might have considerably broader duties and responsibilities. He or she might, in addition to supervising and training employees, be responsible for hiring and firing decisions. He or she might have a limited ability to purchase items, and might have some control over a local advertising budget. He or she might also deal with local suppliers of goods and services. Some organizations, however, prefer to delegate rather limited responsibility to branch managers, and instead rely upon a strong network of regional managers who travel from branch to branch, making key operating decisions.

Factories or service firms with extensive processing requirements employ operations and production managers. While these managers typically supervise many people, their primary responsibility is the overall success of the operation, which may be dependent upon equipment, raw material, purchased goods, or outside vendors. The operations manager at a bank, for example, remains heavily dependent upon data processing equipment, and usually will have an extensive background in this area. The production manager at a petroleum refinery, for another example, remains heavily dependent upon a large variety of specialized equipment, and will usually have a background in engineering or chemistry.

The general manager is responsible for the overall day-to-day operations of the firm or operating unit. He or she must be acquainted with each part of the operation. In a small store, the general manager may spend most of his or her time performing nonmanagerial tasks such as making purchases, or even waiting on customers. In a large corporation, on the other hand, the general manager (who is often the executive vice president) will spend much of his or her time meeting with key executives in each department to ensure that company operations are being conducted successfully.

BACKGROUND AND QUALIFICATIONS:

The educational background of managers and top executives varies as widely as the nature of their diverse responsibilities. Most general managers and top executives have a bachelor's degree in liberal arts or business administration. Graduate and professional degrees are common. Many managers in administrative, marketing, financial, and manufacturing activities have a master's degree in business administration. Larger firms usually have some form of management training program, usually open to recent college graduates. While such programs are usually competitive, they generally offer an excellent opportunity to quickly familiarize oneself with many different aspects of a firm's business. Also, such programs are often open to a broad range of candidates, including both candidates with a BS in business administration, and liberal arts graduates as well.

EARNINGS:

The estimated median annual salary of general managers and top executives was around $34,000 in 1986. Many earned well over $52,000. Salary levels vary substantially depending upon the level of managerial responsibility, length of service, and type, size, and location of the firm.

A college graduate entering a Management Trainee program or position can expect to begin at approximately $300 per week. Some Branch Managers may earn from $20,000 to $30,000 per year. Some firms prefer to pay managers relatively low salaries, but offer profit-sharing or similar incentive bonus-type plans to compensate.

OUTLOOK:

Employment of general managers and top executives is expected to grow about as fast as the average for all occupations through the year 2000.

MANUFACTURERS' SALES WORKERS

DESCRIPTION:

Most manufacturers employ sales workers to market their products to other businesses, mainly to other producers, wholesalers, and retailers. Manufacturers also sell directly to institutions such as schools, hospitals, and libraries. The sales workers who represent a manufacturer to prospective buyers are usually called manufacturers' representatives, although the job title may vary by product line.

Manufacturers' sales workers visit prospective buyers to inform them about the products they sell, analyze the buyer's needs, suggest how their products can meet these needs, and take orders. Sales workers visit firms in their territory, using an approach adapted to their line of merchandise. Sometimes sales workers promote their company's products at trade shows and conferences.

Manufacturers' sales workers spend most of their time visiting prospective customers. They also prepare reports on sales prospects or customers' credit ratings, plan their work schedules, draw up lists of prospects, contact the firm to schedule appointments, handle correspondence, and study literature about their products.

BACKGROUND AND QUALIFICATIONS:

Although a college degree is increasingly desirable for a job as a manufacturer's sales worker, many employers hire individuals without a degree who have previous sales experience. Most entrants to this occupation, even those with college degrees, transfer from other occupations, but some are recent graduates. Entrants are older, on the average, than entrants to other occupations. Sales representatives who have good sales records and leadership ability may advance to sales supervisor, branch manager, or district manager. Those with managerial ability eventually may advance to sales manager or other executive positions; many top executives in industry started as sales representatives. Some people eventually go into business for themselves as independent representatives, while others find opportunities in advertising and marketing research.

EARNINGS:

Manufacturers' sales workers may be paid under different types of compensation plans. Some manufacturers pay experienced sales workers a straight commission, based on the dollar amount of their sales; others pay a fixed salary. Median earnings of full-time manufacturers' sales workers were about $25,600 in 1986.

OUTLOOK:

Little or no change in employment is expected in the occupation through the year 2000. Increased reliance on electronic ordering systems and a trend toward increased utilization of wholesale distribution channels will limit future employment growth.

PERSONNEL AND LABOR RELATIONS SPECIALIST

DESCRIPTION:

Personnel and labor relations specialists provide the necessary link between management and employees which helps management make effective use of employees' skills, and helps employees find satisfaction in their jobs and working conditions. Personnel specialists interview, select, and recommend applicants to fill job openings. They handle wage and salary administration, training and career development, and employee benefits. Labor relations specialists usually deal in union-management relations, and people who specialize in this field work primarily in unionized businesses and government agencies. They help management officials prepare for collective bargaining sessions, participate in contract negotiations with the union, and handle day-to-day matters of labor relations agreements.

In a small company, personnel work consists mostly of interviewing and hiring, and one person usually handles all phases. By contrast, a large organization needs an entire staff, which might include recruiters, interviewers, counselors, job analysts, wage and salary analysts, education and training specialists, as well as technical and clerical workers. Personnel work often begins with the personnel recruiter or employment interviewer who travels around the country, often to college campuses, in the search for promising job applicants. These specialists talk to applicants, and then select and recommend those who appear qualified to fill vacancies. They often administer tests to applicants and interpret the results. Job analysts and salary & wage administrators examine detailed information on jobs, including job qualifications and worker characteristics, in order to prepare manuals and other materials for these courses, and look into new methods of training. They also counsel employees participating in training opportunities, which may include on-the-job, apprentice, supervisory, or management training.

Employee benefits supervisors and other personnel specialists handle the employer's benefits programs, which often include health insurance, life insurance, disability insurance, and pension plans. These specialists also coordinate a wide range of employee services, including cafeterias and snack bars, health rooms, recreational facilities, newsletters and communications, and counseling for work-related personal problems. Counseling employees who are reaching retirement age is a particularly important part of the job. Labor relations specialists give advice on labor management relations. Nearly three out of four work in private industry, for manufacturers, banks, insurance companies, airlines, department stores, and virtually every other business concern.

BACKGROUND AND QUALIFICATIONS:

The educational backgrounds of personnel, training, and labor relations specialists and managers vary considerably due to the diversity of duties and level of responsibility. While some employers look for graduates with degrees in Personnel Administration or Industrial and Labor Relations, others prefer graduates with a general business background. Still others feel that a well-rounded liberal arts education is the best preparation. A college degree in Personnel Administration, Political Science, or Public Administration can be an asset in looking for personnel work with a government agency. Graduate study in industrial or labor relations is often required for work in labor relations. Although a law degree is often required for entry-level jobs, most of the people who are responsible for contract negotiations are lawyers, and a combination of industrial relations courses and a law degree is becoming highly desirable.

New personnel specialists usually enter formal or on-the-job training programs to learn how to classify jobs, interview applicants, or administer employee benefits. Next, new workers are assigned to specific areas in the employee relations department to gain experience. Later, they may advance within their own company, transfer to another employer, or move from personnel to labor relations work. Workers in the middle ranks of a large organization often transfer to a top job in a smaller company. Employees with exceptional ability may be promoted to executive positions, such as director of personnel, or director of labor relations.

EARNINGS:

Beginning personnel/labor relations specialists earned an average of $14,800 per year in 1987. Those with a superior academic record or an additional year of specialized experience started at $18,400 per year. Holders of a master's degree started at $22,500, and those with a doctorate in a personnel field earned $27,200.

OUTLOOK:

The number of jobs in this field is projected to increase through the year 2000, although most job openings will be due to replacement needs. The job market is likely to remain competitive in view of the abundant supply of college graduates and experienced workers with suitable qualifications.

PHYSICIST

DESCRIPTION:

Through systematic observation and experimentation, physicists describe the structure of the universe and the interaction of matter and energy in fundamental terms. Physicists develop theories that describe the fundamental forces and laws of nature. The majority of physicists work in research and development. Some do basic research to increase scientific knowledge. Some engineering-oriented physicists do applied research and help develop new products. Many physicists teach and do research in colleges and universities. A small number work in inspection, quality control, and other production-related jobs in industry, while others do consulting work.

Most physicists specialize in one or more branches of the science. A growing number of physicists are specializing in fields that combine physics and a related science. Furthermore, the practical applications of a physicist's work have become increasingly merged with engineering. Private industry employs more than one half of all physicists, primarily in companies manufacturing chemicals, electrical equipment, and aircraft and missiles. Many others work in hospitals, commercial laboratories, and independent research organizations.

BACKGROUND AND QUALIFICATIONS:

Graduate training in physics or a closely related field is almost essential for most entry-level jobs in physics, and for advancement into all types of work. A PhD is normally required for faculty status at colleges and universities, and for industrial or government jobs administering research and development programs. Those with a Master's Degree qualify for many research jobs in private industry and in the Federal Government. In colleges and universities, some teach and assist in research while studying for their PhD degrees. Those with a BA may qualify for some applied research and development positions in private industry and in government, and some holding Bachelor's degrees are employed as research assistants in colleges and universities while studying for advanced degrees. Many also work in engineering and other scientific fields. Physicists often begin their careers performing routine laboratory tasks. After gaining some experience, they are assigned more complex tasks and may advance to work as project leaders or research directors. Some work in top management jobs. Physicists who develop new products sometimes form their own companies or join new firms to exploit their own ideas.

EARNINGS:

Starting salaries in private industry averaged about $31,200 a year in 1986 for those with a Master's degree, and $42,500 for those with a PhD, according to an American Institute of Physics survey. Average earnings for all Physicists in the Federal Government in 1986 were $45,600 a year.

OUTLOOK:

Physicists with a PhD should experience good employment opportunities by the late 1990s. The employment of Physicists is expected to improve as retirements increase. Related industries: engineers, chemistry, geology, and geophysics.

PUBLIC RELATIONS WORKER

DESCRIPTION:

Public relations workers aid businesses, government, universities, and other organizations build and maintain a positive public image. They apply their talents and skills in a variety of different areas, including press, community, or consumer relations, political campaigning, interest-group representation, fund-raising, or employee recruitment. Public relations is more than "telling the employer's story", however. Understanding the attitudes and concerns of customers, employees, and various other public groups, and effectively communicating this information to management to help formulate policy is an important part of the job.

Public relations staffs in very large firms may number 200 or more, but in most firms the staff is much smaller. The director of public relations, who is often a vice-president of the company, may develop overall plans and policies with a top management executive. In addition, large public relations departments employ writers, research workers, and other specialists who prepare material for the different media, stockholders, and other groups the company wishes to reach.

Manufacturing firms, public utilities, transportation companies, insurance companies, and trade and professional associations employ many public relations workers. A sizeable number work for government agencies, schools, colleges, museums, and other educational, religious, human service, and other organizations. The rapidly expanding health field also offers opportunities for public relations work. A number of workers are employed by public relations consulting firms which furnish services to clients for a fee. Others work for advertising agencies.

BACKGROUND AND QUALIFICATIONS:

A college education combined with public relations experience is excellent preparation for public relations work. Although most beginners in the field have a college degree in communications, public relations, or journalism, some employers prefer a background in a field related to the firm's business. Other firms want college graduates who have worked for the news media. In fact, many editors, reporters, and workers in closely related fields enter public relations work. Some companies, particularly those with large public relations staffs, have formal training programs for new workers. In other firms, new employers work under the guidance of experienced staff members.

Promotion to supervisory jobs may come as workers demonstrate their ability to handle more demanding and creative assignments. Some experienced public relations workers start their own consulting firms. The Public Relations Society accredits public relations officers who have at least five years of experience in the field and have passed a comprehensive six-hour examination.

EARNINGS:

Median earnings for public relations workers who were not self-employed were $26,900 in 1986. The middle 50 percent earned between $19,700 and $41,200 annually; the lowest 10 percent earned less than $14,400; and the top 10 percent earned more than $51,500. In the Federal Government, persons with a bachelor's generally started at $18,400 a year in 1987; those with a master's degree generally started at $22,500 per year.

OUTLOOK:

Employment of public relations workers is expected to increase much faster than the average for all occupations through the year 2000.

PURCHASING AGENT

DESCRIPTION:

Purchasing agents, also called industrial buyers, obtain goods and services of the quality required at the lowest possible cost, and see that adequate supplies are always available. Agents who work for manufacturing firms buy machinery, raw materials, product components, services, and maintenance and repair supplies; those working for government agencies may purchase such items as office supplies, furniture, business machines, or vehicles, to name some.

Purchasing agents usually specialize in one or more specific groups of commodities. Agents are assigned to sections, headed by assistant purchasing managers, who are responsible for a group of related commodities. In smaller organizations, purchasing agents generally are assigned certain categories of goods. About half of all purchasing agents work for manufacturing firms.

BACKGROUND AND QUALIFICATIONS:

Most large organizations now require a college degree, and many prefer applicants who have an MBA degree. Familiarity with the computer and its uses is desirable in understanding the systems aspect of the purchasing profession. Following the initial training period, junior purchasing agents usually are given the responsibility of purchasing standard and catalog items. As they gain experience and develop expertise in their assigned areas, they may be promoted to purchasing agent and then senior purchasing agent. Continuing education is essential for purchasing agents who want to advance their careers. Purchasing agents are encouraged to participate in frequent seminars offered by professional societies, and to take courses in the field at local colleges and universities.

The recognized mark of experience and professional competence is the designation certified purchasing manager (CPM). This designation is conferred by the National Association of Purchasing Management, Inc. upon candidates who have passed four examinations and who meet educational and professional experience requirements.

EARNINGS:

Median annual earnings for purchasing agents were slightly over $23,200 in 1986. The middle 50 percent earned between $17,000 and $21,000. The bottom 10 percent earned less than $13,400, and the top 10 percent earned more than $42,400.

OUTLOOK:

Employment of purchasing agents and managers is expected to increase more slowly than the average for all occupations during the 1990's. Computerization of purchasing coupled with an increased reliance on a smaller number of suppliers should boost the productivity of purchasing personnel.

QUALITY CONTROL SUPERVISOR

DESCRIPTION:

A quality control supervisor may either be involved in the spot checking of items being manufactured or processed, or in assuring that the proper processes are being followed. A quality control system involves selection and training of personnel, product design, the establishment of specifications, procedures and tests, the design and maintenance of facilities and equipment, the selection of materials, and recordkeeping. In an effective quality control system, all these aspects are evaluated on a regular basis, and modified and improved when appropriate.

BACKGROUND AND QUALIFICATIONS:

While some quality control positions involved with the supervision of the production of simpler items might require little background besides on-the-job training, many require a specialized degree in engineering, chemistry, or biology. While all manufacturing firms require some degree of quality control, this is especially important in the chemistry, food and drug industries. Some drug manufacturers for example, may assign one out of six production workers to quality assurance functions alone.

EARNINGS:

Earnings by quality control workers vary widely, depending upon the industry. An entry level position in the food, drug, or chemical industry, for example, requires a BA in Chemistry or Biology, and brought a starting salary in 1986 in the $300-400 per week range.

OUTLOOK:

Also varies greatly, depending upon the industry.

REPORTER/EDITOR

DESCRIPTION:

Newspaper reporters gather information on current events and use it to write stories for daily or weekly newspapers. Large dailies frequently assign teams of reporters to investigate social, economic, or political conditions, and reporters are often assigned to "beats", such as police stations, courthouses, or governmental agencies, to gather news originating in these places. General assignment reporters write local news stories on a wide range of topics, from public meetings to human interest stories.

Reporters with a specialized background or interest in a particular area write, interpret, and analyze the news in fields such as medicine, politics, foreign affairs, sports, fashion, art, theater, consumer affairs, travel, finance, social events, science, education, business, labor, religion, and other areas. Critics review literary, artistic, and musical works and performances while editorial writers present viewpoints on topics of interest. Reporters on small newspapers cover all aspects of local news, and also may take photographs, write headlines, lay out pages, and write editorials. On some small weeklies, they may also solicit advertisements, sell subscriptions, and perform general office work. Reporters must be highly motivated, and are expected to work long hours.

BACKGROUND AND QUALIFICATIONS:

Most newspapers will only consider applicants with a degree in journalism, which includes training in the liberal arts in addition to professional training in journalism. Others prefer applicants who have a bachelor's degree in one of the liberal arts and a master's degree in journalism. Experience as a part-time "stringer" is very helpful in finding full time employment as a reporter.

Most beginning reporters start on weekly or small daily newspapers, with a small number of outstanding journalism graduates finding work with large daily newspapers, although this is a rare exception. Large dailies generally look for at least three years of reporting experience, acquired on smaller newspapers.

Beginning reporters are assigned duties such as reporting on civic and community meetings, summarizing speeches, writing obituaries, interviewing important community leaders or visitors, and covering police, government, or courthouse proceedings. As they gain experience, they may report on more important events, cover an assigned beat, or specialize in a particular field. Newspaper reporters may advance to large daily newspapers or state and national newswire services. However, competition for such positions is fierce, and news executives are flooded with applications from highly qualified reporters every year. Some experienced reporters become columnists, correspondents, editorial writers, editors, or top executives; these people represent the top of the field, and competition for them is extremely keen. Other reporters transfer to related fields, such as public relations, writing for magazines, or preparing copy for radio or television news programs.

EARNINGS:

Reporters working for daily newspapers having contracts negotiated by the Newspaper Guild had starting salaries ranging from about $9,400 to nearly $47,000 a year in 1986. The majority started at between $15,600 and $23,400 a year.

Experienced reporters averaged about $31,200 annually in 1986, according to figures provided by The Newspaper Guild. Virtually all experienced reporters earned over $20,800 a year, while the top contractual salary was $48,300 a year. A number of top reporters on big city dailies earned even more, on the basis of merit. Benefits may vary widely according to length of service and the size and location of the employer. Most reporters, however, receive benefits such as paid vacations, and group insurance and pension plans.

OUTLOOK:

Employment of reporters and correspondents is expected to grow through the year 2000, primarily due to the anticipated increase in the number of smalltown and suburban daily and weekly newspapers.

SECURITIES AND FINANCIAL SERVICES SALES REPRESENTATIVES

DESCRIPTION:

Securities Sales Representatives: Most investors, whether they are individuals with a few hundred dollars or large institutions with millions to invest, use securities sales representatives when buying or selling stocks, bonds, shares in mutual funds, or other financial products. Securities sales representatives also provide many related services for their customers. Depending on a customer's knowledge of the market, they may explain the meaning of stock market terms and trading practices; offer financial counseling; devise an individual financial portfolio including securities, corporate and municipal bonds, life insurance, annuities, and other investments; and offer advice on the purchase or sale of particular securities.

Financial Services Sales Representatives: Financial services sales representatives call on various businesses to solicit applications for loans and new deposit accounts for banks or savings and loan associations. They also locate and contact prospective customers to present their bank's financial services and to ascertain the customer's banking needs. At most small and medium-sized banks, branch managers and commercial loan officers are responsible for marketing the bank's financial services. As banks offer more and increasingly complex financial services, for example, securities brokerage and financial planning-the job of financial services sales representatives will assume greater importance.

BACKGROUND AND QUALIFICATIONS:

A college education is becoming increasingly important, as securities sales representatives must be well informed about economic conditions and trends. Although employers seldom require specialized academic training, courses in business administration, economics, and finance are helpful. Securities sales representatives must meet state licensing requirements, which generally include passing an examination and, in some cases, furnishing a personal bond. In addition, sales representatives must register as representatives of their firm according to regulations of the securities exchanges where they do business or the National Association of Securities Dealers, Inc. (NASD). Before beginners can qualify as registered representatives, they must pass the General Securities Registered Representative Examination.

Banks and other credit institutions prefer to hire college graduates for financial services sales jobs. A business administration degree with a specialization in finance or a liberal arts degree including courses in accounting, economics, and marketing serves as excellent preparation for this job. Financial services sales representatives learn through on-the-job training under the supervision of bank officers. Outstanding performance can lead to promotion to managerial positions.

EARNINGS:

According to the Securities Industry Association, average annual earnings of beginning securities sales representatives were $37,000 in 1986. Financial services sales representatives are paid a salary; some receive bonuses if they meet certain established goals. Average earnings of financial services sales representatives are substantially less than those of securities sales representatives.

OUTLOOK:

The demand for securities sales representatives fluctuates as the economy expands and contracts. Employment of securities sales representatives is expected to expand as economic growth, rising personal incomes, and greater inherited wealth increase the funds available for investment. Employment of financial services sales representatives is also expected to increase through the year 2000, as banks and credit institutions expand the financial services they offer, and issue more loans for personal and commercial use.

STATISTICIAN

DESCRIPTION:

Statisticians devise, carry out, and interpret the numerical results of surveys and experiments. In doing so, they apply their knowledge of statistical methods to a particular subject area, such as economics, human behavior, the natural sciences, or engineering. They may use statistical techniques to predict population growth or economic conditions, develop quality control tests for manufactured products, or help business managers and government officials make decisions and evaluate the results of new programs. Over half of all statisticians are in private industry, primarily in manufacturing, finance, and insurance firms.

BACKGROUND AND QUALIFICATIONS:

A bachelor's degree in statistics or mathematics is the minimum educational requirement for many beginning jobs in statistics. For other entry-level jobs in the field, however, a BA with a major in an applied field of study such as economics or a natural science, and a minor in statistics is preferable. A graduate degree in mathematics or statistics is essential for college and university teaching. Most mathematics statisticians have at least a BA in mathematics and an advanced degree in statistics.

Beginning statisticians who have a BA often spend their time performing routine work under the supervision of an experienced statistician. Through experience, they may advance to positions of greater technical and supervisory responsibility. However, opportunities for promotion are best for those with advanced degrees.

EARNINGS:

In the Federal Government in 1987, the average starting salary of statisticians who had a bachelor's degree and no experience was between $14,800 and $18,400 a year, depending on their grades. Beginning statisticians with a master's degree earned from $22,500 to $27,200. Those with a PhD earned from $27,200 to $32,600. The average annual salary for statisticians in the Federal Government was about $39,400 in 1986.

OUTLOOK:

Employment opportunities for persons who combine training in statistics with knowledge of computer science or a field of application - such as biology, economics or engineering - are generally expected to be favorable through the year 2000.

SYSTEMS ANALYST

DESCRIPTION:

Systems analysts plan efficient methods of processing data and handling the results. Analysts use various techniques, such as cost accounting, sampling, and mathematical model building to analyze a problem and devise a new system. The problems that systems analysts solve range from monitoring nuclear fission in a powerplant to forecasting sales for an appliance manufacturing firm. Because the work is so varied and complex, Analysts usually specialize in either business or scientific and engineering applications. Most systems analysts work in manufacturing firms, banks, insurance companies, and data processing service organizations. In addition, large numbers work for wholesale and retail businesses and government agencies.

BACKGROUND AND QUALIFICATIONS:

College graduates are almost always sought for the position of systems analyst. For some of the more complex positions, persons with graduate degrees are preferred. Employers usually seek analysts with a background in accounting, business management, or economics for work in a business environment, while a background in the physical sciences, mathematics, or engineering is preferred for work in scientifically oriented organizations. A growing number of employers seek applicants who have a degree in Computer Science, Information Systems, or Data Processing. Regardless of the college major, employers seek those who are familiar with programming languages.

In order to advance, systems analysts must continue their technical education. Technological advances come so rapidly in the computer field that continuous study is necessary to keep computer skills up to date. Training usually takes the form of one and two-week courses offered by employers and software vendors. Additional training may come from professional development seminars offered by professional computing societies. An indication of experience and professional competence is the Certificate in Data Processing (CDP). This designation is conferred by the Institute for Certification of Computer Professionals, and is granted to candidates who have five years experience and have passed a five-part examination.

EARNINGS:

Median annual earnings of systems analysts who worked full time in 1986 were about $32,800. In the Federal Government, the entrance salary for recent college graduates with a bachelor's degree was about $14,800 a year in 1987. Salaries tend to be highest in mining and public utilities and lowest in finance, insurance, and real estate.

OUTLOOK:

The demand for systems analysts is expected to rise through the year 2000, as advances in technology lead to new applications for computers. Factory and office automation, advances in telecommunications technology, and scientific research are just a few areas where use of computers will expand.

TECHNICAL WRITER/EDITOR

DESCRIPTION:

Technical writers and technical editors research, write, and edit technical materials, and also may produce publications and audiovisual materials. To ensure that their work is accurate, Technical Writers must be expert in the subject area in which they are writing. Editors are also responsible for the accuracy of material on which they work. Some organizations use job titles other than technical writer/editor, such as staff writer, publications engineer, communications specialist, publications engineer, communications specialist, industrial writer, industrial materials developer, and others.

Technical writers set out either to instruct or inform, and in many instances they do both. They prepare manuals, catalogs, parts lists, and instructional materials needed by sales representatives who sell machinery or scientific equipment and by the technicians who install, maintain, and service it. Technical writers are often part of a team, working closely with scientists, engineers, accountants, and others. Technical editors take the material Technical writers produce and further polish it for final publication and use. Many writers and editors work for large firms in the electronics, aviation, aerospace, ordinance, chemical, pharmaceutical, and computer manufacturing industries. Firms in the energy, communications, and computer software fields also employ many technical writers, and research laboratories employ significant numbers.

BACKGROUND AND QUALIFICATIONS:

Employers seek people whose educational background, work experience, and personal pursuits indicate they possess both writing skills and appropriate scientific knowledge. Knowledge of graphics and other aspects of publication production may be helpful in landing a job in the field. An understanding of current trends in communication technology is an asset, and familiarity with computer operations and terminology is increasingly important. Many employers prefer candidates with a degree in science or engineering, plus a minor in English, journalism, or technical communications. Other employers emphasize writing ability and look for candidates whose major field of study was journalism, English, or the liberal arts. Depending on their line of business, these employees almost always require course work or practical experience in a specific subject as well, computer science, for example.

People with a solid background in science or engineering are at an advantage in competing for such jobs. Those with BA's or MA's in Technical Writing are often preferred over candidates with little or no technical background. Beginning technical writers often assist experienced writers by doing library research and preparing drafts of reports. Experienced technical writers in companies with large writing staffs may eventually move to the job of technical editor, or shift to an administrative position in the publication or technical information departments. The top job is usually that of publications manager (and other titles), who normally supervises all of the people directly involved in producing the company's technical documents. The manager supervises not only the technical writers and editors, but also staff members responsible for illustrations, photography, reproduction, and distribution.

EARNINGS:

In 1986, beginning salaries for writers and editorial assistants ranged from $18,400 to $29,300 annually, according to surveys by the Executive Compensation Service. Salaries for technical writers ranged from $19,300 to $37,800. Experienced editors generally earned between $20,900 and $39,000; supervisory editors, $28,600 to $42,600 a year.

OUTLOOK:

Through the year 2000, the outlook for writing and editing jobs is expected to continue to be keenly competitive. With the increasing complexity of industrial and scientific equipment, more users will depend on the technical writer's ability to prepare precise but simple explanations and instructions.

UNDERWRITER

DESCRIPTION:

Underwriters appraise and select the risks their company will insure. Underwriters decide whether their insurance company will accept risks after analyzing information in insurance applications, reports from loss control consultants, medical reports, and actuarial studies. Most Underwriters specialize in one of the three major categories of insurance: life, casualty, and health. They further specialize in group or individual policies.

BACKGROUND AND QUALIFICATIONS:

For beginning underwriters, most large insurance companies seek college graduates with degrees in liberal arts or business administration. Underwriter trainees begin by evaluating routine applicants under the close supervision of an experienced risk appraiser. Continuing education is a necessity if the underwriter expects to advance to senior level positions. Insurance companies generally place great emphasis on completion of one or more of the many recognized independent study programs. Many companies pay tuition and the cost of books for those who successfully complete underwriting courses; some offer salary increases as an additional incentive. Independent study programs are available through the American Institute of Property and Liability Underwriters, the Health Insurance Association of America, and the Life Office Management Association.

As underwriters gain experience, they can qualify as a "Fellow" of the Academy of Life Underwriters by passing a series of examinations and completing a research paper on a topic in the field. Exams are given by the Institute of Home Office Underwriters and the Home Office Life Underwriters Association. The designation of "Fellow" is recognized as a mark of achievement in the underwriting field. Experienced underwriters who complete a course of study may advance to chief underwriter or underwriting manager. Some underwriting managers are promoted to senior managerial positions after several years.

EARNINGS:

According to a survey of property and liability insurance companies, personal lines (noncommercial) underwriters earned a median salary of $21,300 a year in 1986, while commercial lines underwriters earned $23,600 a year. Senior personal and commercial lines underwriters received a median salary of $28,600.

OUTLOOK:

Employment of underwriters is expected to rise faster than the average for all occupations through the year 2000 as insurance sales continue to expand. Most job openings, however, are expected to result from the need to replace underwriters who transfer to other occupations or stop working altogether.

PART THREE: WHERE THE JOBS ARE

Primary Greater Chicago Employers

ACCOUNTING AND AUDITING

For more information on professional employment opportunities in the accounting industry, contact the following professional and trade organizations, as listed beginning on page 295:

AMERICAN INSTITUTE OF CERTIFIED PUBLIC ACCOUNTANTS
THE EDP AUDITORS ASSOCIATION
INDEPENDENT ACCOUNTANTS ASSOCIATION OF ILLINOIS
INSTITUTE OF INTERNAL AUDITORS/CHICAGO CHAPTER
NATIONAL SOCIETY OF PUBLIC ACCOUNTANTS

CLIFTON GUNDERSON & COMPANY
301 South West Adams
Peoria IL 61602
309/671-4560
Contact Director of Personnel. A full-service accounting firm.

DELOITTE & TOUCHE
200 East Randolph Drive
75th floor
Chicago IL 60601
312/861-1161
Contact John McGrath, Director/Professional Recruiting. A CPA firm. Provides accounting, management advisory services, and tax consultation services. Corporate headquarters location. International.

KPMG/PEAT MARWICK
303 East Wacker Drive
Chicago IL 60601
312/938-1000
Contact Patricia Gamble, Director of Human Resources. One of the largest CPA firms in the world.

LAVENTHOL & HORWATH
300 South Riverside
Chicago IL 60606
312/648-0555
Contact William Haase, Personnel Director. Chicago office of the nationally recognized accounting and consulting firm.

PRICE WATERHOUSE
200 East Randolph
Chicago IL 60601
312/565-1500
Contact Mark Ormond, Recruitment Director. One of the largest international public accounting firms, with 115 United States offices and more than 400 offices in 100 countries. Common positions include: Accountant; Auditor; Attorney-Tax; Computer Programmer; Management Consultant; Systems Analyst; Technical Writer/Editor; Tax Specialist. Principal educational backgrounds sought: Accounting; Computer Science; Economics; Engineering. Training programs offered; Internships offered. Company benefits include: medical insurance; dental insurance; pension plan; life insurance; tuition assistance; disability coverage; daycare assistance; profit sharing; savings plan; 25 days vacation. United States headquarters location: New York, NY. World headquarters location: London, England. Operations at this facility include: regional headquarters; service.

ARTHUR YOUNG & COMPANY
One IBM Plaza
Chicago IL 60611
312/645-3000
Contact Micki Grace, Director of Recruiting-Chicago. Micki Grace can be contacted at 150 South Wacker Drive, Chicago IL 60606. A major international public accounting firm with services in three major areas: auditing and accounting, tax services, and management (consulting) services. Operates more than 90 offices and facilities in the United States, with international offices in over 65 foreign countries. Common positions include: Accountant. Principal educational backgrounds sought: Accounting. Company benefits include: medical, dental, and life insurance; pension plan; tuition assistance; disability coverage; 401K. Corporate headquarters location. Operations at this facility include: regional headquarters

ADVERTISING, MARKETING & PUBLIC RELATIONS

For more information on professional employment opportunities in the advertising and public relations industries, contact the following professional and trade organizations, as listed beginning on page 295:

AMERICAN ADVERTISING FEDERATION
AMERICAN ASSOCIATION OF ADVERTISING AGENCIES
AMERICAN MARKETING ASSOCIATION
BUSINESS-PROFESSIONAL ADVERTISING ASSOCIATION
FINANCIAL RELATIONS BOARD INC.
TELEVISION BUREAU OF ADVERTISING/CHICAGO
PUBLIC RELATIONS SOCIETY OF AMERICA
TELEVISION BUREAU OF ADVERTISING

ADVERTISING METAL DISPLAY
4620 West 19th Street
Cicero IL 60650
708/863-8900
Contact Bob Harris, Personnel. Manufactures and sells point of purchase displays.

N.W. AYER INC
111 East Wacker Drive
2nd Floor
Chicago IL 60601
312/280-0830
Contact department of interest. The Chicago office of the nationally recognized advertising agency.

BBDO CHICAGO INC.
410 North Michigan Avenue
Chicago IL 60611
312/337-7860
Contact Michelle Shotts, Vice President, Human Resources. Chicago office of the nationally known advertising agency. Common positions include: Advertising Worker; Buyer; Commercial Artist; Marketing Specialist; Personnel & Labor Relations Specialist; Public Relations Specialist; Statistician; Systems Analyst. Principal educational backgrounds sought: Art/Design; Business Administration; Communications; Computer Science; Finance; Liberal Arts; Marketing; Mathematics. Training programs offered; Internships offered. Company benefits include: medical, dental, and life insurance; profit sharing. Corporate headquarters location: New York, NY. Parent company: Omnicom. Operations at this facility include: administration; service.

FOOTE CONE AND BELDING COMMUNICATIONS
101 East Erie
Chicago IL 60611
312/751-7000
Contact Joseph Vinci, College Relations Representative. Ranks as the 8th largest advertising agency in the U.S.

BOZELL
625 North Michigan Avenue
Chicago IL 60611
312/988-2000
Contact Barbara King, Manager, Human Resources. Area offices of a major international advertising agency. Services include marketing and community relations.

CHICAGO DISPLAY COMPANY
1301 West Armitage Avenue
Melrose Park IL 60130
312/379-8500
Contact Joan Maddocks, Personnel Manager. Makes advertising displays for merchandisers & manufacturers.

DDB NEEDHAM WORLDWIDE
303 East Wacker Drive
Chicago IL 60601
312/861-0200
Contact Patricia DuBoux, V.P., Director of Human Resources. An advertising agency. Corporate headquarters location: New York, NY. Parent company: Omnicom. Common positions include: Account Executive; Account Supervisor; Media Planner; Media Buyer; Research Supervisor; Copywriter; Art Director; Creative Director; Secretary; Accounting Clerk. Principal educational backgrounds sought: Art/Design; Business Administration; Communications; Liberal Arts; Marketing; Mathematics. Company benefits include: medical insurance; dental insurance; life insurance; pension plan; tuition assistance; disability coverage; profit sharing; employee discounts; savings plan. Operations at this facility include: research/marketing; administration; service.

BERNARD HODES ADVERTISING
205 West Wacker Drive
Suite 1300
Chicago IL 60606
312/222-5800
Contact Mrs. Greta Sherman, Branch Manager. Chicago office of a national recruitment advertising agency

INFORMATION RESOURCES, INC.
150 North Clinton Street
Chicago IL 60606
Contact Thomas Quinn, Senior Corporate Recruiter. A major metropolitan Chicago marketing research firm. Common positions include: Accountant; Computer Programmer; Electrical Engineer. Principal educational backgrounds sought: Accounting; Computer Science; Marketing. Company benefits include: medical, dental, and life insurance; tuition assistance; disability coverage; employee discounts; savings plan. Corporate headquarters location. Operations at this facility include: divisional headquarters; research/development; sales.

KETCHUM COMMUNICATIONS, INC.
142 East Ontario
Chicago IL 60611
312/266-4550
Contact Paula Williams, Administrative Assistant. A Chicago area public relations agency. Common positions include: Public Relations Specialist; Technical Writer/Editor. Principal educational backgrounds sought: Business Administration; Communications; Marketing. Training programs offered; Internships offered. Corporate headquarters location: Pittsburgh, PA. Operations at this facility include: regional headquarters.

SAATCHI SAATCHI DFS
225 North Michigan
Suite 900
Chicago IL 60601
312/856-1046
Contact Mary Palmer, Broadcast Director. Chicago office of the nationally known advertising agency.

J. WALTER THOMPSON USA INC.
875 North Michigan Avenue
Chicago IL 60611
312/951-4000
Contact Barbara Lewis, V.P. & Director of Personnel. Chicago office of the well-known company engaged in advertising, public relations, research, and related activites. Subsidiares include J. Walter Thompson Company, one of the world's largest advertising agencies, which plans and creates consumer, direct response, trade, and corporate advertising, recruitment and medical advertising, and other services, including the design and production of merchandising and sales promotion programs and a wide range of consumer, media, and market research; Hill and Knowlton, Inc., the world's largest public relations firm; Lord, Geller, Federico, Einstein, Inc., a New York-based full-service agency noted for its creative flair and effective execution; and Simmons Market Research Bureau, Inc., a syndicated market research firm, and one of the leading United States authorities on magazine readership and demographics. Company employs more than 8,600 people worldwide.

YOUNG & RUBICAM/CHICAGO
1 South Wacker Drive
Suite 1800
Chicago IL 60606
312/845-4000
Contact Larry Claypoll, Vice President, Business Manager. A major international advertising agency, with 126 agency offices throughout the world. Operates through three divisions: Young & Rubicam International, with offices througghout the world; Marsteller Inc., a worldwide leader in business-to-business and consumer advertising, with offices throughout the

Unites States and worldwide, with subsidiary Burson-Marsteller providing public relations services throughout the world; and Young & Rubicam USA, with 14 consumer advertising agencies operating through four regional groups (except Young & Rubicam Detroit), and five specialized advertising/marketing agencies. Corporate headquarters location: New York, NY.

AMUSEMENT, ARTS, RECREATION

For more information on professional employment opportunities in the arts, entertainment, or leisure industries, contact the following professional and trade organizations, as listed beginning on page 295:

AMERICAN ASSOCIATION OF ZOOLOGICAL PARKS & AQUARIUMS
AMERICAN FEDERATION OF MUSICIANS
AMERICAN FEDERATION OF MUSICIANS/CHICAGO
AMERICAN FEDERATION OF TELEVISION AND RADIO ARTISTS
NATIONAL ENDOWMENT FOR THE ARTS
NATIONAL ENDOWMENT FOR THE ARTS/CHICAGO
NATIONAL RECREATION AND PARKS ASSOCIATION/CHICAGO
THEATRE COMMUNICATIONS GROUP

BALLY MANUFACTURING
8700 West Bryn Mawr Avenue
Chicago IL 60631
312/399-1300
Contact Mrs. Lois Balodis, Personnel Director. Major manufacturers of pinball, video, slot and exercise machines. Also engaged in the ownership and operation of health clubs, hotels, and casinos.

FAIRMONT RACE TRACK/
OGDEN FAIRMONT INC.
Route 40
Collinsville IL 62234
618/345-4300
Contact Brian Zander, General Manager. A major area race track specializing in horse racing. Employs over 400.

FIELD MUSEUM OF NATURAL HISTORY
Roosevelt Road at Lake Shore Drive
Chicago IL 60605
312/922-9410
Contact Human Resources Administrator. A research and education museum.

MUSEUM OF SCIENCE & INDUSTRY
57th Street and Lake Shore Drive
Chicago IL 60637
312/684-1414
Contact Judy Kupfer, Personnel Coordinator. One of the largest museums of science and industry in the world. Corporate headquarters location.

WICKS ORGAN COMPANY
1100 Fifth Street
Highland IL 62249
618/654-2191
Contact Martin Wick, President. A prestigious manufacturer of church pipe organs.

APPAREL & TEXTILES MANUFACTURING

For more information on professional employment opportunities in the apparel, textile or fashion industries, contact the following professional and trade organizations, as listed beginning on page 295:

AMERICAN APPAREL MANUFACTURERS ASSOCIATION
AMERICAN TEXTILE MANUFACTURERS INSTITUTE
NORTHERN TEXTILE ASSOCIATION
TEXTILE RESEARCH INSTITUTE

ARATEX SERVICES, INC.
1834 Walden Office Square
Suite 450
Schaumburg IL 60173
708/397-9500
Contact Connie Melhuse, Area Human Resource Manager. A major garment rental company, serving more than 280,000.

ARTEX INTERNATIONAL INC.
1405 S. Walnut Street
Highland IL 62249
618/654-2114
Contact Personnel Department. Major area apparel company, specializing in the manufacturer of dyed and imprinted tablecloths and napkins. Employs over 100.

BELLEVILLE SHOE MANUFACTURING COMPANY
100 Premier Drive
Belleville IL 62223
618/233-5600
Contact Bill Tripp, Plant Manager. Manufacturers of men's and boy's shoes. Employs over 300.

R.A. BRIGGS & COMPANY
650 North Church Street
Lake Zurich IL 60047
Contact Vincent P. Smyth, Personnel Director. Specializes in textiles with silk screening and embroidery.

FLORSHEIM SHOE COMPANY
130 South Canal Street
Chicago IL 60606.
Contact Personnel Manager. A retailer and manufacturer of footwear.

HARTMARX CORPORATION
101 North Wacker Drive
Chicago IL 60606
312/372-6300
Contact Human Resources Coordinator. A manufacturer and retailer of men's and women's apparel.

LANE BRYANT, INC.
75 Oakbrook Center
Oak Brook IL 60521
708/573-8602
Contact Richard Martin, Regional Manager. Purchases, distributes, & sells apparel, shoes, etc.

LERNER STORES CORPORATION
4190 East North Harlem Avenue
Chicago IL 60634
312/625-3991
Contact Regional Office. Sells moderately priced women's fashions, except shoes.

O'BRYAN BROTHERS
4220 West Belmont Avenue
Chicago IL 60641
312/283-3000
Contact Denis B. O'Keefe, Director of Personnel. An apparel manufacturer specializing in ladies' loungewear and lingerie. Corporate headquarters location.

OXFORD CLOTHES
1220 West Van Buren Street
Chicago IL 60607
312/829-3600
Contact Robert Stepman, Personnel Manager. Manufacturer of men's and boys' suits and coats. A subsidiary of Koracorp Industries, Inc. Corporate headquarters location.

OZITE CORPORATION
1755 Butterfield Road
Libertyville IL 60048
708/362-8210
Contact Kathy Fox, Personnel. Manufactures commercial, automotive, and industrial carpeting and wall covering. Corporate headquarters location. Common positions include: Accountant; Administrator; Bank Officer/Manager; Blue-Collar Worker Supervisor; Buyer; Chemist; Claim Representative; Computer Programmer; Credit Manager; Customer Service Representative; Industrial Engineer; Personnel & Labor Relations Specialist; Purchasing Agent; Quality Control Supervisor; Sales Representative. Principal educational backgrounds sought: Accounting; Business Administration; Engineering; Liberal Arts; Marketing. Company benefits include: medical insurance; dental insurance; pension plan; life insurance; tuition assistance; disability coverage; profit sharing; employee discounts; savings plan.

BANKING/SAVINGS AND LOAN

For more information on professional employment opportunities in the banking industry, contact the following professional and trade organizations, as listed beginning on page 295:

AMERICAN BANKERS ASSOCIATION
BANK ADMINISTRATION INSTITUTE
COMMUNITY BANKERS ASSOCIATION OF ILLINOIS
ILLINOIS BANKERS ASSOCIATION
INDEPENDENT BANKERS ASSOCIATION OF AMERICA
INSTITUTE OF FINANCIAL EDUCATION
NATIONAL COUNCIL OF SAVINGS INSTITUTIONS

AMERICAN NATIONAL BANK AND TRUST
33 North La Salle Street
Chicago IL 60690
312/661-6907
Contact Ron Yenerich, Vice President of Personnel. Provides banking services to corporate clients.

BOATMEN'S NATIONAL BANK OF BELLEVILLE
23 Public Square
Belleville IL 62222-0367
618/233-6600
Contact Personnel Officer. A full-service St. Louis area bank. Employs over 100. Corporate headquarters location: St. Louis MO. Parent company: Boatmen's Bancshares, Inc. Common positions include: Bank Office/Manager; Customer Service Representative; Branch Manager; Department Manager. Principal educational backgrounds sought: Accounting; Business Administration; Finance. Company benfits include: medical, dental, and life insurance; pension plan; tuition assistance; disability coverage; employee discounts; savings plan.

BOULEVARD BANK NATIONAL ASSOCIATION
410 North Michigan Avenue
Chicago IL 60611
312/836-6505
Contact Katie Speth, Senior Human Resources Recruiter. A full-service bank, the 13th largest in the state of IL.

CITICORP SAVINGS OF ILLINOIS
One South Dearborn Street
Chicago IL 60603
312/977-5000
Contact Ian Ostergard, Vice President. A full service consumer banking institution.

CONTINENTAL ILLINOIS NATIONAL BANK
231 South LaSalle Street
Chicago IL 60697
312/828-2345
Contact Joseph Thompson, Personnel Director. One of the largest banks in the Chicago area.

EAGLE BANCORPORATION INC.
1223 Broadway
P.O. Box 70
Highland IL 62249
618/654-4511
Contact Marsh Kennett, Personnel Director. Bank holding company, national member of Federal Reserve System. Employs over 100.

EXCHANGE NATIONAL BANK OF CHICAGO
120 South LaSalle Street
Chicago IL 60603
312/781-8661
Contact Joan Schellhorn, Employment Manager. A commercial middle market bank. Member of FDIC.

FEDERAL RESERVE BANK OF CHICAGO
230 South LaSalle Street
Chicago IL 60604
312/322-5496
Contact Bob DiCosola, Personnel Director. A member of the Federal Reserve, the nation's central bank.

FIRST NATIONAL BANK OF BELLEVILLE
19 Public Square
Belleville IL 62220
618/234-0020
Contact Les Mehrtens, Personnel Dirctor. A leading St. Louis area national banking institution. Employs over 300.

GERMANIA FEDERAL SAVINGS AND LOAN ASSOCIATION
543 E. Broadway
Alton IL 62002
618/465-5543
Contact Joan Springman, Asst. Vice President, Personnel Officer. Federal savings and loan association. Employs over 100.

HARRIS TRUST AND SAVINGS BANK
111 W. Monroe Street
Chicago IL 60690
312/461-7646
Contact Human Resources Department. A full service banking institution.

ILLINI FEDERAL SAVINGS AND LOAN ASSOCIATION
6550 North Illinois Street
Fairview Heights IL 62208
618/397-5300
Contact Bill Bright, Personnel Director. A federal savings and loan association.

LASALLE
135 South LaSalle Street
Chicago IL 60603
312/443-2000
Contact Mary McClay, Personnel. The sixth largest bank in Illinois offering full banking.

LASALLE BANK/LAKEVIEW BANK
3201 North Ashland Avenue
Chicago IL 60657
312/525-2180
Contact Carolyn K. Cacal, Personnel Administrator. A full-service bank with one location in Chicago.

MERCHANDISE NATIONAL BANK
Merchandise Mart
Chicago IL 60654
312/836-8120
Contact Mrs. Metcalfe, Director of Personnel. A commercial bank. Offices in Germania Club, as well as in Merchandise Mart. Corporate headquarters location. Common positions include: Accountant; Bank Officer/Manager; Credit Manager; Customer Service Representative; Teller. Principal educational backgrounds sought: Accounting; Business Administration; Finance. Company benefits include: medical insurance; dental insurance; pension plan; life insurance; tuition assistance; disability coverage; employee discounts; savings plan.

NORTHWEST NATIONAL BANK
4747 W. Irving Park
Chicago IL 60641
312/777-7700
Contact Vice President of Personnel. A commercial bank. A subsidiary of Northwestco, Inc. Corporate headquarters location.

OLD KENT BANK
Sears Tower
Chicago IL 60606
312/876-4200
Contact Personnel Recruiter. Engaged in the commercial banking and trust business, including taking deposits, making secured and unsecured loans, financing commercial transactions, underwriting municipal obligations, renting safe deposit boxes, providing travel services, and performing corporate, pension, and personal trust services.

ST. PAUL FEDERAL BANK FOR SAVINGS
6700 West North Avenue
Chicago IL 60635
312/622-5000
Contact Karen Antink, Employment Manager. Federally chartered savings and loan association. There are multiple branch locations in Chicago and the suburbs. Corporate headquarters location. Common positions include: Accountant; Customer Service Representative; Sales Representative. Principal educational backgrounds sought: Accounting; Finance. Training programs offered. Company benefits include: medical, dental, and life insurance; pension plan; tuition assistance; disability coverage; profit sharing; employee discounts; savings plan. Operations at this facility include: administration; service; sales.

TALMAN HOME FEDERAL SAVINGS AND LOAN ASSOCIATION OF ILLINOIS
5501 South Kedzie Avenue
Chicago IL 60629
312/434-3322
Contact Mr. Robert Brigham, Director of Human Resources. One of the nation's largest savings and loan associations. Branch offices throughout Chicago and its suburbs, and central Illinois. It owns two subsidiaries: Talman Insurance Services, Inc. and Talman Home Mortgage Corporation, which has offices nationwide. Common positions include: Accountant; Advertising Worker; Attorney; Bank Officer/Manager; Claim Representative; Consumer Loan Officer; Credit Manager; Customer Service Representative; Financial Analyst; Financial Counselor; Insurance Agent/Broker; Branch Manager; Department Manager; Consumer Loan Officer; Mortgage Loan Officer; Personnel & Labor Relations Specialist; Public Relations Worker; Purchasing Agent; Systems Analyst; Underwriter. Principal educational backgrounds sought: Accounting; Business Administration; Communications; Computer Science; Economics; Finance; Liberal Arts; Marketing. Company benefits include: medical, dental, and life insurance; pension plan; tuition assistance; disability coverage; savings plan. Corporate headquarters location: 30 West Monroe Street, Chicago, IL 60603. Operations at this facility include: regional headquarters; divisional headquarters; administration; service.

BOOK AND MAGAZINE PUBLISHING

For more information on professional employment opportunities in the book and magazine publishing industries, contact the following professional and trade organizations, as listed beginning on page 295:

AMERICAN BOOKSELLERS ASSOCIATION
ASSOCIATION OF AMERICAN PUBLISHERS
MAGAZINE PUBLISHERS ASSOCIATION
WRITERS GUILD OF AMERICA EAST, INC.
WRITERS GUILD OF AMERICA WEST, INC.

BELL & HOWELL COMPANY
5215 Old Orchard Road
Skokie IL 60077
708/740-7685
Contact Cheryl Haas, Corporate Human Resource Manager. Offices of the publishing/information services company.

CHILDRENS PRESS
5440 North Cumberland Avenue
Chicago IL 60656
312/693-0800
Contact Carol Werkmeister, Personnel Assistant. Children's Press, publishes a wide list of children's books. Common positions include: Accountant; Computer Programmer; Customer Service Representative; Sales Representative; Editor. Company benefits include: medical insurance; dental insurance; pension plan; life insurance; disability coverage; savings plan. Corporate headquarters location: Danbury, CT. Parent company is Grolier, Inc. Operations at this facility include: manufacturing; administration; sales.

CHRISTIANITY TODAY, INC.
465 Gundersen Drive
Carol Stream IL 60188
312/260-6200
Contact Jo Ann Selander, Director of Personnel. A major Chicago area publisher of religious magazines.

COMMERCE CLEARING HOUSE, INC.
4025 West Peterson Avenue
Chicago IL 60646
312/583-8500
Contact Darde Gaertner, Personnel Director. Publishes current information, primarily in tax and law.

DAVID C. COOK PUBLISHING COMPANY
850 North Grove Avenue
Elgin IL 60120
312/741-2400
Contact Jon Kobel, Employment Assistant. Creates, designs, produces, prints, markets, and distributes non-denominational Christian education material. Common positions include: Blue Collar Worker Supervisor; Buyer; Computer Programmer; Customer Service Representative; Department Manager; Operations/Production Manager; Marketing Specialist; Personnel & Labor Relations Specialist; Public Relations Specialist; Purchasing Agent; Sales Representative; Statistician; Systems Analyst. Principal educational backgrounds sought: Accounting; Art/Design; Business Administration; Communications; Computer Science; Finance; Marketing; Mathematics. Company benefits include: medical, dental, and life insurance; tuition assistance; disability coverage; employee discounts; 401 K. Operations at this facility include: manufacturing; research/development; administration; service; sales.

DONNELLEY DIRECTORY
205 North Michigan Avenue
Chicago IL 60601
Contact Bill Sheehan, General Personnel. Engaged in the sales and publishing of Yellow Pages.

ENCYCLOPEDIA BRITANNICA
310 South Michigan Avenue
Chicago IL 60604
312/347-7284
Contact Personnel Manager. Publishers of reference books and educational materials.

FOLLETT CORPORATION
1000 West Washington Boulevard
Chicago IL 60607
312/666-4300
Contact Carl Dickes, Director of Human Resources. Primarily concerned with education products and services.

CHARLES LEVY CIRCULATING COMPANY
1200 North Branch Street
Chicago IL 60622
312/440-4400
Contact Frances Lefkow, Personnel Director. A major area magazine, book and newspaper distributor.

RAND McNALLY & COMPANY
8255 Central Park Avenue
Skokie IL 60076
708/673-9100
Contact Employment Manager. A major book and map publisher. Well-known products include road atlases. Corporate headquarters location.

SCOTT, FORESMAN AND COMPANY
1900 East Lake Avenue
Glenview IL 60025
312/729-3000
Contact Human Resources Department. A subsidiary of SFN Companies, Inc. Publisher of elementary, secondary and college textbooks and materials; also adult and continuing education; and educational software. Common positions include: Accountant; Advertising Worker; Computer Programmer; Credit Manager; Customer Service Representative; Department Manager; Editor; Marketing Specialist; Personnel Specialist; Sales Representative; Systems Analyst. Principal educational backgrounds sought: Accounting; Art/Design; Business Administration; Computer Assisted Instruction; Computer Science; Finance; Liberal Arts; Marketing; Mathematics. Company benefits include: medical insurance; dental insurance; pension plan;

life insurance; tuition assistance; disability coverage; profit sharing; employee discounts; savings plan; benefit reimbursement account. Parent company is Time, Inc. American Stock Exchange. Corporate, regional headquarters location. Operations at this facility include: service; sales.

SCRIPTURE PRESS PUBLICATIONS
1825 College Avenue
Wheaton IL 60187
708/668-6000
Contact Douglas Walton, Employment Manager. Publishers of Christian Education materials, providing Sunday School curriculum, books, training and resources for all ages. Common positions include: Accountant; Advertising Worker; Commercial Artist; Customer Service Representative; Marketing Specialist; Purchasing Agent; Sales Representative; Writer/Editor. Principal educational backgrounds sought: Accounting; Art/Design; Communications; Liberal Arts; Marketing. Company benefits include: medical insurance; dental insurance; pension plan; life insurance; tuition assistance; disability coverage; profit sharing; employee discounts; savings plan. Corporate headquarters location. Operations include: research/development; administration; service; sales; distribution.

STANDARD RATE & DATA
3004 Glenview Road
Wilmette IL 60091
708/256-6067
Contact Ms. Liz Conner, Personnel Director. Subsidiary of Macmillan, Inc. Publishers of specialized directories for advertising agencies. Corporate headquarters location.

BROADCASTING

For more information on professional employment opportunities in the broadcasting industry, contact the following professional and trade organizations, as listed beginning on page 295:

BROADCAST EDUCATION ASSOCIATION
CABLE TELEVISION ASSOCIATION
FEDERAL COMMUNICATIONS COMMISSION
ILLINOIS CABLE TELEVISION ASSOCIATION
INTERNATIONAL RADIO AND TV SOCIETY
NATIONAL ASSOCIATION OF BROADCASTERS
NATIONAL ASSOCIATION OF BROADCASTERS/ILLINOIS
NATIONAL ASSOCIATION OF BUSINESS AND EDUCATIONAL RADIO
TELEVISION BUREAU OF ADVERTISING
TELEVISION BUREAU OF ADVERTISING/CHICAGO
WOMEN IN RADIO AND TV, INC.

NBC INC.
Merchandise Mart
19th Floor
Chicago IL 60654
312/836-5555
Contact Janet Maldonado, Administrator, Personnel. Operating facilities for one television station and a regional office for the national television sales network. Parent company: GE. Common positions include: Accountant; Advertising Worker; Broadcast Engineer and Technician; Broadcast Professional; Electrical Engineer; Financial Analyst; Reporter/Editor; Sales Representative. Principal educational backgrounds sought: Accounting; Business Administration; Communications; Engineering; Finance; Journalism; Liberal Arts. Company benefits include: medical insurance; dental insurance; pension plan; life insurance; tuition assistance; disability coverage; employee discounts; savings plan; dependent life insurance. Regional headquarters location. Corporate headquarters: New York, NY.

A.C. NIELSEN
Nielsen Plaza
Northbrook IL 60062
708/498-6300
Contact Personnel. Provides demographic and related information for the consumer goods industry, such as television audience-rating services and consumer polling. Corporate headquarters location.

CHARITABLE, NON-PROFIT, HUMANITARIAN

For more information on professional employment opportunities with charitable, non-profit or humanitarian organizations, contact the following professional and trade associations, as listed beginning on page 295:

NATIONAL ASSOCIATION OF SOCIAL WORKERS
NATIONAL ORGANIZATION FOR HUMAN SERVICE EDUCATION

AMERICAN NATIONAL RED CROSS
43 East Ohio Street
Chicago IL 60611
312/440-2236
Contact Jean Budza, Employment Specialist. A social services organization committed to the health and safety needs of the community.

INTERNATIONAL ASSOCIATION OF LIONS CLUBS
300 22nd Street
Oak Brook IL 60521-8842
708/571-5466
Contact Peggy Malenchik, Personnel Manager. A major international service club organization.

KNOX COUNTY COUNCIL FOR DEVELOPMENTAL DISABILITIES
Suite 204 Bondi Building
Galesburg IL 61401
309/342-2125
Contact Mary Crittenden, Assistant Administrator. A not-for-profit agency serving the developmentally disabled.

NATIONAL SAFETY COUNCIL
444 North Michigan Avenue
Chicago IL 60611
312/527-4800
Contact Stacey Donovan, Human Resources Department. A non-governmental, not-for-profit public service organization. Common positions include: Accountant; Advertising Worker; Blue-Collar Worker Supervisor; Computer Programmer; Credit Manager; Customer Service Representative; Chemical Engineer; Industrial Hygienest; Metallurgical Engineer; Mining Engineer; Financial Analyst; Marketing Specialist; Personnel & Labor Relations Specialist; Public Relations Specialist; Purchasing Agent; Reporter/Editor; Statistician; Systems Analyst; Technical Writer/Editor; Transportation & Traffic Specialist; Warehouse Worker; Data Entry Operator; Administrative Secretary. Principal educational backgrounds sought: Accounting; Business Administration; Communications; Computer Science; Finance; Journalism; Marketing. Company benefits include: medical insurance; pension plan; life insurance; tuition assistance; disability coverage; savings plan. Corporate headquarters location. Operations at this facility include: regional headquarters; administration; sales

THE WOODLAWN ORGANIZATION
6040 South Harper Street
Chicago IL 60637
312/288-5840
Contact Personnel Director. Neighborhood community organization founded to serve the needs of Woodlawn residents. Provides social services, detox center, child abuse center, mental health facilities, two early childhood development programs, secretarial and word-processing training programs, a youth try-out employment project, and real estate management of property owned by HUD. Social services are available citywide, not limited to Woodlawn residents. Common positions include: Accountant; Administrator; Computer Programmer; Financial Analyst; Department Manager; Purchasing Agent; Social Worker; Alcoholism/Drug Counselor; Nurse; Early Childhood Development Teacher. Principal educational backgrounds sought:

Accounting; Business Administration; Computer Science; Finance; Liberal Arts. Company benefits include: medical, dental and life insurance; tuition assistance. Corporate headquarters location. Operations at this facility include: administration.

CHEMICALS & RELATED:
PRODUCTION, PROCESSING AND DISPOSAL

For more information on professional employment opportunities in the chemical industry, contact the following professional and trade organizations, as listed beginning on page 295:

AMERICAN CHEMICAL SOCIETY
AMERICAN INSTITUTE OF CHEMICAL ENGINEERING
AMERICAN INSTITUTE OF CHEMICAL ENGINEERING/CHICAGO
AMERICAN INSTITUTE OF CHEMISTS
AMERICAN INSTITUTE OF CHEMISTS/CHICAGO
ASSOCIATION OF STATE & INTERSTATE
 WATER POLLUTION CONTROL ADMINISTRATORS
WATER POLLUTION CONTROL FEDERATION

ALLIED CHEMICAL CORPORATON
1701 East Woodfield Rd.
Schaumburg IL 60173
708/884-4882
Contact Personnel Director at 201/455-2000. Business operations are carried out by four operating units: Union Texas Petroleum, Chemicals, Fibers and Eltra Corporation.

BEE CHEMICAL CO.
2700 East 170th Street
Lansing IL 60438
708/474-7000
Contact Craig Vincent, Personnel. A diverse chemical company with three operating divisions.

BP CHEMICAL
COMMERCIAL COMPOSITES
333 North 6th Street
St. Charles IL 60174
708/584-3130
Contact Ms. Jan Johnson, Assistant Personnel Manager. Manufactures cones and plastic products for stereos.

CF INDUSTRIES
Salem Lake Drive
Long Grove IL 60047
708/438-9500
Contact Carla Pritts, Staff Recruiter. Manufactures and distributes chemical fertilizer products.

CHEMICAL WASTE MANAGEMENT
3001 Butterfield Road
Oak Brook IL 60521
708/218-1500
Contact Dave Rogers, Director of Personnel. A garbage and refuse removal company.

FMC CORPORATION
200 East Randolph Drive
Chicago IL 60601.
Contact Staffing Manager. Manufactures and sells a broad range of chemical products.

GENERAL FIRE EXTINGUISHER CORPORATION
1685 Shermer Road
Northbrook IL 60062
312/272-7500
Contact Personnel Supervisor. Manufactures a complete line of fire extinguishers.

W.R. GRACE
300 Genessee Street
Lake Zurich IL 60047
312/438-8241
Contact Director of Human Resources. Markets industrial waste water treatment products.

HARCROS PIGMENTS INC.
2001 Lynch Avenue
East St. Louis IL 62205
618/271-4700
Contact Dave Goeddel, Personnel Director. Manufacture synthetic, natural & magnetic iron oxides, colors, extender pigments, and barytes.

HYSAN CORPORATION
1400 Touhy Avenue
Des Plaines IL 60018
708/390-8100
Contact David Taylor, Director of Human Resources. A major chemical manufacturer and distributor.

INTERNATIONAL MINERALS & CHEMICAL CORPORATION
421 East Hawley Street
Mundelein IL 60060
708/202-2199
Contact Supervisor, Corporate Human Resources. Involved in chemicals and minerals. A Fortune 500 company.

NALCO CHEMICAL COMPANY
1 Nalco Center
Naperville IL 60563-1198
708/305-1000
Contact Karen Nordquist, Employment Manager. Several area locations including: Naperville, Northbrook. Engaged primarily in the manufacture and sale of highly specialized service chemicals used in water treatment, pollution control, energy conservation, oil production and refining, steelmaking, papermaking, mining and other industrial processes. Corporate headquarters location. International. New York Stock Exchange.

OLIN CORPORATION
P.O. Box 2219
Patterson Road
Joliet IL 60434
815/727-4901
Contact Vince Cimino, Personnel Manager. Several area locations including: Oak Brook. Manufacturer of organic and inorganic chemicals, specializing in those used in industry and agriculture. Also manufactures metal and paper products, sports and recreational equipment, and energy systems. Operations at this facility include: manufacturing. Corporate headquarters location: Stamford, CT. New York Stock Exchange. International. Common positions include: Accountant; Chemical Engineer; Industrial Engineer; Mechanical Engineer; Operations/Production Manager; Personnel & Labor Relations Specialist. Principal educational backgrounds sought: Business Administration; Engineering. Company benefits include: medical insurance; dental insurance; pension plan; life insurance; tuition assistance; disability coverage; profit sharing; employee discounts; savings plan.

PITMAN-MOORE, INC.
421 E. Hawley Street
Mundelein IL 60060
708/949-3300
Contact George Hyland, Director, Human Resources. A leader in the animal health and nutrition businesses worldwide and the nation's largest supplier of feed-grade phosphates and potassium products. Common positions include: Accountant; Biochemist; Biologist; Computer Programmer; Customer Service Representative; Marketing Specialist; Systems Analyst. Principal educational backgrounds sought: Accounting; Biology; Computer Science; Marketing.

RHONE-POULENC BASIC CHEMICAL COMPANY
1245 East Diehl Road
Suite 303
Naperville IL 60563
708/505-1450
Contact Glen Hanson, Personnel Manager. Several area locations, including: Chicago Heights and Hammond, IN. A chemical manufacturer specializing in agricultural, specialty and industrial chemicals; food ingredients; and plastics. Corporate headquarters location: Westport, CT. International. New York Stock Exchange.

STEPAN COMPANY
22 West Frontage Road
Northfield IL 60093
708/446-7500
Contact Mr. Richard Larsen, Corporate Personnel Manager. Several area locations. Develops, manufactures, and markets a wide range of chemical intermediates sold to producers of such consumer products as shampoos, toothpastes, household detergents, and other personal care items. Products also used as ingredients in industrial detergents and cleansers, agricultural fertilizers, herbicides, and pesticides, as well as petroleum-based detergents for recovering additional oil from known reservoirs. A major producer of phthalic anhydride, an essential ingredient in plastics and polyesters, and also manufactures urethane foam systems and other specialty products. Has seven production plants; five in United States, including near Joliet, IL. Corporate headquarters location. Operations include: research/development; administration; sales. Common positions include: Accountant; Chemist; Customer Service Representative; Chemical Engineer; Sales Representative; Systems Analyst. Principal educational backgrounds sought: Accounting; Biology; Chemistry; Engineering; Finance; Liberal Arts. Company benefits include: medical, dental, and life insurance; pension plan; tuition assistance; disability coverage; profit sharing; savings plan; employee stock ownership plan. American Stock Exchange

**SUN CHEMICAL CORPORATION/
GENERAL PRINTING INK**
135 West Lake Street
Northlake IL 60164
708/562-0550
Contact Nick Hiller, Personnel Director. One of the world's largest producers of printing inks and organic pigments. Also designs and manufactures graphic arts equipment, aircraft and military instrumentation and a number of diversified products including specialty chemicals, flexible laminates, and automobile cigarette lighters. Products sold primarily by own sales force. Printing ink facilities are located in Chicago, Kankakee, and Northlake. Corporate headquarters location: New York, NY. International. New York Stock Exchange.

WITCO CORPORATION/ MIDWEST REGIONAL OFFICE
2701 West Lake Street
Melrose Park IL 60160
708/344-4300

Contact Ms. D.E. Thoren, Manager, Personnel Services. Produces a wide range of special purpose chemical and petroleum products for industrial and consumer use. Two business segments: Chemical Group, which manufactures chemicals sold to OEMs for use in the manufacture of rubber, plastics, cosmetics, pharmaceuticals, petroleum lubricants, fungicidal compounds, automobiles, building materials, paper, and textiles; and Petroleum Group, which manufactures white oils, petrolatums, natural and synthetic petroleum sulfonates, microcrystalline waxes, greases and other petroleum specialties from refined and semi-refined oils, as well as operating two refineries which primarily produce lubricating oils sold under the Kendall and Amalie trademarks. These products are used in the pharmaceutical, cosmetics, food processing, animal husbandry, paper converting, plastics, chemical processing, textile, and agricultural industries. Other Illinois facilities include four chemical group manufacturing plants in Chicago. Common positions include: Buyer; Credit Manager; Customer Service Representative; Purchasing Agent; Sales Representative. Principal educational backgrounds sought: Business Administration; Marketing. Company benefits include: medical insurance; dental insurance; pension plan; life insurance; tuition assistance; disability coverage; savings plan. Corporate headquarters location: New York, NY. Operations at this facility include: regional headquarters; divisional headquarters; administration; service; sales. International. New York Stock Exchange

COLLEGES AND UNIVERSITIES

BELLEVILLE AREA COLLEGE
2500 Carlyle Road
Belleville IL 62221
618/235-2700

Contact Marg Fraley, Personnel Director. A St. Louis area community college. Employs over 200.

LEWIS & CLARK COMMUNITY COLLEGE
5800 Godfrey Road
Godfrey IL 62035
618/466-3411

Contact Dr. Dale Chapman, V.P. of Administration and Finance. A major area 2-year Junior college.

McKENDREE COLLEGE
701 College Road
Lebanon IL 62254
618/537-4481
Contact Mary Ann Newcomb, Personnel Director. A major St. Louis educational institution with 28 academic majors and an enrollment of over 1,000.

PRINCIPIA COLLEGE
Elsah IL 62028
618/374-2131
Contact Chestnut Booth, Personnel Coordinator. A major St. Louis area 4-year college for Christian Scientists. Common positions include: Accountant; Administrator; Advertising Worker; Blue-Collar Worker Supervisor; Computer Programmer; Credit Manager; Department Manager; General Manager; Personnel & Labor Relations Specialist; Systems Analyst; Faculty; Coach; Administrative Worker; Counselor. Principal educational backgrounds sought: Accounting; Business Administration; Computer Science; Liberal Arts. Some internships offered. Company benefits include: medical and life insurance; pension plan; tuition assistance; disability coverage; daycare assistance; employee discounts.

SOUTHERN ILLINOIS UNIVERSITY AT EDWARDSVILLE
Box 1222
Edwardsville IL 62026
618/692-2000
Contact Personnel Services. A state university offering several graduate programs as well as a 4-year bachelor's degree program.

COMMUNICATIONS: EQUIPMENT & SERVICES

For more information on professional employment opportunities in the communication industry, contact the following professional and trade organizations, as listed beginning on page 295:

COMMUNICATIONS WORKERS OF AMERICA
COMMUNICATIONS WORKERS OF AMERICA/CHICAGO
UNITED STATES TELEPHONE ASSOCIATION

AMERITECH SERVICES
1900 East Golf Road
Floor 3
Schaumberg IL 60173
708/605-2299
Contact Joe Poehlmann, Manager of Employment. Provides services to its five telecommunications companies.

ANDREW CORPORATION
10500 West 153rd Street
Orland Park IL 60462
708/349-3300
Contact Roger Blaylock, Personnel Manager. A diverse telecommunications hardware firm.

ANIXTER BROTHERS, INC.
4711 Golf Road
Skokie IL 60076
708/677-2600
Contact Ed O'Donnell, Personnel. Distributes wire, cable and other products to the telecommunications industry.

CONTROL DATA INSTITUTE
1020 West 31st Street
Suite 300
Box 1500
Downers Grove IL 60515
708/960-9110
Contact Personnel Director. A major worldwide computer manufacturer.

ILLINOIS BELL
225 West Randolph
Floor 10C
Chicago IL 60606
312/727-7861
Contact Management Employment Office. Provides communications systems and services.

RELIABLE ELECTRIC COMPANY
11333 West Addison
Franklin Park IL 60131
708/455-8010
Contact Scott Hodal, Personnel Manager. Manufactures connectors for telecommunication devices used by the telephone industry and power utilities. Corporate headquarters location.

ROCKWELL INTERNATIONAL
8245 South Lemont Road
Downers Grove IL 60516
708/985-9000
Contact Dennis Kedidle, Personnel Director. Designs and manufactures telecommunications products and systems including digital PBX (private branch exchange), switching systems, PCM transmission multiplexers, and miscellaneous telecommunications equipment. A subsidiary of Rockwell

International (Pittsburgh, PA). Divisional headquarters location. International.

TELEPHONE & DATA SYSTEMS INC.
79 West Monroe Street
Suite 905
Chicago IL 60603
312/630-1900
Contact Office Manager. A conglomerate, owning out-of-state telephone companies.

COMPUTER RELATED:
HARDWARE, SOFTWARE AND SERVICES

For more information on professional employment opportunities in the computer industry, contact the following professional and trade organizations, as listed beginning on page 295:

ADAPSO/THE COMPUTER SOFTWARE AND SERVICES
 INDUSTRY ASSOCIATION
ASSOCIATION FOR COMPUTER SCIENCE
ASSOCIATION FOR COMPUTING MACHINERY
IEEE COMPUTER SOCIETY
SEMICONDUCTOR INDUSTRY ASSOCIATION

**ADVANCED SYSTEM APPLICATIONS INC/
DIVISION OF POLICY MANAGEMENT SYSTEMS CORPORATION**
One ASA Plaza
P.O. Box 385
Bloomingdale IL 60108
312/893-9055
Contact Robert Farrell, Recruiting Supervisor. A computer services company specializing in on-lines claim adjustment for the insurance industry. Common positions include: Computer Programmer. Principal educational backgrounds sought include: Computer Science. Training programs offered; Internships offered. Company benfits include: medical, dental, and life insurance; tuition assistance; savings plan; 401 K, fitness center. Corporate headquarters location: Columbia, SC. Parent company: PMSC. Operations at this facility include: divisional headquarters.

APPLIED INFORMATION DEVELOPMENT
823 Commerce Drive
Oak Brook IL 60521
708/654-3030
Contact James Verri, Personnel Director. A computer company involved primarily in data processing and consulting services.

APPLIED LEARNING
1751 W. Diehl Road
Naperville IL 60563
708/369-3000
Contact Director of Personnel. A computer training company. Employs 829.

AUTOMATIC DATA PROCESSING
7350 West Lawrence Avenue
Chicago IL 60656
312/867-6400
Contact Kristin Mooney, Senior Employment Specialist. Engaged in the data processing services business.

COMDISCO
6111 North River Road
Rosemont IL 60018
708/698-3000
Contact Lucie Buford, Vice Presdient, Personnel. A company engaged in the leasing of computer equipment to businesses.

HONEYWELL INC.
1500 W. Dundee Road
Arlington Heights IL 60004
708/394-4000
Contact Mark Hoggay, Senior Human Resources Administrator. An international company dedicated to advanced technology and offering high quality products and services in the fields of information processing, automation and controls.

IBM
One IBM Plaza
Chicago IL 60611
312/245-4048
Contact Don Folkl, Manager of Central Employment. A leading corporation in information technology.

MOORE BUSINESS FORMS & SYSTEMS DIVISION
1205 Milwaukee Avenue
Glenview IL 60025-2496
708/480-3000
Contact Cindy Leitza, Manager of Personnel Services. National headquarters and administrative offices for the international manufacturer of business systems, forms, and equipment. Company has branches in 39 countries, and maintains 280 sales offices worldwide.

NCR CORPORATION
405 South Washington Boulevard
Mundelein IL 60060
312/566-4350
Contact Christine Sitko, Personnel Manager. Multiple area locations including: Rolling Meadows, Mundelein, Niles, Chicago, Springfield IL, Springfield MO, Kansas City, St. Louis. Develops, manufactures, markets, installs, and services total business information processing systems for selected worldwide markets. These markets are primarily in retail, financial, commercial, industrial, health care, education, and government sectors. The NCR total systems concept encompasses one of the broadest hardware and software product lines in the industry. NCR computers range from small business systems to the most powerful general-purpose processors, and are supported by a complete spectrum of terminals, processors, data communications networks, and an extensive library of software products. Supplemental services and products include field engineering, data centers, systems services, educational centers, and a comprehensive line of media. Common positions include: Sales Representative. Principal educational backgrounds sought: Business Administration; Computer Science; Marketing. Company benefits include: medical insurance, dental insurance, pension plan, life insurance, tuition assistance, disability coverage, profit sharing, employee discounts, savings plan. Corporate headquarters location: Dayton, OH. International. Regional headquarters location. Operations at this facility include: administration; sales. New York Stock Exchange.

WALLACE COMPUTER SERVICES INC.
4600 West Roosevelt Road
Hillsdale IL 60162
312/626-2000
Contact Tom Raclaw, Personnel Director. A company engaged in the manufacture and sale of computer oriented business forms, commercial printing, computer labels, machine ribbons, computer software, and computer accessory supplies.

CONSTRUCTION: SERVICES, MATERIALS & RELATED

For more information on professional employment opportunities in the construction industry, contact the following professional and trade organizations, as listed beginning on page 295:

BUILDING OFFICIALS AND CODE
 ADMINISTRATORS INTERNATIONAL, INC
CONSTRUCTION INDUSTRY MANUFACTURERS ASSOCIATION
HOME BUILDERS ASSOCIATION OF GREATER CHICAGO
INTERNATIONAL CONFERENCE OF BUILDING OFFICIALS
NATIONAL ASSOCIATION OF HOME BUILDERS

ANNING-JOHNSON CO.
1959 Anson Drive
Melrose Park IL 60160
312/261-3636
Contact Charles B. Bruggen, Vice President. A construction company dealing in specialty contracting.

BARBER-GREENE CO.
3000 Barber-Greene Road
DeKalb IL 60115
815/756-5600
Contact Corporate Personnel Manager. Designs, manufactures and sells construction machinery.

THE CECO CORPORATION
One Tower Lane
Oak Brook Terrace IL 60181
312/242-2000
Contact Craig Grant, Manager, Human Resources. Manufactures, distributes, & sells products for construction industry.

CONTRACTING & MATERIAL COMPANY
165 Hintz Road
Wheeling IL 60090
708/541-2250
Contact Fran Seabert, Office Manager. Involved in contract construction, electrical and pipeline, heavy, and highway construction.

ECONOMY MECHANICAL INDUSTRIES
77 Wheeling Road
Wheeling IL 60090
708/541-8700
Contact Personnel Director. A mechanical contracting firm, works in commercial plumbing.

GLOBE INDUSTRIES
2638 East 126th Street
Chicago IL 60633
312/646-1300
Contact Vice President/Industrial Relations. Manufactures and sells roofing products.

GOLD BOND BUILDING PRODUCTS
1400 E. Touhy Avenue
Des Plaines IL 60018
312/298-7020
Contact Office Manager. A diversified manufacturer of construction products.

EDWARD GRAY CORPORATION
12233 Avenue O
Chicago IL 60633
312/221-8400
Contact W. Jed Mundell, Treasurer. Engaged in all phases of industrial construction.

H.H. HALL CONSTRUCTION COMPANY
211 South 15th Street
P.O. Box 2439
East St. Louis IL 62202
618/274-2500
Contact Personnel Department. A major area contracting firm engaged in industrial and commercial construction work. Also manufactures ready mix concrete.

HOEFFKEN BROS. INC.
P.O. Box 405
Belleville IL 62222
618/233-0268
Contact Leon Linneman, Personnel Director. An area heavy construction firm specializing in roads and bridges.

KENNY CONSTRUCTION COMPANY
250 Northgate Parkway
Wheeling IL 60090
708/541-8200
Contact Ronald P. Smith, Corporate Secretary. A heavy duty construction contractor.

MILLER-DAVIS COMPANY
4300 North Avenue
Melrose Park IL 60165
312/626-0957
Contact Carl Guse, Senior Vice-President. A major regional general contracting firm. Common positions include: Accounting; Engineering. Company benefits include: medical insurance; pension plan; disability coverage; profit sharing; ESOP. Divisional headquarters location. Corporate headquarters location: Kalamazoo, MI.

PASCHEN CONTRACTORS INC.
2739 North Elston Avenue
Chicago IL 60647
312/278-4700
Contact William Paschen, Vice President. A construction company with 28 different payrolls, including construction sites at the deep tunnel, CTA, and others. Corporate headquarters location.

PHILLIPS, GETSCHOW COMPANY
1913 South Briggs Street
Joliet IL 60433
312/644-6116
Contact Joyce Wilson, Personnel. Another area facility is in Joliet. A construction company working in the areas of mechanical and nuclear construction. Corporate headquarters location.

R&D THIEL INC.
1700 Rand Road
Palatine IL 60074
708/359-7150
Contact Personnel Director. A general contractor. Corporate headquarters location.

RICHARDS BRICK COMPANY
234 Springer Avenue
Box 407
Edwardsville IL 62025
618/656-0230
Contact John Motley, Plant Superintendant. A major manufacturer of building bricks.

SHEFFIELD STEEL CORPORATION
Industry Avenue
P.O. Box 727
Joliet IL 60434-0727
815/723-9335
Contact Bill Winkler, Manager of Employee Relations. Operates the largest subsidiary component of Penn Dixie Industries, a multi-product corporation primarily serving the construction industry, although companies operate independently. Manufactures steel, industrial and welding wire, nails, fence, welded wire fabric, and other products (Kokomo, IN); and hot-rolled steel merchant bars and lightweight structural steel shapes (Joliet, IL). Other facilities operate in several western and midwestern states. Corporate headquarters location: Kokomo, IN.

GEORGE SOLLITT CONSTRUCTION COMPANY
790 North Central
Wooddale IL 60191
708/860-7333
Contact Office Manager. General contractors for schools and hospitals; also public works projects such as sewage treatment plants. Second office in Seattle, WA. Corporate headquarters location.

SYMONS CORPORATION
200 East Touhy
Des Plaines IL 60018
312/298-3200
Contact Richard M. Wolter, Corporate Personnel Manager. Manufacturer of concrete forming equipment: standard, custom and fiberglass. Common positions include: Accountant; Advertising Worker; Buyer; Computer Programmer; Credit Manager; Customer Service Representative; Draftsperson; Civil Engineer; Industrial Engineer; Personnel & Labor Relations Specialist; Purchasing Agent; Quality Control Supervisor; Sales Representative. Principal educational backgrounds sought: Business Administration; Computer Science; Engineering; Marketing; Structural Engineering. Company benefits include: medical insurance; dental insurance; pension plan; life insurance; tuition assistance; disability coverage; employee discounts; savings plan. Corporate headquarters location. Operations at this facility include: manufacturing; administration; sales. International.

USG CORPORATION
101 South Wacker Drive
Chicago IL 60606
312/606-4390
Contact Greg Puchalski, Manager of Employment and Development. A major manufacturer of building materials in the United States. Produces a wide range of products for use in new building construction, repair and remodeling, and in many industry processes. Operates more than 100 plants in the United States, Canada, Mexico, and Europe. Corporate headquarters location. International. New York Stock Exchange. Common positions include: Accountant; Attorney; Buyer; Computer Programmer; Chemical Engineer; Civil Engineer; Electrical Engineer; Industrial Engineer; Mechanical Engineer; Mining Engineer; Financial Analyst; Industrial Designer; Systems Analyst; Technical Writer/Editor. Principal educational backgrounds sought: Accounting; Art/Design; Business Administration; Engineering; Finance; Liberal Arts; Marketing. Company benefits include: medical insurance; dental insurance; pension plan; life insurance; tuition assistance; disability coverage; employee discounts; savings plan. Operations at this facility include: administration.

W.E. O'NEIL CONSTRUCTION
2751 North Clybourn Avenue
Chicago IL 60614
312/327-1611
Contact Personnel Department. A construction company. Common positions include: Civil Engineer; Electrical Engineer; Mechanical Engineer; Construction Engineer. Principal educational background sought: Engineering. Company benefits include: medical insurance; dental insurance; life insurance; disability coverage; profit sharing; savings plan. Corporate headquarters location.

ELECTRICAL AND ELECTRONIC: MANUFACTURING & DISTRIBUTION

For more information on professional employment opportunities in the electrical and electronics industries, contact the following professional and trade organizations, as listed beginning on page 295:

AMERICAN ELECTROPLATERS AND SURFACE FINISHERS SOCIETY
AMERICAN ELECTROPLATERS AND SURFACE
 FINISHERS SOCIETY/ CHICAGO BRANCH
INSTITUTE OF ELECTRICAL AND ELECTRONICS ENGINEERS/
 CHICAGO
ELECTROCHEMICAL SOCIETY
ELECTRONIC INDUSTRIES ASSOCIATION
ELECTRONICS TECHNICIANS ASSOCIATION
INSTITUTE OF ELECTRICAL AND ELECTRONICS ENGINEERS
INTERNATIONAL BROTHERHOOD OF ELECTRICAL WORKERS
INTERNATIONAL SOCIETY OF CERTIFIED
 ELECTRONICS TECHNICIANS
NATIONAL ELECTRICAL MANUFACTURERS ASSOCIATION
NATIONAL ELECTRONICS SALES AND SERVICES ASSOCIATION

ADVANCE TRANSFORMER CO.
10275 West Higgins Road
Rosemont IL 60018
708/390-5000
Contact Personnel Director. Manufactures ballasts for lighting components.

APPLETON ELECTRIC CO.
1701 W. Wellington
Chicago IL 60657
312/327-7200
Contact L.W. McElhinny, Vice President/Industrial Relations. Manufactures electrical components.

BASLER ELECTRIC COMPANY
Route 143
P.O. Box 269
Highland IL 62249
618/654-2341
Contact Marilyn Frey, Personnel Director. Manufacturers of transformers and electronic systems. Employs over 400.

BLUE M ELECTRIC COMPANY
2218 W. 138th Street
Blue Island IL 60406
708/385-9000
Contact Bruce Leonard, Manager of Human Resources. Designs equipment with special temperature controls.

BODINE ELECTRIC COMPANY
2500 West Bradley Place
Chicago IL 60618
312/478-3515
Contact David C. McClenahan, Director, Human Resources. Manufacturer of specialized electrical equipment.

BRUSH FUSES INC.
2070 Maple Street
Des Plaines IL 60018
708/299-2211
Contact C.D. Rundle, Employee Relations Manager. Manufactures fuses. Common positions include: Accountant; Blue-Collar Worker Supervisor; Buyer; Computer Service Representative; Draftsperson; Industrial Engineer; Mechanical Engineer; Financial Analyst; General Manager; Operations/Production Manager; Personnel & Labor Relations Specialist; Purchasing Agent; Quality Control Supervisor. Educational backgrounds sought: Accounting; Business Administration; Computer Science; Engineering; Finance. Company benefits include: medical insurance; dental insurance; life insurance; tuition assistance; disability coverage; profit sharing. Corporate headquarters location. Parent company: Hawker Siddeley. Operations at this facility include: manufacturing; research/development; administration; sales. London Stock Exchange.

COMMERCIAL LIGHT COMPANY
245 Fencl Lane
Hillside IL 60162
708/449-6900
Contact Al Oliver, Personnel Director. An electrical contractor.

R. DRON ELECTRICAL COMPANY INC.
P.O. Box 753
Granite City IL 62040
618/452-1363
Contact June Idoux, Office Manager. An on site electrical contracting company. Employs over 100.

DUCHOSSOIS INDUSTRIES, INC,
845 Larch Avenue
Elmhurst IL 60126
708/279-3600
Contact Christ Wright, Corporate Recruiter. A diversified manufacturer of electronic products.

DYNASCAN CORPORATION
6460 West Cortland Street
Chicago IL 60635
312/889-8870
Contact Celeste Boucher, Human Resources Director. Designs and markets consumer electronics products.

EATON CONTROLS DIVISION
191 East North Avenue
Carol Stream IL 60188
312/260-3400
Contact Nick Blaukwiekel, Manager of Staffing & Recruitment. Designs, manufactures, and sells electronic and electromechanical divices to automotive, appliance, and air conditioning and refrigeration manufacturers.

FURNAS ELECTRIC COMPANY
1000 McKee Street
Batavia IL 60510
708/879-6000
Contact Leslie H. Nord, Manager of Professional Employment. Manufactures electromotor products such as motor controls.

G&W ELECTRIC COMPANY
3500 West 127th Street
Blue Island IL 60406
708/388-5010
Contact Personnel Director. Produces power cable terminals, switches, splices.

GUARDIAN ELECTRIC MANUFACTURING CO.
1425 Lake Avenue
Woodstock IL 60098
815/337-0050
Contact Sharon McFarlin, Director of Personnel. Manufactures electromechanical components and relays.

HYRE ELECTRIC COMPANY
2320 West Ogden Avenue
Chicago IL 60608
312/738-7200
Contact Rick Freeman, Treasurer. An electrical contracting company.

INTERMATIC, INC.
Intermatic Plaza
Spring Grove IL 60081
815/675-2321
Contact Director, Employee Relations. A manufacturer of electro-mechanical and electronic timers, photo controls, Malibu lights, outdoor lighting systems, and portable heaters.

JAKEL INCORPORATED
400 Broadway
Highland IL 62249
618/654-2371
Contact Human Resources. Manufacturer of sub-fractional horse power electric motors.

JOHNSON CONTROLS
300 South Glengarry
Geneva IL 60134
708/232-4270
Contact Donna Brucher, Personnel Director. Manufactures storage batteries for sale to private labels.

KALMUS & ASSOCIATES, INC.
2424 South 25th Avenue
Broadview IL 60153
708/343-7004
Contact Colleen Brown, Personnel Manager. Manufactures printed circuit boards.

KNOWLES ELECTRONICS, INC.
3100 North Mannheim Road
Franklin Park IL 60131
708/455-3600
Contact Richard Lane, Personnel Director. Manufactures miniature electronic components.

McGRAW-EDISON COMPANY/MACOMB
510 North Pearl Street
Macomb IL 61455
309/833-4171
Contact Larry Baker, Personnel Manager. A subsidiary of Cooper Industries in Houston, TX. Manufactures electrical porcelain insulators. Operations at this facility include: manufacturing. Corporate headquarters location: Rolling Meadows, IL. New York Stock Exchange. Common positions include: Accountant; Buyer; Draftsperson; Engineer; Ceramics Engineer; Industrial Engineer; Mechanical Engineer; Personnel & Labor Relations Specialist; Quality Control Supervisor. Principal educational backgrounds sought: Accounting; Business Administration; Engineering. Company benefits include: medical insurance; dental insurance; life insurance; pension plan; tuition assistance; disability coverage; profit sharing; savings plan.

METHODE ELECTRONICS INC.
7447 Wilson Avenue
Harwood Heights IL 60656
708/867-9600
Contact Personnel Manager. Several area locations. Manufactures component devices that connect, convey, and control electrical and electronic energy and pulse. Products include printed circuit boards, connectors, and transportation control and connection components. Chief customers include the telecommunications, computer, transportation, military, aerospace, industrial, and entertainment electronics industries. Operates seven facilities in the Chicago area: Harwood Heights, housing headquarters and manufacturing facilities; Chicago (manufacturing facility); Skokie (currently being leased); Rolling Meadows (manufacturing); and three facilities in Chicago Ridge. Also has facilities in Carthage and Warsaw, IL. Corporate headquarters location.

MOLEX INCORPORATED
2222 Wellington Court
Lisle IL 60532
708/969-4550
Contact Director/Employee Relations. Several area locations including: Downers Grove, Schaumburg, Addison. Designs, manufactures, and distributes electrical and electronic devices such as terminals, connectors, switches, and related application tooling. Products are used by television, stereo, home computer, electronic game, audio, video, refrigeration, laundry, and many other consumer manufacturing firms, as well as by the automotive, truck, leisure vehicle, and farm equipment industries. Sold through independent sales representatives located throughout the United States Corporate headquarters location. International.

MOTOROLA INC.
1303 East Algonquin Road
Schaumburg IL 60196
708/576-5260
Contact Jim Donnelly, V.P./Corporate Director of Personnel. Several area locations including: Carol Stream, Franklin Park. One of the world's leading manufacturers of electronic equipment and components, engaged in the design, manufacture, and sale of a diversified line of products such as 2-way radios and other electronic communication systems; semiconductors, including integrated circuits, and other components, primarily for aerospace use; electronic engine controls; digital appliance controls; automobile radios, citizens band radios, and other automotive and industrial electronic equipment; and data communication products such as low, medium and high speed modems, multiplexers, and network processors. In addition to Schaumburg executive offices, other Illinois facilities include plants in Carol Stream, Franklin Park, and a manufacturing plant in Schaumburg. Corporate headquarters location. International. New York Stock Exchange.

NEWARK ELECTRONICS
4801 North Ravenswood Avenue
Chicago IL 60640
312/784-5100
Contact James D. Runtz, Director of Recruitment. A broad-line electronics distributor with sales offices throughout North America and Europe. Divisional headquarters: Premium Industrial Corporation. Corporate headquarters location: Cleveland, OH. New York Stock Exchange. Common positions include: Accountant; Advertising Worker; Buyer; Computer Programmer; Credit Representative; Financial Analyst; Industrial Engineer; Branch Manager; Management Trainee; Purchasing Agent; Sales Representative; Systems Analyst. Principal educational backgrounds sought: Accounting; Business Administration; Communications; Computer Science; Engineering; Finance; Liberal Arts; Marketing. Company benefits include: medical insurance; pension plan; life insurance; tuition assistance; disability coverage; employee discounts; savings plan; stock options. Operations at this facility include: divisional headquarters.

OAK SWITCH SYSTEMS INC.,
SUBSIDIARY OF OAK INDUSTRIES INC.
100 South Main Street
P.O. Box 517
Crystal Lake IL 60014
815/459-5000
Contact Martin Davis, Director/Employee Relations. Components division manufactures products such as electrical switches, controls and components for home appliances, high frequency crystals, oscillators, and potentiometers. Parent company: Oak Industries Inc. Illinois facilities in Crystal Lake, Hinsdale, Mt. Prospect, Princeton, and Sterling. Common positions include: Accountant; Blue-Collar Worker Supervisor; Buyer; Computer Programmer;

Credit Manager; Draftsperson; Electrical Engineer; Industrial Engineer; Mechanical Engineer; Marketing Specialist; Purchasing Agent; Quality Control Supervisor; Sales Representative; Systems Analyst. Principal educational backgrounds sought: Accounting; Business Administration; Computer Science; Engineering; Marketing; Physics. Company benefits include: medical insurance; dental insurance; pension plan; life insurance; tuition assistance; disability coverage; savings plan; stock purchase plan. Operations at this facility include: manufacturing; research/development; administration; sales. Divisional headquarters location. Corporate headquarters location: Rancho Bernardo, CA. International facilities. New York Stock Exchange.

RAULAND-BORG CORPORATION
3450 West Oakton
Skokie IL 60076
708/679-0900
Contact Carl Bank, Personnel Manager. Manufactures electronic communications and professional sound equipment. Corporate headquarters location.

RICHARDSON ELECTRONICS, LTD.
40W267 Keslinger Road
La Fox IL 60147
Contact Patricia A. Salas, Employment & Benefits Manager. Distributes and manufactures industrial and electronic components. Common positions include: Accountant; Computer Programmer; Credit Manager; Customer Service Representative; Electrical Engineer; Financial Analyst; Marketing Specialist; Purchasing Agent; Quality Control Supervisor; Sales Representative; Systems Analyst. Principal educational backgrounds sought: Accounting; Business Administration; Computer Science; Engineering; Finance; Marketing. Company benefits include: medical, dental and life insurance; tuition assistance; disability coverage; profit sharing; savings plan. Corporate headquarters location. International. Operations at this facility include: manufacturing; research/development; administration; service; sales.

SCHUMACHER ELECTRIC CORPORATION
7474 North Rogers Avenue
Chicago IL 60626
312/973-1600
Contact Ralph Cernohouz, Controller. Manufactures transformers.

SHURE BROTHERS INC.
222 Hartrey Avenue
Evanston IL 60202-3696
708/866-2235
Contact Jack Shea, Personnel Manager. Several area locations. Manufactures electronics equipment. Corporate headquarters location. Principal educational backgrounds sought include: Engineering. Company benefits

include: medical, dental, and life insurance; pension plan; tuition assistance; disability coverage; employee discounts; savings plan. Corporate headquarters location. Operations at this facility include: manufacturing; research/development; administration; service; sales.

SOLA ELECTRIC
1717 Busse Road
Elk Grove Village IL 60007
708/439-2800
Contact Jack Allen, Employee Relations Manager. Manufactures transformers, power supplies, and voltage regulators. A unit of General Signal Corporation. Corporate headquarters location.

SQUARE D COMPANY
1415 South Roselle
Palatine IL 60067-7399
708/397-2600
Contact Barry Leon, Corporate Personnel Manager. Several area locations. An electronics firm operating in two major business segments: Electrical Equipment and Electronics Products. Electrical Equipment segment designs, manufactures and sells a broad range of products generally used in the distribution and control of electricity. Products include circuitbreakers, safety switches, panel boards, switchboards, switchgear, busways, transformers, and wiring devices; motor-starters, relays, limit switches, pressure switches, vacuum switches, programmable controllers, and energy management systems. Electronics Products segment includes the manufacture and sale of electro-deposited copper foil through subsidiary Yates Electronics. Other products include semiconductor devices manufactured by subsidiary General Semiconductor Industries. Corporate headquarters location. International. New York Stock Exchange.

SUN ELECTRIC COMPANY
One Sun Parkway
Crystal Lake IL 60014
815/459-7700
Contact Betty Zambon, Supervisor, Human Resources. Several area locations including: Chicago. Designs, manufactures, and markets diagnostic test and service equipment for the transportation industry, utilizing microcomputer applications and advanced electronics. Product line includes engine and emission analyzers; wheel service equipment (balancers, aligners, brake service equipment), a line of hand-held engine test equipment, collision repair equipment, and air conditioning and electrical systems testers. Corporate headquarters location. International. New York Stock Exchange.

SWITCHCRAFT, INC.
5555 North Elston Avenue
Chicago IL 60630
312/792-2700
Contact Elaine Lysandrou, Human Resource Manager. Major manufacturer of electronic switches. A subsidiary of Raytheon (Lexington, MA). Corporate headquarters location.

TRI-CITY ELECTRIC COMPANY
7455 Duvan Drive
Tinley Park IL 60477
708/532-0200
Contact Personnel. Engaged in industrial electrical contracting. Corporate headquarters location. International.

WEBER MARKING SYSTEMS, INC.
711 West Algonquin Road
Arlington Heights IL 60005
708/364-8500
Contact Mrs. Shirley A. Hurley, Director of Employee Relations. Several area locations. International distributor of product identification addressing, labeling, industrial, marking machines and devices. Corporate headquarters location.

WELLS-GARDNER ELECTRONICS CORPORATION
2701 North Kildare Avenue
Chicago IL 60639
312/252-8220
Contact Mary Ann Mikol, Director of Industrial Relations. Business activities in three industry segments: video monitors, including game and display monitors sold to arcade game and computer manufacturers; television receivers; and intrusion alarms. All manufacturing, sales, and administration at Chicago facility. Corporate headquarters location.

WESTINGHOUSE ELECTRIC
10 South Riverside Plaza
Chicago IL 60606
312/454-7200
Contact Bill Hoffman, Regional Administration Manager. Engaged principally in the manufacture, sale, and service of equipment used for the generation and control of electricity. Its products are segmented into three parts: Power Systems, Industry Products, and Public Systems. The principal products include large generators, motors, steam and combustion turbines, transformers, marine and missile launching equipment, lamps and lamp parts, electrical apparatus and equipment. Over 125 subsidiaries are based in the United States, the United Kingdom, Brazil, Puerto Rico, Saudi Arabia, Sweden, Spain, and Australia. Corporate headquarters location: Pittsburgh, PA. New York Stock Exchange.

ENGINEERING & ARCHITECTURE

For more information on professional employment opportunities in the engineering and architecture industries, contact the following professional and trade organizations, as listed beginning on page 295:

AMERICAN INSTITUTE OF ARCHITECTS
AMERICAN SOCIETY FOR ENGINEERING EDUCATION
AMERICAN SOCIETY OF CIVIL ENGINEERS
AMERICAN SOCIETY OF HEATING, REFRIGERATING AND AIR CONDITIONING ENGINEERS
AMERICAN SOCIETY OF HEATING, REFRIGERATING AND AIR CONDITIONING ENGINEERS/CHICAGO
AMERICAN SOCIETY OF LANDSCAPE ARCHITECTS/CHICAGO
AMERICAN SOCIETY OF NAVAL ENGINEERS
AMERICAN SOCIETY OF PLUMBING ENGINEERS
AMERICAN SOCIETY OF SAFETY ENGINEERS
ILLINOIS SOCIETY OF PROFESSIONAL ENGINEERS
ILLUMINATING ENGINEERING SOCIETY OF NORTH AMERICA
INSTITUTE OF INDUSTRIAL ENGINEERS
INSTITUTE OF INDUSTRIAL ENGINEERS/CHICAGO
NATIONAL ACADEMY OF ENGINEERING
NATIONAL SOCIETY OF PROFESSIONAL ENGINEERS
SOCIETY OF FIRE PROTECTION ENGINEERS
SOCIETY OF FIRE PROTECTION ENGINEERS/CHICAGO
UNITED ENGINEERING TRUSTEES

ABB RAYMOND COMBUSTION ENGINEERING INC.
650 Warrenville Road
Lisle IL 60532
708/971-2500
Contact Rob Sentell, Vice President, Human Resources. Several local facilities, including Lisle and Naperville. Other locations in Cleveland, OH; Abilene, Kansas; Enterprise, Kansas; and Concordi, Kansas. Engineering, sales, and manufacturing firm serving the power, cement, gypsum, chemical, mineral, and environmental and foundry industries. Common positions include: Accountant; Buyer; Computer Programmer; Draftsperson; Chemical Engineer; Electrical Engineer; Mechanical Engineer; Department Manager; Marketing Specialist; Personnel & Labor Relations Specialist; Purchasing Agent; Sales Representative; Systems Analyst. Principal educational backgrounds sought: Accounting; Business Administration; Computer Science; Engineering; Finance; Marketing. Company benefits include: medical, dental, and life insurance; pension plan; tuition assistance; disability coverage; profit sharing; savings plan. Corporate headquarters location: Stamford, CT. Parent company: Asea Brown Boveri. Operations at this facility include: divisional headquarters; research/development. New York Stock Exchange

AUSTIN COMPANY
2001 Rand Road
Des Plaines IL 60016
708/391-4300
Contact Ranjit Roy, Manager of Engineering. A design/building company providing architectural services.

CONSOER, TOWNSEND, & ASSOCIATES, INC.
303 East Wacker Drive
Suite 600
Chicago IL 60601
618/463-4432
Contact Carla Hickey, Director of Human Resources. Consulting engineers.

FLOUR DANIEL
200 W. Monroe Street
Chicago IL 60606
312/368-3681
Contact Director of Personnel. Provides a wide range of services to the power industry.

GREELEY AND HANSEN
222 South Riverside Plaza, Suite 900
Chicago IL 60606
312/648-1155
Contact Personnel Administrator. A consulting engineering firm specializing in wastewater.

DAVY McKEE CORPORATION
300 South Riverside
Suite 1800
Chicago IL 60606
312/902-1200
Contact John G. Gatto, Director/Human Resources. Provides industrial engineering and contracting services to industries such as food service and pharmaceuticals. Above address is Midwest region sales and administrative offices location. Parent company: Davy Ltd., London. Common positions include: Chemical Engineer; Civil Engineer; Electrical Engineer; Mechanical Engineer; Structural Engineer. Principal educational background sought: Engineering. Company benefits include: medical insurance; pension plan; life insurance; tuition assistance; disability coverage; savings plan. Divisional headquarters location. Corporate headquarters: Pittsburgh, PA. London Exchange.

SALEM TECHNICAL SERVICES
1333 Butterfield Road
Downers Grove IL 60515
800/323-7200
Contact Recruiting. This office recruits for our 30 offices nationally from coast to coast. Salem is one of the nation's largest and most respected contract technical service firms with 30 offices nationally: contract, or temporary assignments, are available throughout the US in all engineering disciplines - from aircraft to nuclear. Common positions include: Architect; Computer Programmer; Draftsperson; Aerospace Engineer; Agricultural Engineer; Biomedical Engineer; Ceramics Engineer; Chemical Engineer; Civil Engineer; Electrical Engineer; Industrial Engineer; Mechanical Engineer; Metallurgical Engineer; Mining Engineer; Petroleum Engineer; Systems Analyst; Technical Writer/Editor; Aviation Mechanics. Principal educational backgrounds sought: Engineering. Company benefits include: medical insurance; life insurance. Corporate and national headquarters location. Parent company: The SEC Companies.

SARGENT & LUNDY
55 East Monroe Street
Chicago IL 60603
312/269-3578
Contact Carol Talaronek, Supervisor of Employment. A consulting engineering firm engaged in the design of nuclear and fossil fueled power plants for the electric utility industry. Employs 4,500 people. Corporate headquarters location. Common positions include: Computer Programmer; Draftsperson; Civil Engineer; Electrical Engineer; Mechanical Engineer; Reporter/Editor; Systems Analyst; Technical Writer/Editor. Principal educational backgrounds sought: Engineering; Chemical Engineering; Instrumentation Engineering. Company benefits include: medical insurance; dental insurance; pension plan; life insurance; tuition assistance; disability coverage; employee discounts; savings plan.

SCHMIDT, GARDEN & ERIKSON, INC.
104 South Michigan Avenue
Chicago IL 60603
312/332-5070
Contact Mary Ann Underhill, Personnel Director. A full-service architectural/engineering firm. Specializes in the design of commercial and industrial space, hospitals and schools. Corporate headquarters location. Common positions include: Architect; Draftsperson; Engineer; Civil Engineer; Electrical Engineer; Mechanical Engineer; Quality Control Supervisor; Sales Representative. Principal educational backgrounds sought: Architectural; Engineering; Interior Design; Marketing. Company benefits include: medical insurance; dental insurance; life insurance; disability coverage.

SKIDMORE, OWINGS & MERILL
33 West Monroe
Chicago IL 60603
312/641-5959
Contact Arleen DeSmet, Personnel Director. An architectural/engineering consulting firm. Common positions include: Architect; Electrical Engineer; Mechanical Engineer; Structural Engineer. Principal educational backgrounds sought: Engineering; Architecture. Company benefits include: medical insurance; dental insurance; life insurance; tuition assistance; disability coverage; profit sharing.

TAD TECHNICAL SERVICES CORPORATION
1717 North Naper Boulevard
Suite 101
Naperville IL 60563
708/505-1913
Contact Personnel. A contract engineering services company serving the midwest since 1944. Common positions include: Architect; Biochemist; Blue-Collar Worker Supervisor; Chemist; Commercial Artist; Computer Programmer; Draftsperson; Biomedical Engineer; Ceramics Engineer; Civil Engineer; Electrical Engineer; Industrial Engineer; Mechanical Engineer; Metallurgical Engineer; Petroleum Engineer; Quality Control Supervisor; Systems Analyst; Technical Writer/Editor; Computer Aided Designer; Machine And Product Designer. Princpal educational backgrounds sought: Art/Design; Biology; Chemistry; Communications; Engineering; Mathematics; Physics. Training programs offered; Internships offered. Company benefits include: medical, dental, and life insurance. Corporate headquarters location: Cambridge, MA. Operations at this facility include: divisional headquarters; research/development; administration; service; sales.

FABRICATED METAL PRODUCTS/PRIMARY METALS

For more information on professional employment opportunities in the fabricated metal industry, contact the following professional and trade organizations, as listed beginning on page 295:

AMERICAN CASTE METALS ASSOCIATION
AMERICAN POWDER METALLURGY INSTITUTE
ASSOCIATION OF IRON AND STEEL ENGINEERS
NATIONAL ASSOCIATION OF METAL FINISHERS

ALLIED TUBE AND CONDUIT
16100 Lathrop Avenue
Harvey IL 60426
312/955-6000
Contact Vice President/Personnel. Manufactures steel tubing/conduits.

AMAX ZINC CO.
Route 3 and Monsanto Ave.
E. St. Louis IL 62201
618/274-5000
Contact Personnel Department. A major area foundry, producing primary zinc.

AMERICAN SPRING AND WIRE SPECIALTY CO.
816 North Spaulding Avenue
Chicago IL 60651
312/826-0800
Contact Patti A. Buffington, Manager of Human Resources. Manufacturer of springs and wire formed products.

AMERICAN STEEL FOUNDRIES
1700 Walnut St.
Granite City IL 62040
618/452-2111
Contact Gwen Pitchford, Personnel Director. Manufacturers of railroad castings, and wholesalers of steel castings. Employs over 1,000.

B-LINE SYSTEMS INC.
509 W. Monroe
Highland IL 62249
618/654-2184
Contact Personnel Department. A leading greater St. Louis metal fabricating company, engaged primarily in the production of roll formers, and the welding of all sorts on steel and aluminum products for the electrical and mechanical industry. Employs over 400.

A.M. CASTLE & COMPANY
3400 North Wolf Road
Franklin Park IL 60131
708/455-7111
Contact Tom Prendergast, Personnel Director. A large metals service center company.

CBI INDUSTRIES INC.
800 Jorie Boulevard
Oak Brook IL 60522
800/572-7722
Contact Hugh Fewin, Personnel Director. Designs, fabricates, and constructs large metal plate structures and related systems.

CENTRAL STEEL AND WIRE COMPANY
3000 West 51st Street
Chicago IL 60632
312/471-3800
Contact Mr. Kukowski, Personnel Director. Distributes processed and non processed ferrous metals.

DANVILLE METAL STAMPING COMPANY, INC.
20 Oakwood Avenue
Danville IL 61832
217/446-0647
Contact Greg Allard, Personnel Director. Develops and produces fabricated metal components.

A. FINKL & SONS
2011 North Southport Avenue
Chicago IL 60614
312/975-2622
Contact Personnel Manager. A steel mill that manufactures custom forgings.

GRANITE CITY STEEL DIVISION/ NATIONAL STEEL COMPANY
20th and State Streets
Granite City IL 62040
618/451-3456
Contact Roy Paulsen, Director/Human Resources. A major area manufacturer of steel. Employs over 3,000.

HANDY BUTTON MACHINE
1750 North 25th Avenue
Melrose Park IL 60160
708/450-9000
Contact Corinne Amati, Personnel Director. Manufactures metal stampings and forms.

HARRIS-HUB/DRESHER
7200 South Mason
P.O. Box 8
Bedford Park IL 60499
708/331-5030
Contact Personnel Director. Manufacturer of metal furniture for the consumer market.

INLAND STEEL INDUSTRIES
30 West Monroe Street
Chicago IL 60603
312/346-0300
Contact Personnel Supervisor. A large integrated steel manufacturer.

KROPP FORGE DIVISION
5301 West Roosevelt Road
Chicago IL 60650
312/242-1900
Contact Frank Greco, Personnel Director. A producer of steel forgings.

LINDBERG CORPORATION
6133 North River Road
Rosemont IL 60018
708/823-2021
Contact Office Manager. Operating in the field of metallurgical processing.

METAL REMOVAL TOOLING
5740 North Tripp Avenue
Chicago IL 60646
312/583-8200
Contact Personnel Manager. Manufacturer of rotary tools, circuit board drills and fibre glass routers, master carbide drills, special tooling, and regrinding. Operations at this facility include: manufacturing. Common positions include: Accountant; Computer Programmer; Customer Service Representative; Industrial Engineer; Mechanical Engineer; Personnel & Labor Relations Specialist; Purchasing Agent; Sales Representative; Computer-Aided Manufacturing Engineer. Principal educational backgrounds sought: Accounting; Business Administration; Computer Science; Engineering. Company benefits include: medical insurance; dental insurance; pension plan; life insurance; tuition assistance; disability coverage; savings plan

MODERN DROP FORGE COMPANY
13810 South Western Avenue
P.O. Box 429
Blue Island IL 60406
708/388-1806, 568-3030
Contact Gregg Heim, Personnel Manager. Operates a steel forging plant. Corporate headquarters location.

NATIONAL CASTINGS DIVISION
1400 South Laramie Avenue
Cicero IL 60650
312/863-4800
Contact Personnel Manager. Operates a steel foundry, as part of the heavy industry division of Midland-Ross. Corporate headquarters location: Cleveland, OH.

NATIONAL METALWARES INC.
900 North Russell Avenue
Aurora IL 60506
708/892-9000
Contact Bert Hilding, Management Research. Wholly-owned subsidiary of Varlen Corporation. Manufacturer of fabricated steel tubing. Corporate headquarters location.

NATIONAL STEEL CORPORATION
2850 West Golf Road
Suite 402
Rolling Meadow IL 60008
312/640-3300
Contact Tamela Olt, Personnel Manager. A widely diversified company engaged in a wide range of metal products manufacturing. Engaged in the following business segments: Transportation (steel for automotive and rail markets); Containers; Service Centers (36 stores specializing in cut-to-order steel sheet); Metal Buildings and Components; Appliances; Tubing (for cars, chairs, and chemicals); Electrical Products and Components; Construction Products (steel used for doors, heating and cooling systems); Research and Development; National Mineral Resources; and Environment. Chicago area subsidiaries include Midwest Steel (which is involved in Appliances, Tubing, and Construction products divisions). Common positions include: Customer Service Representative; Management Trainee; Sales Representative. Principal educational backgrounds sought: Business Administration; Communications; Marketing. Training programs offered. Company benefits include: medical, dental, and life insurance; pension plan; tuition assistance; disability coverage; profit sharing; savings plan. Corporate headquarters location: Pittsburgh, PA. Parent company: NKK/NII. Operations at this facility include: sales. New York Stock Exchange.

NESCO STEEL BARREL COMPANY
P. O. Box N
Granite City IL 62040
618/452-1190
Contact Albert Zamarione, President. A leading manufacturer of steel drums for food, chemicals and oil.

NORTHWESTERN STEEL AND WIRE COMPANY
121 Wallace Street
Sterling IL 61081
815/625-2500, ext. 700
Contact Don Simpson, Manager of Employment. A producer of basic steel and wire products. Operations at this facility include: manufacturing; sales. Corporate headquarters location. Common positions include: Accountant; Chemist; Computer Programmer; Credit Manager; Engineer; Electrical Engineer; Industrial Engineer; Mechanical Engineer; Metallurgical Engineer; Financial Analyst; Management Trainee; Marketing Specialist;

Personnel & Labor Relations Specialist. Principal educational backgrounds sought: Accounting; Chemistry; Computer Science; Engineering; Finance; Marketing; Mathematics. Company benefits include: medical insurance; dental insurance; pension plan; life insurance; disability coverage; profit sharing.

PARKVIEW METAL PRODUCTS
4931 West Armitage
Chicago IL 60639
312/622-8414
Contact John Harrington, Personnel Director. A metal stampings manufacturer servicing metal trades industries nationwide. Builds and maintains progressive dies. Common positions include: Blue-Collar Worker Supervisor; Mechanical Engineer; Operations/Production Manager; Purchasing Agent; Quality Control Supervisor. Principal educational backgrounds sought: Business Administration; Engineering. Company benefits include: medical insurance; life insurance; disability coverage; profit sharing. Corporate headquarters location. Operations at this facility include: manufacturing; administration; sales.

REYNOLDS METALS COMPANY
1st and 47th Street
McCook IL 60525
708/485-9000
Contact Cornell Ward, Manager, Industrial Relations. A producer of primary aluminum and fabricated aluminum products. Founded in 1928. Operates 50 plants in the United States. Mines and processes bauxite, refines it into alumina, reduces it to aluminum and then processes finished product. It produces Reynolds Wrap foil, beverage cans, plastic films, electric wire and cable, building products, and solar hot water heating systems. Operations include: manufacturing. Corporate headquarters location: Richmond, VA. International. New York Stock Exchange. Common positions include: Accountant; Chemist; Computer Programmer; Customer Service Representative; Draftsperson; Electrical Engineer; Industrial Engineer; Mechanical Engineer; Metallurgical Engineer; Operations/Production Manager; Personnel & Labor Relations Specialist; Quality Control Supervisor; Systems Analyst; Technical Writer/Editor; Transportation & Traffic Specialist. Principal educational backgrounds sought: Accounting; Business Administration; Computer Science; Engineering; Liberal Arts; Marketing. Company benefits include: medical insurance; dental insurance; pension plan; life insurance; tuition assistance; disability coverage; savings plan.

RHEEM MANUFACTURING COMPANY/ WATER HEATER DIVISION
7600 South Kedzie Avenue
Chicago IL 60652
312/434-7500
Contact Mr. John Blanz, Personnel Director. Manufacturer of steel shipping containers and steel drums. Corporate headquarters location: New York, NY.

ROESCH INC.
100 North 24th Street
P.O. Box 328
Belleville IL 62222
618/233-2760
Contact Bonnie Voges, Personnel Director. Major Southern Illinois manufacturers of steel stampings and porcelain enameling, refrigerated ice merchandisers.

SLOAN VALVE COMPANY
10500 Seymour
Franklin Park IL 60131
708/671-4300
Contact K. Peter Blut, Employment Manager. Several area locations including: Franklin Park, and Melrose Park. Manufacturers of a variety of valves such as Royal Flush valves for toilets, railroad car valves, air brake valves and faucets. A privately-owned company. Corporate headquarters location. International. Common positions include: Accountant; Computer Programmer; Industrial Engineer; Mechnical Engineer; Q.A. Engineer. Principal educational backgrounds sought: Accounting; Business Administration; Computer Science; Engineering. Company benefits include: medical, dental, and life insurance; pension plan; tuition assistance; disability coverage; 401 K. Corporate headquarters location. Operations at this facility include: manufacturing; research/development; administration.

TARACORP INDUSTRIES
16th and Cleveland
Granite City IL 62040
618/451-4400
Contact Carla R. Jones, Personnel Administrator. Manufactures and sells lead products. Common positions include: Accountant; Administrator; Blue-Collar Worker Supervisor; Buyer; Chemist; Claim Representative; Customer Service Representative; Engineer; Industrial Engineer; Purchasing Agent; Quality Control Supervisor; Transportation & Traffic Specialist. Currently in a hiring freeze. Principal educational backgrounds sought: Accounting; Chemistry; Engineering. Company benefits include: medical insurance; pension plan; life insurance; disability coverage; profit sharing. Divisional headquarters location. Corporate headquarters location: Atlanta, GA. Operations at this facility include: manufacturing; sales.

TEMPEL STEEL COMPANY
1939 West Bryn Mawr
Chicago IL 60660
312/282-9400
Contact Arthur Canning, Manager Industrial Relations. Several area locations including: Arlington Heights, Elk Grove Village. Manufacturer of magnetic steel laminations for electric motors and transformers. Corporate headquarters location.

THOMPSON STEEL COMPANY
9470 King Street
Franklin Park IL 60131
708/678-0400
Contact Personnel Director. Cold-roll reducers of strip steel. Corporate headquarters location.

UDDEHOLM CORPORATION
2 Crossroads of Commerce #600
Rolling Meadows IL 60008
312/577-2220
Contact Personnel Office. A major area steel distributorship. Corporate headquarters location.

USS/A DIVISION OF USX CORPORATION
208 South LaSalle Street
Chicago IL 60604
312/933-3000
Contact Corporate Employment Manager. Several area locations, including: Joliet, Chicago Heights, and Moline. One of the world's largest vertically integrated steel manufacturers. Also involved in mining, transporting, processing and construction. Active in many other industries including chemicals, cement, plastics and wire products. Divisions include: USS Products, USS Supply, USS Chemicals and Plastics, USS Agri-Chemicals, USS Realty, American Bridge, Oilwell Supply, Universal Atlas Cement. Local operations include Illinois Manufacturing Division: Chicago Plant (South Works): produces steel ingots, billets. Steel Supply Division: produces strapping, strapping equipment, wire rope, fence, metal conveyor belts, nails, paint, and containers. Corporate headquarters location: Pittsburgh, PA. New York Stock Exchange.

VERSON
A DIVISION OF ALLIED PRODUCTS CORP
1355 East 93rd Street
Chicago IL 60619
312/933-8303
Contact Larry Farnesi, Manager, Employee Relations. Designs and manufactures metal forming equipment. Corporate headquarters location.

Common positions include: Computer Programmer; Customer Service Representative; Electrical Engineer; Industrial Engineer; Mechanical Engineer; Sales Representative. Principal educational backgrounds sought: Computer Science; Engineering; Mathematics. Company benefits include: medical and life insurance; tuition assistance; disability coverage; savings plan; 401 K. Corporate headquarters location: Chicago, IL. Parent company: Allied Products Corp. Operations at this facility include: divisional headquarters; manufacturing. New York Stock Exchange.

WELDED TUBE COMPANY OF AMERICA
1855 East 122nd Street
Chicago IL 60633
312/646-4500
Contact John Perish, Personnel Director. Engaged in the manufacture and sale of welded steel tubing, in square, rectangular, and special shapes and sizes. Manufacturing facilities are located in Chicago. Products are used in low- and medium-rise construction; automotive, railroad and industrial equipment; farm implements and equipment; boat, car, and truck trailers; and industrial storage facilities. Future plans include supplying the oil and gas industries with a line of tubular products, to be added to the current Chicago manufacturing plants. Corporate headquarters location: Philadelphia, PA. American Stock Exchange.

WELLS MANUFACTURING COMPANY
7800 North Austin Avenue
Skokie IL 60077
708/463-5050
Contact Robert Engelhardt, Vice President & Personnel Director. Several area locations. National distributor of electric furnace gray and alloyed iron castings, and cast iron bar stock. Corporate headquarters location.

FINANCIAL SERVICES/CONSULTANTS

For more information on professional employment opportunities in the financial services and management consulting industries, contact the following professional and trade organizations, as listed beginning on page 295:

AMERICAN FINANCIAL SERVICES ASSOCIATION
AMERICAN SOCIETY OF APPRAISERS
AMERICAN SOCIETY OF APPRAISERS/CHICAGO
ASSOCIATION OF MANAGEMENT CONSULTING FIRMS
CHICAGO ASSOCIATION OF BUSINESS ECONOMISTS
CHICAGO ASSOCIATION OF CREDIT MANAGEMENT
COUNCIL OF CONSULTANT ORGANIZATIONS
FEDERATION OF TAX ADMINISTRATORS
FINANCIAL ANALYSTS FEDERATION
FINANCIAL ANALYSTS FEDERATION/CHICAGO

FINANCIAL EXECUTIVES INSTITUTE
FINANCIAL EXECUTIVES INSTITUTE/CHICAGO
INSTITUTE OF FINANCIAL EDUCATION
INSTITUTE OF MANAGMENT CONSULTANTS/
 GREATER CHICAGO CHAPTER
NATIONAL ASSOCIATION OF CREDIT MANAGEMENT
NATIONAL ASSOCIATION OF REAL ESTATE INVESTMENT TRUSTS
NATIONAL CORPORATE CASH MANAGEMENT ASSOCIATION
SECURITIES INDUSTRY ASSOCIATION

CHICAGO BOARD OF OPTIONS EXCHANGE
400 South LaSalle
Chicago IL 60605
312/786-5600
Contact Human Resources Department. A financial institution engaged in the trading of options.

THE CHICAGO BOARD OF TRADE
141 West Jackson Boulevard
Chicago IL 60604
312/435-3494
Contact Amy Smith, Employment Specialist. Commodity futures exchange.

CHICAGO MERCANTILE EXCHANGE
30 South Wacker Drive
Chicago IL 60606
312/930-8243
Contact Steven Timmons, Employment Manager. A large commodities exchange company.

CHICAGO METROPOLITAN MUTUAL ASSURANCE COMPANY
4455 Martin Luther King Jr. Drive
Chicago IL 60653
312/285-3030
Contact Alzater Timmons, Personnel Director. Mortgage holders. Corporate headquarters location.

CHICAGO MILWAUKEE CORPORATION
547 West Jackson Boulevard
Suite 310
Chicago IL 60606
312/822-0400
Contact Dianne Barango, Personnel Director. A financial investment company with 2 subsidiaries involved in real estate sales.

THE CONTINENTAL CORPORATION
200 South Wacker Drive
Chicago IL 60606
312/876-5000
Contact Joyce E. Heidemann, AVP Human Resources. A large diversified financial company.

DRESSER FINANCE CORPORATION
3201 North Wolf Road
Franklin Park IL 60131
708/451-3500
Contact Debra Zeman, Personnel Department. Offers finance services.

EQUIFAX INC.
P.O. Box 3115
Naperville IL 60566
708/505-1099
Contact Personnel Department. A diversified credit reporting agency.

FIRST CHICAGO CORPORATION
1 First National Plaza
Suite 0016
Chicago IL 60670-0016
312/407-4908
Contact Cynthia Causey, Executive Recruiter. A holding company that is primarily concerned with the operation of The First National Bank of Chicago. The bank provides a broad range of commercial and investment banking, trust services, financial and other services on a worldwide basis to individuals, businesses and governmental units. Maintains 14 major departments dealing with the different aspects of operation: Commercial Lending, Trading Products, Corporate Trust Services, Retail Banking (including Personal Trust), Financial Products, Service Products, Risk Insurance, Credit Policy, Community Affairs, Personnel, Systems & MIS, Corporate Planning, Credit Administration, Law, Control, Audit, Bond, Economics, Communications and Administration. Corporate headquarters location. International. New York Stock Exchange. Common positions include: Accountant; Attorney; Seasoned Commercial Lender; Computer Programmer; Customer Service Representative; Mining Engineer; Petroleum Engineer; Financial Analyst; Systems Analyst; Mergers & Acquisitions Specialist; Leveraged Buyout Specialist. Principal educational backgrounds sought: Accounting; Business Administration; Computer Science; Finance; Law. Company benefits include: medical insurance; pension plan; life insurance; tuition assistance; disability coverage; 401 K.

A.T. KEARNEY, INC.
222 South Riverside Plaza
Chicago IL 60606
312/648-0111
Contact V.P./Executive Search Department. A general management consulting firm.

HELLER FINANCIAL
200 North LaSalle
Chicago IL 60601
312/621-7700
Contact Susan Gallen, V.P. of Organizational Staffing. Provides businesses with a variety of financial services.

HOUSEHOLD INTERNATIONAL
2700 Sanders Road
Prospect Heights IL 60070
708/564-5000
Contact Personnel Department. A multi-billion dollar financial services company.

KEMPER GROUP
Route 22
Long Grove IL 60049
708/540-2000
Contact Director of Corporate Personnel. A holding company operating in six business segments.

LESTER B. KNIGHT & ASSOCIATES, INC.
549 West Randolph Street
Chicago IL 60606
312/346-2100
Contact Jim Turner, Director of Human Resources. A management consulting firm.

MAY & SPEH DATA PROCESSING
1501 Opus Place
Downers Grove IL 60515
708/964-1501
Contact Claudia Colalillo, Director/Human Resources. Provides data processing services to business and industry. Common position is: Computer Programmer. Corporate headquarters location.

MERRILL LYNCH
141 West Jackson Boulevard
Chicago IL 60604
312/347-6000
Contact Director of Personnel. Provides financial services in securities, extensive insurance, and real estate and related areas. Its major subsidiary, Merrill Lynch, Pierce, Fenner & Smith, Inc., is one of the largest securities brokerage firms in the United States. It also brokers commodity futures and options, is a dealer in corporate and municipal securities, and engages in investment banking activities. Other major subsidiaries include Merrill Lynch Government Securities, Inc., Family Life Insurance Company and AMIC Corporation. Corporate headquarters location: New York, NY. New York Stock Exchange.

MIDWEST STOCK EXCHANGE INC.
440 South LaSalle
Suite 425
Chicago IL 60605
312/663-2012
Contact Bruce Handler, Employee Relations Specialist. The second largest stock exchange in the United States. Securities trading and depository services. Common positions include: Accountant; Computer Programmer; Customer Service Representative; Financial Analyst; Department Manager; Operations/Production Manager; Technical Writer/Editor; Research Analyst. Company benefits include: medical insurance; dental insurance; pension plan; life insurance; tuition assistance; disability coverage; savings plan. Corporate headquarters location. New York Stock Exchange and American Stock Exchange.

STEIN ROE & FARNHAM
1 South Wacker Drive
Chicago IL 60606
312/368-7705
Contact Susan C. Esque, Manager, Human Resources. Investment counsel offering professional advice and service to individuals, institutions and other organizations. Also manages several no-load mutual funds. Approximately 60 officers and 400 employees. Regional offices in Arizona, New York, Cleveland, Minneapolis, Ft. Lauderdale, and Puerto Rico. Corporate headquarters location. Common positions include: Accountant; Administrator; Attorney; Computer Programmer; Customer Service Representative; Economist; Financial Analyst; Department Manager; Operations/Production Manager; Department Manager; Statistician; Systems Analyst; Research Assistant. Principal educational backgrounds sought: Accounting; Business Administration; Finance; MBA for Analyst or Manager of Investment. Company benefits include: medical insurance; life insurance; tuition assistance; disability coverage; profit sharing.

THE NORTHERN TRUST COMPANY
50 South LaSalle
Chicago IL 60675
312/630-6000
Contact Personnel Department. A major full service bank engaged in commercial lending, trust and financial services, bond, financial management, operations and capital markets among other services.

**FOOD AND BEVERAGE RELATED:
PROCESSING AND DISTRIBUTION**

For more information on professional employment opportunities in the food processing and distributing industries, contact the following professional and trade organizations, as listed beginning on page 295:

AMERICAN ASSOCIATION OF CEREAL CHEMISTS
AMERICAN SOCIETY OF AGRICULTURAL ENGINEERS
AMERICAN SOCIETY OF BREWING CHEMISTS
DAIRY AND FOOD INDUSTRIES SUPPLY ASSOCIATION
ILLINOIS ASSOCIATION OF CEREAL CHEMISTS
NATIONAL AGRICULTURAL CHEMICALS ASSOCIATION
NATIONAL DAIRY COUNCIL
UNITED FOOD AND COMMERCIAL
 WORKERS INTERNATIONAL UNION

ARCHER DANIEL MIDLAND CO.
P.O. Box 1470
Decatur IL 62525
217/424-5239
Contact Sheila Witts-Mannweiler, Personnel Manager. One of the nation's leading agricultural products firms.

GEORGE J. BALL, INC.
622 Town Road
West Chicago IL 60185
708/231-3500
Contact Dennis Johnson, Personnel Director. Chicago-area horticultural business.

CAMPBELL SOUP COMPANY
2550 West 35th Street
Chicago IL 60632
312/376-3700 ext. 408
Contact Lew Bechtol, Personnel Assistant. Area locations: West Chicago/Downers Grove. The Chicago Campbell Soup plant manufactures a full line of Campbell Soup products including Swanson's Dinners, Vlassic Pickles, Godiva Chocolates, and Franco American products. Pepperidge Farm is a subsidiary. New York Stock Exchange. Common positions include:

Accountant; Administrator; Blue-Collar Worker Supervisor; Chemist; Engineer; Electrical Engineer; Industrial Engineer; Mechanical Engineer; Food Technologist; Manager; Department Manager; General Manager; Management Trainee; Operations/Production Manager; Personnel & Labor Relations Specialist; Purchasing Agent; Quality Control Supervisor; Sales Representative; Transportation & Traffic Specialist. Principal educational backgrounds sought: Business Administration; Engineering. Company benefits include: medical insurance; dental insurance; pension plan; life insurance; tuition assistance; disability coverage; profit sharing; employee discounts. Operations at this facility include: manufacturing. Corporate headquarters location: Camden, NJ.

CONAGRA FLOUR MILLING COMPANY
145 West Broadway
Alton IL 62002
618/463-4432
Contact Oren Cummins, Manager. Grain terminal operators engaged in the milling of flour and animal feed. Employs over 100.

CONTINENTAL GRAIN COMPANY
10 South Riverside Plaza
Chicago IL 60606
312/930-1050
Contact Mr. Jochum, Personnel Director. An international food company, involved mostly in grain.

CPC INTERNATIONAL/BEST FOODS DIVISION
P.O. Box 448
6400 South Archer
Argo IL 60501
312/563-2400
Contact Robert Swanson, Human Resources Manager. A worldwide family of food and related businesses.

CULINARY FOODS, INC.
1240 West George Street
Chicago IL 60657
312/528-7300
Contact Howard Davis, President. Buys raw food products, processes and distributes them.

DOMINICK'S FINER FOODS
505 Railroad Avenue
Northlake IL 60164
708/562-1000
Contact Gary J. Bosco, Human Resources Manager. Retail grocery firm.

EDWARD DON & COMPANY
2500 South Harlem Avenue
North Riverside IL 60546
708/442-9400
Contact Jim Walsh, Human Resources Manager. Distributor of food service equipment and supplies.

ENVIRODYNE INDUSTRIES, INC.
701 Harger Road
Oak Brook IL 60521
708/571-8800
Contact Personnel Department. A holding company for sausage casing and disposable plastic cutlery and straws company.

FLOUR MILLS DIVISION/ CON-AGRA
145 West Broadway
Alton IL 62002
618/463-4411
Contact Cindy Holt, Office Manager. A major division of the national agricultural products corporation, specializing in the manufacture of grain terminal operators; and the production of millers-flour and animal feed.

FORT HOWARD CUP CORP.
7575 South Kostner
Chicago IL 60652
312/767-3300
Contact Dorothy Stanis, Employment Manager. Several area locations. Engaged in the manufacture and distribution of a variety of food serviceware including plates, cups, bowls, drinking straws, ice cream cones, as well as containers for use in packaging food and dairy products. Principal trademarkes include Sweetheart, Guildware, and Eat-it-All. Corporate headquarters location: Green Bay, WI. Parent company: Fort Howard Paper Company. New York Stock Exchange.

GENERAL BISCUIT BRANDS, INC.
7777 North Caldwell Avenue
Niles IL 60648
312/774-2000
Contact Barbara Grant, Manager of Human Resources. A producer and distributor of cookies and crackers.

GOLDEN GRAIN
7700 W. 71st Street
Bridgeview IL 60455
708/585-1400
Contact David Futts, General Manager. Producers of Rice-a-roni. Makers of all types of macaroni.

GONNELLA BAKING COMPANY
2002-14 West Erie Street
Chicago IL 60612
312/733-2020
Contact Lou Pasquesi, Jr., Personnel. Makers of bread and other bakery products.

G. HEILEMAN BREWING CO.
STAG BREWERY
1201 West E. Street
Belleville IL 62221
618/234-1234
Contact Personnel Director. A major regional brewery.

ILLINOIS FARM BUREAU
1701 Towanda Avenue
Bloomington IL 61701
309/557-2209
Contact Jack Fowler, Director of Employment & Training. Sell production supplies, provide insurance protection, market farm products and provide business and personal services for members.

INTERSTATE BRANDS CORPORATION
40 East Garfield Boulevard
Chicago IL 60615
312/536-7700
Contact William Schwab, Associate Personnel Manager. Manufacturers & wholesalers of break & cake products.

JAYS FOODS, INC.
825 East 99th Street
Chicago IL 60628
312/731-8400
Contact Personnel Director. Produces and distributes popcorn & potato chips.

KEEBLER COMPANY
One Hollow Tree Lane
Elmhurst IL 60126
312/379-1525
Contact Dennis Christensen, V.P./Human Resources. A producer biscuits, cookies, and other bakery products.

KITCHENS OF SARA LEE
500 Waukegan Road
Deerfield IL 60015
Contact Human Resources/Staffing. An area producer of frozen baked goods. Parent company, Sara Lee Corporation, is a diversified consumer goods company. Common positions include: Accountant; Buyer; Chemist; Computer Programmer; Industrial Engineer; Mechanical Engineer; Packaging Engineer; Financial Analyst; Food Technologist; Experimental Baker. Principal educational backgrounds sought: Business Administration; Computer Science; Engineering; Finance; Marketing; Packaging Design. Company benefits include: medical, dental, and life insurance; pension plan; tuition assistance; disability coverage; employee discounts. Corporate, regional and divisional headquarters location. Operations at this facility include: research/development; administration; service; sales.

KRAFT, INC.
2211 Sanders Road
Northbrook IL 60062
312/498-8000
Contact Dave Ahlers, Manager of Employee Relations. An international leader in consumer food products.

KRAFT HOLLEB
800 Supreme Drive
Bensonville IL 60106
708/595-1200
Contact Personnel Director. Ditributes prepared foods to institutional customers.

LEAF, INC.
2355 Waukegan Road
Bannockburn IL 60015
708/940-7500
Contact Joel Dant, Vice President, Personnel. A confectionery and candy company (manufacturing & sales)

NATIONAL BAKING COMPANY
5001 West Polk
Chicago IL 60644
312/261-6000
Contact Harry Carson, Executive Vice President/General Manager. Specializes in preparation and baking of breads and rolls. Trucks deliver products east of the Rocky Mountains. Institutional route system locally. Corporate headquarters location.

NESTLE FOODS CORPORATION
2101 Adams Street
Granite City IL 62040
618/225-4242
Contact Dennis Martin, Manager, Human Resources. The St. Louis office of the nationally-known manufacturer of a wide range of food products. Also produces a wide range of ingredients for the food-processing and beverage industries. A wholly-owned subsidiary of Nestle SA (Vevey, Switzerland), a major international food products firm. Corporate headquarters: Purchase, NY. Common positions include: Accountant; Blue-Collar Worker Supervisor; Draftsperson; Chemical Engineer; Industrial Engineer; Mechanical Engineer; General Manager; Management Trainee; Operations/Production Manager; Personnel & Labor Relations Specialist; Quality Control Supervisor. Principal educational backgrounds sought: Engineering. Company benefits include: medical, dental, and life insurance; pension plan; tuition assistance; disability coverage; savings plan. Operations at this facility include: manufacturing.

OSCAR MAYER FOODS CORPORATION
320 Scott Street
Chicago IL 60610
312/642-1200
Contact Don Culburson, Assistant Personnel Manager. Operates meat packing and processing facilities in the United States and abroad. Company produces more than 750 food service and consumer processed meat products, including wieners, sausage, bacon, sandwich spreads, turkey products, and ham products, as well as many others. Company's products are sold throughout the United States by approximately 450 salespersons operating out of 32 distribution centers in most major cities. A processing plant in Chicago. Company has a distribution center in Chicago, and subsidiary Claussen Pickle Company is located in Woodstock. Operates 20 processing plants nationwide. Operations at this facility include: manufacturing. Corporate headquarters location: Madison, WI. Parent company: Phillip Morris. New York Stock Exchange. International. Common positions include: Accountant; Blue-Collar Worker Supervisor; Buyer; Credit Manager; Engineer; Customer Service Representative; Draftsperson; Chemical Engineer; Electrical Engineer; Industrial Engineer; Mechanical Engineer; Food Technologist; Department Manager; Operations/Production Manager; Personnel & Labor Relations Specialist; Purchasing Agent; Quality Control Supervisor. Principal educational backgrounds sought: Accounting; Biology; Business Administration; Computer Science; Engineering; Finance; Food Science; Liberal Arts. Company benefits include: medical insurance; dental insurance; pension plan; life insurance; tuition assistance; disability coverage; employee discounts; profit sharing; savings plan.

PRAIRIE FARMS DAIRY INC.
P.O. Box W
1800 Adams Street
Granite City IL 62040
618/451-5600
Contact Personnel Department. Major St. Louis area producer and wholesaler of dairy products.

THE QUAKER OATS COMPANY
Merchandise Mart Plaza
Chicago IL 60654
Contact Placement Office for information. Engaged in research, manufacturing, and marketing of foods, pet foods, toys and specialty retailing. Established in 1877. Employs 32,000 people worldwide. Corporate headquarters location. New York Stock Exchange.

SARA LEE
3 First National Plaza
70 West Madison
Chicago IL 60602
312/726-2600
Contact Vice President of Human Resources. The corporate office of the cake, cake-mix, and dessert snacks producer.

SUPERIOR COFFEE COMPANY
990 Supreme Drive
Bensenville IL 60106
708/860-1400
Contact Mr. Lee Ashmann, V.P./Human Resources Department. Several area locations, including: Bensenville, Chicago, Elk Grove Village. Produces and sells coffee, tea, salad dressings, syrups, and vending products. Corporate headquarters location.

SYSCO FOOD SERVICES
250 Wieboldt Drive
Des Plaines IL 60017
708/699-5400
Contact Personnel Department. Manufactures, sells, and distributes food products.

TOPCO ASSOCIATES, INC.
7711 Gross Point Road
Skokie IL 60076
312/676-3030
Contact Garry J. Lunt, Employment Manager. Cooperative buying organization engaged in procurement of private label grocery products, meat products, produce and general merchandise items. Serves 35 member supermarket chains located nationwide. Common positions include:

Accountant; Food Technologist; Transportation & Traffic Specialist; Food & Non-food Buyers; Marketing Research Analyst; Produce Buyer. Principal educational backgrounds sought: Accounting; Biology; Business Administration; Computer Science; Finance; Liberal Arts; Marketing. Company benefits include: medical, dental, and life insurance; pension plan; tuition assistance; disability coverage; savings plan. Corporate headquarters location. Operations at this facility include: administration; procurement; finance; MIS; Accounting; Marketing; Quality Assurance.

VIENNA BEEF LTD.
2501 North Damen Avenue
Chicago IL 60647
312/278-7800
Contact Mr. Jamie Eisenberg, Vice President, Personnel. National distributor and processor of meat and sausage. Also a meat cutting facility. Corporate headquarters location. International. Common positions include: Accountant; Computer Programmer; Customer Service Representative; Food Technologist; Sales Representative. Principal educational backgrounds sought: Accounting; Business Administration; Computer Science. Company benefits include: medical, dental, and life insurance; pension plan; disability coverage; profit sharing; employee discounts. Operations at this facility include: regional headquarters; manufacturing; administration; service; sales.

WORLD'S FINEST CHOCOLATE
4801 South Lawndale
Chicago IL 60632
312/847-4600
Contact Greg Serratore, Personnel Director. Manufactures chocolate and cocoa products. Corporate headquarters location. International.

WILLIAM WRIGLEY, JR. COMPANY
410 North Michigan Avenue
Chicago IL 60611
312/644-2121
Contact Edgar W. Swanson, Vice President/Personnel. Several area locations. Manufactures and markets chewing gums, under such well-known name brands as Wrigley's Spearmint, Doublemint, Juicy Fruit, Freedent, Big Red, Orbit, Spurt, Hubba Bubba, and others, in 14 factories worldwide. Gum factories are located in Chicago and Naperville, a raw materials processing plant is located in West Chicago, and the Wrigley Building is located in Chicago (houses corporate offices). A Fortune 500 company. New York Stock Exchange.

GENERAL MERCHANDISE/RETAIL

For more information on professional employment opportunities in the retail industry, contact the following professional and trade organization, as listed beginning on page 295:

NATIONAL RETAIL MERCHANTS ASSOCIATION

AMES CORPORATION
11535 South Central
Worth IL 60482
708/597-3500
Contact Associate Relations Manager. A retail department store chain. Basic full-line mass merchandiser. Operates more than 270 stores nationwide. Regional headquarters. Corporate headquarters location: Framingham, MA. New York Stock Exchange. Common positions include: Management Trainee. Principal educational backgrounds sought: Business Administration; Economics; Liberal Arts. Company benefits include: medical insurance; pension plan; life insurance; tuition assistance; disability coverage; profit sharing; employee discounts; savings plan.

EVANS, INC.
36 South State Street
Chicago IL 60603
312/855-2000
Contact Robert Parraga, Vice President of Personnel. A retailer of fur garments, cloth coats and suits.

FIRESTONE TIRE
205 North Michigan Avenue
Chicago IL 60601
312/819-0001
Contact Personnel Director. Operates a chain of 280 retail outlets marketing tires and automotive services in Ohio, Michigan, Indiana, Illinois, Wisconsin, Minnesota, Iowa, Nebraska, North Dakota, and South Dakota. 1,400 retail outlets nationally.

GATELY'S PEOPLE STORE
6901 West 159th Street
Tinley Park IL 60477
708/429-2400
Contact Mary Walsh, Director of Personnel. A retail department store. Corporate headquarters location.

HOME NURSERY GREENHOUSES INC.
P.O. Box 307
Edwardsville IL 62025
618/656-1790
Contact Carol Balke, Personnel Director. A major area nursery engaged in the wholesale and retail sales of lawn and garden supplies.

K'S MERCHANDISE
3103 North Charles Street
Decatur IL 62526
217/875-1440
Contact John Bell, Director of Personnel. An expanding retail catalog showroom chain.

K-MART CORPORATION
2300 B West Higgins Road
Hoffman Estates IL 60195
708/884-3795
Contact Larry Foster, Director of Personnel & Training. A major nationwide discounts department store chain.

KROCH'S & BRENTANO'S, INC.
29 South Wabash Avenue
Chicago IL 60603
312/332-7500
Contact Dolores A. Sledz, Vice President, Human Resources. Operates retail stores, selling books, gift items, etc.

MONTGOMERY WARD & COMPANY
One Montgomery Ward Plaza
Chicago IL 60671
312/467-2000
Contact Susan Rayner, Executive Placement Director. Nationwide mass merchandiser in the retail and catalog areas. Operates more than 300 stores. Corporate headquarters location. International.

J.C. PENNEY COMPANY INC./ NORTHWEST REGION
1750 East Golf Road
Schaumburg IL 60173-5049
708/517-4600
Contact Don Brewer, Regional Career Development Coordinator. Multiple area locations including: Schaumburg, Ford City, Lombard, North Riverside. A national, $14-billion retail merchandise sales and service corporation. Regional headquarters. Corporate headquarters location: Dallas, TX. International. New York Stock Exchange. Common positions include: Buyer; Department Manager; Management Trainee. Principal educational backgrounds sought: Accounting; Business Administration; Communications;

Computer Science; Liberal Arts; Economics; Marketing. Company benefits include: medical insurance; dental insurance; pension plan; life insurance; disability coverage; profit sharing; employee discounts; savings plan.

POLK BROTHERS
8311 West North Avenue
Melrose Park IL 60160
708/216-3030
Contact Mike Crane, Personnel Director. Multiple area locations. A furniture and appliances sales company selling a wide variety of products with name brands. Corporate headquarters location.

SAKS FIFTH AVENUE
669 North Michigan
Chicago IL 60611
312/944-6500
Contact Mrs. Christine Warman, Personnel Director. Fashion-forward, specialized department store chain. Branches of greatly varying sizes in 30 cities throughout the country. Soft goods products only, particularly apparel for men, women and children. Emphasis on high-quality fashion items. Subsidiary companies conduct a catalogue operation and a corporate gift service. A subsidiary of Gimbel Brothers, Inc., but is operated autonomously with respect to current operations, personnel, merchandising, purchasing, etc. Corporate headquarters location: New York, NY.

SAXON PAINT & HOME CARE CENTERS
3840 West Fullerton
Chicago IL 60647
312/252-8100
Contact Howard R. Kraus, Director of Personnel. Several area locations. A chain of retail stores in northern Illinois, Indiana, and Wisconsin. 44 stores are located in Chicago metropolitan area. Saxon specializes in paint, wallpaper, window fashions and other home decorating products. Also manufacture own paint. Corporate headquarters location. Common positions include: Advertising Worker; Buyer; Management Trainee; Store Manager; Salesperson. Principal educational backgrounds sought: Accounting; Art/Design; Liberal Arts. Training programs offered. Company benefits include: medical, dental, and life insurance; disability coverage; profit sharing; employee discounts; savings plan.

G.D. SEARLE & COMPANY
5200 Old Orchard Road
P.O. Box 1045, Skokie IL 60077
708/982-7000
Contact Human Resources. Engaged in four groups: Research and Development, Pharmaceutical/Consumer Products, Medical Products, and the Optical Group. Products include ethical pharmaceuticals, healthcare

products, high-purity compressed gases, eyewear, lenses and sunglasses. Corporate headquarters location. International. New York Stock Exchange.

SEARS, ROEBUCK & COMPANY
Sears Tower, D-707-2
Chicago IL 60684
312/875-2500
Contact Mary Misar, Professional Employment. One of the world's largest retailers with subsidiaries engaged in the insurance, securities brokerage, and real estate businesses. The company's principal business groups are: Merchandise, which distributes broad lines of merchandise and services in the United States through more than 850 retail stores and 2,700 sales offices and other facilities; Allstate, which engages in the property/liability insurance, life insurance and financial services businesses, principally in the United States and Canada; Coldwell Banker, which invests in, develops, and operates real estate and performs financial services, which include savings and loan, mortgage banking and mortgage guaranty insurance activities; and Dean Witter Reynolds, which provides a complete range of securities brokerage services. The company employs approximately 390,000 people worldwide, including part-time employees. Corporate headquarters location. International. New York Stock Exchange.

SHERWIN-WILLIAMS COMPANY
11541 South Champlain
Chicago IL 60628
312/821-3011
Contact Mr. Murphy, Personnel Director. Operates nationally in six segments: Retail Stores, Coatings, Chemicals, Packaging Products, Specialty Products, and International. Products include Sherwin-Williams, Dutch Boy, Martin Seymour, Baltimore and Kem paints, as well as such related packaging products as paint cans, sprays and labels. Corporate headquarters location: Cleveland, OH. International. New York Stock Exchange.

JOHN M. SMYTH'S HOMEMAKERS
1013 Butterfield Road
Downers Grove IL 60515
708/665-7241
Contact Rex Slocum, Personnel Director. Multiple area locations. Large, high quality retail furniture chain. One store in downtown Chicago and five suburban locations. Corporate headquarters location. Common positions include: Administrator; Buyer; Customer Service Representative; Department Manager; Management Trainee; Sales Representative. Principal educational backgrounds sought: Art/Design; Business Administration; Liberal Arts; Marketing. Company benefits include: medical insurance; life insurance; disability coverage; employee discounts.

VENTURE STORES
17 West 734 22nd Street
Oakbrook Terrace IL 60181
708/627-9750
Contact Ellen Pritchett, Regional Personnel Manager. Department store chain. A subsidiary of May Department Stores Company. Corporate headquarters location.

F.W. WOOLWORTH COMPANY
915 Lee Street
Des Plaines IL 60016
708/827-7731
Contact Roger Boe, Regional Director. An international retailing firm with more than 6,000 retail stores and leased departments in the United States, Puerto Rico, U.S. Virgin Islands, Canada, Germany, Mexico, Spain, Australia, Great Britain, Ireland, and the Caribbean Islands, operating under the names Woolworth, Woolco, Kinney, and Richman, as well as other names regionally. Annual sales in excess of $6 billion. Corporate headquarters location: New York, NY. International. New York Stock Exchange.

HEALTH CARE & PHARMACEUTICALS: PRODUCTS & SERVICES

For more information on professional employment opportunities in the health care and pharmaceutical industries, contact the following professional and trade organizations, as listed beginning on page 295:

AMERICAN ACADEMY OF PHYSICIAN ASSISTANTS
AMERICAN COLLEGE OF HEALTHCARE EXECUTIVES
AMERICAN DENTAL ASSOCIATION
AMERICAN HEALTH CARE ASSOCIATION
AMERICAN MEDICAL ASSOCIATION
AMERICAN OCCUPATIONAL THERAPY ASSOCIATION
AMERICAN PHARMACEUTICAL ASSOCIATION
AMERICAN PHYSICAL THERAPY ASSOCIATION
AMERICAN SOCIETY FOR BIOCHEMISTRY
 AND MOLECULAR BIOLOGY
AMERICAN SOCIETY OF HOSPITAL PHARMACISTS
AMERICAN VETERINARY MEDICAL ASSOCIATION
CARDIOVASCULAR CREDENTIALING INTERNATIONAL
CHICAGO PHYSICAL THERAPY ASSOCIATION
ILLINOIS ACADEMY OF PHYSICIAN ASSISTANTS
ILLINOIS SOCIETY OF HOSPITAL PHARMACISTS
MEDICAL GROUP MANAGEMENT ASSOCIATION
MEDICAL GROUP MANAGEMENT ASSOCIATION/
 SPRINGFIELD BRANCH
NATIONAL HEALTH COUNCIL
NATIONAL MEDICAL ASSOCIATION

ABBOTT LABORATORIES
Abbott Park
Corporate Placement (AP6D)
North Chicago IL 60064
Contact Michael Omelanuk, Manager of Corporate Placement. Manufactures a wide variety of health care products, including pharmaceuticals, hospital products, diagnostic products, chemicals, and nutritional products. Common positions at this facility include: Accountant; Attorney; Biochemist; Biologist; Chemist; Computer Programmer; Biomedical Engineer; Chemical Engineer; Civil Engineer; Electrical Engineer; Mechanical Engineer; Financial Analyst; Personnel & Labor Relations Specialist; Systems Analyst. Principal educational backgrounds sought: Accounting; Biology; Business Administration; Chemistry; Computer Science; Engineering; Personnel/Industrial Relations. Company benefits include: medical insurance; dental insurance; pension plan; life insurance; tuition assistance; disability coverage; profit sharing; employee discounts; savings plan. Corporate headquarters location. Operations at this facility include: divisional headquarters; manufacturing; research/development; administration; service; sales. New York Stock Exchange

ALTON MEMORIAL HOSPITAL
1 Memorial Drive
Alton IL 62002
618/463-7311
Contact Scott Seaborn, Vice-President of Human Resources & Faci. A major St.Louis area general hospital.

ALTON MENTAL HEALTH CENTER
4500 College Avenue
Alton IL 62002
618/465-5593
Contact Joe Fophrkolv, Head of Personnel. A major metropolitan St. Louis medical facility, specializing in treatment of psychiatric developmental disabilities. Employs over 300.

AMERICAN DENTAL ASSOCIATION
211 E. Chicago Ave
Chicago IL 60611-9985
312/440-2500
Contact Thomas Dorsch, Director of Human Resources. A professional association serving the dental community.

AMERICAN HOSPITAL ASSOCIATION
840 N. Lake Shore Drive
Chicago IL 60690
312/280-6092
Contact Cal Gilbert, Recruitment Manager. A $50 million organization serving the medical industry.

BAXTER HEALTHCARE
One Baxter Parkway
Deerfield IL 60015
708/948-2000
Contact Robert DeBaun, Corporate Recruitment Director. A multinational manufacturer and distributor of a wide range of products and services used primarily in the health care field. Sells domestically and internationally to hospitals, clinical and medical research laboratories, medical and dental offices, rehabilitation centers, nursing homes, and related facilities and institutions. Company operates in three domestic market segments (Hospital, Laboratory, Medical Specialties), and one international market segment. A small sampling of the company's products include disposable medical and surgical instruments, hospital apparel and furniture, disposable plastic products, food service products and systems, blood-typing serums, laboratory controls, specialty glassware, diagnostic reagents and associated instrumentation, a wide range of medical and dental devices and instruments, diagnostic equipment, prosthetic devices, plastic lenses, intravenous fluids and fluid delivery systems, and ethical pharmaceuticals. Corporate headquarters location. International. New York Stock Exchange.

BEVERLY FARM FOUNDATION INC.
6301 Humbert Road
Godfrey IL 62035
618/466-0367
Contact Rebecca Hutt, Personnel Director. A residential care facility for mentally handicapped children and adults from ages 5 to 85. Employs over 200.

CENTREVILLE TOWNSHIP HOSPITAL
5900 Bond Avenue
East St. Louis IL 62207
618/332-3060
Contact Ms. Willa Bates, Administrative Assistant. A major area medical facility. Employs over 300.

HELENE CURTIS INDUSTRIES, INC.
325 North Wells
Chicago IL 60610
312/661-0222
Contact Jack Calabro, Director of Human Resources. Operates in beauty & hair products, & sealing products.

DAMON LABS
3231 South Euclid
Berwyn IL 60402
312/282-9500
Contact Georgianna Casey, Personnel Manager. An around-the-clock clinical testing lab.

FOUR FOUNTAINS CONVALESCENT
101 S. Belt West
Belleville IL 62220
618/277-7700
Contact Personnel Department. A major area skilled nursing care facility. Employs over 100.

GROEN COMPANY
DOVER CORPORATION
1900 Pratt Boulevard
Elk Grove Village IL 60007
708/439-2400
Contact Personnel Director. Manufactures food processing equipment.

JOHNSON PRODUCTS COMPANY
8522 South Lafayette Avenue
Chicago IL 60620
312/483-4100
Contact Personnel Manager. A leading manufacturer of hair care and cosmetic products.

MEMORIAL HOSPITAL
4501 North Park Drive
Belleville IL 62223
618/233-7750
Contact Barbara Nicely, Director of Personnel. A major St. Louis general hospital with 346 adult and pediatric beds and 32 cribs.

PACKARD INSTRUMENT COMPANY
2200 Warrenville Road
Downers Grove IL 60515
708/969-6000
Contact Marcella Huff, Manager, Human Resources. A division of Cranberra Industries, Inc. manufactures biomedical instruments such as the scintillation gamma counter (tests blood for disease). Sells to hospitals and universities. Corporate headquarters location: Meriden, CT. International. Company benefits include: medical, dental, and life insurance; pension plan; tuition assistance; disability coverage; profit sharing; employee discounts; savings plan. Parent company: Canberra Industries. Operations at this facility include: manufacturing; research/development; service. Common positions

include: Chemist; Electrical Engineer; Mechanical Engineer. Principal educational backgrounds sought: Business Administration; Engineering; Liberal Arts.

RESPIRATORY CARE INC. (RCI)
900 West University Drive
Arlington Heights IL 60004
708/259-7400
Contact Althea Schuler, Human Resource Manager. Specialized manufacturer of sterile disposable products for respiratory therapy. Common positions include: Accountant; Blue-Collar Worker Supervisor; Buyer; Computer Programmer; Credit Manager; Customer Service Representative; Draftsperson; Biomedical Engineer; Chemical Engineer; Electrical Engineer; Industrial Engineer; Mechanical Engineer; Department Manager; General Manager; Operations/Production Manager; Purchasing Agent; Quality Control Supervisor; Transportation & Traffic Specialist. Principal educational backgrounds sought: Accounting; Business Administration; Chemistry; Computer Science; Engineering; Liberal Arts. Company benefits include: medical insurance; dental insurance; pension plan; life insurance; tuition assistance; disability coverage; employee discounts. Corporate headquarters location: Temecula, CA. Parent company: Hudson Respiratory Care Inc. Operations at this facility include: manufacturing; research/development; administration; service; sales.

ST. CLEMENT HOSPITAL
325 Spring Street
Red Bud IL 62278
618/282-3831
Contact Personnel Director. A major St. Louis-area general hospital.

ST. ELIZABETH'S HOSPITAL
211 South 3rd Street
Belleville IL 62222
618/234-2120
Contact Norman Theisman, Personnel Director. A major Southern Illinois general hospital.

ST. JOSEPH HOSPITAL
915 East 5th Street
Alton IL 62002-6434
618/463-5151
Contact Neil Godar, Personnel Director. A major Southern Ilinois general hospital.

ST. JOSEPH HOSPITAL
1515 Main Street
Highland IL 62249
618/654-7421
Contact Kim Kampwerth, Personnel Assistant. A major Southern Illinois general hospital. Company benefits include: medical, dental, and life insurance; pension plan; tuition assistance; disability coverage.

ST. PAUL'S HOMES FOR THE AGED
1021 West E Street
Belleville IL 62220
618/233-2095
Contact Arthur H. Peters, Administrator. Residential and nursing care for the aged.

WESLEY-JESSEN CORP.
400 West Superior Street
Chicago IL 60610
312/751-6200
Contact Gene Tucker, Director of Personnel. Develops, manufactures and markets contact lenses and lens products. A wholly owned subsidiary of Schering-Plough Corporation (Madison, NJ). Common positions include: Accountant; Administrator; Blue-Collar Worker Supervisor; Buyer; Chemist; Computer Programmer; Credit Manager; Customer Service Representative; Draftsperson; Industrial Engineer; Mechanical Engineer; Financial Analyst; Industrial Manager; Marketing Specialist; Personnel & Labor Relations Specialist; Purchasing Agent; Quality Control Supervisor; Sales Representative; Statistician; Systems Analyst; Technical Writer/Editor. Principal educational backgrounds sought: Accounting; Chemistry; Communications; Computer Science; Engineering; Finance; Liberal Arts; Marketing. Internships offered. Company benefits include: medical insurance; dental insurance; pension plan; life insurance; tuition assistance; disability coverage; profit sharing; employee discounts; savings plan. Divisional headquarters location. Operations include: manufacturing; research/development; administration; sales. Corporate headquarters location: Madison, NJ. New York Stock Exchange

WOOD RIVER TOWNSHIP HOSPITAL
Edwardsville Road
Wood River IL 62095
618/254-3821
Contact Personnel Department. A major general hospital.

HIGHLY DIVERSIFIED

FARLEY INDUSTRIES
233 S. Wacker Drive
Chicago IL 60606
312/876-7000
Contact Human Resources Director. A diversified holding company.

ITEL
2 North Riverside Plaza
Chicago IL 60606
312/902-1515
Contact Gloria Waber, Manager of Corporate Relations. A company with 4 current sources of cash flow: container and railcar leasing, marine dredging & wiring systems products for voice data and video communications.

NEWELL
29 East Stephenson Street
Freeport IL 61032
815/235-4171
Contact Manager, Corporate Recruitment. Newell Company is a manufacturer of staple, volume comsumer and industrial products for the volume purchaser. Manufacturing is decentralized by product line. Common positions include: Accountant; Administrator; Credit Manager; Financial Analyst; General Manager; Personnel & Labor Relations Specialist; Systems Analyst; Technical Writer/Editor. Principal educational backgrounds sought: Accounting; Business Administration; Computer Science; Finance; Mathematics. Company benefits include: medical, dental, and life insurance; pension plan; tuition assistance; disability coverage; profit sharing; employee discounts; credit union. Operations at this facility include: administration. New York Stock Exchange.

ST. LOUIS NATIONAL STOCK YARDS COMPANY
P.O. Box 97
National Stock Yards IL 62071
618/271-2405
Contact Personnel Department. A diversified livestock company engaged in a variety of activities, including livestock marketing; the operation of public stock yards and dry bulk warehousing; the operation of a switching railroad system; the operation of area restaraunts; and the sale of real estate.

UNR INDUSTRIES, INC.
332 South Michigan Avenue
Chicago IL 60604
312/341-1234
Contact Personnel Department. Several area locations including: Evanston, Hammond, IN, Paris and Peoria. A diversified corporation with five

operating groups: Industrial Products, Commercial Products, Consumer Products, Communications Products and Transportation Products. The first group manufactures and sells mechanical and structural electric resistance-welded steel tubing. The commercial products group manufactures and sells grocery shopping carts, self-service luggage carts, office and other carts and continuous shelving systems. The consumer products group includes the wholesale and retail sale of Unarco-West Corporation. Sales include name brand appliances, TV and sound equipment. Also, manufactures roller skate wheels, outdoor barbecue grills, a line of casual indoor/outdoor furniture, and stainless steel sinks. The communications group includes the manufacture and marketing of towers with related accessories used principally to support communications equipment for microwave transmissions, broadcasting, home television and amateur broadcasting. The transportation group includes the manufacture and sale of loading equipment and box car doors for railroads. Corporate headquarters location. New York Stock Exchange.

HOTELS AND RESTAURANTS

For more information on professional employment opportunities in the hotel and restaurant industries, contact the following professional and trade organizations, as listed beginning on page 295:

THE AMERICAN HOTEL AND MOTEL ASSOCIATION
THE EDUCATION FOUNDATION OF
 THE NATIONAL RESTAURANT ASSOCIATION
COUNCIL ON HOTEL, RESTAURANT
 & INSTITUTIONAL EDUCATION

ARA SERVICES
2000 Spring Road
Suite 300
Oak Brook IL 60521
708/572-2800
Contact Nora McCarthy, Human Resources Manager. A leading provider of institutional dining services.

CARSON PIRIE SCOTT
1 South State Street
Chicago IL 60603
312/641-8000
Contact Mark Case, College Recruitment. Provides hotel management and direct mail marketing.

COLLINSVILLE HOLIDAY INN
1000 Eastport Plaza Drive
Collinsville IL 62234
618/345-2800
Contact Ms. Gami Lauer, Accounting Department. Operates a full service hotel as part of the Holiday Inn chain, whose operations include the management of more than 1,750 company-owned and franchised hotels, gaming operations, restaurants, and a sea transportation subsidiary. Corporate headquarters location: Memphis, TN. Employs over 100.

COLLINSVILLE MAC INC./ McDONALD'S RESTAURANT OFFICE
3673 Highway 111
Granite City IL 62040
618/931-2100
Contact Jim Burns, Head of Operations. A regional home office which owns and operates 15 area fast food restaurants. Parent company is a worldwide developer, operator, franchisor, and servicer of a system of restaurants which process, package, and sell a limited menu of fast foods. Internationally, company is one of the largest restaurant chains, and the largest food service organization, operating more than 6,000 McDonald's restaurants in all 50 states and in more than 25 foreign countries. Corporate headquarters location: Oak Brook, IL. New York Stock Exchange. Employs over 100.

DRAKE HOTEL
140 East Walton Place
Chicago IL 60611
312/787-2200
Contact Miss Bodell, Personnel Director. A Hilton International hotel and restaurant.

EXECUTIVE HOUSE HOTEL
71 East Wacker Drive
Chicago IL 60601
312/346-7100
Contact Margaret Lord, Personnel Director. A major Chicago hotel.

FABER ENTERPRISES
55 E. Monroe Street
Chicago IL 60603
312/558-8989
Contact Personnel Manager. A chain of restuarants, retail drug and gift stores.

FISCHER'S RESTAURANT
2100 W. Main Street
Belleville IL 62220
618/233-1131
Contact Vel Crabtree, Manager. A major area restaurant which also provides catering services. Employs over 100.

HOLIDAY INNS, INC.
300 East Ohio Street
Chicago IL 60611
708/932-9600
Contact Regional Human Resources Director. One of the world's largest hotel chains.

HYATT REGENCY CHICAGO
151 East Wacker Drive
Chicago IL 60601
312/565-1000
Contact Carla Thomas, Director of Human Resources. A regional office for the Hyatt chain of hotels.

PHEASANT RUN INC.
P.O. Box 64
St. Charles IL 60174
708/584-6300
Contact Debbie Edwards, Personnel Director. Operates a hotel. Corporate headquarters location. Common positions include: Department Manager. Company benefits include: medical insurance.

RAMADA HOTEL O'HARE
6600 North Mannheim Road
Rosemont IL 60018
708/827-5131
Contact Janet Hartzler, Personnel Director. Operates a major hotel as part of the international hotel chain. Parent company: Ramada Inns Inc. Common positions include: Accountant; Credit Manager; Hotel Manager/Assistant Manager; Department Manager; Personnel & Labor Relations Specialist; Purchasing Agent; Sales Representative. Principal educational backgrounds sought: Accounting; Business Administration; Communications; Finance; Liberal Arts; Marketing. Company benefits include: medical insurance; dental insurance; pension plan; life insurance; tuition assistance; disability coverage; profit sharing; employee discounts; savings plan; stock options. Corporate headquarters location: Phoenix, AZ. New York Stock Exchange

RITZ CARLTON HOTEL
160 East Pearson Street
Chicago IL 60611
312/266-1000
Contact Michael Denison, Director of Personnel. An exclusive Chicago hotel with convention and banquet facilities. A subsidiary of Four Seasons Hotels, Ltd. Common positions include: Administrator; Credit Manager; Customer Service Representative; Hotel Manager/Assistant Manager; Department Manager; General Manager; Management Trainee; Marketing Specialist; Personnel & Labor Relations Specialist; Purchasing Agent; Sales Representative. Principal educational backgrounds sought: Business Administration; Hotel Administration; Marketing. Company benefits include: medical insurance; dental insurance; pension plan; life insurance; tuition assistance; disability coverage; profit sharing; employee discounts; savings plan. Operations at this facility include: service; sales. Corporate headquarters location: Toronto, Canada.

TRI-R VENDING SERVICE
1401 West North Avenue
Chicago IL 60622
312/235-9100
Contact Ms. Linda Sprunk, Personnel Director. Provides vending and food services throughout the Chicago area. Corporate headquarters location.

THE WESTIN HOTEL
909 North Michigan Avenue
Chicago IL 60611
312/943-7200
Contact Jeff Sablich, Director of Human Resources. A 747-room luxury hotel with three restaurants, a health club, 18 fully-equipped meeting rooms, two ballrooms, parking facilities, swimming pool. Located on Chicago's Magnificent Mile.

INSURANCE

For more information on professional employment opportunities in the insurance industry, contact the following professional and trade organizations, as listed beginning on page 295:

ALLIANCE OF AMERICAN INSURERS
AMERICAN COUNCIL OF LIFE INSURANCE
AMERICAN INSURANCE ASSOCIATION
INSURANCE INFORMATION INSTITUTE
INSURANCE INFORMATION INSTITUTE OF CHICAGO
NATIONAL ASSOCIATION OF LIFE UNDERWRITERS
SOCIETY OF ACTUARIES

ALLSTATE INSURANCE CO.
Allstate Plaza South
Building G1C
Northbrook IL 60062
708/402-7182
Contact Deborah Cross, Employment Manager. One of the nation's largest insurance companies.

AON CORPORATION
123 North Wacker Drive
14th Floor
Chicago IL 60606
312/701-3200
Contact Rebecca Hogue, Director of Corporate Staffing. A leading metropolitan Chicago insurance agency specializing in accident and health coverage but also provides life, property, and casualty insurance and brokerage and related services. Common positions include: Accountant; Actuary; Administrator; Claim Representative; Customer Service Representative; Branch Manager; Department Manager; Personnel & Labor Relations Specialist. Company benefits include: medical, dental, and life insurance; pension plan; tuition assistance; disability coverage; profit sharing; employee discounts; savings plan. Corporate headquarters location. New York Stock Exchange.

BANKERS LIFE AND CASUALTY
4444 W. Lawrence Avenue
Chicago IL 60630
312/777-7000
Contact Director of Human Resources. Specializes in life and health insurance policies.

BENEFIT TRUST LIFE INSURANCE CO.
1771 West Howard Street
Chicago IL 60626
312/274-8100
Contact Susan Harris, Manager of Human Resources. A legal reserve insurance company.

CNA INSURANCE COMPANIES
CNA Plaza
Floor 41S
Chicago IL 60685
312/822-4100
Contact Employment Manager. A multiline insurer underwriting several various policies.

COMBINED INSURANCE COMPANY
5050 North Broadway
Chicago IL 60640
312/769-8698
Contact Rebecca Hogue, Vice President, Personnel Director. Writes accident, health, and life policies.

THE COUNTRY COMPANIES
1701 Towanda Street
Bloomington IL 61701
309/557-2786
Contact Ruth Woeful, Personnel. A multi-line insurance and financial services organization.

FEDERAL KEMPER INSURANCE COMPANY
2001 East Mound Avenue
Decatur IL 62526
217/877-9510
Contact Linda Koter, Personnel Manager. An insurance agency.

FOURTH DEARBORN/BLUE CROSS
233 North Michigan Avenue
Chicago IL 60601
Contact Personnel Director. Group life insurance company. Multiple area locations.

ILLINOIS FARMERS INSURANCE COMPANY
150 South Lincoln Way
P.O. Box 948
Aurora IL 60507
708/844-4700
Contact Mr. W. Patrick Dooley CPCU, Regional Personnel Manager. A subsidiary of Farmers Insurance Company, Los Angeles, CA. Farmers maintains a regional office and four branch claims offices in the area. Handles property, life, and casualty insurance. Corporate headquarters location. Common positions at this facility include: Accountant; Claim Representative; Management Trainee; Underwriter. Principal educational backgrounds sought: Accounting; Business Administration; Finance; Marketing; All majors qualify. Company benefits include: medical insurance; pension plan; life insurance; tuition assistance; disability coverage; profit sharing. Regional headquarters.

LIBERTY MUTUAL INSURANCE GROUP
555 West Pierce Road
Itasca IL 60143-2691
312/250-7100
Contact Roland Stanton, Director of Human Resources. Several area locations including: Lisle, Des Plaines, Matteson. A full-line insurance firm

offering life, medical, and business insurance, as well as investment and retirement plans. Common positions include: Accountant; Administrator; Attorney; Claim Representative; Computer Programmer; Electrical Engineer; Industrial Engineer; Mechanical Engineer; Financial Analyst; Insurance Agent/Broker; Management Trainee; Sales Representative; Systems Analyst; Underwriter. Principal educational backgrounds sought: Accounting; Art/Design; Business Administration; Communications; Computer Science; Economics; Engineering; Finance; Liberal Arts; Marketing; Mathematics. Company benefits include: medical, dental, and life insurance; pension plan; tuition assistance; disability coverage; employee discounts; savings plan. Corporate headquarters location: Boston, MA. Operations at this facility include: divisional headquarters (midwest only).

NORTH AMERICAN COMPANY
FOR LIFE & HEALTH INSURANCE
222 South Riverside Plaza
Chicago IL 60606
312/648-7600
Contact Mary Bresnahan, Staffing and Development Specialist. Writes a wide variety of individual life insurance policies. Common positions include: Accountant; Actuary; Attorney; Claim Representative; Computer Programmer; Customer Service Representative; Purchasing Agent; Systems Analyst; Underwriter; Insurance Clerk. Principal educational backgrounds sought: Accounting; Business Administration; Communications; Computer Science; Finance; Liberal Arts; Marketing; Mathematics. Company benefits include: medical insurance; dental insurance; pension plan; life insurance; tuition assistance; disability coverage; employee discounts. Corporate headquarters location. Operations at this facility include: administration; service; sales.

OLD REPUBLIC INTERNATIONAL
307 North Michigan Avenue
Chicago IL 60601
312/346-8100
Contact Charles Strizak, Personnel Director. A life, health, home, and finance insurance corporation.

ROTARY INTERNATIONAL
1560 Sherman Avenue
Evanston IL 60201
708/866-3000
Contact Jacquelyn McGuire, Employment Supervisor. Rotary is an international organization of more than one million service-minded business and professional leaders. The Evanston headquarters is involved in administration and service to the clubs, publicity for the organization and the administration of the humanitarian programs funded by the rotary. Common positions include: Accountant; Commercial Artist; Computer Programmer; Financial Analyst; Department Manager; Personnel & Labor Relations

Specialist; Public Relations Worker; Editor/Feature Writer. Principal educational backgrounds sought: Accounting; Business Administration; Communications; Finance; Liberal Arts; International Studies; Foreign Languages; Journalism. Company benefits include: medical insurance, dental, and life insurance; pension plan; tuition assistance; disability coverage. Corporate headquarters location.

SAFECO INSURANCE COMPANIES
1900 West Hassell Road
Hoffman Estates IL 60196
708/490-2900
Contact Christopher Higman, Personnel Manager. An insurance company offering Personal Lines Insurance, homeowners and auto; Commercial Insurance, all lines in property and casualty; and Life and Health Insurance products. Common positions include: Attorney; Claim Representative; Customer Service Representative; Financial Analyst; Management Trainee; Sales Representative; Underwriter. Principal educational backgrounds sought: Accounting; Art/Design; Biology; Business Administration; Chemistry; Communications; Computer Science; Economics; Engineering; Finance; Geology; Liberal Arts; Marketing; Mathematics; Physics; all educational backgrounds accepted. Company benefits include: medical insurance; dental insurance; pension plan; life insurance; disability coverage; profit sharing; employee discounts; savings plan. Corporate headquarters location: Seattle, WA. Operations at this facility include: regional and divisional headquarters.

SENTRY INSURANCE COMPANY
75 Executive Drive
Aurora IL 60504
708/844-8105
800/323-0863
Contact Thomas Skillman, Human Resources Manager. Concentrates on the business insurance market. Sentry is a multi-line insurer whose primary markets are: hardware stores, auto parts stores, printers, metal workers, and other small businesses. Common positions include: Insurance Agent/Broker; Sales Representative. Principal educational backgrounds sought: Business Administration; Communications; Finance; Liberal Arts. Company benefits include: medical, dental, and life insurance; pension plan; disability coverage; profit sharing; savings plan. Corporate headquarters location: Stevens Point, WI. Operations at this facility include: divisional headquarters.

TICOR TITLE INSURANCE
203 North LaSalle Street
Suite 1400
Chicago IL 60601
312/621-5058
Contact Gail A. Burke, Personnel Representative. Several area locations, including Arlington Heights, Joliet, Mattson, and Oaklawn. Specializes in real

estate title insurance and escrow services. Corporate headquarters location: Los Angeles, CA.

TRAVELERS INSURANCE COMPANY
100 Park Street
Naperville IL 60566-1029
708/961-8700
Contact Ralph Schulz, Assistant Manager/Personnel Administration. One of the world's largest investor-owned financial service organizations. Offers many different financial services including every principal form of insurance for life, health and property. Corporate headquarters location: Hartford, CT. New York Stock Exchange. International.

UNITED EQUITABLE INSURANCE GROUP
7373 North Cicero
Lincolnwood IL 60646
708/677-4800
Contact Marlene Gaffney, Supervisor of Employment. Provides accident, health, and life insurance as well as extended service contracts for automobiles. Common positions include: Accountant; Actuary; Claim Representative; Computer Programmer; Customer Service Representative; Financial Analyst; Marketing Specialist; Systems Analyst; Underwriter. Principal educational backgrounds sought: Accounting; Business Administration; Computer Science; Marketing; Mathematics; Actuarial Science. Company benefits include: medical insurance; dental insurance; life insurance; tuition assistance; long-term disability coverage; profit sharing; credit union. Corporate headquarters location.

WASHINGTON NATIONAL CORPORATION
1630 Chicago Avenue
Evanston IL 60201
708/570-3186
Contact Michael Richardson, Human Resources Department. A financial services holding company with subsidiaries engaged primarily in marketing and underwriting life insurance, annuities, and health insurance for groups and individuals. With life insurance in force of $30 billion and assets of $2.9 billion, Washington National Corporation had 1989 revenues of over $800 million. Washington National also involved in real estate development. Corporate headquarters location. New York Stock Exchange. Common positions include: Accountant; Actuary; Computer Programmer; Financial Analyst; Sales Representative; Systems Analyst; Underwriter. Principal educational backgrounds sought: Accounting; Business Administration; Computer Science; Finance; Marketing; Mathematics. Training programs offered; Internships offered. Company benefits include: medical, dental, and life insurance; pension plan; tuition assistance; disability coverage; employee discounts; savings plan; health club membership discounts

WAUSAU INSURANCE COMPANIES
901 Warren Road
Suite 500
Lisle IL 60532-4307
312/719-9700
Contact James Hofman, Personnel Specialist. Regional office for major insurance company; offers a full line of business insurance services in 17 regional offices and 200 service offices across the United States. Common positions include: Claim Representative; Sales Representative; Underwriter. Principal educational backgrounds sought: Business Administration; Communications; Economics; Finance; Marketing. Company benefits include: medical, dental, and life insurance; pension plan; tuition assistance; disability coverage; savings plan. Corporate headquarters location: Wassau, WI. Operations at this facility include: regional headquarters.

ZURICH-AMERICAN INSURANCE COMPANIES
1400 American Lane
Schaumburg IL 60196
708/605-6000
Contact Dan Borbas, Vice-President/Human Resources. A large international insurance company with worldwide operations. Corporate headquarters location.

LEGAL SERVICES

For more information on professional employment opportunities in the legal services industry, contact the following professional and trade organizations, as listed beginning on page 295:

FEDERAL BAR ASSOCIATION
FEDERAL BAR ASSOCIATION/CHICAGO CHAPTER
NATIONAL ASSOCIATION FOR LAW PLACEMENT
NATIONAL ASSOCIATION OF LEGAL ASSISTANTS
NATIONAL FEDERATION OF PARALEGAL ASSOCIATIONS
NATIONAL PARALEGAL ASSOCIATION

AMERICAN BAR ASSOCIATION
750 N. Lake Shore Drive
Chicago IL 60611
Contact Manager of Employment. The world's largest voluntary professional association.

ARNSTEIN AND LEHR
120 South Riverside Plaza
Suite 1200
Chicago IL 60606
312/876-7100
Contact Jackie Van Fossan, Personnel Director. A general practice legal services firm.

BAKER & McKENZIE
One Prudential Plaza,
130 East Randolph Street
Chicago IL 60601
312/861-2905
Contact Cathy Delfino, Recruiter. A metropolitan Chicago law firm

CHAPMAN AND CUTLER
111 West Monroe Street
16th Floor
Chicago IL 60603
312/845-3000
Contact Linda O'Donnell, Personnel Director. A leading area general practice law firm.

GARDNER, CARTON, & DOUGLAS
Quaker Tower
Suite 3400
321 North Clark Street
Chicago IL 60610-4795
312/644-3000
Contact Anita McGaugh, Assistant Personnel Director. A Chicago area law firm concentrating on corporate and real estate law.

KECK, MAHIN, & CATE
8300 Sears Tower
233 S. Wacker Drive
Chicago IL 60606-6589
312/876-3400
Contact Personnel Director. A metropolitan Chicago general practice law firm.

LORD, BISSELL, & BROOK
115 South LaSalle Street
Suite 3400
Chicago IL 60603
312/443-0700
Contact Jean Bouslog, Personnel Director. A leading Chicago law firm specializing in corporate law.

PETERSON, ROSS, SCHLOERB & SEIDEL
200 East Randolph Street
Suite 7000
Amoco Building
Chicago IL 60601
312/861-1400
Contact Laura Geyer, Manager of Personnel. An area law firm offering a variety of legal services. Common positions include: Accountant. Company benefits include: medical, dental, and life insurance; pension plan; disability coverage; savings plan. Corporate headquarters location. Operations at this facility include: service.

RUDNICK & WOLFE
203 North LaSalle Street
Suite 1500
Chicago IL 60601
312/368-4000
Contact Personnel. A metropolitan Chicago law firm

VEDDER, PRICE, KAUFMAN, & KAMMHOLZ
222 North LaSalle Street
Chicago IL 60601-1003
312/609-7500
Contact Leslie Thomas, Personnel. A firm engaged in a variety of legal services including labor, litigation, corporate, health, and pro bono law.

MANUFACTURING: MISCELLANEOUS CONSUMER

ACE HARDWARE CORPORATION
2200 Kensington Court
Oak Brook IL 60521
312/990-6600
Contact Don Wallner, Human Resources Representative. A wholesaler of hardware and related products.

ALBERTO-CULVER CO.
2525 Armitage Avenue
Melrose Park IL 60160
708/450-3000
Contact Cindy Lange, Manager of Staffing. Develops, manufactures and promotes personal use products.

BALLY MANUFACTURING/GAMING DIVISION
90 O'Leary Drive
Bensenville IL 60106
708/860-7777
Contact Scott D. Robinson, Director of Human Resources/Administration. A manufacturer of electronic/mechanical slot machines and gaming equipment. Divisional headquarters location. Common positions include: Accountant; Blue-Collar Worker Supervisor; Buyer; Computer Programmer; Credit Manager; Customer Service Representative; Draftsperson; Electrical Engineer; Industrial Engineer; Mechanical Engineer; Operations/Production Manager; Marketing Specialist; Personnel & Labor Relations Specialist; Purchasing Agent; Quality Control Supervisor; Systems Analyst; Transportation & Traffic Specialist. Principal educational backgrounds sought: Accounting; Computer Science; Engineering; Finance. Company benefits include: medical, dental, and life insurance; pension plan; tuition assistance; disability coverage; profit sharing; employee discounts; savings plan. Corporate headquarters location: Chicago, IL. Operations at this facility include: divisional headquarters; manufacturing; research/development; administration; service; sales. New York Stock Exchange.

CALSTAR CORPORATION
1191 South Wheeling Road
Wheeling IL 60090
708/541-9000
Contact Marilyn Alexander, Personnel Manager. Manufactures and sells paint.

CHICAGO LOCK COMPANY
4311 West Belmont Avenue
Chicago IL 60641
312/282-7177
Contact Victor Novak, Personnel Director. Manufactures a variety of locks.

COTTER COMPANY
2740 North Clybourn Avenue
Chicago IL 60614-1088
312/975-2700
Contact A. Fred Lobo, Director of Human Resources. A member-owned wholesaler of hardware, variety and related products.

COUNSELOR COMPANY
2107 Kishwaukee Street
Rockford IL 61101
815/968-9621
Contact Tim Jahnke, Director of Employee Relations. A manufacturer of digital and mechanical bathroom scales.

CUMMINS ALLISON CORPORATION
891 Feehanville Drive
Mt. Prospect IL 60056
312/299-9550
Contact J.A. Panarale, Vice President, Employee Relations. Manufacturer of office products, mostly for banking use.

DESOTO, INC.
1700 South Mount Prospect Road
Box 5030
Des Plaines IL 60017
708/391-9000
Contact Personnel Representative. A diversified manufacturer of coatings (consumer paints and industrial coatings), and specialty products.

EMPIRE STOVE COMPANY
918 Freeburg Avenue
P.O. Box 529
Belleville IL 62222
618/233-7420
Contact Betty Senulis, Personnel Director. Manufacturers of gas heating appliances. Employs over 100.

EUREKA COMPANY
1201 E. Bell Street
Bloomington IL 61701
309/823-5285
Contact Martha E. Campbell, Employment Manager. A manufacturer of vacuum cleaners.

HAEGER POTTERIES
7 Maiden Lane
Dundee IL 60118
708/426-3441
Contact Lorraine Ritt, Personnel Manager. Manufactures ceramic artware and decorations.

KLEIN TOOLS, INC.
7200 McCormick Boulevard
Chicago IL 60645
312/588-6821
Contact Tom Dragon, Industrial Relations Manager. A manufacturer of utility tools & protective equipment.

LAKEWOOD ENGINEERING & MANUFACTURING COMPANY
502 North Sacramento Boulevard
Chicago IL 60612
312/722-4300
Contact Bob Brueck, Director of Personnel. Manufacturers of ventilating fans, electric heaters, etc.

LEEWARDS
1200 St. Charles Street
Elgin IL 60120
Contact Mark Walters, Recruiting Manager. A major manufacturer and retailer of crafts and hobbycrafts. Common positions include: Buyer; Computer Programmer; Management Trainee. Company benefits include: medical, dental, and life insurance; tuition assistance; disability coverage; employee discounts. Corporate headquarters location. Operations at this facility include: regional headquarters; divisional headquarters; administration.

LIGHTOLIER
1600 Fleetwood Drive
Elgin IL 60123
312/742-2266
Contact David Waltmire, Personnel/Labor Relations. Manufacturer of quality lighting fixtures.

LLOYD'S ELECTRONICS/
A DIVISION OF DYNASCAN CORPORATION
700 North Commerce Street
P.O. Box 2066
Edison IL 60507-2066
708/820-6699
Contact Carol Kurth, Human Resources. Designs, imports, and markets home and portable audio entertainment products for sale to dealers throughout the United States. The company also markets its products on a minor scale in Latin America and South Africa. Leading products include home stereo systems, portable radios and digital clock radios, cassette recorders and personal tape players. Company purchases its home entertainment products and components from several manufacturers in Taiwan, South Korea, China, Japan, the Philippines, and Hong Kong. International. Common positions include: Accountant; Administrator; Blue-Collar Worker Supervisor; Customer Service Representative; Financial Analyst; Department Manager; Operations/Production Manager; Sales Representative; Computer Operator. Principal educational backgrounds sought: Accounting; Business Administration; Finance; Marketing. Company benefits include: medical, dental and life insurance; disability coverage. Operations at this facility include: administration; sales; warehouse

LOCKE HOME PRODUCTS
4200 St. Clair Avenue
P.O. Box 1040
East St. Louis IL 62204
618/271-1272
Contact Christine Bearden, Personnel Director. Manufacture heat stoves (wood & gas), gas fired incinerators.

MITEK CORPORATION
One Mitek Plaza
Winslow IL 61089
815/367-3000
Contact Dave Roskam, Director, Human Resources. Engaged in the development, manufacture, and marketing of automotive, home and professional loudspeakers. Common positions include: Accountant; Blue-Collar Worker Supervisor; Buyer; Credit Manager; Customer Service Representative; Draftsperson; Electrical Engineer; Department Manager; General Manager; Operations/Production Manager; Marketing Specialist; Personnel & Labor Relations Specialist; Purchasing Agent; Quality Control Supervisor; Sales Representative; Systems Analyst; Transportation & Traffic Specialist. Principal educational backgrounds sought: Accounting; Art/Design; Business Administration; Communications; Computer Science; Engineering; Finance; Marketing. Company benefits include: medical insurance; life insurance; tuition assistance; disability coverage; profit sharing; employee discounts; savings plan; 401k. Corporate headquarters location. Operations at this facility include: manufacturing; research/development; administration; sales; service.

NUARC COMPANY INC.
6200 Howard Street
Niles IL 60648
708/967-4400
Contact Barbara Morgenstern, Personnel Director. Manufacturers of graphic art equipment. Corporate headquarters location.

NYSTROM COMPANY
3333 Elston Avenue
Chicago IL 60618
312/463-1144
Contact June Dains, Personnel Director. Manufactures and publishes charts, maps, globes and other visual learning systems. Corporate headquarters location.

OUTBOARD MARINE CORPORATION
100 Sea-Horse Drive
Waukegan IL 60085
708/689-5289
Contact Wayne Applegate, Personnel Director. Several area locations including: Galesburg. Engaged principally in the manufacture of powered products for leisure-time use. Three industry segments and their principal product names are: marine products, which includes Evinrude outboard motors, Johnson outboard motors, OMC stern drive inboard-outboard engines; power mowers, primarily Lawn-Boy rotary power mowers; and other products, which includes Cushman light industrial vehicles, Ryan turf care equipment, and miscellaneous products. Corporate headquarters location. International. New York Stock Exchange.

R.S. OWENS AND COMPANY INC.
5535 North Lynch Avenue
Chicago IL 60630
312/282-6000
Contact Personnel Department. Manufactures trophies, plaques and awards. Common positions include: Blue-Collar Worker Supervisor; Credit Manager; Mechanical Engineer; Department Manager; Personnel & Labor Relations Specialist; Purchasing Agent; Quality Control Supervisor; Sales Representative. Principal educational backgrounds sought: Business Administration; Computer Science; Finance; Liberal Arts; Marketing. Company benefits include: medical insurance; life insurance; disability coverage; profit sharing; employee discounts; savings plan. Corporate, regional headquarters location. Operations at this facility include: manufacturing; administration; service; sales.

PAYMASTER CORPORATION
1811 West Winnemac
Chicago IL 60640
312/878-9200
Contact Larry Hamilton, Personnel Director. Manufactures and sells check-writing machines and check protectors. Corporate headquarters location.

QUASAR COMPANY
1325 Pratt Boulevard
Elk Grove Village IL 60007
708/228-6366
Contact Bill Schupp, Personnel Manager. Manufacturer of consumer electronic appliances such as televisions, microwave ovens, and video tape machines. A subsidiary of Matsushita Electronics Corporation of America. Corporate headquarters location.

RAM GOLF CORPORATION
2020 Indian Boundary Drive
Melrose Park IL 60160
312/681-5800
Contact Allen P. Norby, Director of Personnel. Manufacturer of golf clubs, bags, balls, and related accessories. Corporate headquarters location. Common positions include: Accountant; Advertising Worker; Computer Programmer; Credit Manager; Marketing Specialist. Principal educational backgrounds sought: Accounting; Business Administration; Computer Science; Finance; Marketing. Company benefits include: medical and life insurance; pension plan; disability coverage; employee discounts; savings plan. Corporate headquarters location. Operations at this facility include: manufacturing.

ROADMASTER CORPORATION
P.O. Box 344
Olney IL 62450
618/393-2991
Contact Carol Erwin, Personnel Supervisor. Manufactures bicycles, tricycles, and ride-in toys for children; and fitness equipment. Other facility sites in Tyler, Texas and Delavan, Wisconsin. Common positions include: Accountant; Blue-Collar Worker Supervisor; Buyer; Chemist; Computer Programmer; Credit Manager; Customer Service Representative; Draftsperson; Industrial Engineer; Mechanical Engineer; Financial Analyst; Department Manager; Operations/Production Manager; Purchasing Agent; Quality Control Supervisor; Sales Representative; Systems Analyst; Technical Writer/Editor; Transporation & Traffic Specialist; Industrial Designer. Principal educational backgrounds sought: Accounting; Art/Design; Business Administration; Engineering; Finance; Marketing; Industrial Technology. Company benefits include: medical insurance; pension plan; life insurance; tuition assistance; disability coverage; employee discounts. Corporate headquarters location. Operations at this facility include: manufacturing; administration; service; sales. NASDAQ.

ROCK-OLA MANUFACTURING CORPORATION
313 South Rohlwing Road
Addison IL 60101
708/629-9200
Contact Laverne Sebastian, Personnel. Manufactures juke boxes and soda machines. Corporate headquarters location.

RUST-OLEUM CORPORATION
11 Hawthorne Parkway
Vernon Hills IL 60061
708/367-7700
Contact Steve Gillmann, Manager of Human Resources. Several area locations including: Vernon Hills and Evanston. Leading manufacturer of rust-preventative paints and coatings. Corporate headquarters location.

SCHWINN BICYCLE COMPANY
217 North Jefferson
Chicago IL 60606
312/454-7400
Contact Brian D. Fiala, Vice President, Human Resources. Manufacturer and distributor of bicycles and exercisers. Common positions include: Accountant; Buyer; Computer Programmer; Credit Manager; Draftsperson; Industrial Engineer; Mechanical Engineer; Financial Analyst; Industrial Manager; Department Manager; Management Trainee; Marketing Specialist; Personnel & Labor Relations Specialist; Purchasing Agent; Systems Analyst. Principal educational backgrounds sought: Accounting; Art/Design; Business Administration; Computer Science; Engineering; Finance; Marketing. Internships offered. Company benefits include: medical insurance; pension plan; life insurance; tuition assistance; disability coverage; profit sharing; employee discounts. Corporate headquarters location. Operations at this facility include: national headquarters; administration.

SKIL CORPORATION
4300 West Peterson Avenue
Chicago IL 60646
312/286-7330
Contact Ellen S. Reese, Human Resource Manager/Headquarters. Several area locations including: Skokie, and Elk Grove Village. Manufacturers of hand and power tools. A subsidiary of Emerson Electric Company. Corporate headquarters location. International. Common positions include: Accountant; Computer Programmer; Credit Manager; Customer Service Representative; Draftsperson; Electrical Engineer; Industrial Engineer; Mechanical Engineer; Financial Analyst; Marketing Specialist; Personnel & Labor Relations Specialist; Purchasing Agent; Quality Control Supervisor; Systems Analyst. Principal educational backgrounds sought: Accounting; Business Administration; Engineering; Marketing. Training programs offered; Internships offered. Company benefits include: medical, dental, and life insurance; pension plan; tuition assistance; disability coverage; employee discounts; savings plan. Corporate headquarters location. Parent company: Emerson Electric. Operations at this facility include: divisional headquarters; research/development; administration.

SPACEMASTER
1400 North 25th Avenue
Melrose Park IL 60160
312/345-2500
Contact Linda Lazzaro, Personnel Director. Several area locations. Manufactures store fixtures, office furniture and library equipment. Corporate headquarters location.

SPIEGEL INC.
1515 West 22nd Street
Oak Brook IL 60522
708/986-8800
Contact Greg Powell, Employment Manager. A catalog merchandising company specializing in upscale merchandise for the home, as well as current fashion for women, men and children. Corporate headquarters location. Common positions include: Accountant; Advertising Worker; Architect; Attorney; Buyer; Computer Programmer; Customer Service Representative; Industrial Engineer; Financial Analyst; Manager; Department Manager; Management Trainee; Operations/Production Manager; Marketing Specialist; Quality Control Supervisor; Systems Analyst; Fashion Copywriter; Auditing. Principal educational backgrounds sought: Accounting; Business Administration; Communications; Marketing; Fashion Merchandising. Company benefits include: medical insurance; life insurance; tuition assistance; disability coverage; profit sharing; employee discounts; savings plan; dental insurance. NASDAQ.

ST. CHARLES MANUFACTURING
1611 East Main Street
St. Charles IL 60174
708/584-3800
Contact Ms. Chris Knox, Employee Relations Manager. The company manufactures cabinetry for residential and institutional use through sheet metal fabrication. Institutional users are laboratories, schools and hospitals. The company also makes grocery store checkout counters and exhaust hoods for fumes in laboratories. There are other plants in North Carolina and Utah. Corporate headquarters location. International.

UNITED STATES TOBACCO MANUFACTURING COMPANY
11601 Copenhagen Court
Franklin Park IL 60131
708/595-8200
Contact Val Racich, Personnel Manager. Several area locations, including: Franklin Park. Manufacturing plant for moist, smokeless tobacco products, and warehouse for distribution of various products. Products include Skoal, Copenhagen and Happy Days smokeless tobaccos. Corporate headquarters location: Greenwich, CT. New York Stock Exchange.

UNITED STATIONERS SUPPLY COMPANY
2200 East Golf Road
Des Plaines IL 60016
708/699-5000
Contact Mrs. Pat Zatto, Personnel Director. Wholesale distributors of office furniture, office machines, stationery, and a variety of writing instruments. Corporate headquarters location.

WEN PRODUCTS, INC.
5810 Northwest Highway
Chicago IL 60631
312/763-6060
Contact Ray Reimnitz, Vice-President of Operations. Manufactures electronic soldering guns, sanders, electric saws, and a complete line of power tools. Corporate headquarters location.

RICHARD WILCOX MANUFACTURING
600 South Lake Street
Aurora IL 60506
708/897-6951
Contact Larry French, Personnel. Several area locations, including: Belvidere, East Chicago (IN), Aurora, Mattoon. Engaged in the manufacture and distribution of a wide range of products and services for industry and the consumer. Four principal business segments are: products for the home, including home comfort products (air conditioners, etc., sold under names such as White-Westinghouse, Kelvinator, Gibson, and Frigidaire) and kitchen appliances (freezers, refrigerators, dishwashers, etc., sold under above brand names and others), laundry appliances, refrigeration compressors and motors, and sewing machines; machinery and metal castings, including such products as military armor, machine tools machinery for the graphic arts industry, rolls, rolling mills, castings and finishing and processing machinery for the steel industry; spinning and twisting equipment for the textile industry; and general industrial equipment such as commercial air conditioning and heating equipment, commercial laundry equipment, commercial refrigeration products, construction equipment, conveyor systems, food and chemical processing equipment, safety products, storage equipment and wall partitions, and valves, controls, and instrumentation. Corporate headquarters location: Cleveland, OH. New York Stock Exchange.

WILSON SPORTING GOODS CO.
2233 West Street
River Grove IL 60171
708/456-6100
Contact Mary Lally, Personnel Manager. Manufacturer of sporting goods for golf, tennis, and team sports. Approximately $400 million in sales. Common position include: Accountant; Administrator; Architect; Buyer; Chemist; Commercial Artist; Computer Programmer; Credit Manager; Customer Service Representative; Draftsperson; Aerospace Engineer; Chemical Engineer; Electrical Engineer; Industrial Engineer; Mechanical Engineer; Financial Analyst; Operations/Production Manager; Marketing Specialist; Public Relations Worker; Quality Control Supervisor; Sales Representative; Statistician; Technical Writer/Editor. Principal educational backgrounds sought: Accounting; Art/Design; Business Administration; Chemistry; Communications; Computer Science; Economics; Engineering; Finance; Liberal Arts; Marketing; Mathematics; Physics. Company benefits include:

medical, dental, and life insurance; pension plan; tuition assistance; disability coverage; employee discounts; savings plan. Corporate headquarters location. Operations at this facility include: regional headquarters; research/development; administration; service; sales.

ZENITH ELECTRONICS CORPORATION
1000 Milwaukee Avenue
Glenview IL 60025
312/391-7000
Contact Personnel. Designs, manufactures and markets consumer electronics products including televisions, video cassette recorders, video cameras, related components and systems, and cable television decoders. Products sold through extensive distributor network, most of which are independently owned. Company maintains facilities throughout the U.S. and in Canada, Mexico, Ireland and Taiwan. Common positions include: Electrical Engineer; Mechanical Engineer; Financial Analyst. Principal educational backgrounds sought: Business Administration; Computer Science; Engineering; Finance. Company benefits include: medical insurance; dental insurance; life insurance; tuition assistance; disability coverage; profit sharing; employee discounts; savings plan. Corporate, headquarters location. Operations include: research/development; administration. International. New York Stock Exchange.

MANUFACTURING:
MISCELLANEOUS INDUSTRIAL

For more information on professional employment opportunities in manufacturing, contact the following professional and trade organizations, as listed beginning on page 295:

NATIONAL ASSOCIATION OF MANUFACTURERS
NATIONAL ASSOCIATION OF MANUFACTURERS/
 PARK RIDGE BRANCH
NATIONAL MACHINE TOOL BUILDERS
NATIONAL SCREW MACHINE PRODUCTS ASSOCIATION
NATIONAL SCREW MACHINE PRODUCTS ASSOCIATION/
 NORTHERN ILLINOIS CHAPTER
NATIONAL TOOLING AND MACHINING ASSOCIATION
NATIONAL TOOLING AND MACHINING ASSOCIATION/
 CHICAGO CHAPTER

ACCO INTERNATIONAL
770 South Acco Plaza
Wheeling IL 60090
708/541-9500
Contact Janet Petitt, Personnel Recruiter. Manufacturer of school, office and computer supplies.

AIRCO, INC.
2100 Western Court
Lisle IL 60532
708/287-9336
Contact Lou Stevens, Personnel. Industrial gases, welding and cutting equipment.

ALLIED PRODUCTS CORPORATION
10 South Riverside Plaza
Suite 1600
Chicago IL 60606
312/454-1020
Contact Mr. Leo Simmermeyer, Vice President. Agricultural equipment, industrial components.

ALLSTEEL INC.
Allsteel Drive
Aurora IL 60507-0871
708/844-7191
Contact Employee Relations Representative. Manufacturer of steel office furniture systems.

AMSTED INDUSTRIES
205 North Michigan Boulevard
44th Floor
Chicago IL 60601
312/645-1700
Contact Shirley Whitesell, Personnel Manager. Manufactures industrial products through 11 subsidiaries.

ARMSTRONG-BLUM MANUFACTURING CO.
1441 Business Center Drive
Mount Prospect IL 60056
708/803-4000
Contact Gary Nordhaus, Personnel. Manufactures metal cutting saws.

ARROW GROUP INDUSTRIES
1101 North 4th Street
Breese IL 62230
618/526-4546
Contact Patty Sellers, Director, Personnel. Manufacturers of utility storage buildings. Employs over 200.

BARCO CORPORATION
500 North Hough Street
Barrington IL 60010
312/381-1700
Contact Karen Borre, Human Resources Manager. Manufactures fluid power and fluid systems components.

BEALL MANUFACTURING DIVISION/ VARLEN CORP.
P.O. Box 70
East Alton IL 62024
618/259-8154
Contact Scott Patsaros, Personnel. Manufacturers of spring lock washers, agriculture implement parts, leaf spring steel items, flat washers. Employs over 100.

BELDING CORPORATION
130 West Grand Lake Boulevard
West Chicago IL 60185
708/231-5200
Contact Jacquie Boyd, Personnel Manager. Moves and installs heavy equipment; millwork, ironworking.

BERKELEY-DAVIS, INC.
1020 Bahls Street
Danville IL 61832
217/446-9500
Contact Phillip J. Thomas, Manager of Production and Personnel. Custom designed resistance and arc welding equipment.

BINKS MANUFACTURING CO.
9201 West Belmont Avenue
Franklin Park IL 60131
708/671-3000
Contact Jim Linquist, Personnel Director. Spray finishing and coating application equipment.

BORG-WARNER CORPORATION
200 South Michigan Avenue
Chicago IL 60604
312/322-8500
Contact Angela D'Aversa, Director, Human Resources. A $3.5-billion diversified manufacturing and services company. Most products are components made for manufacturers serving the transportation industry. The company also has extensive operations that provide protective services for business. Common positions include: Accountant; Attorney; Computer Programmer; Management Trainee; Personnel & Labor Relations Specialist; Systems Analyst; Underwriters. Principal educational backgrounds sought:

Accounting; Business Administration; Computer Science; Economics; Finance. Company benefits include: medical, dental and life insurance; pension plan; tuition assistance; disability coverage; savings plan. Corporate headquarters location. International. Operations at this facility include: administration.

CHICAGO BLOWER CORPORATION
1675 Glen Ellyn Road
Glendale Heights IL 60139
708/858-2600
Contact Ron M. Mrowiec, Personnel Manager. Manufactures industrial fans and blowers.

CHICAGO EXTRUDED METALS COMPANY
1601 South 54th Avenue
Cicero IL 60650
708/656-7900
Contact Al Pristaze, Controller. Manufactures screw machine products, brass wire rods, etc.

CHICAGO FAUCET COMPANY
2100 South Nuclear Drive
Des Plaines IL 60018
312/694-4400
Contact Brian Downing, Personnel Manager. Manufactures brass plumbing fittings.

CHICAGO RAWHIDE MANUFACTURING COMPANY
900 North State Street
Elgin IL 60123
708/379-2500
Contact Doug Riker, Manager of Employee Relations. Manufactures and markets sealing products.

CHICAGO RIVET & MACHINE COMPANY
901 Frontenac Road
Naperville IL 60566-7061
708/357-8500
Contact Mr. Steven Voss, Controller. Operates a fastener and wire producing firm.

CINCH CONNECTORS
1501 Morse Avenue
Elk Grove Village IL 60007
708/981-6000
Contact Randall Hori, Manager, Human Resources. Produces connectors, interconnection systems, IC sockets, relay sockets, tube sockets, terminal strips, barrier blocks, crimp terminals, communications cross-connect

systems, harness assemblies, and adapters. Major markets served: Military/Aerospace; Telecommunications; Computer & Instrumentation; and Automodine. Common positions include: Accountant; Buyer; Chemist; Computer Programmer; Customer Service Representative; Draftsperson; Electrical Engineer; Industrial Engineer; Mechanical Engineer; Metallurgical Engineer; Marketing Specialist; Systems Analyst. Principal educational backgrounds sought: Accounting; Chemistry; Computer Science; Engineering; Marketing. Company benefits include: medical insurance; dental insurance; pension plan; life insurance; tuition assistance; disability coverage; savings plan. Operations at this facility include: divisional headquarters; manufacturing; research/development; administration; service; sales.

COMMERCIAL STAMPING & FORGING, INC.
5757 West 65th Street
Bedford Park IL 60638
312/767-8500
Contact Frank Kosteki, Director of Personnel. Manufactures fabrications for underground tunnels.

CULLIGAN INTERNATIONAL
1 Culligan Parkway
Northbrook IL 60062
708/205-5902
Contact Debbie Wheeler, Employment Supervisor. Manufacturer of water equipment and systems.

DANA CORPORATION/
VICTOR PRODUCT DIVISION
5750 West Roosevelt Road
Chicago IL 60650
312/287-6180
Contact Gloria Reichert, Employment Specialist. Several area locations. Manufacturers of sealing products; gaskets, rubber seals primarily used on heavy-vehicle trucks and earth-moving equipment. Division of Dana Corporation. International facilities located in Canada, Mexico, South America, Europe, England, Scandinavia, Singapore, and Korea. Corporate headquarters location: Lisle, IL. International. New York Stock Exchange.

DANLY MACHINE DIVISION/
CONNELL LIMITED PARTNERSHIP
215 South 54th Avenue
Cicero IL 60650
312/242-1800
Contact Gene Elliot, Director of Employee Relations. A manufacturer of machine tools.

DEERE & COMPANY
John Deere Road
Moline IL 61265
309/765-8000
Contact Richard Van Bell, Director of Personnel. Manufactures, distributes and finances the sale of heavy equipment and machinery for use in the agricultural equipment and industrial equipment industries. The agricultural equipment sector manufactures tractors, and soil, seeding, and harvesting equipment. The industrial equipment segment manufactures a variety of earth moving equipment, tractors, loaders, and excavators; while the consumer products division manufactures a variety of tractors and products for the homeowner. Financial services, including personal and commercial lines of insurance, retail, and managed health care services are offered. Common positions include: Accountant. Principal educational backgrounds sought include: Accounting. Company benefits include: medical, dental, and life insurance; pension plan; tuition assistance; disability coverage; profit sharing; employee discounts; savings plan. Corporate headquarters location. Operations at this facility include: administration. New York Stock Exchange.

DEXTER CORPORATION
1 East Water Street
Waukegan IL 60085
312/623-4200
Contact John Nuebel, Manager/Human Resources. Manufacturer of industrial coatings and finishes. A Fortune 500 company heavily engaged in research and development. New York Stock Exchange. Common positions include: Accountant; Chemist; Computer Programmer; Chemical Engineer; General Manager; Operations/Production Manager; Personnel & Labor Relations Specialist; Purchasing Agent; Quality Control Supervisor; Sales Representative; Systems Analyst; Transportation & Traffic Specialist. Principal educational backgrounds sought: Accounting; Chemistry; Engineering. Company benefits include: medical insurance; dental insurance; pension plan; life insurance; tuition assistance; disability coverage; profit sharing; savings plan. Operations at this facility include: manufacturing; research/development; administration; sales. Corporate headquarters location: Windsor Locks, CT.

A.B. DICK COMPANY
5700 West Touhy Avenue
Chicago IL 60648
312/763-1900
Contact Karen Harling, Director of Employee & Staffing Relations. A manufacturer of office machines.

THE DO-ALL COMPANY
254 North Laurel Avenue
Des Plaines IL 60016
312/824-1122
Contact Kevin Hennessy, Personnel Director. Distributor of machine tools and other industrial supplies.

DUDEK & BOCK SPRING MANUFACTURING
5100 West Roosevelt Road
Chicago IL 60650
312/379-4100
Contact Walter Dudek, President. Manufactures springs, platforms, and wire forms.

DUO-FAST CORPORATION
3702 North River Road
Franklin Park IL 60131-2176
708/678-0100
Contact George Meyer, Personnel Director. Manufacturer of industrial staples and nailing tools.

DURO METAL PRODUCTS COMPANY
2649 North Kildare Avenue
Chicago IL 60639
312/235-5000
Contact Jack Fairbrother, Personnel Manager. Manufacturer of mechanic's hand tools.

EATON CORPORATION/ CONTROLS DIVISION
191 East North Avenue
Carol Stream IL 60188
708/260-3400
Contact Patricia Konisha, Employment Manager. Manufacturer of automotive appliance controls.

ELGIN NATIONAL INDUSTRIES
120 South Riverside Plaza
Chicago IL 60606
312/454-1900
Contact Thomas K. Shay, Vice President/Finance & Administration. A diverse company operating in three basic areas: Engineering and Construction, Coal Manufacturing, and Industrial Products.

EQUIPTO
225 S. Highland Avenue
Aurora IL 60507
708/859-1000
Contact Bill Corrigan, Personnel Director. Manufactures industrial shelving, work benches, lockers.

FEDERAL SIGNAL CORPORATION
2645 Federal Signal Drive
University Park IL 60466
708/534-3400
Contact Vice President of Human Resources. A diversified manufacturer of signs, signals, and tools.

FIATALLIS NORTH AMERICA, INC.
245 East North Avenue
Carol Stream IL 60188
708/260-4000
Contact Rosemarie Herrlin, Personnel Administrator. Distributes moving equipment and components.

FLUID POWER SYSTEMS
511 Glenn Avenue
Wheeling IL 60090
708/459-2800
Contact Personnel Manager. Several locations. A subsidiary of United Technologies (Hartford, CT), a major diversified industrial firm; this company manufactures hydraulic valves. Common positions include: Accountant; Blue-Collar Worker Supervisor; Buyer; Customer Service Representative; Draftsperson; Industrial Engineer; Mechanical Engineer; Department Manager; Personnel & Labor Relations Specialist; Quality Control Supervisor; Sales Representative. Principal educational backgrounds sought: Engineering. Company benefits include: medical insurance; dental insurance; pension plan; life insurance; tuition assistance; disability coverage; employee discounts; savings plan. Corporate headquarters location: Detroit, MI. Parent company: United Technologies Automotive, Inc. Operations at this facility include: manufacturing, administration, service, sales. New York Stock Exchange.

FOOTE JONES
603 Roger Street
Downers Grove IL 60515
708/968-5400
Contact Personnel Department. Supplies precision gears and gear boxes.

GBC
One GBC Plaza
Northbrook IL 60062
708/272-3700, ext.327
Contact Allison Paggi, Senior Recuiter. Office binding and laminating systems.

GRAINGER, INC.
1250 Busch Parkway
Buffalo Grove IL 60089
708/459-5445
Contact Rick Gossman, Recruiter. Manufactures/distributes a variety of industrial motors.

HOLLYMATIC CORPORATION
600 East Plainfield Road
Countryside IL 60525
312/579-3700
Contact Marylyn Krische, Human Resources Manager. Manufactures machines and parts, and paper products.

**IDEAL ROLLER COMPANY/
DIVISION OF ROTATION DYNAMICS, INC.**
2512 West 24th Street
Chicago IL 60608
312/247-5600
Contact Lillian Hastak, Personnel Director. Manufacturer of mechanical and rubber rollers. Owned by Wheelabrator-Frye. Common positions at this facility include: Accountant; Blue-Collar Worker Supervisor; Chemist; Computer Programmer; Credit Manager; Customer Service Representative; Draftsperson; Industrial Engineer; Branch Manager; Department Manager; Management Trainee; Operations/Production Manager; Marketing Specialist; Purchasing Agent; Quality Control Supervisor; Sales Representative. Principal educational backgrounds sought: Accounting; Business Administration; Computer Science; Engineering; Finance; Marketing. Company benefits include: medical insurance; dental insurance; pension plan; life insurance; tuition assistance; disability coverage; profit sharing; savings plan. Corporate headquarters location: Hinsdale, IL. Operations at this facility include: divisional headquarters; manufacturing; research/development; service.

**ILLINOIS GEAR/
A HOUSEHOLD INTERNATIONAL COMPANY**
2102 North Natchez Avenue
Chicago IL 60635
312/622-8000
Contact Director of Industrial Relations. Manufacturer of gears, sprockets, & other machine parts.

ILLINOIS TOOL WORKS
8501 West Higgins Road
Chicago IL 60631
312/693-3040
Contact Personnel Manager. Develops, produces, and markets specially engineered products and systems.

INTERNATIONAL HOUGH DIVISION/DRESSER INDUSTRIES
East Sunnyside Avenue
Libertyville IL 60048
708/367-2000
Contact Personnel Department. Provides crawler dozers, crawler loaders, wheel loaders and scrapers to a variety of customers.

ITT McDONNELL & MILLER
3500 North Spaulding Avenue
Chicago IL 60618
312/267-1600
Contact Al Landini, Personnel Director. Produces water control valves and boiler equipment for heating and air conditioning systems.

ITT/FLUID HANDLING DIVISION
8200 North Austin Avenue
Morton Grove IL 60053
708/966-3700
Contact Don Flowers, Manager of Employee Relations. Producer of heat exchangers, plumbing equipment, & pumps.

MARSH COMPANY
707 East 'B' Street
P.O. Box 388
Belleville IL 62222.
Contact Personnel Department. A major St. Louis company engaged in the manufacture of microprocessor controlled and mechanical marking, coding, and packing equipment for industrial use.

McMASTER-CARR SUPPLY COMPANY
600 North County Line Road
Elmhurst IL 60126
708/834-9600
Contact Karla Kauffman Keehn, Personnel. A distributor of industrial products and supplies. Primary selling tool is the firm's catalog, which contains descriptions of a variety of products necessary to maintain a manufacturing facility. Corporate headquarters location. Common positions include: Computer Programmer; Customer Service Representative; Management Trainee; Purchasing or Marketing Assistant. Principal educational backgrounds sought: Business Administration; Communications;

Computer Science; Economics; Engineering; Finance; Liberal Arts; Marketing. Company benefits include: medical insurance; dental insurance; life insurance; pension plan; tuition assistance; disability coverage; profit sharing; employee discounts.

MILLER FLUID POWER CORPORATION
800 North York Road
Bensenville IL 60106
708/766-3400
Contact Tom Parker, Human Resources Director. Manufacturer of pneumatic and hydraulic cylinders and components. Corporate headquarters location. Common positions include: Accountant; Buyer; Computer Programmer; Credit Manager; Customer Service Representative; Draftsperson; Engineer; Industrial Engineer; Mechanical Engineer; Industrial Designer; Branch Manager; Department Manager; Operations/Production Manager; Marketing Specialist; Personnel & Labor Relations Specialist; Purchasing Agent; Quality Control Engineer; Sales Representative; Systems Analyst; Manufacturing Engineer. Principal educational backgrounds sought: Accounting; Art/Design; Business Administration; Computer Science; Engineering; Finance; Liberal Arts; Marketing. Company benefits include: medical insurance; pension plan; life insurance; tuition assistance; disability coverage; profit sharing; savings plan. Operations at this facility include: manufacturing; research/development; administration; service; sales.

F.E. MORAN
2265 Carlson Drive
Northbrook IL 60062
708/498-4800
Contact Richard Maloni, President. Mechanical contractors specializing in fire detection heating, air conditioning, plumbing, and ventilation systems. Corporate headquarters location. International.

NAVISTAR INTERNATIONAL CORPORATION
455 North Cityfront Plaza Drive
Chicago IL 60611
312/836-2000
Contact Jim Gats, Personnel Director. Several area locations including: Hinsdale, Libertyville, Broadview, Schaumburg. A worldwide enterprise having numerous subsidiaries, licensees and joint ventures. Manufactures and markets self-propelled heavy machinery and vehicles for use on and off the highways. Corporate headquarters location. International. New York Stock Exchange.

OLIN CORPORATION/ BRASS AND WINCHESTER GROUPS
East Alton IL 62024
618/258-2909
Contact Mr. Schnieder, Personnel. A major St. Louis company engaged in the manufacture of commercial and military ammunition; ramset powder activated fastening systems; copper and alloy sheet and strip, stamped and drawn parts and clad metals.

OTIS ELEVATOR COMPANY
550 West Jackson Boulevard
Chicago IL 60606
312/454-1323
Contact Diane Kosec, Personnel Representative. One of the world's largest producers of elevators and escalators. The company is primarily engaged in the manufacture, installation, and service of elevators and escalators. Corporate headquarters location: Farmington, CT.

PARKER-HANNIFIN CORPORATION
500 South Wolf Road
Des Plaines IL 60016
708/298-2400
Contact Lou Ford, Personnel Manager. Several area locations. A fluid power firm making one of the most complete lines of components and replacement parts for hydraulic and pneumatic power systems for the industrial, automotive, aviation, space, and marine industries. Company has also recently entered the biomedical market to research and help produce equipment and products for treatment of chronic illnesses. Employs more than 20,000 people at 131 manufacturing plants, 37 administrative and sales offices, and 63 distribution and service centers. Illinois properties are located in Broadview (refrigeration components headquarters), Des Plaines, and Dixon (3 facilities). Corporate headquarters location: Cleveland, OH. International. New York Stock Exchange.

PEABODY MYERS CORPORATION
1621 South Illinois
Streator IL 61364
815/672-3171
Contact B. W. Collins, Personnel Director. Manufacturer of truck-mounted vacuum loading and cleaning equipment for cleaning city sewer line systems, industrial vacuum cleaning operations, and municipal street cleaning requirements. Common positions include: Accountant; Computer Programmer; Draftsperson; Engineer; Mechanical Engineer; Operations/Production Manager; Marketing Specialist; Sales Representative. Principal educational backgrounds sought: Accounting; Business Administration; Engineering; Finance. Company benefits include: medical insurance; pension plan; life insurance; tuition assistance; disability coverage; profit sharing; savings plan. Operations at this facility include: manufacturing;

research/development; administration; sales. Corporate headquarters location: Stamford, CT. New York Stock Exchange.

PEERLESS OF AMERICA
5800 North Pulaski Road
Chicago IL 60646
312/509-2700
Contact W.C. Buettgen, Director of Personnel. Several area locations, including: Chicago, Effingham. A privately owned manufacturer of heat exchanger coils. These coils are used in refrigerators, freezers, dehumidifiers, and air conditioners. Corporate headquarters location: Chicago, IL. Common positions include: Accountant; Blue-Collar Worker Supervisor; Department Manager; Operations/Production Manager; Quality Control Supervisor. Principal educational backgrounds sought: Accounting; Computer Science; Engineering; Marketing. Training programs offered; Internships offered. Company benfits include: medical, dental, and life insurance; disability coverage; profit sharing; 401 K. Operations at this facility include: manufacturing; administration; service; sales.

PIONEER SCREW & NUT COMPANY
2700 York Road
Elk Grove Village IL 60007
Contact Human Resources Manager. A manufacturer of fasteners and nuts and bolts. Parent company of American Cold Heating Corporation. Common positions include: Customer Service Representative; Metallurgical Engineer; Purchasing Agent; Quality Control Supervisor; Sales Representative. Principal educational backgrounds sought: Business Administration; Engineering; Marketing. Company benefits include: medical, dental, and life insurance; tuition assistance; disability coverage; profit sharing; savings plan. Corporate headquarters location. Operations at this facility include: manufacturing.

PITTWAY CORPORATION
333 Skokie Boulevard
Northbrook IL 60065-3012
708/498-1260
Contact Peggy Odegaard, Administrative Assistant to President. Several area locations, including: Aurora, Crystal Lake, Niles. A diverse corporation engaged in four industry segments: Burglar and Fire Alarms, produces security systems and fire alarms under brand names First Alert and BRK; Packaging, manufactures aerosol valves, pumps and closures; Publishing, publishes 27 national business and trade magazines; and Real Estate Developing, operates a 950-unit condominium in Florida. Corporate headquarters location. International. American Stock Exchange.

REVCOR, INC.
251 Edwards Avenue
Carpentersville IL 60110
708/428-4411
Contact Larry Brigman, Personnel Director. Manufactures fans and blowers. Corporate headquarters location.

**SCIAKY BROTHERS INC/
MEMBER COMPANY OF ALLEGHENY INTERNATIONAL**
4915 West 67th Street
Chicago IL 60638
708/594-3800
Contact James D. Schmitt, Manager/Employee Relations. A leading manufacturer of automated welding systems, including electron beam, laser, resistance and fusion welding systems. A manufacturer of industrial systems automation. Corporate headquarters location: Pittsburgh, PA. New York Stock Exchange. Common positions include: Accountant; Blue-Collar Worker Supervisor; Buyer; Computer Programmer; Draftsperson (CAD/CAM); Electrical Engineer; Industrial Engineer; Mechanical Engineer; Financial Analyst; Industrial Designer; Operations/Production Manager; Marketing Specialist; Personnel & Labor Relations Specialist; Physicist; Quality Control Supervisor; Sales Representative; Systems Analyst; Technical Writer/Editor; Service Engineer. Principal educational backgrounds sought: Art/Design; Business Administration; Computer Science; Engineering; Finance; Marketing; Physics; Metallurgy; Computer Engineering. Company benefits include: medical insurance; dental insurance; pension plan; life insurance; tuition assistance; disability coverage; profit sharing; employee discounts; savings plan. Divisional headquarters location. Operations include: manufacturing; research/development; administration; service; sales.

SCULLY-JONES CORPORATION
1901 South Rockwell
Chicago IL 60608
312/247-5900
Contact Gerald Walton, Personnel Director. An employee-owned manufacturer of precision toolholders for machine tools. Operations include: manufacturing; administration. Corporate headquarters location. Common positions include: Accountant; Customer Service Representative; Industrial Engineer; Mechanical Engineer; Programmer; Purchasing Agent; Quality Control Supervisor; Systems Analyst. Principal educational backgrounds sought: Business Administration; Computer Science; Engineering. Company benefits include: medical insurance; dental insurance; life insurance; tuition assistance; disability coverage; profit sharing; savings plan.

SPOTNAILS INC.
1100 Hicks Road
Rolling Meadows IL 60008
708/259-1620
Contact Karen Yoder, Employee Relations Manager. Manufactures pneumatic tools and fasteners. Common positions include: Accountant; Administrator; Blue-Collar Worker Supervisor; Customer Service Representative; Industrial Engineer; Mechanical Engineer. Principal educational backgrounds sought: Accounting; Business Administration; Engineering. Company benefits: medical, dental, and life insurance; pension plan; tuition assistance; disability coverage. Corporate headquarters location. Operations include: regional headquarters; manufacturing; administration; service; sales.

STEPHENS-ADAMSON, INC.
850 Ridgeway Avenue
Aurora IL 60506
708/892-4311
Contact Personnel. A subsidiary of Allis-Chalmers. Manufacturer of heavy equipment used for handling bulk material. Corporate headquarters location.

TC INDUSTRIES
P.O. Box 477
Crystal Lake IL 60014
815/459-2400
Contact John McGrath, Personnel Director. A diversified company with interests in commercial heat treating, heavy equipment, and military components. Corporate headquarters location.

TEMPLETON, KENLY & CO. INC.
2525 South Gardner Road
Broadview IL 60153
312/865-1500
Contact Ms. Kathleen Mohr, Manager of Personnel. Manufactures hydraulic and mechanical jacks. Common positions include: Accountant; Computer Programmer; Credit Manager; Customer Service Representative; Draftsperson; Industrial Engineer; Mechanical Engineer; General Manager; Operations/Production Manager; Personnel & Labor Relations Specialist; Purchasing Agent; Quality Control Supervisor; Transportation & Traffic Specialist. Principal educational backgrounds sought: Accounting; Computer Science; Engineering; Marketing. Company benefits include: medical, dental, and life insurance; tuition assistance; disability coverage; profit sharing; savings plan; EAP (Employee Assistance Plan). Operations at this facility include: manufacturing; research/development; administration; service; sales. Corporate headquarters location.

TUTHILL PUMP DIVISION
12500 South Pulaski
Chicago IL 60658
708/389-2500
Contact Karen Angelucci, Personnel Director. International distributor and manufacturer of pumps (rotary), positive displacement gear, test plugs, and tube connectors. Corporate headquarters location: Hindsdale, IL. International. Common positions include: Accountant; Blue-Collar Worker Supervisor; Buyer; Computer Programmer; Credit Manager; Customer Service Representative; Draftsperson; Engineer; Electrical Engineer; Mechanical Engineer; Metallurgical Engineer; Purchasing Agent; Quality Control Supervisor; Sales Representative.

UNION CARBIDE CORPORATION/ MIDWEST REGION
10 South Riverside Plaza
Suite 2200
Chicago IL 60606
312/454-2000
Contact Jim Carey, Employee Relations Manager. Among the nation's 25 largest industrial companies with sales over $9 billion. It is engaged in three major lines of business: chemicals and plastics; gases, metals and carbons. Union Carbide is primarily a manufacturer of basic products used by the chemicals, plastics, and metal industries. Union Carbide is a major multinational company with about one third of its sales coming from international operations. The company employs 100,000 people, operates about 500 plants, mines and mills in over 30 countries, and has over 170,000 stockholders. Corporate headquarters location: Danbury, CT. International. New York Stock Exchange.

UNITED AIR CLEANER COMPANY/ A UNIT OF DOLLINGER/ A FILTRONA COMPANY
9705 South Cottage Grove Avenue
Chicago IL 60628
312/734-5000
Contact John J. Dreznes, Vice President - Sales. International distributors and manufacturers of air cleaners, automotive, and tractor engines. Corporate headquarters location: Richmond, VA. Parent company is American Filtrona Corporation.

UPPCO, INC.
5610 West Bloomingdale
Chicago IL 60639
312/622-7010
Contact Salvador Isais, Personnel Manager. Designs and manufactures specialized motors. Corporate headquarters location.

VULCAN MATERIALS COMPANY/ MIDWEST DIVISION
500 West Plainfield Road
Countryside IL 60525
312/482-7000
Contact J. Wayne Houston, Manager, Administration & Human Resources. A multi-industry company operating in three businesses: one of the nation's largest producers of construction aggregates; a leading chemicals manufacturer; and a principal producer of secondary aluminum, detinned steel scrap and tin chemicals. Chicago operations produce limestone materials. A Fortune 500. Common positions include: Accountant; Buyer; Computer Programmer; Credit Manager; Customer Service Representative; Draftsperson; Industrial Engineer; Mining Engineer; Financial Analyst; Geologist; Operations/Production Manager; Marketing Specialist; Personnel & Labor Relations Specialist; Purchasing Agent; Quality Conrol Supervisor; Sales Representative; Systems Analyst. Principal educational background sought: Accounting; Business Administration; Computer Science; Engineering; Finance; Marketing. Training programs offered. Company benfits include: medical, dental, and life insurance; pension plan; tuition assistance; disability coverage; profit sharing; savings plan. Corporate headquarters location: Birmingham, AL. Operations at this facility include: divisional headquarters; administration; sales. New York Stock Exchange.

WHITING CORPORATION
15700 Lathrop Avenue
Harvey IL 60426
708/331-4000
Contact Manager of Human Resources. Manufacturer of heavy overhead gantry cranes; metallurgical process equipment; transportation maintenance/repair equipment; and special products. Common positions include: Draftsperson; Electrical Engineer; Industrial Engineer; Mechanical Engineer; Metallurgical Engineer; Department Manager; Sales Representative. Principal educational backgrounds sought: Business Administration; Engineering; Finance; Mathematics. Company benefits include: medical insurance; dental insurance; pension plan; life insurance; tuition assistance; disability coverage; profit sharing. Operations at this facility include: manufacturing; service; sales. Corporate headquarters location.

WOODSTOCK DIE CASTING
555 North Wheeler Street
Woodstock IL 60098
815/338-0700
Contact Pauline Gray, Manager/Personnel Administration. Manufactures automotive and industrial die castings. Division of Allied Corporation (Morristown, NJ). Corporate headquarters location.

YEOMANS CHICAGO
1999 Ruby Street
Melrose Park IL 60160
708/344-9600
Contact John Lillis, Personnel Director. Several area locations including: Melrose Park, Westmont, Bensenville, Carol Stream. Manufactures and sells goods and services for conveying, controlling, and treating water and waste water. Principal products include ductile iron pressure pipe and fittings, plastic pipe, waterworks valves, fire hydrants, vitrified clay pipe for sewer lines, waste treatment equipment, and water treatment chemicals. Municipalities, water and sewer line contractors, and piping contractors are the principal customers. Products sold by both company salespersons and distributors. Corporate headquarters location. International.

MISCELLANEOUS SERVICES

BURNS INTERNATIONAL SECURITY SERVICES
6323 North Avondale
Chicago Il 60631
312/774-6200
Contact Lester Kerr, Personnel Director. Provides private security guards to a variety of users.

GREAT LAKES MAINTENENCE & SECURITY CORPORATION
201 North Wells Street
Room 408
Chicago IL 60606
312/332-1638
Contact Barbara Dennis, Personnel Department. Provides maintenence, cleaning and security guard services

PINKERTON'S, INC.
9930 West Derby Lane
Westchester IL 60153
312/450-2360
Contact Larry Gallina, Personnel Manager. Provides uniformed security officers and investigative services. District headquarters. Corporate headquarters location: New York, NY. New York Stock Exchange. Common positions include: Accountant; Blue-Collar Worker Supervisor; Branch Manager; Department Manager; General Manager; Management Trainee; Personnel & Labor Relations Specialist; Sales Representative. Principal educational backgrounds sought: Accounting; Business Administration; Liberal Arts; Law Enforcement. Company benefits include: medical insurance; life insurance; tuition assistance; profit sharing.

SAFETY-KLEEN
777 Big Timber Road
Elgin IL 60123
708/697-8460
Contact Robert Burian, Vice President of Personnel. A company engaged in the cleaning of industrial machinery and the recycling of industrial cleaning solvents after their use.

NEWSPAPER PUBLISHERS

For more information on professional employment opportunities in the newspaper journalism industry, contact the following professional and trade organizations, as listed beginning on page 295:

AMERICAN NEWSPAPER PUBLISHERS ASSOCIATION
AMERICAN SOCIETY OF NEWSPAPER EDITORS
THE DOW JONES NEWSPAPER FUND
INTERNATIONAL CIRCULATION MANAGERS ASSOCIATION
NATIONAL NEWSPAPER ASSOCIATION
NATIONAL PRESS CLUB
THE NEWSPAPER GUILD
THE NEWSPAPER GUILD/CHICAGO LOCAL

ALTON TELEGRAPH PRINTING COMPANY
111 East Broadway
Alton IL 62002
618/463-2500
Contact Personnel Department. A major regional newspaper publisher. Employs over 100.

CHICAGO TRIBUNE
435 North Michigan
Chicago IL 60611
312/222-4572
Contact Ronald Williams, Director of Human Resources. Publishes one of the nation's largest newspapers.

THE DAILY HERALD-PADDOCK PUBLICATIONS
P.O. Box 280
Arlington Heights IL 60006
312/870-3722
Contact Sharon Nestmann or Karen Lowery, Employment Recruiters. Publishes a daily newspaper with circulation of 100,000.

LERNER NEWSPAPERS, INC.
8135 River Drive
Morton Grove IL 60053
708/966-5555
Contact Personnel Director. Publishes 52 mastheads in the Chicago area.

THE NEWS DEMOCRAT
120 South Illinois
P.O. Box 427
Belleville IL 62222
618/234-1000
Contact Personnel Director. A major Southern Illinois newspaper publisher.

**THE NEWS-SUN/
COPLEY PRESS INC.**
100 West Madison
Waukegan IL 60085
708/336-7000
Contact Personnel Director. Several area locations including: Libertyville. A communications firm publishing a daily newspaper, The News-Sun (Waukegan) and a weekly newspaper, The Independent-Register (Libertyville).

SOUTHTOWN ECONOMIST, INC.
5959 South Harlem Avenue
Chicago IL 60638
312/586-8800
Contact Sue Buckles, Personnel. Publisher of neighborhood newspapers. Corporate headquarters location.

PAPER, PACKAGING & FOREST PRODUCTS/ CONTAINERS & GLASS PRODUCTS

For more information on professional employment opportunities in the paper and packaging industries, contact the following professional and trade organizations, as listed beginning on page 295:

**AMERICAN PAPER INSTITUTE
PAPER INDUSTRY MANAGEMENT ASSOCIATION
TECHNICAL ASSOCIATION OF THE PULP AND PAPER INDUSTRY**

ARVEY CORPORATION
A DIVISION OF HAMMERHILL PAPER CO.
3450 N. Kimball
Chicago IL 60618
312/463-0030
Contact Randall Rakow, Corporate Vice President. A manufacturer and retailer of paper products.

BAGCRAFT OF AMERICA
3900 West 43rd Street
Chicago IL 60632
312/254-8000
Contact Charles F. Gaul, Industrial Relations Manager. Manufacturer of flexible packaging, laminating materials.

BENNETT INDUSTRIES
515 First Street
Peotone IL 60468
708/258-3211
Contact Robert Rundin, Director of Industrial Relations. Manufacturers of plastic and metal shipping containers.

BOISE CASCADE CORPORATION
800 West Bryn Mawr
Itasca IL 60143
312/773-5000
Contact Human Resource Director. Manufacture, distribute, and sell paper & office products.

CENTRAL CAN COMPANY
3200 South Kilbourn Avenue
Chicago IL 60623
312/254-8700
Contact Raymond Mielkus, Assistant Personnel Manager. Manufactures shipping containers and paint cans.

JOHN CRANE, INC.
6400 Oakton Street
Morton Grove IL 60053
312/967-2460
Contact George Pinder, Senior Human Resources Representative. Manufactures & markets mechanical seals & packaging, and Teflon products.

GARDEN CITY ENVELOPE COMPANY
3001 North Rockwell Street
Chicago IL 60618
312/267-3600
Contact John Arciszewski, Employee Relations Manager. Specializes in the manufature of all types of envelopes.

GEE COMPANY
2600 W. 79th Street
Chicago IL
312/476-7400
Contact President. A forest products firm with offices throught the area.

GEORGIA-PACIFIC
HOPPER PAPER DIVISION
P.O. Box 369
Taylorville IL 62568
217/824-9611
Contact Bob Morrison, Personnel Director. Manufactures printing papers.

GEORGIA PACIFIC
Old Route 66
P.O. Box 100
Mt. Olive IL 62069
217/999-2511
Contact Personnel Department. One of several area divisions of the well-known diversified manufacturer of packaging products. Company's principal products are glass containers, although the company also produces and sells containerboard, corrugated containers, printing plates and ink, plywood and demension lumber, blown plastic containers, plastic beverage bottles, plastic drums, metal and plastic closures, tamper-resistant closures, plastic and glass prescription containers, pharmaceutical items, labels, and multipack plastic carriers for containers. Specialized glass products made and sold by the company include Libbey Tumblers, stemware, and decorative glassware, television bulbs for picture tubes, and Kimble scientific and laboratory ware. Some overseas affiliates also manufacture flat glass and related products.

GREIF BROTHERS CORPORATION
615 Northwest Avenue
Northlake IL 60164
708/562-1800
Contact Barbara Bradford, Personnel. Manufactures shipping containers for bulk products.

HIGHLAND SUPPLY CORPORATION
1111 6th Street
Highland IL 62249
618/654-2161
Contact Donald J. Frolker, Personnel Manager. Manufacture foils, polypropolene film, cellophane and film bags (printed and plain). Common positions include: Accountant; Chemist; Computer Programmer; Mechanical Engineer; General Manager; Operations/Production Manager; Quality Control Supervisor; Sales Representative. Principal educational backgrounds sought: Accounting; Business Administration; Chemistry; Computer Science; Engineering; Marketing. Company benefits include: medical insurance; life insurance; tuition assistance. Corporate headquarters location. Operations at this facility include: manufacturing; administration; sales.

INLANDER-STEINDLER PAPER COMPANY
2100 Devon Avenue
Elk Grove Village IL 60007
708/952-2000
Contact Sales Manager. A paper distributor with five branches in IL, IN, & WI.

INTERNATIONAL PAPER COMPANY/ NORTHLAKE
635 Northwest Avenue
Northlake IL 60164
312/562-6900 or 562-9300
Contact Phil Kohner, Regional Manager/Employee Relations. One of the largest natural resource management companies. It produces solid wood products, including plywood, lumber, poles, and cabinets and a variety of pulp and paper products, packaging, packaging materials, and packaging systems.

IVEX CORPORATION
50 South Mannheim Road
Hillside IL 60162
708/547-2400
Contact Personnel Director. Manufactures corrugated packaging.

JEFFERSON-SMURFIT/ CONTAINER DIVISION
6th and Zscholkke Sts.
Highland IL 62249
618/654-2141
Contact Don Walker, Personnel Controller. A metropolitan manufacturer of corrugated containers.

JEFFERSON SMURFIT CORPORATION/
ALTON PACKAGING CORPORATION
401 Alton Street
Alton IL 62002
618/463-6000
Contact Mr. Tom Hardy, Personnel Director. Mr. Tom Hardy can be contacted at P.O. Box 66820, St. Louis MO 63166. Manufacture paperboard packaging, boxes, paper cores.

KERR GLASS MANUFACTURING CORPORATION
1500 North Route 59
Plainfield IL 60544
312/242-4592
Contact Charles Worden, Manager, Industrial Relations. Manufactures and sells glass containers.

MEAD CONTAINER
7601 South 78th Avenue
Bridgeview IL 60455
708/458-8100
Contact Beverly Grybas, Administrative Manager. Several area locations including: Chicago (2) and Hillside. A multi-industry firm with segments operating primarily in the forest products industry (paper, pulp, lumber, etc.), but also in such areas as balance-engineered castings, molded rubber parts, distribution of piping and electrical supplies, and the manufacture of advanced digital information systems. Forest products segment includes three major subsidiaries: Georgia Kraft Company, Brunswick Pulp and Paper, and Northwood Forest Industries. Bridgeview facility produces corrugated shipping containers; facility at 9540 South Dorchester Avenue, Chicago (60628) produces folding cartons; subsidiary facility (Bermingham and Prosser) at 125 Fencl Lane, Hillside (60162) is responsible for distributing paper products; and subsidiary Ft. Dearborn Paper Company, 2901 West 36th Place, Chicago (60632) produces and converts paper. Parent company is divided into five operating segments: Paper, Paperboard, Consumer and Distribution, Industrial Products, and Advanced Systems. Corporate headquarters location: Dayton, OH. International.

MILLS-AMERICAN ENVELOPE
3001 North Rockwell
Chicago IL 60618
312/533-6700
Contact John Arciszewski, Human Resource Manager. An envelope manufacturer. A subsidiary of Stanwood Industries. Corporate headquarters location.

OWENS-ILLINOIS INC./
MOLD SHOP
1625 East Broadway
Alton IL 62002
618/463-3130
Contact L. Krietner, Personnel Coordinator. One of several area divisions of the well-known diversified manufacturer of packaging products. Company's principal products are glass containers, although the company also produces and sells blown plastic containers, plastic beverage bottles, plastic drums, metal and plastic closures, tamper-resistant closures, plastic and glass presciption containers, pharmaceutical items, labels, and mulipack pstic carriers for containers. Specialized glass products made and sold by the company include Libbey Tumblers, stemware, and decorative glassware, television blubs for picture tubes, and Kimble scientific and laboratory ware. Some overseas affiliates also manufacture flat glass and related products. Common positions include: Moldmaker. Principal educational backgrounds sought: Moldmaker Apprenticeship. Training programs offered. Company benefits include: medical, dental, and life insurance; pension plan; tuition assistance; disability coverage; savings plan. Corporate headquarters location: Toledo, OH. Parent company: manufacturing.

OWENS-ILLINOIS INC./
MACHINE DIVISION
315 Tolle Lane
Godfrey IL 62035
618/466-8811
Contact Verlene Schwalb, Assistant Industrial Relations Director. One of several area divisions of the well-known diversified manufacturer of packaging products. Company's principal products are glass containers, blown plastic containers, plastic beverage bottles, plastic drums, metal and plastic closures, tamper-resistant closures, plastic and glass prescription containers, pharmaceutical items, labels, and multipack plastic carriers for containers. Specialized glass products made and sold by the company include Libbey Tumblers, stemware, and decorative glassware, television bulbs for picture tubes, and Kimble scientific and laboratory ware. Some overseas affiliates also manufacture flat glass and related products. Common positions include: Machinist. Training programs offered. Company benefits include: medical, dental, and life insurance; pension plan; tuition assistance; disability coverage; savings plan. Corporate headquarters location: Toledo, OH. Parent company: Owens-Illinois Inc. Operations at this facility include: manufacturing.

PACKAGING CORPORATION OF AMERICA
1603 Orrington Avenue
Evanston IL 60204
708/492-4458
Contact Barb White, Administrative Assistant. A worldwide manufacturer of paper, corrugated cardboard, paper board, aluminum, and plastics packaging

material with 60 plant location and 9,000 employees. Products are used in the packaging of food, paper and paper products, metal products, rubber and plastics, automotive products, and point of purchase displays; packaging soap, detergent, and food products; and residential construction. Operates more than 60 plants throughout the Midwest, South, and East. Common positions include: Accountant; Industrial Engineer; Mechanical Engineer; Operations/Production Manager; Sales Representative. Principal educational backgrounds sought: Accounting; Engineering; Marketing. Training programs offered; Internships offered. Company benefits include: medical, dental, and life insurance; tuition assistance; disability coverage; daycare assistance; profit sharing; employee discounts; savings plan. Corporate headquarters location. Parent company: Tenneco Inc. Operations at this facility include: divisional headquarters; research/development; administration. New York Stock Exchange (Tenneco Inc).

PLASTOFILM INDUSTRIES, INC.
P.O. Box 531
Wheaton IL 60189
312/668-2838
Contact Sue Finley, Personnel Manager. A manufacturer of plastic packaging for pharmaceuticals, cosmetics, toys and small tools. Corporate headquarters location.

SCHOLLE CORPORATION
200 West North Avenue
Northlake IL 60164
708/562-7290
Contact Kevin Breese, Director of Corporate Personnel. Manufacturer and distributor of flexible film packaging for the food and beverage industries; specialty chemical solutions for coating and related industries; bulk and packaged acid; automotive products solutions; and prefabricated industrial and agricultural buildings. Also manufactures filling equipment for food and beverage bag-in-box. Operations include: manufacturing; research/development; administration; service; sales. Corporate headquarters location. Common positions include: Accountant; Blue-Collar Worker Supervisor; Buyer; Chemist; Credit Manager; Customer Service Representative; Draftsperson; Chemical Engineer; Industrial Engineer; Mechanical Engineer; Financial Analyst; Department Manager; Management Trainee; Operations/Production Manager; Personnel & Labor Relations Specialist; Purchasing Agent; Quality Control Supervisor; Sales Representative; Transportation & Traffic Specialist. Principal educational backgrounds sought: Accounting; Business Administration; Chemistry; Engineering; Finance; Marketing. Company benefits include: medical insurance; dental insurance; pension plan; life insurance; tuition assistance; disability coverage; employee discounts.

SIGNODE INDUSTRIES INC.
3650 West Lake
Glenview IL 60025
708/724-6100
Contact Manager of Professional Recruiting. Signode is one of the leading manufacturers and distributors of strapping systems for use in packaging and materials handling by a broad range of industries. Common positions include: Accountant; Computer Programmer; Chemical Engineer; Mechanical Engineer; Financial Analyst; Sales Representative; Systems Analyst. Principal educational backgrounds sought: Business Administration; Computer Science; Engineering. Company benefits include: medical insurance; dental plan; life insurance; tuition assistance; disability coverage; profit sharing; savings plan. Operations at this facility include: manufacturing; research/development; administration; sales. Corporate headquarters location.

H.P. SMITH DIVISION
JAMES RIVER CORPORATION
5001 West 66th Street
Bedford Park IL 60638
708/458-0777
Contact Robert E. Jones, Human Resources Manager. The company does paper converting for the release paper market. Common positions include: Accountant; Chemist; Customer Service Representative; Chemical Engineer; Mechanical Engineer; Operations/Production Manager; Marketing Specialist; Sales Representative. Principal educational backgrounds sought: Accounting; Chemistry; Engineering; Marketing. Company benefits include: medical, dental, and life insurance; pension plan; tuition assistance; disability coverage; profit sharing; employee discounts; savings plan. Corporate headquarters location: Richmond, VA. Parent company: James River Corp. Operations at this facility include: divisional headquarters; manufacturing; research/development; administration; service; sales. New York Stock Exchange

SOLO CUP COMPANY
1501 East 96th Street
Chicago IL 60628
312/721-3600
Contact Chuck Keegan, Personnel Office. Manufacturer and distributor of paper cups, plates, etc. Corporate headquarters location: Champaign, IL.

STONE CONTAINER CORPORATION
150 North Michigan Avenue
Chicago IL 60601
312/580-4764
Contact Jeanne Seufert, Recruiting Specialist. A major multinational paper company, operating principally in the production and sale of commodity pulp, paper, and packaging products. More than 100 locations nationwide

Common positions include: Accountant; Computer Programmer; Credit Manager; Customer Service Representative; Financial Analyst; Systems Analyst; Transportation & Traffic Specialist. Principal educational backgrounds sought: Accounting; Business Administration; Computer Science; Finance. Company benefits include: medical, dental and life insurance; pension plan; tuition assistance; disability coverage; employee discounts; savings plan. Corporate headquarters location. New York Stock Exchange.

WALDORF CORPORATION
4200 South Pulaski Road
Chicago IL 60632
312/847-2500
Contact Personnel Department. Manufacturer of folding cartons for foods, detergents, personal hygiene products, and soaps. Principal educational background sought: Business Administration. Company benefits include: medical insurance; dental insurance; pension plan; life insurance; disability coverage; profit sharing; savings plan. Operations at this facility include: manufacturing; sales. Corporate headquarters location: St. Paul, MN.

WESTERN KRAFT PAPER GROUP
1001 Knell Street
Montgomery IL 60538
708/896-2061
Contact Personnel Department. Manufacturers of corrugated cartons. Common positions include: Customer Service Representative; General Manager; Sales Representative. Principal educational backgrounds sought: Accounting; Marketing. Company benefits include: medical insurance; dental insurance; pension plan; life insurance; tuition assistance; disability coverage; profit sharing; employee discounts; savings plan. Operations at this facility include: manufacturing. Corporate headquarters location: Portland, OR.

WEYERHAEUSER PAPER COMPANY
3001 Otto Street
Belleville IL 62223
618/233-5460
Contact Human Resource Manager. Manufacturer of corrugated cardboard shipping containers. Common positions include: Accountant; Customer Service Representative; Electrical Engineer; Industrial Engineer; Mechanical Engineer; Department Manager; Management Trainee; Operations/Production Manager; Marketing Specialist; Personnel & Labor Relations Specialist; Purchasing Agent; Quality Control Supervisor; Sales Representative. Principal educational backgrounds sought: Accounting; Business Administration; Engineering. Training programs offered; Internships offered. Company benefits include. medical, dental, and life insurance; pension plan; tuition assistance; disability coverage; profit sharing; savings plan. Corporate headquarters location: Tacoma, Washington.

Operations at this facility include: manufacturing; administration; service; sales. New York Stock Exchange. American Stock Exchange.

WOODWORK CORPORATION OF AMERICA
1432 West 21st Street
Chicago IL 60608
312/226-4800
Contact Bruce Stulik, Controller. Manufacturers of architectural woodwork. Corporate headquarters location.

PETROLEUM & ENERGY RELATED: MINING & DRILLING

For more information on professional employment opportunities in the petroleum, energy, and mining industries, contact the following professional and trade organizations, as listed beginning on page 295:

AMERICAN ASSOCIATION OF PETROLEUM GEOLOGISTS
AMERICAN GAS ASSOCIATION
AMERICAN GEOLOGICAL INSTITUTE
AMERICAN INSTITUTE OF MINING,
 METALLURGICAL AND PETROLEUM
AMERICAN INSTITUTE OF MINING, METALLURGICAL
 AND PETROLEUM/CHICAGO
AMERICAN NUCLEAR SOCIETY
AMERICAN PETROLEUM INSTITUTE
CLEAN ENERGY RESEARCH INSTITUTE
GEOLOGICAL SOCIETY OF AMERICA
SOCIETY OF EXPLORATION GEOPHYSICISTS
SOCIETY OF TRIBOLOGISTS AND LUBRICATION ENGINEERS

AMOCO CORPORATION
200 E. Randolph Drive
Chicago IL 60601
312/856-5551
Contact Human Resources Department. One of the nation's leading energy and petroleum companies.

AMOCO PETROLEUM ADDITIVES COMPANY
P.O. Box 182
Wood River IL 62095
618/251-2200
Contact Mr. George A. Preston, Director, Human Resources. Manufacturers of petroleum additives products. Employs over 300.

BLACKSTONE MANUFACTURING COMPANY
4630 West Harrison Street
Chicago IL 60644
312/378-7800
Contact Juan J. Gomez, Personnel Manager. A manufacturer of fuel pumps. Divisional headquarters.

CLARK OIL AND REFINING CORPORATION
P.O. Box 7
Hartford IL 62048
618/254-7301
Contact James Stewart, Manager of Industrial Relations. Manufacturers of petroleum products. Employs over 300.

CLARK OIL & REFINING
131 st and Kedzie Avenue
Blue Island IL 60406
708/385-5000
Contact Tom Fredette, Personnel Director. A refiner and retail marketer of gasoline.

COLUMBIA QUARRY COMPANY/ PLANTS #9, #3, AND #1
800 Quarry Road
Valmeyer IL 62295
618/935-2201
Contact Kevin Wilder, Foreman. Manufacturers of calcium carbonate and crushed stone. Employs over 100.

GOODMAN EQUIPMENT CORPORATION
5430 W. 70th Place
Bedford Park IL 60638
708/496-1188
Contact Employee Relations Manager. Manufacturer of underground mining locomotives.

T.J. GUNDLACH MACHINE COMPANY
1 Freedom Drive
P.O. Box 385
Belleville IL 62223
618/233-7208
Contact T.E. Dinges, Vice President, Administration. Engaged in the manufacture and sales of mining machinery and equipment

**LIQUID AIR CORPORATION/
AMERICAN AIR LIQUIDE**
5230 South East Avenue
Countryside IL 60525
312/482-8400
Contact Ronald J. Nowak, Manager of Administration. Engaged in the sale of industrial gases and related.

LIQUID CARBONIC CORPORATION
135 Lasalle Street
Chicago IL 60603
312/855-2834
Contact Carol Bosco, Director of Employee Relations. Produces a wide range of gas products.

MISSISSIPPI LIME COMPANY
Alby Street
Alton IL 62002
618/465-7741
Contact Personnel Department. A leading St. Louis company engaged in the manufacture of limestone, sand and rock.

SHELL OIL COMPANY/WOOD RIVER
Box 262
Wood River IL 62095
618/254-7371
Contact Personnel Department. Area office of the widely-recognized petroleum products company. Engaged in the exploration, development, production, purchase, transportation, and marketing of crude oil and natural gas and related chemical products. The Oil Products segment is engaged primarily in the marketing and sale of its oil products in the United States. The Chemical Products segment is engaged principally in the production of detergent alcohols, agricultural herbicides and insecticides, and other petrochemicals. Corporate headquarters: Houston, TX. New York Stock Exchange.

SHELL OIL COMPANY
1415 West 22nd Street
Oak Brook IL 60521
708/572-5976
Contact Shiela Austin, Employee Relations Assistant. Several area locations including: Argo, Arlington Heights, and Hammond, IN. Engaged in the exploration for, and development, production, purchase, transportation, and marketing of crude oil and natural gas and related chemical products. The oil products segment is engaged primarily in the marketing and sale of its oil products in the United States. The chemical products segment is engaged principally in the production of detergent alcohols, epoxy resins, solvents, and

agricultural herbicides and insecticides. Corporate headquarters location: Houston, TX. New York Stock Exchange.

PRINTING

For more information on professional employment opportunities in the printing and graphic arts industries, contact the following professional and trade organizations, as listed beginning on page 295:

ASSOCIATION OF GRAPHIC ARTS
BINDING INDUSTRIES OF AMERICA
NATIONAL ASSOCIATION OF PRINTERS AND LITHOGRAPHERS
PRINTING INDUSTRIES OF AMERICA
TECHNICAL ASSOCIATION OF THE GRAPHIC ARTS

ALDEN PRESS, INC.
2000 Arthur Avenue
Elk Grove Village IL 60007
708/640-6000
Contact Jim Lillie, Personnel Director. A commercial printing company.

AM INTERNATIONAL
333 W. Wacker Drive
Suite 900
Chicago IL 60606-1265
312/558-7934
Contact Marianne Gruber, Manager of Personnel. Sells and services design and display products.

AMERICAN PRINTERS AND LITHOGRAPHERS
6701 West Oakton
Chicago IL 60648
312/267-6500
Contact William Wahl, Director of Purchasing. A commercial printer.

BASF/COATING AND INKS DIVISION
4000 W. 40th Street
Chicago IL 60632
312/737-7400
Contact Personnel Director. Manufactures printing inks and container coatings.

INTERNATIONAL PAPER COMPANY/PEORIA
8401 North University
Peoria IL 61615
309/692-7221
Contact Charles Harper or Bernice Sommer, Supervisor, Employee Relations. A large printing facility of consumer labels.

SCHAWK GRAPHICS INC.
1695 River Road
Des Plaines IL 60018
312/694-9080
Contact Bob Drew, Personnel Director. Several area locations. Lithographers with clients in the printing, publishing and advertising industries. Corporate headquarters location: Park Ridge, IL.

UARCO INC.
West County Line Road
Barrington IL 60010
708/381-7000
Contact Mr. Fritz Kauffmann, Personnel Manager. Several area locations, including: Chicago and Watseka. Engaged in the design, manufacture and sale of business forms. Forms are used by data processing equipment firms as well as for typical business concerns. Products include such items as sales slips, invoices, purchase orders, and payroll checks. Company has 19 plants and 230 sales offices nationwide. Parent company: Pace Industries, NY. Common job positions include: Accountant; Chemist; Computer Programmer; Credit Manager; Chemical Engineer; Industrial Engineer; Mechanical Engineer; Sales Representative (resumes referred from Barrington to appropriate location near applicant's home). Principal educational backgrounds sought: Accounting; Business Administration; Chemistry; Computer Science; Engineering; Marketing. Company benefits include: medical insurance; dental insurance; pension plan; life insurance; disability coverage. Corporate headquarters location. Operations at this facility include: research/development; administration.

WILSON JONES COMPANY
6150 West Touhy Avenue
Chicago IL 60648
312/774-7700
Contact Industrial Relations Manager. Manufactures business forms and binders. A subsidiary of American Brands, Inc. (New York, NY). Corporate headquarters location.

REAL ESTATE: SERVICES; MANAGEMENT; DEVELOPMENT

For more information on professional employment opportunities in the real estate industry, contact the following professional and trade organizations, as listed beginning on page 295:

APARTMENT OWNERS AND MANAGERS ASSOCIATION
BUILDING OWNERS AND MANAGERS ASSOCIATION
BUILDING OWNERS AND MANAGERS ASSOCIATION/
 SUBURBAN CHICAGO
INSTITUTE OF REAL ESTATE MANAGEMENT
INTERNATIONAL ASSOCIATION OF CORPORATE
 REAL ESTATE EXECUTIVES/CHICAGO CHAPTER
NATIONAL ASSOCIATION OF REALTORS
INTERNATIONAL ASSOCIATION OF CORPORATE
 REAL ESTATE EXECUTIVES
INTERNATIONAL REAL ESTATE INSTITUTE
NATIONAL ASSOCIATION OF REAL ESTATE INVESTMENT TRUSTS

BAIRD & WARNER
200 W. Madison Street
Suite 2500
Chicago IL 60606
312/368-5864
Contact Norb Michalak, Vice President of Human Resources. Full service real estate company.

CHICAGO TITLE & TRUST COMPANY
30 North LaSalle Street Suite 3700
Chicago IL 60602
312/630-2408
Contact Carol Denlinger or Lauren Pahos, Human Resources Officers. Provides title insurance on real estate property as well as conventional trust services and escrow services. Parent company: Alleghany Corporation. Common positions include: Accountant; Attorney; Computer Programmer; Financial Analyst; Personnel & Labor Relations Specialist; Sales Representative; Systems Analyst; Title Examiner; Escrow Closer. Principal educational backgrounds sought: Accounting; Business Administration; Computer Science; Finance; Law; Title Insurance Related. Company benefits include: medical insurance; dental insurance; pension plan; life insurance; tuition assistance; long term & short term disability coverage; 401K - savings and profit sharing plan. Corporate headquarters location. Parent company: Alleghany Corp. Operations at this facility include: administration; service; sales.

MERCHANDISE MART PROPERTIES, INC.
Suite 470
(Office of the Building)
Merchandise Mart Plaza
Chicago IL 60654
312/527-7792
Contact Tom Fitzpatrick, Manager, Human Resources. Management and leasing agent for the Merchandise Mart Building. Common positions include: Accountant; Advertising Worker; Attorney; Computer Programmer; Credit Manager; Draftsperson; Construction Project Engineer; Department Manager; Marketing Specialist; Personnel & Labor Relations Specialist; Systems Analyst; Technical Writer/Editor. Principal educational backgrounds sought: Accounting; Communications; Computer Science; Engineering. Company benefits include: medical, dental and life insurance; pension plan; disability coverage; profit sharing. Corporate headquarters location. Operations at this facility include: administration; service.

RESEARCH AND DEVELOPMENT

FERMI NATIONAL ACCELERATOR LABORATORY
P.O. Box 500
Batavia IL 60510
708/840-3324
Contact James L. Thompson, Employment Manager. A federally-funded, not-for-profit organization dedicated to basic research in the field of high energy physics. Parent company: Universities Research Association. Common positions include: Electrical Engineer; Mechanical Engineer. Principal educational backgrounds sought: Computer Science; Engineering; Physics. Company benefits include: medical insurance; dental insurance; pension plan; life insurance; tuition assistance; disability coverage; savings plan. Corporate headquarters location: Washington, D.C. Operations at this facility: research/development.

SARGENT-WELCH SCIENTIFIC COMPANY
7400 North Linder Avenue
Skokie IL 60076
708/677-0600
Contact Personnel Director. For over 130 years, this company has supplied material for scientific research, education and applied science. Both a distributor and manufacturer of a wide range of analytical instruments, scientific apparatus, lab equipment, supplies, chemicals and specialized furniture. Common positions include: Accountant; Administrator; Advertising Worker; Attorney; Biochemist; Blue-Collar Worker Supervisor; Buyer; Chemist; Computer Programmer; Credit Manager; Customer Service Representative; Draftsperson; Electrical Engineer; Industrial Engineer; Mechanical Engineer; Financial Analyst; Branch Manager; Department

Manager; Operations/Production Manager; Marketing Specialist; Personnel & Labor Relations Specialist; Physicist; Purchasing Agent; Quality Control Supervisor; Sales Representative; Systems Analyst; Technical Writer/Editor. Principal educational backgrounds sought: Accounting; Biology; Business Administration; Chemistry; Computer Science; Engineering; Finance; Liberal Arts; Marketing; Physics. Company benefits include: medical insurance; dental insurance; life insurance; tuition assistance; disability coverage; profit sharing; employee discounts; savings plan. Corporate headquarters location. Parent company: Artra Group. Operations at this facility include: manufacturing; research/development; administration; service; sales. International. New York Stock Exchange

RUBBER AND PLASTICS

For more information on professional employment opportunities in the rubber and plastics industries, contact the following professional and trade organizations, as listed beginning on page 295:

SOCIETY OF PLASTIC ENGINEERS
SOCIETY OF PLASTICS INDUSTRY
SOCIETY OF PLASTICS INDUSTRY/DES PLAINES

FLEX-O-GLASS
4647 West Augusta Boulevard
Chicago IL 60651
312/261-5200
Contact Paul Neville, Personnel Director. A plastics manufacturer.

HOFFER PLASTICS CORPORATION
500 Collins Street
South Elgin IL 60177
708/741-5740, ext. 275
Contact Personnel Director. A custom injection molder of termoplastics products.

INGRID DIVISION OF SEVKO, INC.
1419 Lake Cook Road
Suite 200
Deerfield IL 60015
708/940-8788
Contact Personnel. Manufacturer of plastic housewares and other plastic parts.

MIDWEST RUBBER RECLAIMING COMPANY
3101 Mississippi Avenue
Box 2349
East St. Louis IL 62202
618/337-6400
Contact Horace Drake, Personnel Director. A leading St. Louis company engaged in the manufacture of reclaimed rubber.

PANDUIT CORPORATION
17301 South Ridgeland Avenue
Tinley Park IL 60477
312/532-1800, ext. 1246
Contact Employment Department. Several area locations including: Tinley Park, New Lenox, Burr Ridge, Romeoville. Manufactures plastic wiring devices, mass-terminated connectors, terminals, and installation tools associated with these products. Multinational manufacturing facilities with sales and distribution offices in most major world capitals. Operations at this facility include: manufacturing; research/development; administration. Corporate headquarters location. International. Common positions include: Computer Programmer; Draftsperson; Mechanical Engineer; Systems Analyst; Sales Representative. Principal educational backgrounds sought: Business Administration; Computer Science; Engineering; Marketing. Company benefits include: medical insurance; dental insurance; pension plan; life insurance; tuition assistance; disability coverage; profit sharing; employee discounts; savings plan. Operations at this facility include: manufacturing; research/development; administration; service; sales.

PREMARK INTERNATIONAL
1717 Deerfield Road
Deerfield IL 60015
708/405-6000
Contact Pat Lloyd, Supervisor of Staffing. A holding company with several subsidiaries operating in the area of plastics manufacturing.

REPUBLIC MOLDING CORPORATION
6330 West Touhy Avenue
Chicago IL 60648
312/647-8977
Contact Michael Handzel, Vice President. Manufactures plastic housewares primarily through the process of injection molding. Corporate headquarters location.

W.H. SALISBURY & COMPANY
7520 North Long Avenue
Skokie IL 60077
312/679-6700
Contact Vice President. Several area locations. A manufacturer of molded, extruded and cut rubber products such as electrician's gloves.

SIGNAL PLASTICS
3445 North Kimball Avenue
Chicago IL 60618
312/267-3100
Contact Human Resources. Molds and manufactures plastic tail lights for cars. A division of T.L. Swint Industries, Inc. Common positions at this facility include: Accountant; Administrator; Blue-Collar Worker Supervisor; Buyer; Customer Service Representative; Draftsperson; Purchasing Agent; Quality Control Supervisor; Sales Representative. Principal educational backgrounds sought: Accounting; Business Administration; Engineering; Marketing. Company benefits include: medical insurance; life insurance; tuition assistance; disability coverage. Operations at this facility include: manufacturing; research/development; administration.

TRANSPORTATION

For more information on professional employment opportunities in the transportation industry, contact the following professional and trade organizations, as listed beginning on page 295:

AIR LINE EMPLOYEES ASSOCIATION
AIR TRANSPORT ASSOCIATION OF AMERICA
AIR TRANSPORT ASSOCIATION OF CHICAGO
AMERICAN INSTITUTE OF AERONAUTICS AND ASTRONAUTICS
AMERICAN TRUCKING ASSOCIATION
ASSOCIATION OF AMERICAN RAILROADS
ASSOCIATION OF AMERICAN RAILROADS/CHICAGO
AUTOMOTIVE SERVICE INDUSTRY ASSOCIATION
AUTOMOTIVE SERVICE ASSOCIATION
AUTOMOTIVE SERVICE ASSOCIATION/CHICAGO
AVIATION MAINTENANCE FOUNDATION
ILLINOIS TRUCKING ASSOCIATION
INSTITUTE OF TRANSPORTATION ENGINEERS
MARINE TECHNOLOGY SOCIETY
MOTOR VEHICLE MANUFACTURERS ASSOCIATION
NATIONAL AERONAUTIC ASSOCIATION OF USA
NATIONAL AUTOMOTIVE DEALERS ASSOCIATION
NATIONAL INSTITUTE FOR AUTOMOTIVE SERVICE EXCELLENCE
NATIONAL MARINE MANUFACTURERS ASSOCIATION
PROFESSIONAL AVIATION MAINTENANCE ASSOCIATION
SHIPBUILDERS COUNCIL OF AMERICA

ABF
2020 Albright Road
Montgomery IL 60538
708/896-4626
Contact Branch Manager. A common carrier trucking firm.

AIRCRAFT GEAR CORPORATION
6633 West 65th Street
Chicago IL 60638
708/594-2100 ext. 701
Contact Kenneth Zuncic, Personnel Manager. Manufacturer of aircraft gears, precision parts, rotors and gear boxes. Corporate headquarters location. Common positions include: Industrial Engineer. Principal educational backgrounds sought: Business Administration; Computer Science; Engineering; Finance; Marketing. Company benefits include: medical insurance; dental insurance; pension plan; life insurance; tuition assistance; disability coverage; profit sharing. Operations at this facility include: manufacturing; administration; sales.

ALLEN INDUSTRIES
Route 2
Herrin IL 62948
Contact Industrial Relations Manager. Suppliers of original equipment to the automotive industry.

ALLIED VAN LINES/
CORPORATE HEADQUARTERS
300 Park Plaza
Naperville IL 60563
708/717-3150
Contact Human Resource Department. The world's leading mover of families.

THE ALTON AND SOUTHERN RAILWAY COMPANY
1000 S. 22nd Street
East St. Louis IL 62207
618/482-3232
Contact F.E. Cooper, Superintendant. A major metropolitan St. Louis-based railroad. Employs over 400.

AMERICAN WARRANTY CORPORATION
7373 North Cicero
Lincolnwood IL 60646
708/677-4800
Contact Director of Human Resources. Provides services contracts for extended auto repair.

AMMCO TOOLS INC.
Wacker Park
North Chicago IL 60064
708/689-1111
Contact John Lauten, Personnel Manager. Manufacturer of automotive tools and equipment for brake service, engine repair and wheel alignment. Corporate headquarters location.

ATCHISON TOPEKA & SANTA FE RAILWAY
80 East Jackson Boulevard
Chicago IL 60604
312/347-2457
Contact L.G. Wright, Manager, EEO and Employment. One of the largest rail carriers in the U.S.

BELT RAILWAY CO. OF CHICAGO
6900 South Central Avenue
Chicago IL 60638
708/468-4112
Contact M.D. McCarthy, Personnel. A major railroad company, with sales office in Chicago.

BRINK'S, INC.
234 East 24th Street
Chicago IL 60616
312/567-7100
Contact Personnel Director. Transports money & valuables domestically & internationally.

BURTON SPRING
2441 West 48th Street
Chicago IL 60632
312/376-1200
Contact Sandy Thompson, Personnel Manager. A manufacturer of truck and trailer leaf springs.

CATERPILLAR TRACTOR COMPANY
P.O. Box 504
Joliet IL 60434
815/729-6250
Contact Employee Relations Manager. Designs, manufactures, and markets earthmoving equipment.

**CNW
CHICAGO NORTHWESTERN CORPORATION**
165 North Canal Street
Chicago IL 60606
312/559-7000
Contact Robert F. Ard, Vice President of Personnel. A major railroad company offering freight rail service.

CONTINENTAL AIR TRANSPORT
730 West Lake Street
Chicago IL 60606
312/454-7829
Contact Linda Hawkins, Personnel Director. Provides ground transporation for customers around Chicago and O'Hare Airport.

ECHLIN MANUFACTURING COMPANY
1600 North Industrial Drive
McHenry IL 60050
815/385-7000
Contact Tom Zimmerman, Employment Relations Manager. Supplier of aftermarket parts and supplies for motor vehicles.

**ELECTRO-MOTIVE DIVISION/
GENERAL MOTORS**
9301 West 55th Street
La Grange IL 60525
708/387-6428
Contact Salaried Employment. Manufacturer of diesel-electric locomotives for railroads.

ELGIN, JOLIET & EASTERN RAILWAY COMPANY
P.O. Box 88
Joliet IL 60434
815/740-6738
or 740-6760
Contact L.M. Frye, Assistant Dir./Personnel Administration. A common carrier freight line operating in IN & IL.

F&B MANUFACTURING CO.
5480 North Northwest Highway
Chicago IL 60630
312/774-6300
Contact Dan Powell, Personnel Director. Manufactures small auto parts and components.

FIRESTONE TIRE AND RUBBER COMPANY
NORTH CENTRAL REGION
361 Frontage Road
Suite 121
Burr Ridge IL 60521
Contact Robert Gilman, Personnel Manager. Operates a chain of retail tire outlets.

G.R. GROUP, INC.
P.O. Box 159
East St. Louis IL 62202
618/271-1866
Contact Doug Wood, Personnel Director. Wholesalers of transportation equipment and supplies. Employs over 100.

GARRETT GENERAL AVIATION
SERVICES DIVISION
P.O. Box 2177
Capital Airport
Springfield IL 62705
217/544-3431
Contact Jay Davis, Manager Human Resources. Provides a comprehensive group of services to the aircraft industry. Parent company, Allied Signal Corporation, serves a broad spectrum of industries through its more than 40 strategic businesses, which are grouped into three sectors: Aerospace; Automotive; and Engineered Materials. Allied Signal is one of the nation's largest industrial organizations, and has 115,000 employees in over 30 countries. Common positions include: Accountant; Administrator; Customer Service Representative; Operations/Production Manager; Personnel & Labor Relations Specialist; Purchasing Agent; Quality Control Supervisor; Blue-Collar Worker Supervisor; Computer Programmer; Department Manager; A&P Mechanics; Structural Sheet Metal Trim and Upholsters; Cabinet Makers. Principal educational backgrounds sought: Aviation Applied Sciences; Aviation Management; Aviation Maintenance; Accounting; Liberal Arts; Business Administration; Computer Science; Marketing. Company benefits include: medical, dental, and life insurance; pension plan; tuition assistance; disability coverage; profit sharing; savings plan; paid vacation. Corporate headquarters: Morristown, NJ. Parent company: Allied Signal Inc. New York Stock Exchange.

GATX CORPORATION
120 South Riverside Plaza
Chicago IL 60606
312/621-6200
Contact Maureen A. Kelly, Personnel Manager. Holding company engaged in the lease or sale of rail cars.

GE RAILCAR SERVICES CORPORATION
33 West Monroe
Chicago IL 60603
312/853-5000
Contact Julie Dreixler, Manager of Employment/Hourly Relations. Lease and repair of specialized types of railcars.

GOODYEAR TIRE AND RUBBER COMPANY
1501 Nicholas Boulevard
Elk Grove Village IL 60007
708/640-5000
Contact Personnel Department. One of the largest makers of tire and rubber products.

HENDRICKSON INTERNATIONAL
P.O. Box 249
Burr Ridge IL 60521-0249
312/986-2500
Contact Peter Quagliana, Director, Human Resources. A worldwide supplier of quality engineered products to the truck/automotive industry. Company designs, develops, and manufactures suspension systems, leaf springs, and heavy stampings primarily for heavy-duty trucks. Several area locations include: Chicago, Crest Hill, and Burr Ridge. Common positions at this facility include: Buyer; Draftperson; Industrial Engineer; Mechanical Engineer; Sales Representative. Principal educational backgrounds sought: Business Administration; Engineering; Mathematics; Industrial Technology. Internships offered. Company benfits include: medical, dental, and life insurance; pension plan; tuition assistance; disability coverage; savings plan (401 K). Corporate headquarters: Itasca, IL. Parent company: Boler Company. Operations at this facility include: research/development; administration.

ILLINOIS CENTRAL GULF RAILROAD COMPANY
233 North Michigan Avenue
Chicago IL 60601
312/819-7500
Contact Personnel. Corporate offices for a major midwestern railroad.

ITEL/PULLMAN
200 South Michigan Avenue
Chicago IL 60604
312/322-7070
Contact Diane Kreja, Personnel Manager. Works in railcar leasing, repair, and administration.

LAWSON PRODUCTS
1666 East Touhy Avenue
Des Plaines IL 60018
708/827-9666
Contact Hank Kvintus, V.P. of Human Resources. Distributors of automotive and industrial parts.

ROCKWELL GRAPHIC SYSTEMS
700 Oakmont Lane
Westmont IL 60559
708/850-5600
Contact Anson Cranmer, Personnel Director. Operations are conducted in four industry segments: Automotive (develops, manufactures, and markets various components for heavy-duty trucks, special purpose vehicles, light trucks and passenger cars); Aerospace (engaged in research, development, and manufacture of space systems and rocket engines, military and general aviation aircraft); Electronics (research, development, and manufacture of guidance controls, avionics, telecommunication, and micro-electronics systems and equipment); and General Industries (Energy Graphics, Textile and Power Tools divisions). International operations. Corporate headquarters location: Pittsburgh, PA. New York Stock Exchange.

SANTA FE SOUTHERN PACIFIC CORPORATION
224 South Michigan Avenue
Chicago IL 60604
312/786-6000
Contact Mr. Robert Edwards, Human Resources Director. Corporate office of the Atchinson, Topeka, and Santa Fe railway. The company is also involved in the exploration, development, production, and marketing of petroleum and natural resources.

SUNSTRAND
4949 Harrison Avenue
Rockford IL 61125
815/226-6000
Contact Phil Polgreen, Corporate V.P. of Personnel & Public Relations. Corporate office of an aeronautics and aviation equipment parts manufacturer. Designs and develops high-technology components for aerospace, aviation, power transmission, and fluid and heat transfer.

TERMINAL RAILROAD ASSOCIATION/ST. LOUIS
2016 Madison Avenue
Granite City IL 62040
314/231-5378
Contact Mr. R.P. Mathewson, Director Labor Relations/Personnel. Railroad terminal and switching operations.

THRALL CAR MANUFACTURING COMPANY
2521 South State Street
Chicago Heights IL 60411
708/757-5900
Contact Craig Dowden, Vice President, Human Resources. Manufactures railway freight cars. Common positions include: Accountant; Buyer; Computer Programmer; Draftsperson; Industrial Engineer; Mechanical Engineer; Personnel & Labor Relations Specialist; Purchasing Agent; Sales Representative. Principal educational backgrounds sought: Accounting; Computer Science; Engineering; Marketing. Company benefits include: medical, dental, and life insurance; pension plan; tuition assistance; disability coverage; profit sharing; savings plan Operations at this facility include: manufacturing.

UNITED AIRLINES
P.O. Box 66100
Chicago IL 60666
708/952-4000
Contact Professional Employment. Passenger and cargo air transportation company. Common positions include: Accountant; Attorney; Buyer; Computer Programmer; Customer Service Representative; Industrial Engineer; Financial Analyst; Marketing Specialist; Personnel & Labor Relations Specialist; Public Relations Worker; Purchasing Agent; Reporter/Editor; Systems Analyst; Technical Writer/Editor; Transportation & Traffic Specialist. Principal educational backgrounds sought: Accounting; Business Administration; Computer Science; Finance; Marketing. Company benefits include: medical, dental, and life insurance; pension plan; disability coverage; employee discounts. Corporate headquarters location. Parent company: UAL, Inc. Operations at this facility include: administration. New York Stock Exchange.

VAPOR CORPORATION
6420 West Howard Street
Niles IL 60648
312/631-9200
Contact Sandi Reid, Recruiting Coordinator. Manufacturers of railroad passenger car heating and air conditioning equipment, steam generators, electronic controls for transit rails, and railroad speed indicating/pacesetting controls. Corporate headquarters location.

UTILITIES

For more information on professional employment opportunities in the utilities industry, contact the following professional and trade organizations, as listed beginning on page 295:

AMERICAN WATER WORKS ASSOCIATION
AMERICAN WATER WORKS FOUNDATION/CHICAGO

CENTRAL ILLINOIS LIGHT COMPANY
300 Liberty Street
Peoria IL 61602
309/672-7961
Contact Lee Edwards, Employment Manager. An electric and gas utility serving the greater Peoria area. Common positions include: Accountant; Computer Programmer; Civil Engineer; Electrical Engineer; Industrial Engineer; Mechanical Engineer. Principal educational backgrounds sought: Accounting; Business Administration; Computer Science; Engineering. Training programs offered. Company benefits include: medical, dental, and life insurance; pension plan; tuition assistance; disability coverage; savings plan. Corporate headquarters location. Operations at this facility include: regional headquarters; divisional headquarters; administration; service; sales. New York Stock Exchange.

CENTRAL ILLINOIS PUBLIC SERVICE
607 East Adams Street
Springfield IL 62739
217/523-3600
Contact Jack Herron, Personnel Manager. An electric and gas utility company serving the Central and Southern Illinois area.

COMMONWEALTH EDISON COMPANY
One First National Plaza
P.O. Box 767
Chicago IL 60690
312/294-4489
Contact W.R. Wroblewski, Supervisor of Professional Placement. An investor-owned utility engaged in electricity.

ILLINOIS POWER
500 South 27th Street
Decator IL 62525
217/424-6817
Contact Robert Teel, Professional Recruiting Specialist. An electric utilities company servicing approximately 1/4 of the state of Illinois. Common positions include: Accountant; Chemist; Computer Programmer; Customer Service Representantive; Economist; Civil Engineer; Electrical Engineer; Mechnical Engineer; Marketing Specialist; Public Relations Specialist; Statistician. Principal educational backgrounds sought: Accounting; Business Administration; Chemistry; Communications; Computer Science; Economics; Engineering; Finance; Marketing. Company benefits include: medical, and life insurance; pension plan; tuition assistance; disability coverage; 401 K.

Corporate headquarters location. Operations at this facility include: administration; sales. New York Stock Exchange.

ILLINOIS POWER COMPANY
330 North 29th Street
East St. Louis IL 62205
618/874-1041
Contact Personnel Department. An electric and gas utility serving the East St. Louis region.

ILLINOIS POWER COMPANY
1050 West Boulevard
Belleville IL 62221
618/234-3400
Contact Personnel Department. An electric and gas utility servinig the Belleville region.

NICOR
1700 West Ferry Road
Naperville IL 60566
708/242-4470
Contact Jean Smolios, Senior Personnel Coordinator. A petroleum and natural gas distributor servicing Illinois.

NORTHERN ILLINOIS GAS COMPANY
P.O. Box 190
Aurora IL 60507-0190
312/983-8888
Contact Steve Webber, Management Recruiting Administrator. Multiple area locations including: Bellwood, Glen Ellyn, Glenwood, Glenview, Crystal Lake, Joliet, and Rockford. A gas supply company serving many communities in Northern Illinois. A subsidiary of NICOR, Inc. Common positions include: Accountant; Computer Programmer; Chemical, Civil, Petroleum, Industrial, and Mechanical Engineers; Sales Representative. Principal educational backgrounds sought: Accounting; Business Administration; Computer Science; Engineering; Marketing. Company benefits include: medical insurance; dental insurance; pension plan; life insurance; tuition assistance; disability coverage; savings plan. Corporate headquarters location: Naperville, FL. New York Stock Exchange.

PEOPLES GAS COMPANY
122 South Michigan Avenue
Chicago IL 60603
312/431-4000
Contact Mr. John Ibach, Personnel Director. A gas distributing company servicing the Chicago area.

Professional Employment Services

PERSONNEL AGENCIES AND TEMPORARY SERVICES

ACCORD INC.
1543 Westchester Boulevard
Westchester IL 60153
Contact Chester Dombrowski, Mechanical Manager, or John Fawcett, Electronic Manager. 708/345-7900. Employment agency. Founded 1981. Specializes in the areas of: Computer Hardware and Software; Engineering; Manufacturing; MIS/EDP; Technical and Scientific. Common positions filled include: Computer Programmer; Customer Service Representative; Draftsperson; EDP Specialist; Electrical Engineer; General Manager; Industrial Designer; Industrial Engineer; MIS Specialist; Mechanical Engineer; Quality Control Supervisor; Sales Representative; Software Engineer; Technical Writer/Editor; Technician. Company pays fee. Number of placements per year: 51-100.

ADVANTAGE PERSONNEL
1011 East State Street
Rockford IL 61104
815/964-2666. Temporary help service. Appointment requested. Founded 1954. A member of Victor Temporary Services. Victor Temporary Services has over 100 offices throughout the United States. Nonspecialized. Positions commonly filled include: Bookkeeper; Clerk; Computer Operator; Customer Service Representative; Data Entry Clerk; Demonstrator; Draftsperson; Electronic Assembler; Factory Worker; General Laborer; Legal Secretary; Light Industrial Worker; Medical Secretary; Office Worker; Receptionist; Secretary; Stenographer; Technician; Typist; Word Processing Specialist. Company pays fee. Number of placements per year: 1001+.

AMERICAN ASSOCIATION OF RETIRED PERSONS SENIOR COMMUNITY SERVICE EMPLOYMENT PROGRAM
Post Office Box 630
1210 North Main
Edwardsville IL 62025
Contact June M. Nealy, Project Director. 618/656-5710. Employment agency; temporary help agency. Appointment recommended. Founded 1974. This is a fee-free employment office sponsored by American Association of Retired Persons to serve persons 55 years of age and older; we offer subsidized employment for eligible persons (under low income) and help in finding permanent employment and vocational counselling to all over 55 years. Nonprofit. Nonspecialized. Positions commonly filled include: Bookkeeper; Clerk; Dietician/Nutritionist; Driver; General Laborer; Receptionist; Secretary; Typist. Placements per year: 51-100.

APT (ABLE'S POOL OF TEMPORARIES)
36 South Wabash, Suite 1133
Chicago IL 60603
Contact Gladys Wolff, Director. 312/726-0474. Temporary help service. Appointment requested. Founded 1982. Specializes in placing older workers aged 50 and over. Positions commonly filled include: Bookkeeper; Clerk; Data Entry Clerk; Legal Secretary; Office Worker; Receptionist; Secretary; Stenographer; Typist. Company pays fee.

E.J. ASHTON & ASSOCIATES, LTD
3125 N. Wilke Road, Suite A
Arlington Heights IL 60004
Contact Ed Ashton, President. 708/577-7900. Employment agency. Appointment required. Founded 1979. Recruiting in and for the Insurance and Financial Services industries with emphasis on Insurance professionals and Management. Specializes in the areas of: Accounting; Banking and Finance; Health and Medical; Insurance; Real Estate. Positions commonly filled include: Accountant; Actuary; Attorney; Claims Representative; Economist; Financial Analyst; Insurance Agent/Broker; Management Consultant; Marketing Specialist; Sales Representative; Statistician.Company pays fees. Number of placements per year: 51-100.

AVAILABILITY, INC.
659 A East Broadway
Alton IL 62002
Contact Lee J. Hamel, Manager. 618/462-8831. Employment agency; temporary help service. No appointment required. Founded 1964. Specializes in the areas of: Accounting and Finance; Banking; Clerical; Computer Hardware and Software; Engineering; MIS/EDP; Sales and Marketing; Technical and Scientific. Positions commonly filled include: Accountant; Administrative Assistant; Aerospace Engineer; Agricultural Engineer; Bank Officer/Manager; Biomedical Engineer; Bookkeeper; Ceramics Engineer; Chemical Engineer; Civil Engineer; Claim Representative; Clerk; Computer Operator; Computer Programmer; Credit Manager; Customer Service Representative; Data Entry Clerk; EDP Specialist; Electrical Engineer; Financial Analyst; General Manager; Industrial Engineer; Legal Secretary; MIS Specialist; Marketing Specialist; Mechanical Engineer; Medical Secretary; Metallurgical Engineer; Mining Engineer; Office Worker; Personnel and Labor Relations Specialist; Petroleum Engineer; Public Relations Worker; Purchasing Agent; Receptionist; Sales Representative; Secretary; Statistician; Stenographer; Systems Analyst; Technical Writer/Editor; Typist; Word Processing Specialist. Company pays fee; individual pays fee. Number of placements per year: 101-200.

B-W AND ASSOC., INC.
4415 W. Harrison
Hillside IL 60162
Contact Bill Wennlund, Owner. 708/449-5400. Employment agency. Appointment required. Founded 1973. The entrepreneurial spirit in today's search of Construction and Engineering personnel. Specializes in the areas of: Architecture; Construction; Engineering; Food Industry; Health and Medical; Manufacturing; Real Estate. Positions commonly filled include: Architect; Civil Engineer; Construction Manager; Electrical Engineer; Mechanical Engineer; Petroleum Engineer. Company pays fee. Number of placements per year: 51-100.

BRITT ASSOCIATES, INC.
53 West Jackson Boulevard
Chicago IL 606041
Contact William Lichtenaller, President. 312/427-9450. Employment agency. Appointment requested. Founded 1971. Member NAPC. Specializes in the areas of: Distribution; Inventory and Production Control; Materials Management; Transportation. Positions commonly filled include: Buyer; Inventory Controller; Production Controller; Purchasing Agent; Traffic Manager; Warehouse Manager. Company pays fee.

CAREER MANAGEMENT ASSOCIATES
262 North Phelps
Rockford IL 61108
Contact Brad Marion, Vice President. 815/229-7815. Employment agency. No appointment required. Founded 1971. Midwest division of national firm specializing in Health Care, Manufacturing and Financial services. Specializes in the areas of: Accounting; Banking and Finance; Computer Hardware and Software; Engineering; Health and Medical; Insurance; Manufacturing; MIS/EDP; Secretarial and Clerical. Positions commonly filled include: Accountant; Actuary; Administrative Assistant; Aerospace Engineer; Bank Officer/Manager; Bookkeeper; Claims Representative; Clerk; Computer Programmer; Credit Manager; Customer Service Rep; Data Entry Clerk; EDP Specialist; Electrical Engineer; Executive Secretary; Financial Analyst; General Manager; Hotel Manager; Industrial Engineer; Legal Secretary; Management Consultant; Marketing Specialist; Mechanical Engineer; Medical Secretary; Metallurgical Engineer; Nurse; Personnel Director; Purchasing Agent; Receptionist; Sales Representative; Secretary; Stenographer; Systems Analyst; Technical Writer/Editor; Typist; Underwriter; Word Processor. Company pays fee. Number of placements per year: 201-500.

CASEY FOR ACCOUNTANTS
632 West Algonquin Road, Suite 202
Des Plaines IL 60016
708/981-0200. Employment agency; temporary help agency. Appointment required. Founded 1975. Permanent and temporary Accounting, Finance and

DP. Specializes in the areas of: Accounting; Banking and Finance; Computer Hardware and Software; MIS/EDP. Positions commonly filled include: Accountant; Attorney; Bank Officer/Manager; Bookkeeper; Computer Programmer; Credit Manager; Data Entry Clerk; EDP Specialist; Financial Analyst; Personnel Director; Systems Analyst; Word Processor. Company pays fee. Number of placements per year: 201-500.

CEMCO SYSTEMS
2015 Spring Road, Suite 250
Oak Brook IL 60521
Contact David R. Gordon, General Manager. 708/573-5050. Employment agency. Appointment required. Founded 1974. Provides career counseling, resume assistance and "skills vs. salary" evaluation. Accurate representation to both applicant and client. Specializes in the areas of: Computer Hardware and Software; MIS/EDP. Positions commonly filled include: Computer Programmer; EDP Specialist. Company pays fee. Number of placements per year: 101-500.

CORRUGATED BOX CONSULTANTS
50 West 75th Street, Suite 101
Willowbrook IL 60514-2383
Contact Richard Dantzer, President. 708/325-2743. Employment agency. Appointment required. Founded 1979. Specializes in the area of: Corrugated Boxes. Positions commonly filled include: Accountant; Computer Programmer; Customer Service Rep; Electrical Engineer; General Manager; Industrial Designer; Industrial Engineer; Marketing Specialist; Middle Management Personnel; Personnel Director; Sales Representative; Supervisor. Company pays fee. Number of placements per year: 51-100.

CPU ASSOCIATES
1717 North Naper Boulevard
Suite 101
Naperville IL 60563
Contact L.A. Smith, President. 708/505-0082. Employment agency; temporary help agency. Appointment required. Founded 1982. CPU Assoc. has expanded into DP Temps to service client needs. Specializes in the areas of: Computer Hardware and Software; MIS/EDP. Positions commonly filled include: Computer Programmer; EDP Specialist; Marketing Specialist; Sales Representative; Systems Analyst. Company pays fee. Number of placements per year: 51-100.

CREATIVE OPTIONS, INC.
206 Whispering Hills
Naperville IL 60540
Contact Therese Paul, Owner. 708/717-9102. Employment agency. Specializes in projects and overflow work in the following areas: Clerical; Health and Medical; Insurance; Manufacturing; Sales and Marketing.

DICKEY & ASSOCIATES, INC.
Post Office Box 1598
Rockford IL 61110
Contact Ned Dickey, President. 815/968-1883. Employment agency. Founded 1965. Specializes in the areas of: Engineering; Manufacturing; Personnel/I.R. Positions commonly filled include: Accountant; Aerospace Engineer; Agricultural Engineer; Ceramics Engineer; Electrical Engineer; General Manager; Industrial Engineer; Marketing Specialist; Metallurgical Engineer; Personnel Director; Sales Representative; Purchasing Agent. Company pays fee. Number of placements per year: 0-50.

DUNHILL OF CHICAGO
230 North Michigan Avenue, 30th Floor
Chicago IL 60601
Contact George Baker, Owner. 312/346-0933. Employment agency. Founded 1967. Specializes in the areas of: Accounting and Finance; Banking; Computer Hardware and Software; Sales and Marketing. Positions commonly filled include: Accountant; Bank Officer/Manager; Computer Operator; Computer Programmer; Sales Representative.

DUNHILL OF NORTHSIDE CHICAGO
5701 North Sheridan Road
Chicago IL 60660
Contact Geoff Mayhew, President. 312/334-1600. Employment agency. Founded 1982. Specializes in the areas of: Computer Hardware and Software. Positions commonly filled include: Computer Operator; Computer Programmer; Systems Analyst.

DYNAMIC SEARCH SYSTEMS, INC.
3800 N. Wilke Road, Suite 485
Arlington Heights IL 60004
Contact Michael J. Brindise, Principal. 708/259-3444. Employment agency. Appointment required. Founded 1983. We provide Data Processing personnel to Chicago and suburban employers. Primary focus covers Applications Development, Technical services and Consulting. Positions commonly filled include: Computer Programmer; EDP Specialist; Systems Analyst. Company pays fee. Number of placements per year: 101-500.

EDP TEMPS AND CONTRACT SERVICES
2115 Butterfield Road
Oak Brook IL 60521
708/620-7171. Temporary help service. No appointment required. Founded 1976. Branch offices located in: California; Connecticut; Illinois; Maryland; Massachusetts; Michigan; New York; Ohio; Pennsylvania; Virginia. Specializes in the areas of: Accounting and Finance; Banking; Computer Hardware and Software; Engineering; Insurance; Manufacturing; MIS/EDP; Nonprofit; Personnel and Human Resources; Printing and Publishing; Technical and Scientific. Positions commonly filled include: Computer

Operator; Computer Programmer; EDP Specialist; MIS Specialist; Systems Analyst; Technical Writer/Editor. Company pays fee. Number of placements per year: 1001+.

ELITE PERSONNEL SERVICE, INC.
925 East Rand Road, Suite 202
Arlington Heights IL 60004
Contact Carolyn Reed, Business Manager and Consultant. 708/577-8820. Employment agency. No appointment required. Founded 1980. Specializes in the areas of: Clerical and Secretarial. Positions commonly filled include: Administrative Assistant; Bookkeeper; Clerk; Customer Service Representative; Data Entry Clerk; Legal Secretary; Medical Secretary; Office Worker; Receptionist; Secretary; Stenographer; Typist; Word Processing Specialist. Company pays fee.

ESQUIRE PERSONNEL SERVICES, INC.
222 S. Riverside Plaza, Suite 320
Chicago IL 60606
Contact Scott F. Fischer, Vice President. 312/648-4600; temp services: 312/715-1111. Employment agency; temporary help agency. Appointment required. Founded 1955. Specializes in the areas of: Accounting; Advertising; Banking and Finance; Health and Medical; Insurance; Legal; Sales and Marketing; Secretarial and Clerical. Positions commonly filled include: Accountant; Actuary; Administrative Assistant; Advertising Executive; Attorney; Bank Officer/Manager; Claims Representative; Clerk; Computer Programmer; Credit Manager; Customer Service Rep; Data Entry Clerk; EDP Specialist; Executive Secretary; Financial Analyst; Insurance Agent/Broker; Legal Secretary; Marketing Specialist; Medical Secretary; Personnel Director; Public Relations Worker; Purchasing Agent; Receptionist; Sales Representative; Secretary; Statistician; Stenographer; Systems Analyst; Technical Writer/Editor; Typist; Underwriter; Word Processor. Company pays fee. Number of placements per year: 201-500.

FARDIG ASSOCIATES
176 W. Adams, Suite 1611
Chicago IL 60603
Contact Maria Ferry, Vice President. 312/332-1480. Employment agency. Appointment required. Founded 1969. Specializes in the areas of: Accounting; Banking and Finance; Insurance; Legal; Manufacturing; Sales and Marketing; Secretarial and Clerical. Positions commonly filled include: Accountant; Administrative Assistant; Bookkeeper; Clerk; Customer Service Rep; Data Entry Clerk; Executive Secretary; Legal Secretary; Marketing Specialist; Receptionist; Sales Representative; Secretary; Typist; Word Processor. Company pays fee. Number of placements per year: 51-100.

GENERAL EMPLOYMENT ENTERPRISES INC.
2200 E. Devon Avenue, Suite 246
Des Plaines IL 60018
Contact Steve Leibovitz, Agency Manager. 708/299-1233. Employment agency. No appointment required. Founded 1893. GEE owns and operates 28 branches throughout the U.S. and Canada. "Service Second to None." Specializes in the areas of: Computer Hardware and Software; Engineering; MIS/EDP; Technical and Scientific. Positions commonly filled include: Biomedical Engineer; Computer Programmer; EDP Specialist; Electrical Engineer; Mechanical Engineer; Systems Analyst; Technical Writer/Editor; Technician. Company pays fees. Number of placements per year: 201-500.

GODFREY PERSONNEL INC.
300 W. Adams, Suite 612
Chicago IL 60606
Contact James Godfrey, President. 312/236-4455 Employment agency. Appointment required. Founded 1950. To be the leader in Chicago area with placements in the Insurance industry. Positions commonly filled include: Actuary; Claims Representative; General Manager; Insurance Agent/Broker; Secretary; Typist; Underwriter; Word Processor. Company pays fee. Number of placements per year: 201-500.

GROVE PERSONNEL SERVICES
1411 Opus Place, Suite 118
Downers Grove IL 60515
Contact Raejean Fellows C.P.C., President. 708/399-2000. Employment agency; temporary help agency. Appointment required. Founded 1979. A progressive personnel agency specializing in permanent and temporary placement of Office professionals and entry to mid-level management. Specializes in the areas of: Banking and Finance; Insurance; Sales and Marketing; Secretarial and Clerical. Positions commonly filled include: Accountant; Actuary; Administrative Assistant; Bank Officer/Manager; Bookkeeper; Claims Representative; Customer Service Rep; Data Entry Clerk; EDP Specialist; Executive Secretary; Legal Secretary; Marketing Specialist; Medical Secretary; Personnel Director; Receptionist; Sales Representative; Secretary. Company pays fee. Number of placements per year: 201-500.

HILTON RESEARCH ASSOCIATES-MID WEST
1920 Highland Avenue, Suite 300
Lombard IL 60148
708/916-3124. Employment agency. Appointment requested. Founded 1979. Specializes in the areas of: Health and Medical; MIS/EDP; Sales and Marketing. Positions commonly filled include: Biochemist; Biomedical Engineer; Chemist; Computer Programmer; Customer Service Representative; MIS Specialist; Marketing Specialist; Nurse; Sales Representative. Company pays fee. Number of placements per year: 201-500

J.C.G. LIMITED, INC.
2300 E. Higgins Road
Elk Grove Village IL 60007
Contact James Greene, President. 708/439-1400. Employment agency. Appointment required. Founded 1970. Specializes in the areas of: Engineering; Manufacturing; Transportation. Positions commonly filled include: Accountant; Bank Officer/Manager; Bookkeeper; Civil Engineer; Credit Manager; Draftsperson; Electrical Engineer; Executive Secretary; Insurance Agent/Broker; Marketing Specialist; Mechanical Engineer; Medical Secretary; Physicist; Receptionist; Sales Representative; Secretary; Systems Analyst; Technical Writer/Editor; Underwriter. Company pays fee. Number of placements per year: 51-100.

KINGSLEY EMPLOYMENT
208 South LaSalle Street, Suite 1877
Chicago IL 60604
Contact Edward Friedman, Owner. 312/726-8190. Employment agency. No appointment required. Founded 1968. Specializes in: Advertising; Banking. Positions commonly filled include: Administrative Assistant; Advertising Worker; Financial Analyst; Office Worker; Receptionist; Secretary; Stenographer; Typist; Word Processing Specialist. Company pays fee. Number of placements per year: 51-100.

MACINTYRE EMPLOYMENT SERVICES, LTD.
830 E. Rand Road, Unit #9
Mt. Prospect IL 60056
Contact Elizabeth E. MacIntyre, President. 708/577-8860. Employment agency. No appointment required. Founded 1980. Specializes in the areas of: Accounting; Advertising; Architecture; Computer Hardware and Software; Construction; Engineering; Health and Medical; Manufacturing; MIS/EDP; Printing and Publishing; Sales and Marketing; Secretarial and Clerical; Technical and Scientific; Transportation. Company pays fee.

MICHAEL DAVID ASSOCIATES, INC.
133 East Ogden Avenue, Room 202
Hinsdale IL 60521
Contact Director, Administrative Services. 708/654-4460. Employment agency. Appointment requested. Founded 1982. Specializes in the areas of: Accounting and Finance; Clerical; Computer Hardware and Software; Engineering; Food Industry; Health and Medical; Insurance; Legal; Manufacturing; Personnel and Human Resources; Sales and Marketing; Technical and Scientific. Company pays fee. Number of placements per year: 201-500.

THE MURPHY GROUP
122B Calender Court Mall
La Grange IL 60525
Contact Susan M. Oja, Owner/Manager. 708/352-8350. Employment agency. No appointment required. Founded 1957. Nonspecialized. Positions commonly filled include: Accountant; Actuary; Administrative Assistant; Advertising Worker; Bank Officer/Manager; Bookkeeper; Buyer; Civil Engineer; Claim Representative; Clerk; Computer Operator; Computer Programmer; Credit Manager; Customer Service Representative; Data Entry Clerk; Demonstrator; Draftsperson; Driver; EDP Specialist; Economist; Electrical Engineer; Financial Analyst; General Manager; Industrial Designer; Industrial Engineer; Insurance Agent/Broker; Legal Secretary; MIS Specialist; Marketing Specialist; Mechanical Engineer; Medical Secretary; Metallurgical Engineer; Office Worker; Operations/Production Specialist; Personnel and Labor Relations Specialist; Public Relations Worker; Purchasing Agent; Quality Control Supervisor; Receptionist; Reporter/Editor; Sales Representative; Secretary; Statistician; Stenographer; Systems Analyst; Technical Writer/Editor; Technician; Typist; Underwriter; Word Processing Specialist. Company pays fee. Number of placements per year: 101-200.

THE MURPHY GROUP
555 E. Butterfield, Suite 207
Lombard IL 60148
Contact Dee Comstock, Owner. 708/960-1898. Employment agency. Appointment required. Nonspecialized. Positions commonly filled include: Accountant; Actuary; Advertising Executive; Aerospace Engineer; Agricultural Engineer; Architect; Bank Officer/Manager; Biochemist/Chemist; Biologist; Biomedical Engineer; Bookkeeper; Ceramics Engineer; Civil Engineer; Claims Representative; Clerk; Commercial Artist; Computer Programmer; Credit Manager; Customer Service Rep; Data Entry Clerk; Dietician/Nutritionist; Draftsperson; EDP Specialist; Economist; Electrical Engineer; Executive Secretary; Financial Analyst; General Manager; Hotel Manager; Industrial Designer; Industrial Engineer; Insurance Agent/Broker; Interior Designer; Legal Secretary; Management Consultant; Marketing Specialist; Mechanical Engineer; Medical Secretary; Metallurgical Engineer; Mining Engineer; Personnel Director; Petroleum Engineer; Physicist; Public Relations Worker; Purchasing Agent; Receptionist; Reporter/Editor; Sales Representative; Secretary; Statistician; Stenographer; Systems Analyst; Technical Writer/Editor; Technician; Typist; Underwriter. Company pays fee. Number of placements per year: 201-500.

THE MURPHY GROUP
1211 West 22, Suite 200
Oak Brook IL 60521
Contact William A. Murphy II, Vice President/General Manager. 708/574-2840. Employment agency; temporary help agency. Founded 1957. A regional network of personnel consultants, the only one in existence. A multiple listing

of job orders and candidates. Specializes in the areas of: Accounting; Advertising; Banking and Finance; Computer Hardware and Software; Engineering; Food Industry; Insurance; Manufacturing; MIS/EDP; Printing and Publishing; Sales and Marketing; Secretarial and Clerical; Technical and Scientific. Positions commonly filled include: Accountant; Administrative Assistant; Advertising Executive; Bookkeeper; Civil Engineer; Claims Representative; Clerk; Computer Programmer; Credit Manager; Customer Service Representative; Data Entry Clerk; Draftsperson; EDP Specialist; Electrical Engineer; Executive Secretary; Financial Analyst; General Manager; Industrial Engineer; Legal Secretary; Marketing Specialist; Mechanical Engineer; Medical Secretary; Personnel Director; Purchasing Agent; Receptionist; Sales Representative; Secretary; Stenographer; Systems Analyst; Technician; Typist; Underwriter; Word Processor. Company pays fee. Number of placements per year: 1000+

**OPERATION ABLE/
ABLE WORKER INSTITUTE**
36 South Wabash
Chicago IL 60603
312/580-0390. Individual job search assistance and outplacement counseling. Appointment requested. Founded 1977. Specializes in the areas of: Clerical; Elderly; Minorities; Nonprofit; Sales and Marketing; Technical and Scientific; Women. Positions commonly filled include: Accountant; Administrative Assistant; Advertising Worker; Bookkeeper; Chemical Engineer; Chemist; Claim Representative; Clerk; Computer Programmer; Data Entry Clerk; Demonstrator; Draftsperson; Electrical Engineer; Factory Worker; Financial Analyst; Food Technologist; General Laborer; General Manager; Hotel Manager/Assistant Manager; Industrial Engineer; Insurance Agent/Broker; Light Industrial Worker; Marketing Specialist; Mechanical Engineer; Nurse; Office Worker; Operations and Production Specialist; Purchasing Agent; Quality Control Supervisor; Receptionist; Sales Representative; Secretary; Stenographer; Systems Analyst; Typist. Individual pays fee.

**OPERATION ABLE/
OAK PARK TOWNSHIP SENIOR EMPLOYMENT CENTER**
500 South Maple
Oak Park IL 60304
708/386-6445. Employment agency. Appointment requested. Founded 1980. Specializes in the areas of: Elderly; Nonprofit. Positions commonly filled include: Administrative Assistant; Babysitter; Bookkeeper; Clerk; Companion; Customer Service Representative; Demonstrator; Driver; General Laborer; Handyman; Housekeeper; Janitor/Custodian; Light Industrial Worker; Maintenance Worker; Messenger; Office Worker; Receptionist; Sales Representative; Secretary; Typist. Number of placements per year: 501-1000.

OPPORTUNITY PERSONNEL SERVICE
200 West Adams
Chicago IL 60606
Contact Gwen Hudson, President; Marian Long, Executive Director; Charlene Langford, Consultant; or John Drykacz, Consultant. 312/704-9898. Employment agency. Appointment requested. Founded 1955. Specializes in the areas of: Accounting and Finance; Clerical; Computer Hardware and Software; Insurance; Legal; Manufacturing; Personnel and Human Resources; Sales and Marketing. Positions commonly filled include: Accountant; Actuary; Administrative Assistant; Bank Officer/Manager; Bookkeeper; Buyer; Claim Representative; Clerk; Computer Operator; Credit Manager; Customer Service Representative; Data Entry Clerk; Financial Analyst; General Manager; Hotel Manager/Assistant Manager; Legal Secretary; Office Worker; Purchasing Agent; Receptionist; Sales Representative; Secretary; Stenographer; Typist; Underwriter; Word Processing Specialist. Company pays fee; individual pays fee.

PAIGE PERSONNEL/PAIGE TEMPORARY
5215 Old Orchard Road, Suite 940
Skokie IL 60077
708/966-0700. Employment agency; temporary help service. No appointment required. Founded 1964. Specializes in the area of: Clerical. Positions commonly filled include: Administrative Assistant; Bookkeeper; Clerk; Computer Operator; Customer Service Representative; Data Entry Clerk; Legal Secretary; Medical Secretary; Office Worker; Personnel and Labor Relations Specialist; Public Relations Worker; Purchasing Agent; Receptionist; Secretary; Stenographer; Typist; Word Processing Specialist. Company pays fee. Number of placements per year: 501-1000.

PERMANENT PEOPLE, INC.
7900 N. Milwaukee Avenue
Niles IL 60648
Contact Miriam Walchirk, Manager. 708/966-1220. Employment agency. Appointment required. Specializes in the areas of: Secretarial and Clerical. Positions commonly filled include: Customer Service Rep; Executive Secretary; Legal Secretary; Medical Secretary; Personnel Director; Receptionist; Secretary; Typist; Word Processor. Company pays fee. Number of placements per year: 51-100.

POLLAK AND SKAN, INC.
120 W. Center Court
Schaumburg IL 60193
Contact Central Recruiting. 708/359-5227. Temporary help agency. No appointment required. Founded 1951. Pollak and Skan is a diversified contract technical services company serving a wide range of technologies for over 30 years. We are a charter member of the National Technical Services Assoc. and practice its code of ethics. Specializes in the areas of: Computer Hardware and Software; Engineering; Industrial and Interior Design;

Manufacturing; MIS/EDP; Technical and Scientific. Positions commonly filled include: Aerospace Engineer; Agricultural Engineer; Biochemist/Chemist; Biomedical Engineer; Ceramics Engineer; Civil Engineer; Computer programmer; Draftsperson; EDP Specialist; Electrical Engineer; Industrial Designer; Industrial Engineer; Mechanical Engineer; Metallurgical Engineer; Mining Engineer; Petroleum Engineer; Systems Analyst; Technical Writer/Editor; Technician.

PRESTIGE PERSONNEL
2066 Ridge Road
Homewood IL 60430
Contact Estelle Harris, Vice President/Manager. 219/931-1338 or 708/798-9010. Employment agency. Appointment preferred. Founded 1964. Nonspecialized. Positions commonly filled include: Accountant; Administrative Assistant; Aerospace Engineer; Agricultural Engineer; Attorney; Bank Officer/Manager; Biochemist/Chemist; Biologist; Biomedical Engineer; Bookkeeper; Ceramics Engineer; Civil Engineer; Claims Representative; Clerk; Computer Programmer; Credit Manager; Customer Service Rep; Data Entry Clerk; Industrial Designer; Draftsperson; EDP Specialist; Economist; Electrical Engineer; Executive Secretary; Factory Worker; Financial Analyst; General Manager; Hotel Manager; Industrial Engineer; Insurance Agent/Broker; Legal Secretary; Management Consultant; Marketing Specialist; Mechanical Engineer; Medical Secretary; Metallurgical Engineer; Mining Engineer; Personnel Director; Petroleum Engineer; Physicist; Public Relations Worker; Purchasing Agent Receptionist; Sales Representative; Secretary; Statistician; Stenographer; Systems Analyst; Technical Writer/Editor; Technician; Typist; Underwriter; Word Processor. Company pays fee. Number of placements per year: 100-201.

PRESTIGE TEMPORARIES-CALUMET DIVISION
2066 Ridge Road
Homewood IL 60430
Contact Estelle Harris, Vice President/Manager. 219/931-1171 or 708/798-7666. Temporary help agency. Appointment preferred. Founded 1976. Specializes in the areas of: Secretarial and Clerical. Positions commonly filled include: Accountant; Administrative Assistant; Bookkeeper; Clerk; Computer Programmer; Construction Worker; Customer Service Rep; Data Entry Clerk; Executive Secretary; Factory Worker; General Laborer; Legal Secretary; Light Industrial Worker; Marketing Specialist; Medical Secretary; Receptionist; Secretary; Stenographer; Typist; Word Processor. Company pays fee. Number of placements per year: 1000+.

PRESTIGE TEMPORARIES-HOMEWOOD DIVISION
2066 Ridge Road
Homewood IL 60430
Contact Estelle Harris, Vice President/Manager. 708/798-4490. Temporary help agency. Appointment prefered. Founded 1976. Specializes in the areas

of: Accounting; Advertising; Construction; Health and Medical; Legal; Manufacturing; MIS/EDP; Real Estate; Sales and Marketing; Secretarial and Clerical; Transportation. Positions commonly filled include: Administrative Assistant; Bank Officer/Manager; Bookkeeper; Civil Engineer; Claims Representative; Commercial Artist; Computer Programmer; Credit Manager; Customer Service Rep; Data Entry Clerk; Draftsperson; Executive Secretary; Financial Analyst; Industrial Designer; Legal Secretary; Light Industrial Worker; Mechanical Engineer; Medical Secretary; Public Relations Worker; Purchasing Agent; Receptionist; Sales Representative; Secretary; Stenographer; Systems Analyst; Technical Writer/Editor; Technician; Typist; Word Processor. Company pays fee. Number of placements per year: 100+.

PROFILE PERSONNEL, INC.
55 West Wacker Drive, Suite 400
Chicago IL 60601
Contact David Hodge, Operations Manager. 312/641-0540. Employment agency. Appointment preferred. Founded 1969. Specializes in the areas of: Advertising; Banking; Bilingual; Clerical; Insurance; Legal; Manufacturing; Personnel and Human Resources; Real Estate; Sales and Marketing; Secretarial. Positions commonly filled include: Actuary; Administrative Assistant; Bank Teller; Bookkeeper; Claim Representative; Clerk; Computer Operator; Customer Service Representative; Data Entry Clerk; Insurance Agent/Broker; Legal Secretary; Medical Secretary; Office Worker; Public Relations Worker; Receptionist; Sales Representative; Secretary; Stenographer; Typist; Underwriter; Word Processing Specialist. Company pays fee. Number of placements per year: 1001+.

PROFILE TEMPORARY SERVICE, INC.
55 West Wacker Drive, Suite 400
Chicago IL 60601
Contact Cheryl L. Davis, C.P.C., Executive Director. 312/641-1920. Temporary help service. Appointment preferred. Founded 1979. Specializes in the areas of: Accounting and Finance; Advertising; Banking; Clerical; Insurance; Legal; Manufacturing; Real Estate. Positions commonly filled include: Accountant; Administrative Assistant; Advertising Worker; Bookkeeper; Claim Representative; Clerk; Customer Service Representative; Data Entry Clerk; Demonstrator; Legal Secretary; Light Industrial Worker; Model; Office Worker; Receptionist; Secretary; Statistician; Stenographer; Typist; Word Processing Specialist. Company pays fee. Number of placements per year: 1001+.

RICHARD ALLEN WINTER ASSOC. INC.
2275 Half Day Road
Bannockburn IL 60015
708/948-8222. Recruiting agency. Appointment required. Founded 1961. Nonspecialized. Positions commonly filled include: Accountant; Actuary; Advertising Executive; Aerospace Engineer; Agricultural Engineer;

Architect; Attorney; Bank Officer/Manager; Biochemist/Chemist; Biologist; Biomedical Engineer; Bookkeeper; Ceramics Engineer; Civil Engineer; Claims Representative; Commercial Artist; Computer Programmer; Credit Manager; Customer Service Rep; Industrial Designer; Dietician/Nutritionist; EDP Specialist; Economist; Electrical Engineer; Financial Analyst; General Manager; Hotel Manager; Industrial Engineer; Management Consultant; Marketing Specialist; Mechanical Engineer; Metallurgical Engineer; Mining Engineer; Personnel Director; Petroleum Engineer; Phyicist; Public Relations Worker; Purchasing Agent; Reporter/Editor; Sales Representative; Statistician; Systems Analyst; Technical Writer/Editor; Underwriter. Number of placements per year: 51-100.

RITT - RITT AND ASSOCIATES
1400 E. Touhy Avenue
Des Plaines IL 60018
Contact Art Ritt, President. 708/298-2510. Employment agency. Appointment required. Founded 1976. One of the largest independant executive placement firms in the country specializing in Hospitality. All account executives have previous experience working in the Food and Hospitality industries in top positions. "We speak the language." Highly professional and recognized as one of the best companies to work with. Positions commonly filled include: Accountant; Advertising Executive; Architect; Dietician/Nutritionist; Economist; Food and Hospitality Specialist; General Manager; Hotel Manager; Marketing Specialist; Purchasing Agent. Company pays fee. Number of placements per year: 201-500.

SALEM TECHNICAL SERVICES OF OAK BROOK
1333 Butterfield Road
Downers Grove IL 60515
Contact Barry Jones, Manager. 800/323-7200. Temporary help service. No appointment required. Founded 1967. Branch offices located in: Atlanta, GA; Austin, TX; Beloit, WI; Bloomington, MN; Burlington, MA; Charlotte, NC; Cincinnati, OH; Cleveland, OH; Dallas, TX; Grand Rapids, MI; McLean, VA; Houston, TX; Milwaukee, WI; Phoenix, AZ; San Jose, CA; Golden, CO; San Jose, CA. Specializes in the areas of: Architecture; Computer Hardware and Software; Engineering; Manufacturing; MIS/EDP; Personnel and Human Resources; Technical and Scientific. Positions commonly filled include: Aerospace Engineer; Architect; Buyer; Chemical Engineer; Chemist; Civil Engineer; Commercial Artist; Computer Operator; Computer Programmer; Data Entry Clerk; Draftsperson; Driver; EDP Specialist; Electrical Engineer; Industrial Designer; Industrial Engineer; MIS Specialist; Manufacturing Engineer; Mechanical Engineer; Metallurgical Engineer; Operations and Production Specialist; Personnel and Labor Relations Specialist; Purchasing Agent; Quality Control Supervisor; Reporter/Editor; Software Engineer; Systems Analyst; Technical Illustrator; Technical Recruiter; Technical Writer/Editor; Technician; Word Processing Specialist. Number of placements per year: 201-500.

SEARCH DYNAMICS INC.
9420 West Foster Avenue, Suite 200
Chicago IL 60656
Contact J. C. Pappas, President. 312/992-3900. Employment agency. Appointment requested. Founded 1979. Specializes in the areas of: Computer Hardware and Software; Engineering; Manufacturing; Technical and Scientific. Positions commonly filled include: Aerospace Engineer; Agricultural Engineer; Architect; Biomedical Engineer; Ceramics Engineer; Chemical Engineer; Civil Engineer; Draftsperson; Electrical Engineer; General Manager; Industrial Engineer; Marketing Specialist; Mechanical Engineer; Metallurgical Engineer; Mining Engineer; Petroleum Engineer; Physicist; Quality Control Supervisor. Company pays fee. Number of placements per year: 101-200.

SELECTABILITY PERSONNEL
1011 East State Street
Rockford IL 61104
815/964-0078. Temporary help service. Appointment requested. Founded 1954. A member of Victor Temporary Services. Victor Temporary Services has over 100 offices throughout the United States. Nonspecialized. Positions commonly filled include: Bookkeeper; Clerk; Computer Operator; Customer Service Representative; Data Entry Clerk; Demonstrator; Draftsperson; Electronic Assembler; Factory Worker; General Laborer; Legal Secretary; Light Industrial Worker; Medical Secretary; Office Worker; Receptionist; Secretary; Stenographer; Technician; Typist; Word Processing Specialist. Company pays fee. Number of placements per year: 1001+.

SEVILLE TEMPORARY SERVICES
180 N. Michigan Avenue, Suite 707
Chicago IL 60601
Contact Sue Sterling. 312/368-1144. Temporary help agency. Appointment required. Founded 1979. Specializes in the areas of: Accounting; Clerical; Secretarial. Positions commonly filled include: Accountant; Bookkeeper; Data Entry Clerk; Executive Secretary; Legal Secretary; Medical Secretary; Receptionist; Secretary; Stenographer; Typist; Word Processor. Company pays fee.

SHEETS EMPLOYMENT SERVICE, INC.
Four West Miner Street
Arlington Heights IL 60004
Contact Glenn E. Sheets, President. 708/392-6100. Employment agency. Appointment required. Specializes in the areas of: Accounting; Manufacturing; Secretarial and Clerical. Positions commonly filled include: Accountant; Administrative Assistant; Bookkeeper; Clerk; Computer Programmer; Credit Manager; Customer Service Rep; Data Entry Clerk; Draftsperson; EDP Specialist; Executive Secretary; Legal Secretary; Personnel Director; Purchasing Agent; Secretary; Stenographer; Typist;

Underwriter; Typist; Word Processor. Company pays fee. Number of placements per year: 201-500.

SNELLING AND SNELLING OF DES PLAINES
999 East Touhy Avenue, Suite 160
Des Plaines IL 60018
Contact Tom Malloy, President. 708/296-1026. Employment agency. Appointment requested. Founded 1974. Specializes in the areas of: Clerical; Food Industry; Sales and Marketing. Positions commonly filled include: Accountant; Clerk; Credit Manager; Customter Service Representative; Data Entry Clerk; General Manager; Office Worker; Receptionist; Sales Representative; Secretary; Stenographer. Company pays fee. Number of placements per year: 101-200.

SNELLING AND SNELLING OF ROLLING MEADOWS
5105 Tollview Drive, Suite 120
Rolling Meadows IL 60008
Contact James Salerno, Manager. 708/255-2770. Employment agency. No appointment required. Founded 1979. Specializes in the areas of: Banking; Clerical; Food Industry; Sales and Marketing. Positions commonly filled include: Accountant; Bookkeeper; Clerk; Legal Secretary; Office Worker; Receptionist; Sales Representative; Secretary; Typist. Company pays fee. Number of placements per year: 51-100.

STAFF BUILDERS INC. OF ILLINOIS
185 North Wabash Street, Suite 1515
Chicago IL 60601
312/263-0834. Temporary help service. Appointment requested. Founded 1961. Branch offices located in: Arizona; California; Connecticut; District of Columbia; Florida; Georgia; Illinois; Indiana; Kansas; Louisiana; Maryland; Massachusetts; Michigan; Minnesota; Missouri; Nevada; New Jersey; New Mexico; New York; Ohio; Oklahoma; Oregon; Pennsylvania; Rhode Island; Tennessee; Texas; Virginia; Washington. Nonspecialized. Positions commonly filled include: Accountant; Administrative Assistant; Bookkeeper; Clerk; Companion; Computer Operator;Computer Programmer; Customer Service Representative; Data Entry Clerk; Demonstrator; Draftsperson; Driver; EDP Specialist; Factory Worker; General Laborer; Health Aide; Legal Secretary; Light Industrial Worker; Medical Secretary; Nurse; Office Worker; Public Relations Worker; Receptionist; Sales Representative; Secretary; Stenographer; Technician; Typist; Word Processing Specialist. Company pays fee. Number of placements per year: 1001+.

STIVERS TEMPORARY PERSONNEL, INC.
1225 Corporate Boulevard, Suite 200
Aurora IL 60504
708/851-9330. Temporary help service. Appointment requested. Founded 1945. Specializes in the areas of: Accounting and Finance; Banking; Clerical; Engineering; Health and Medical; Insurance; Legal; Manufacturing; MIS and

EDP; Personnel and Human Resources; Real Estate; Transportation. Positions commonly filled include: Administrative Assistant; Bookkeeper; Claim Representative; Clerk; Customer Service Representative; Data Entry Clerk; EDP Specialist; Legal Secretary; Medical Secretary; Office Worker; Receptionist; Secretary; Stenographer; Systems Analyst; Typist; Underwriter; Word Processing Specialist.

STONE ENTERPRISES, LTD
405 North Wabash Street
Chicago IL 60611
Contact Susan L. Stone, President. 312/836-0470. Employment agency and executive search firm. Appointment requested. Founded 1980. Specializes in the areas of: Accounting and Finance; Advertising; Banking; Clerical; Legal; Personnel and Human Resources. Positions commonly filled include: Accountant; Actuary; Administrative Assistant; Advertising Worker; Attorney; Bookkeeper; Claim Representative; Clerk; Computer Operator; Computer Programmer; Credit Manager; Customer Service Representative; Financial Analyst; Hotel Manager and Assistant Manager; Insurance Agent and Broker; Legal Secretary; MIS Specialist; Marketing Specialist; Medical Secretary; Office Worker; Purchasing Agent; QC Supervisor; Receptionist; Sales Representative; Secretary; Stenographer; Systems Analyst; Typist; Underwriter; Word Processing Specialist. Company pays fee. Number of placements per year: 201-500.

SYSTEMS RESEARCH INC.
600 Woodfield Drive, Suite 1075
Schaumburg IL 60173
Contact Bonnie Albrecht, Administrative Assistant. 708/330-1222. Employment agency. Appointment requested. Founded 1969. Specializes in the areas of: Engineering; Manufacturing; Technical and Scientific. Positions commonly filled include: Aerospace Engineer; Agricultural Engineer; Biomedical Engineer; Ceramics Engineer; Chemical Engineer; Draftsperson; Electrical Engineer; Industrial Designer; Industrial Engineer; Marketing Specialist; Mechanical Engineer; Metallurgical Engineer; Mining Engineer; Petroleum Engineer; Operations/Production Specialist; Purchasing Agent; Quality Control Supervisor; Systems Analyst; Technical Writer/Editor; Technician. Company pays fee. Number of placements per year: 201-500.

TALENT TREE OF ILLINOIS
2 North LaSalle, Suite 950
Chicago IL 60602
Contact Lee Nidetz, Vice President. 312/855-1390. Employment agency. No appointment required. Founded 1964. Specializes in the area of: Clerical. Positions commonly filled include: Administrative Assistant; Bookkeeper; Clerk; Customer Service Representative; Data Entry Clerk; Demonstrator; Legal Secretary; Medical Secretary; Office Worker; Personnel and Labor Relations Specialist; Receptionist; Secretary; Stenographer; Typist; Word Processing Specialist. Company pays fee.

TEMP FORCE OF ILLINOIS
345 West Prairie Street, Suite 10
Decatur IL 62522
Contact Deanna Dowling, Manager. 217/429-7147. Temporary help service. No appointment required. Founded 1965. Branch offices located in: Alabama; Arkansas; California; Colorado; Connecticut; Florida; Illinois; Indiana; Kansas; Maryland; Massachusetts; Michigan; Mississippi; Nevada; New Jersey; New Mexico; New York; Ohio; Oklahoma; Pennsylvania; Tennessee; Utah; Vermont; Virginia. Nonspecialized. Positions commonly filled include: Accountant; Bookkeeper; Clerk; Computer Operator; Computer Programmer; Customer Service Representative; Data Entry Clerk; Demonstrator; Driver; Factory Worker; General Laborer; Legal Secretary; Light Industrial Worker; Medical Secretary; Office Worker; Purchasing Agent; Receptionist; Secretary; Statistician; Stenographer; Typist; Word Processing Specialist.

TEMP FORCE OF ILLINOIS
10251 Lincoln Trail
Fairview Heights IL 62208
Contact Jan Lawrence, Manager. 618/398-0650. Temporary help service. No appointment required. Founded 1965. Branch offices located in: Alabama; Arkansas; California; Colorado; Connecticut; Florida; Illinois; Indiana; Kansas; Maryland; Massachusetts; Michigan; Mississippi; Nevada; New Jersey; New Mexico; New York; Ohio; Oklahoma; Pennsylvania; Tennessee; Utah; Vermont; Virginia. Nonspecialized. Positions commonly filled include: Accountant; Bookkeeper; Clerk; Computer Operator; Computer Programmer; Customer Service Representative; Data Entry Clerk; Demonstrator; Driver; Factory Worker; General Laborer; Legal Secretary; Light Industrial Worker; Medical Secretary; Office Worker; Purchasing Agent; Receptionist; Secretary; Statistician; Stenographer; Typist; Word Processing Specialist.

TEMP FORCE OF ILLINOIS
2201 5th Avenue, Suite 6
Moline IL 61265
Contact Juanita Herrell, Manager. 309/797-1108. Temporary help service. No appointment required. Founded 1965. Branch offices located in: Alabama; Arkansas; California; Colorado; Connecticut; Florida; Illinois; Indiana; Kansas; Maryland; Massachusetts; Michigan; Mississippi; Nevada; New Jersey; New Mexico; New York; Ohio; Oklahoma; Pennsylvania; Tennessee; Utah; Vermont; Virginia. Nonspecialized. Positions commonly filled include: Accountant; Bookkeeper; Clerk; Computer Operator; Computer Programmer; Customer Service Representative; Data Entry Clerk; Demonstrator; Driver; Factory Worker; General Laborer; Legal Secretary; Light Industrial Worker; Medical Secretary; Office Worker; Purchasing Agent; Receptionist; Secretary; Statistician; Stenographer; Typist; Word Processing Specialist.

TEMPSTATT, INC.
202 Campbell Street
Geneva IL 60134
Contact Manager. 708/232-1883. Temporary help agency. Founded 1981. Specializes in the areas of: Computer Hardware and Software; Health and Medical; Legal; Manufacturing. Positions commonly filled include: Administrative Assistant; Customer Service Rep; Executive Secretary; General Laborer; Legal Secretary; Light Industrial Worker; Medical Secretary; Nurse; Secretary; Stenographer; Systems Analyst; Typist; Word Processor.

TRI-ASSOCIATES, INC.
819 South Wabash Street, Suite 300
Chicago IL 60605
Contact Pat Brown, Supervisor of Recruitment and Placement. 312/663-1851. Employment agency; temporary help service. Founded 1976. Nonspecialized. Positions commonly filled include: Accountant; Administrative Assistant; Bookkeeper; Claim Representative; Clerk; Computer Operator; Computer Programmer; Customer Service Representative; Data Entry Clerk; EDP Specialist; Electrical Engineer; Financial Analyst; Industrial Engineer; Legal Secretary; MIS Specialist; Marketing Specialist; Mechanical Engineer; Medical Secretary; Operations/Production Specialist; Personnel and Labor Relations Specialist; Receptionist; Sales Representative; Secretary; Stenographer; Systems Analyst; Technical Writer/Editor; Technician; Typist; Word Processing Specialist. Company pays fee. Number of placements per year: 101-200.

VICTOR INTERIM
2217 Grand Avenue
Waukegan IL 60085
708/336-0164. Temporary help service. Appointment requested. Founded 1954. A member of Victor Temporary Services. Victor Temporary Services has over 100 offices throughout the United States. Nonspecialized. Positions commonly filled include: Bookkeeper; Clerk; Computer Operator; Customer Service Representative; Data Entry Clerk; Demonstrator; Draftsperson; Electronic Assembler; Factory Worker; General Laborer; Legal Secretary; Light Industrial Worker; Medical Secretary; Office Worker; Receptionist; Secretary; Stenographer; Technician; Typist; Word Processing Specialist. Company pays fee. Number of placements per year: 1001+.

VICTOR INTERIM SERVICES OF EVANSTON
1608 Maple Street
Evanston IL 60201
708/475-2707. Temporary help service. Appointment requested. Founded 1954. Victor Temporary Services has over 100 offices throughout the United States. Nonspecialized. Positions commonly filled include: Bookkeeper; Clerk; Computer Operator; Customer Service Representative; Data Entry

Clerk; Demonstrator; Draftsperson; Electronic Assembler; Factory Worker; General Laborer; Legal Secretary; Light Industrial Worker; Medical Secretary; Office Worker; Receptionist; Secretary; Stenographer; Technician; Typist; Word Processing Specialist. Company pays fee. Number of placements per year: 1001+.

VICTOR PERSONNEL STAFFING
700 North Milwaukee, Suite 102
Vernon Hills IL 60001
708/680-3875. Temporary help service. Appointment requested. Founded 1954. A member of Victor Temporary Services. Victor Temporary Services has over 100 offices throughout the United States. Nonspecialized. Positions commonly filled include: Bookkeeper; Clerk; Computer Operator; Customer Service Representative; Data Entry Clerk; Demonstrator; Draftsperson; Electronic Assembler; Factory Worker; General Laborer; Legal Secretary; Light Industrial Worker; Medical Secretary; Office Worker; Receptionist; Secretary; Stenographer; Technician; Typist; Word Processing Specialist. Company pays fee. Number of placements per year: 1001+.

VICTOR INTERIM SERVICES OF OAK BROOK
2625 Butterfield Road, Suite 112 South
Oak Brook IL 60521
312/571-8350. Temporary help service. Appointment requested. Founded 1954. Victor Temporary Services has over 100 offices throughout the United States. Nonspecialized. Positions commonly filled include: Bookkeeper; Clerk; Computer Operator; Customer Service Representative; Data Entry Clerk; Demonstrator; Draftsperson; Electronic Assembler; Factory Worker; General Laborer; Legal Secretary; Light Industrial Worker; Medical Secretary; Office Worker; Receptionist; Secretary; Stenographer; Technician; Typist; Word Processing Specialist. Company pays fee. Number of placements per year: 1001+.

WORD PROCESSORS PERSONNEL SERVICE
233 N. Michigan, #2229
Chicago IL 60601
312/856-1117. Employment agency; temporary agency. Appointment required. Founded 1978. Corporate office in Palo Alto, CA with 13 branches nationwide. Specializes in Word Processing and PC, Office Administration staffing, temporary and permanent. Positions commonly filled included: Administrative Assistant; Executive Secretary; Legal Secretary; Medical Secretary; PC Operator; Receptionist; Secretary; Statistician; Typist; Word Processing Supervisor; Word Processor. Company pays fee. Number of placements per year: 0-50(permanent); 501-1000+(temporary).

WORKING WORLD TEMPORARY PERSONNEL
Post Office Box 1036
101 N. Main Street
Crystal Lake IL 60014
Contact Barbara Kalemba, President. 815/455-4490. Temporary help agency. Appointment required. Founded 1980. Specializes in the areas of: Manufacturing; Secretarial and Clerical. Positions commonly filled include: Bookkeeper; Clerk; Computer Programmer; Construction Worker; Customer Service Rep; Data Entry Clerk; Draftsperson; Driver; Executive Secretary; Factory Worker; General Laborer; Legal Secretary; Light Industrial Worker; Marketing Specialist; Medical Secretary; Public Relations Worker; Receptionist; Sales Representative; Secretary; Stenographer; Typist; Underwriter; Word Processor. Number of placements per year: 1000+

EXECUTIVE SEARCH FIRMS OF GREATER CHICAGO

ACCORD, INC.
1543 Westchester Boulevard
Westchester IL 60153
Contact Chester Dombrowski, Manager (Mechanical) or John Fawcett, Manager (Electronic). 708/345-7900. Executive search firm. Founded 1981. Specializes in the areas of: Computer Hardware and Software; Engineering; Manufacturing; MIS/EDP; Technical and Scientific. Number of searches conducted per year: 51-100.

E.J. ASHTON & ASSOCIATES, LTD.
3125 North Wilke Road, Suite A
Arlington Heights IL 60004
Contact Ed Ashton, President. 708/577-7900. Executive search firm. Appointment requested; unsolicited resumes accepted. Founded 1979. Specializes in the areas of: Accounting; Banking; Insurance. Contingency; noncontingency. Number of searches conducted per year: 26-50.

CATALYST SEARCH, INC.
900 Jorie Boulevard, Suite 110
Oak Brook IL 60521
Contact Manager. 708/990-8610. Executive search firm. Appointment requested. Founded 1977. Member of National Association of Physician

Recruiters. Specializes in the areas of: Health and Medical. Number of searches conducted per year: 50.

CHICAGO FINANCIAL SEARCH
2 North Riverside Plaza, Suite 2400
Chicago IL 60606
Contact Sherri Budkowski, Vice President. 312/207-0400. Executive search firm. Appointment requested; unsolicited resumes accepted. Founded 1983. Specializes in the areas of: Banking; Brokerage; Commodities. Number of searches conducted per year: 101-200.

COMPUSEARCH OF BARRINGTON HILLS
960 Route 22, Stone Hill Center, Suite 207
Fox River Grove IL 60021-1905
Contact Ed Leed, Manager. 708/639-1112. Executive search firm. Appointment required; no phone calls; unsolicited resumes accepted. Founded 1965. World's largest contingency search firm. Five hundred offices nationwide, doing business under the names "Management Recruiters", "Sales Consultants", "CompuSearch" and "OfficeMates5". Specializes in mid-management/professional positions, $25,000-75,000 per annum. Specializes in the areas of: Accounting; Administration, MIS/EDP; Advertising; Affirmative Action; Architecture; Banking and Finance; Chemicals and Pharmaceuticals; Communications; Computer Hardware and Software; Construction; Electrical; Engineering; Food Industry; General Management; Health and Medical; Human Resources; Industrial and Interior Design; Insurance; Legal; Manufacturing; Operations Management; Printing and Publishing; Procurement; Real Estate; Retailing; Sales and Marketing; Technical and Scientific; Textiles; Transportation. Contingency.

COMPUSEARCH OF CHAMPAIGN
2110 North Market Street
Champaign IL 61821
Contact Ken Williams, Manager. 217/398-0050. Executive search firm. Appointment required; no phone calls; unsolicited resumes accepted. Founded 1965. World's largest contingency search firm. Five hundred offices nationwide, doing business under the names "Management Recruiters", "Sales Consultants", "CompuSearch" and "OfficeMates5". Specializes in mid-management/professional positions, $25,000-75,000 per annum. Specializes in the areas of: Accounting; Administration, MIS/EDP; Advertising; Affirmative Action; Architecture; Banking and Finance; Chemicals and Pharmaceuticals; Communications; Computer Hardware and Software; Construction; Electrical; Engineering; Food Industry; General Management; Health and Medical; Human Resources; Industrial and Interior Design; Insurance; Legal; Manufacturing; Operations Management; Printing and Publishing; Procurement; Real Estate; Retailing; Sales and Marketing; Technical and Scientific; Textiles; Transportation. Contingency.

COMPUSEARCH OF DES PLAINES
1400 East Touhy Avenue, Suite 220
Des Plaines IL 60018-3374
Contact Dick Kurz, Manager. 708/297-7102. Executive search firm. Appointment required; no phone calls; unsolicited resumes accepted. Founded 1965. World's largest contingency search firm. Five hundred offices nationwide, doing business under the names "Management Recruiters", "Sales Consultants", "CompuSearch" and "OfficeMates5". Specializes in mid-management/professional positions, $25,000-75,000 per annum. Specializes in the areas of: Accounting; Administration, MIS/EDP; Advertising; Affirmative Action; Architecture; Banking and Finance; Chemicals and Pharmaceuticals; Communications; Computer Hardware and Software; Construction; Electrical; Engineering; Food Industry; General Management; Health and Medical; Human Resources; Industrial and Interior Design; Insurance; Legal; Manufacturing; Operations Management; Printing and Publishing; Procurement; Real Estate; Retailing; Sales and Marketing; Technical and Scientific; Textiles; Transportation. Contingency.

CORPORATE ENVIRONMENT, LTD.
Post Office Box 798
Crystal Lake IL 60014
Contact Thomas P. McDermott, President. 815/455-6070. Executive search firm. Appointment required; no phone calls; unsolicited resumes accepted. Founded 1979. Key specialists, mid-management and senior level executives in heavy Technical industries, Environmental, Chemical Process, Equipment/Instruments and other industries requiring a technological background. Functions include Management; Engineering; Manufacturing; and Sales and Marketing. Specializes in the areas of: Chemicals and Pharmaceuticals; Construction; Engineering; Food Industry; General Management; Manufacturing; Operations Management; Sales and Marketing; Technical and Scientific. Noncontingency. Number of searches conducted per year: 0-50.

CREATIVE STAFFING ENTERPRISES, INC.
164 Division Street, Suite 310
Elgin IL 60120
Contact Donald Taylor, President. 708/888-4691. Executive search firm. Appointment requested; unsolicited resumes accepted. Specializes in the areas of: Computer Hardware and Software; Engineering; Technical and Scientific. Number of searches conducted per year: 51-100.

DUNHILL PERSONNEL SYSTEM OF ILLINOIS
2500 South Highland, Suite 103
Lombard IL 60148
Contact Tom Barbeau, Owner. 708/916-7300. Executive search firm Specializes in the areas of: Sales and Marketing.

ELSKO EXECUTIVE SEARCH
3601 Algonquin, Suite 130
Rolling Meadows IL 60008
708/394-2400. Executive search firm. Appointment requested; unsolicited resumes accepted. Founded 1976. Specializes in the areas of: Accounting; Finance. Contingency. Number of searches conducted per year: 101-200.

FIRST SEARCH, INC.
4709 West Golf Road, Suite 812
Skokie IL 60076
Contact Michael Zarnek, President. 708/282-8810. Executive search firm. No appointment required; unsolicited resumes accepted. Founded 1984. Specializes in Telecommunication/Data Comm. industry nationwide, Engineering to Executive levels. Specializes in the areas of: Communications; Engineering; Sales and Marketing; Technical and Scientific; Telecommunications. Contingency. Nummber of searches conducted per year: 0-50.

FORESIGHT
414 Plaza Drive, Suite 304
Westmont IL 60559
Contact Greg Hufford or Joe Scavuzza, Co-owners. 708/655-0550. Executive search firm. No appointment required; unsolicited resumes accepted. Founded 1978. Specializes in the areas of: Computer Hardware and Software; Engineering; Manufacturing; Sales and Marketing; Technical and Scientific; Technical Marketing; Telecommunicaions. Contingency. Number of searches conducted per year: 26-50.

GEER, GRICE & HOLDENER
39 South Barrington Road
South Barrington IL 60010
Contact Michael Geers, Vice President. 708/382-2950. Executive search firm. Appointment required. Founded 1978. Low-profile; results-oriented. Specializes in the areas of: Computer Hardware and Software; MIS/EDP; Sales and Marketing. Positions commonly filled include: Computer Programmer; EDP Specialist; Management Consultant; Marketing Specialist; Sales Representative; Systems Analyst. Company pays fee. Number of placements per year: 51-100.

GRAHAM ROBERTS ASSOCIATES
4300 North Brandywine Drive, Suite 104
Peoria IL 61614
Contact Robert M. Evans, C.P.C., President. 309/685-6225. Executive search firm. Appointment requested; unsolicited resumes accepted. Founded 1967. Specializes in the areas of: Accounting; Administration, MIS/EDP; Advertising; Computer Hardware and Software; Engineering; Food Industry; Insurance; Manufacturing; Personnel and Human Resources; Printing and

Publishing; Sales and Marketing; Technical and Scientific. Contingency; noncontingency. Number of searches conducted per year: 51-100.

HEALTH STAFFERS
5636 North Broadway
Chicago IL 60660
Contact Rose Houston, President. 312/561-5400. Executive search firm. Appointment requested; unsolicited resumes accepted. Founded 1975. Specializes in the areas of: Health and Medical. Contingency; noncontingency. Number of searches conducted per year: 50.

THOMAS HIRTZ & ASSOCIATES
150 North Wacker Drive, Suite 1700
Chicago IL 60606
Contact Thomas Hirtz, President. 312/977-1555. Executive search firm. Appointment requested; unsolicited resumes accepted. Founded 1968. Services the Data Processing industry. Specializes in the areas of: Computer Hardware and Software.

JACOBSON ASSOCIATES
150 N. Wacker Drive, Suite 1120
Chicago IL 60606
Contact David Jacobson, President. 312/726-1578. Executive search firm. Appointment required. Founded 1971. National executive recruiting firm providing comprehensive professional service to the Insurance and related industries. Positions commonly filled include: Actuary; EDP Specialist; Management Consultant. Company pays fee.

MANAGEMENT RECRUITERS OF ALBION
129 South 4th Street
Albion IL 62806
Contact Tom Christensen, Manager. 618/445-2333; FAX 618/445-4061. Executive search firm. Appointment required; no phone calls; unsolicited resumes accepted. Founded 1965. World's largest contingency search firm. Five hundred offices nationwide, doing business under the names "Management Recruiters", "Sales Consultants", "CompuSearch" and "OfficeMates5". Specializes in mid-management/professional positions, $25,000-75,000 per annum. Specializes in the areas of: Accounting; Administration, MIS/EDP; Advertising; Affirmative Action; Architecture; Banking and Finance; Chemicals and Pharmaceuticals; Communications; Computer Hardware and Software; Construction; Electrical; Engineering; Food Industry; General Management; Health and Medical; Human Resources; Industrial and Interior Design; Insurance; Legal; Manufacturing, Operations Management; Printing and Publishing; Procurement; Real Estate; Retailing; Sales and Marketing; Technical and Scientific; Textiles Transportation. Contingency

MANAGEMENT RECRUITERS OF ARLINGTON HEIGHTS
220 Campus Court, Suite 100
Arlington Heights IL 60004
Contact John Dowiat, Manager. 708/577-9800. Executive search firm. Appointment required; no phone calls; unsolicited resumes accepted. Founded 1965. World's largest contingency search firm. Five hundred offices nationwide, doing business under the names "Management Recruiters", "Sales Consultants", "CompuSearch" and "OfficeMates5". Specializes in mid-management/professional positions, $25,000-75,000 per annum. Specializes in the areas of: Accounting; Administration, MIS/EDP; Advertising; Affirmative Action; Architecture; Banking and Finance; Chemicals and Pharmaceuticals; Communications; Computer Hardware and Software; Construction; Electrical; Engineering; Food Industry; General Management; Health and Medical; Human Resources; Industrial and Interior Design; Insurance; Legal; Manufacturing; Operations Management; Printing and Publishing; Procurement; Real Estate; Retailing; Sales and Marketing; Technical and Scientific; Textiles; Transportation. Contingency.

MANAGEMENT RECRUITERS OF BANNOCKBURN
2205 Lakeside Drive
Bannockburn IL 60015
Contact Dennis Gross, Manager. 708/295-6780. Executive search firm. Appointment required; no phone calls; unsolicited resumes accepted. Founded 1965. World's largest contingency search firm. Five hundred offices nationwide, doing business under the names "Management Recruiters", "Sales Consultants", "CompuSearch" and "OfficeMates5". Specializes in mid-management/professional positions, $25,000-75,000 per annum. Specializes in the areas of: Accounting; Administration, MIS/EDP; Advertising; Affirmative Action; Architecture; Banking and Finance; Chemicals and Pharmaceuticals; Communications; Computer Hardware and Software; Construction; and Electrical; Engineering; Food Industry; General Management; Health and Medical; Human Resources; Industrial and Interior Design; Insurance; Legal; Manufacturing; Operations Management; Printing and Publishing; Procurement; Real Estate; Retailing; Sales and Marketing; Technical and Scientific; Textiles; Transportation. Contingency.

MANAGEMENT RECRUITERS OF BARRINGTON HILLS
Stone Hill Center, Suite 207
960 Route 22
Fox River Grove IL 60021-1954
Contact Ed Leed, Manager. 708/639-1112. Executive search firm. Appointment required; no phone calls; unsolicited resumes accepted. Founded 1965. World's largest contingency search firm. Five hundred offices nationwide, doing business under the names "Management Recruiters", "Sales Consultants", "CompuSearch" and "OfficeMates5". Specializes in mid-management/professional positions, $25,000-75,000 per annum. Specializes in the areas of: Accounting; Administration, MIS/EDP; Advertising; Affirmative Action; Architecture; Banking and Finance; Chemicals and

Pharmaceuticals; Communications; Computer Hardware and Software; Construction; Electrical; Engineering; Food Industry; General Management; Health and Medical; Human Resources; Industrial and Interior Design; Insurance; Legal; Manufacturing; Operations Management; Printing and Publishing; Procurement; Real Estate; Retailing; Sales and Marketing; Technical and Scientific; Textiles; Transportation. Contingency.

MANAGEMENT RECRUITERS OF CHAMPAIGN
2110 North Market Street
Champaign IL 61821
Contact Ken Williams, Manager. 217/398-0050; FAX 217/398-2043. Executive search firm. Appointment required; no phone calls; unsolicited resumes accepted. Founded 1965. World's largest contingency search firm. Five hundred offices nationwide, doing business under the names "Management Recruiters", "Sales Consultants", "CompuSearch" and "OfficeMates5". Specializes in mid-management/professional positions, $25,000-75,000 per annum. Specializes in the areas of: Accounting; Administration, MIS/EDP; Advertising; Affirmative Action; Architecture; Banking and Finance; Chemicals and Pharmaceuticals; Communications; Computer Hardware and Software; Construction; Electrical; Engineering; Food Industry; General Management; Health and Medical; Human Resources; Industrial and Interior Design; Insurance; Legal; Manufacturing; Operations Management; Printing and Publishing; Procurement; Real Estate; Retailing; Sales and Marketing; Technical and Scientific; Textiles; Transportation. Contingency.

MANAGEMENT RECRUITERS OF CHERRY VALLEY
Point East, 1740 Bell School Road
Cherry Valley IL 61016
Contact D. Michael Carter, Manager. 815/332-5646. Executive search firm. Appointment required; no phone calls; unsolicited resumes accepted. Founded 1965. World's largest contingency search firm. Five hundred offices nationwide, doing business under the names "Management Recruiters", "Sales Consultants", "CompuSearch" and "OfficeMates5". Specializes in mid-management/professional positions, $25,000-75,000 per annum. Specializes in the areas of: Accounting; Administration, MIS/EDP; Advertising; Affirmative Action; Architecture; Banking and Finance; Chemicals and Pharmaceuticals; Communications; Computer Hardware and Software; Construction; Electrical; Engineering; Food Industry; General Management; Health and Medical; Human Resources; Industrial and Interior Design; Insurance; Legal; Manufacturing; Operations Management; Printing and Publishing; Procurement; Real Estate; Retailing; Sales and Marketing; Technical and Scientific; Textiles; Transportation. Contingency.

MANAGEMENT RECRUITERS OF CHICAGO (DOWNTOWN)
Two North Riverside Plaza
Suite 1815
Chicago IL 60606
Contact Dave Baranski, Manager. 312/648-1800. Executive search firm. Appointment required; no phone calls; unsolicited resumes accepted. Founded 1965. World's largest contingency search firm. Five hundred offices nationwide, doing business under the names "Management Recruiters", "Sales Consultants", "CompuSearch" and "OfficeMates5". Specializes in mid-management/professional positions, $25,000-75,000 per annum. Specializes in the areas of: Accounting; Administration, MIS/EDP; Advertising; Affirmative Action; Architecture; Banking and Finance; Chemicals and Pharmaceuticals; Communications; Computer Hardware and Software; Construction; Electrical; Engineering; Food Industry; General Management; Health and Medical; Human Resources; Industrial and Interior Design; Insurance; Legal; Manufacturing; Operations Management; Printing and Publishing; Procurement; Real Estate; Retailing; Sales and Marketing; Technical and Scientific; Textiles; Transportation. Contingency.

MANAGEMENT RECRUITERS OF CHICAGO-SOUTHWEST
College Drive Office Center
7804 West College Drive
Palos Heights IL 60463
Contact Victor Persico, Manager. 708/361-8778. Executive search firm. Appointment required; no phone calls; unsolicited resumes accepted. Founded 1965. World's largest contingency search firm. Five hundred offices nationwide, doing business under the names "Management Recruiters", "Sales Consultants", "CompuSearch" and "OfficeMates5". Specializes in mid-management/professional positions, $25,000-75,000 per annum. Specializes in the areas of: Accounting; Administration, MIS/EDP; Advertising; Affirmative Action; Architecture; Banking and Finance; Chemicals and Pharmaceuticals; Communications; Computer Hardware and Software; Construction; Electrical; Engineering; Food Industry; General Management; Health and Medical; Human Resources; Industrial and Interior Design; Insurance; Legal; Manufacturing; Operations Management; Printing and Publishing; Procurement; Real Estate; Retailing; Sales and Marketing; Technical and Scientific; Textiles; Transportation. Contingency.

MANAGEMENT RECRUITERS OF DES PLAINES
1400 East Touhy Avenue, Suite 220
Des Plaines IL 60018-3374
Contact Dick Kurz, Manager. 708/297-7102; FAX 708/297-8477. Executive search firm. Appointment required; no phone calls; unsolicited resumes accepted. Founded 1965. World's largest contingency search firm. Five hundred offices nationwide, doing business under the names "Management Recruiters", "Sales Consultants", "CompuSearch" and "OfficeMates5". Specializes in mid-management/professional positions, $25,000-75,000 per annum. Specializes in the areas of: Accounting; Administration, MIS/EDP;

Advertising; Affirmative Action; Architecture; Banking and Finance; Chemicals and Pharmaceuticals; Communications; Computer Hardware and Software; Construction; Electrical; Engineering; Food Industry; General Management; Health and Medical; Human Resources; Industrial and Interior Design; Insurance; Legal; Manufacturing; Operations Management; Printing and Publishing; Procurement; Real Estate; Retailing; Sales and Marketing; Technical and Scientific; Textiles; Transportation. Contingency.

MANAGEMENT RECRUITERS OF ELGIN
472 North McLean Boulevard
Suite 201
Elgin IL 60123
Contact Ron Reeves, Manager. 708/697-2201. Executive search firm. Appointment required; no phone calls; unsolicited resumes accepted. Founded 1965. World's largest contingency search firm. Five hundred offices nationwide, doing business under the names "Management Recruiters", "Sales Consultants", "CompuSearch" and "OfficeMates5". Specializes in mid-management/professional positions, $25,000-75,000 per annum. Specializes in the areas of: Accounting; Administration, MIS/EDP; Advertising; Affirmative Action; Architecture; Banking and Finance; Chemicals and Pharmaceuticals; Communications; Computer Hardware and Software; Construction; Electrical; Engineering; Food Industry; General Management; Health and Medical; Human Resources; Industrial and Interior Design; Insurance; Legal; Manufacturing; Operations Management; Printing and Publishing; Procurement; Real Estate; Retailing; Sales and Marketing; Technical and Scientific; Textiles; Transportation. Contingency.

MANAGEMENT RECRUITERS OF ST. CHARLES
10 East State Avenue, Suite 201
St. Charles IL 60174-1470
Contact Daniel Lasse, Manager. 708/377-6466. Executive search firm. Appointment required; no phone calls; unsolicited resumes accepted. Founded 1965. World's largest contingency search firm. Five hundred offices nationwide, doing business under the names "Management Recruiters", "Sales Consultants", "CompuSearch" and "OfficeMates5". Specializes in mid-management/professional positions, $25,000-75,000 per annum. Specializes in the areas of: Accounting; Administration, MIS/EDP; Advertising; Affirmative Action; Architecture; Banking and Finance; Chemicals and Pharmaceuticals; Communications; Computer Hardware and Software; Construction; Electrical; Engineering; Food Industry; General Management; Health and Medical; Human Resources; Industrial and Interior Design; Insurance; Legal; Manufacturing; Operations Management; Printing and Publishing; Procurement; Real Estate; Retailing; Sales and Marketing; Technical and Scientific; Textiles; Transportation. Contingency.

MANAGEMENT RECRUITERS OF WHEELING
Suite 220, 401 S. Milwaukee Avenue
Wheeling IL 60090
Contact James Wooten, Manager. 708/520-1710. Executive search firm. Appointment required; no phone calls; unsolicited resumes accepted. Founded 1965. World's largest contingency search firm. Five hundred offices nationwide, doing business under the names "Management Recruiters", "Sales Consultants", "CompuSearch" and "OfficeMates5". Specializes in mid-management/professional positions, $25,000-75,000 per annum. Specializes in the areas of: Accounting; Administration, MIS/EDP; Advertising; Affirmative Action; Architecture; Banking and Finance; Chemicals and Pharmaceuticals; Communications; Computer Hardware and Software; Construction; Electrical; Engineering; Food Industry; General Management; Health and Medical; Human Resources; Industrial and Interior Design; Insurance; Legal; Manufacturing; Operations Management; Printing and Publishing; Procurement; Real Estate; Retailing; Sales and Marketing; Technical and Scientific; Textiles; Transportation. Contingency.

MANAGEMENT WORLD
7200 North Ridge Boulevard
Chicago IL 60645
Contact James P. Daly, President. 312/274-1608. Executive search firm. Appointment requested; unsolicited resumes accepted. Founded 1980. Services the Hospitality industry. Specializes in the areas of: Food Industry. Contingency. Number of searches conducted per year: 51-100.

OFFICEMATES5 OF BANNOCKBURN
2205 Lakeside Drive
Bannockburn IL 60015
Contact Dennis Gross, Manager. 708/295-6920. Executive search firm. Appointment required; no phone calls; unsolicited resumes accepted. Founded 1965. World's largest contingency search firm. Five hundred offices nationwide, doing business under the names "Management Recruiters", "Sales Consultants", "CompuSearch" and "OfficeMates5". Specializes in mid-management/professional positions, $25,000-75,000 per annum. Specializes in the areas of: Accounting; Administration, MIS/EDP; Advertising; Affirmative Action; Architecture; Banking and Finance; Chemicals and Pharmaceuticals; Communications; Computer Hardware and Software; Construction; Electrical; Engineering; Food Industry; General Management; Health and Medical; Human Resources; Industrial and Interior Design; Insurance; Legal; Manufacturing; Operations Management; Printing and Publishing; Procurement; Real Estate; Retailing; Sales and Marketing; Technical and Scientific; Textiles; Transportation. Contingency.

OFFICEMATES5 OF DES PLAINES
1400 East Touhy Avenue, Suite 220
Des Plaines IL 60018-3374
Contact Dick Kurz, Manager. 708/297-7102. Executive search firm. Appointment required; no phone calls; unsolicited resumes accepted. Founded 1965. World's largest contingency search firm. Five hundred offices nationwide, doing business under the names "Management Recruiters", "Sales Consultants", "CompuSearch" and "OfficeMates5". Specializes in mid-management/professional positions, $25,000-75,000 per annum. Specializes in the areas of: Accounting; Administration, MIS/EDP; Advertising; Affirmative Action; Architecture; Banking and Finance; Chemicals and Pharmaceuticals; Communications; Computer Hardware and Software; Construction; Electrical; Engineering; Food Industry; General Management; Health and Medical; Human Resources; Industrial and Interior Design; Insurance; Legal; Manufacturing; Operations Management; Printing and Publishing; Procurement; Real Estate; Retailing; Sales and Marketing; Technical and Scientific; Textiles; Transportation. Contingency.

OFFICEMATES5 OF NILES
5940 West Touhy Avenue, Suite 200
Niles IL 60648
Contact Joyce Schechtman, Manager. 708/647-7474; FAX 708/967-2238. Executive search firm. Appointment required; no phone calls; unsolicited resumes accepted. Founded 1965. World's largest contingency search firm. Five hundred offices nationwide, doing business under the names "Management Recruiters", "Sales Consultants", "CompuSearch" and "OfficeMates5". Specializes in mid-management/professional positions, $25,000-75,000 per annum. Specializes in the areas of: Accounting, Administration, MIS/EDP; Advertising; Affirmative Action; Architecture; Banking and Finance; Chemicals and Pharmaceuticals; Communications; Computer Hardware and Software; Construction; Electrical; Engineering; Food Industry; General Management; Health and Medical; Human Resources; Industrial and Interior Design; Insurance; Legal; Manufacturing; Operations Management; Printing and Publishing; Procurement; Real Estate; Retailing; Sales and Marketing; Technical and Scientific; Textiles; Transportation. Contingency.

OFFICEMATES5 OF NORTHFIELD
181 Waukegan Road, Suite 103
Northfield IL 60093
Contact Lynne Goldberg, Manager. 708/446-7737; FAX 708/446-0990. Executive search firm. Appointment required; no phone calls; unsolicited resumes accepted. Founded 1965. World's largest contingency search firm. Five hundred offices nationwide, doing business under the names "Management Recruiters", "Sales Consultants", "CompuSearch" and "OfficeMates5". Specializes in mid-management/professional positions, $25,000-75,000 per annum. Specializes in the areas of: Accounting; Administration, MIS/EDP; Advertising; Affirmative Action; Architecture;

Banking and Finance; Chemicals and Pharmaceuticals; Communications; Computer Hardware and Software; Construction; Electrical; Engineering; Food Industry; General Management; Health and Medical; Human Resources; Industrial and Interior Design; Insurance; Legal; Manufacturing; Operations Management; Printing and Publishing; Procurement; Real Estate; Retailing; Sales and Marketing; Technical and Scientific; Textiles; Transportation. Contingency.

OFFICEMATES5 OF WHEELING
401 South Milwaukee Avenue
Wheeling IL 60090
Contact Manager. 708/459-6160. Executive search firm. Appointment required; no phone calls; unsolicited resumes accepted. Founded 1965. World's largest contingency search firm. Five hundred offices nationwide, doing business under the names "Management Recruiters", "Sales Consultants", "CompuSearch" and "OfficeMates5". Specializes in mid-management/professional positions, $25,000-75,000 per annum. Specializes in the areas of: Accounting; Administration, MIS/EDP; Advertising; Affirmative Action; Architecture; Banking and Finance; Chemicals and Pharmaceuticals; Communications; Computer Hardware and Software; Construction; Electrical; Engineering; Food Industry; General Management; Health and Medical; Human Resources; Industrial and Interior Design; Insurance; Legal; Manufacturing; Operations Management; Printing and Publishing; Procurement; Real Estate; Retailing; Sales and Marketing; Technical and Scientific; Textiles; Transportation. Contingency.

OFFICEMATES5 OF WOODFIELD
1111 Plaza Drive, Suite 655
Schaumburg IL 60173
Contact Anita Kurz, Manager. 312/310-1600. Executive search firm. Appointment required; no phone calls; unsolicited resumes accepted. Founded 1965. World's largest contingency search firm. Five hundred offices nationwide, doing business under the names "Management Recruiters", "Sales Consultants", "CompuSearch" and "OfficeMates5". Specializes in mid-management/professional positions, $25,000-75,000 per annum. Specializes in the areas of: Accounting; Administration, MIS/EDP; Advertising; Affirmative Action; Architecture; Banking and Finance; Chemicals and Pharmaceuticals; Communications; Computer Hardware and Software; Construction; Electrical; Engineering; Food Industry; General Management; Health and Medical; Human Resources; Industrial and Interior Design; Insurance; Legal; Manufacturing; Operations Management; Printing and Publishing; Procurement; Real Estate; Retailing; Sales and Marketing; Technical and Scientific; Textiles; Transportation. Contingency.

PINKERTON AND ASSOCIATES, INC.
320 North Michigan Avenue, Suite 2100
Chicago IL 60601
Contact Tom Pinkerton, President. 312/266-8669. Executive search firm. Appointment required; unsolicited resumes accepted. Founded 1979. A small firm dedicated to quality search, work on retainer assignments only in middle and upper management positions. Specializes in the areas of: Accounting; Administration, MIS/EDP; Advertising; Banking and Finance; Broadcasting; Chemicals and Pharmaceuticals; Communications; Construction; Education; Electrical; Engineering; Food Industry; General Management; Health and Medical; Human Resources; Industrial and Interior Design; Insurance; Legal; Manufacturing; Nonprofit; Operations Management; Printing and Publishing; Procurement; Real Estate; Retailing; Sales and Marketing; Technical and Scientific; Textiles; Transportation; Women. Noncontingency. Number of searches conducted per year: 0-50.

PROFILE FINANCIAL SEARCH
55 West Wacker Drive, Suite 400
Chicago IL 60601
Contact Joseph Lagattuta, Owner/Controller. 312/641-0555. Executive search firm. Appointment requested. Founded 1977. Specializes in the areas of: Accounting and Finance; Banking; Insurance; Manufacturing. Number of searches conducted per year: 501+.

RECRUITING RESOURCES GROUP
35 East Wacker Drive, Suite 2700
Chicago IL 60601
Contact Glenda Peters, Vice President. 312/836-1200. Executive search firm. Appointment required; unsolicited resumes accepted. Founded 1966. Specializes in the areas of: Accounting; Administration, MIS/EDP; Advertising; Banking and Finance; Chemicals and Pharmaceuticals; Communications; Computer Hardware and Software; Engineering; Food Industry; General Management; Health and Medical; Human Resources; Insurance; Legal; Manufacturing; Nonprofit; Operations Management; Printing and Publishing; Real Estate; Sales and Marketing; Technical and Scientific; Textiles; Transportation; Women. Contingency. Number of searches conducted per year: 501+.

ROMAC AND ASSOCIATES OF CHICAGO, INC.
20 N. Wacker, Suite 2420
Chicago IL 60606
Contact Receptionist. 312/263-0902. Executive search firm. Appointment required. Specializes in the areas of Accounting; Banking and Finance. Positions commonly filled include: Accountant; Bank Officer/Manager; Financial Analyst. Company pays fee.

ROY TALMAN & ASSOCIATES
203 North Wabash, Suite 1120
Chicago IL 60601
Contact Ilya R. Talman, President. 312/630-0130. Executive search firm. Appointment requested; unsolicited resumes accepted. Founded 1983. Specializes in the areas of: Computer Hardware and Software; Engineering; Technical and Scientific. Contingency. Number of searches conducted per year: 51-100.

SALES CONSULTANTS OF BARRINGTON HILLS, INC.
Stone Hill Center, 960 Route 22
Fox River Grove IL 60021-1905
Contact Ed Leed, General Manager. 708/639-1112. Executive search firm. Appointment required; no phone calls; unsolicited resumes accepted. Founded 1965. World's largest contingency search firm. Five hundred offices nationwide, doing business under the names "Management Recruiters", "Sales Consultants", "CompuSearch" and "OfficeMates5". Specializes in mid-management/professional positions, $25,000-75,000 per annum. Specializes in the areas of: Accounting; Banking and Finance; Computer Hardware and Software; Engineering; Food Industry; General Management; Health and Medical; Insurance; Manufacturing; MIS/EDP; Printing and Publishing; Sales and Marketing; Technical and Scientific; Transportation. Company pays fee. Number of placements per year: 51-100.

SALES CONSULTANTS OF CHICAGO (DOWNTOWN)
420 North Wabash, Suite 201
Chicago IL 60611
Contact Bob Bowes, Manager. 312/836-9100. Executive search firm. Appointment required; no phone calls; unsolicited resumes accepted. Founded 1965. World's largest contingency search firm. Five hundred offices nationwide, doing business under the names "Management Recruiters", "Sales Consultants", "CompuSearch" and "OfficeMates5". Specializes in mid-management/professional positions, $25,000-75,000 per annum. Specializes in the areas of: Accounting; Administration, MIS/EDP; Advertising; Affirmative Action; Architecture; Banking and Finance; Chemicals and Pharmaceuticals; Communications; Computer Hardware and Software; Construction; Electrical; Engineering; Food Industry; General Management; Health and Medical; Human Resources; Industrial and Interior Design; Insurance; Legal; Manufacturing; Operations Management; Printing and Publishing; Procurement; Real Estate; Retailing; Sales and Marketing; Technical and Scientific; Textiles; Transportation. Contingency.

SALES CONSULTANTS OF CHICAGO (SOUTHWEST)
6420 127th Street, Suite 209
Palos Heights IL 60463-2248
Contact Carroll White or Jack White, Co-Managers. 312/371-9677. Executive search firm. Appointment required; no phone calls; unsolicited resumes accepted. Founded 1965. World's largest contingency search firm. Five

hundred offices nationwide, doing business under the names "Management Recruiters", "Sales Consultants", "CompuSearch" and "OfficeMates5". Specializes in mid-management/professional positions, $25,000-75,000 per annum. Specializes in the areas of: Accounting; Administration, MIS/EDP; Advertising; Affirmative Action; Architecture; Banking and Finance; Chemicals and Pharmaceuticals; Communications; Computer Hardware and Software; Construction; Electrical; Engineering; Food Industry; General Management; Health and Medical; Human Resources; Industrial and Interior Design; Insurance; Legal; Manufacturing; Operations Management; Printing and Publishing; Procurement; Real Estate; Retailing; Sales and Marketing; Technical and Scientific; Textiles; Transportation. Contingency.

SALES CONSULTANTS OF FOX VALLEY
Suite 23, 1700 N. Farnsworth
Aurora IL 60505
Contact John Seebert, Manager. 708/820-8000. Executive search firm. Appointment required; no phone calls; unsolicited resumes accepted. Founded 1965. World's largest contingency search firm. Five hundred offices nationwide, doing business under the names "Management Recruiters", "Sales Consultants", "CompuSearch" and "OfficeMates5". Specializes in mid-management/professional positions, $25,000-75,000 per annum. Specializes in the areas of: Accounting; Administration, MIS/EDP; Advertising; Affirmative Action; Architecture; Banking and Finance; Chemicals and Pharmaceuticals; Communications; Computer Hardware and Software; Construction; Electrical; Engineering; Food Industry; General Management; Health and Medical; Human Resources; Industrial and Interior Design; Insurance; Legal; Manufacturing; Operations Management; Printing and Publishing; Procurement; Real Estate; Retailing; Sales and Marketing; Technical and Scientific; Textiles; Transportation. Contingency.

SALES CONSULTANTS OF LINCOLNSHIRE
Oak Tree Corners, Suite 6
430 Milwaukee Avenue
Prairie View IL 60069
Contact Steve Briody, General Manager, or Caroline Wright, Manager. 708/634-0300. Executive search firm. Appointment required; no phone calls; unsolicited resumes accepted. Founded 1965. World's largest contingency search firm. Five hundred offices nationwide, doing business under the names "Management Recruiters", "Sales Consultants", "CompuSearch" and "OfficeMates5". Specializes in mid-management/professional positions, $25,000-75,000 per annum. Specializes in the areas of: Accounting; Administration, MIS/EDP; Advertising; Affirmative Action; Architecture; Banking and Finance; Chemicals and Pharmaceuticals; Communications; Computer Hardware and Software; Construction; Electrical; Engineering; Food Industry; General Management; Health and Medical; Human Resources; Industrial and Interior Design; Insurance; Legal; Manufacturing; Operations Management; Printing and Publishing; Procurement; Real

Estate; Retailing; Sales and Marketing; Technical and Scientific; Textiles; Transportation. Contingency.

SALES CONSULTANTS OF OAK BROOK
The Corporate Center, Suite 210
1100 Jorie Boulevard
Oak Brook IL 60521-2273
Contact Gary Miller, Manager. 708/990-8233; FAX 708/990-2973. Executive search firm. Appointment required; no phone calls; unsolicited resumes accepted. Founded 1965. World's largest contingency search firm. Five hundred offices nationwide, doing business under the names "Management Recruiters", "Sales Consultants", "CompuSearch" and "OfficeMates5". Specializes in mid-management/professional positions, $25,000-75,000 per annum. Specializes in the areas of: Accounting; Administration, MIS/EDP; Advertising; Affirmative Action; Architecture; Banking and Finance; Chemicals and Pharmaceuticals; Communications; Computer Hardware and Software; Construction; Electrical; Engineering; Food Industry; General Management; Health and Medical; Human Resources; Industrial and Interior Design; Insurance; Legal; Manufacturing; Operations Management; Printing and Publishing; Procurement; Real Estate; Retailing; Sales and Marketing; Technical and Scientific; Textiles; Transportation. Contingency.

SALES CONSULTANTS OF SCHAUMBURG
One Woodfield Place, Suite 415
1701 E. Woodfield Road
Schaumburg IL 60173
Contact Steve Briody, Manager. 312/330-1110. Executive search firm. Appointment required; no phone calls; unsolicited resumes accepted. Founded 1965. World's largest contingency search firm. Five hundred offices nationwide, doing business under the names "Management Recruiters", "Sales Consultants", "CompuSearch" and "OfficeMates5". Specializes in mid-management/professional positions, $25,000-75,000 per annum. Specializes in the areas of: Accounting; Administration, MIS/EDP; Advertising; Affirmative Action; Architecture; Banking and Finance; Chemicals and Pharmaceuticals; Communications; Computer Hardware and Software; Construction; Electrical; Engineering; Food Industry; General Management; Health and Medical; Human Resources; Industrial and Interior Design; Insurance; Legal; Manufacturing; Operations Management; Printing and Publishing; Procurement; Real Estate; Retailing; Sales and Marketing; Technical and Scientific; Textiles; Transportation. Contingency.

SAMUELSON ASSOCIATES
27 East Monroe, Suite 1400
Chicago IL 60603
Contact Don S. Samuelson, Owner. 312/263-0033. Executive search firm. Appointment requested; unsolicited resumes accepted. Founded 1983. Specializes in the area of: Legal. Contingency; noncontingency. Number of searches conducted per year: 26-50.

RAYMOND JAMES SMITH & CLINICAL LEGAL SEARCH
8807 Cary-Algonquin Road
Cary IL 60013
Contact Raymond J. Smith, President. 708/639-8250. Executive search firm. No appointment required; unsolicited resumes accepted. Founded 1976. Specializes in the area of: Legal. Contingency; noncontingency. Number of searches conducted per year: 51-100.

SRS DATA SEARCH
6 N. Michigan, Suite 1401
Chicago IL 60602
Contact William Scothorn, Partner. 312/346-6383. Executive search firm. Appointment required; unsolicited resumes accepted. Founded 1980. Specializes in Data Processing field, Chicago area; Blue chip client base; employees average 7+ years in business, placing programmers through managers. Specializes in the areas of: Administration, MIS/EDP; Computer Hardware and Software. Contingency. Number of searches conducted per year: 201-500.

SYNERGISTICS ASSOCIATES
320 North Michigan Avenue, Suite 1803
Chicago IL 60601
Contact Al Borenstine, President. 312/346-8782. Executive search firm. Appointment required. Founded 1971. Specializes in the areas of: Computer Software and Hardware; MIS/EDP. Positions commonly filled include: EDP Executive; EDP Specialist; Management Consultant. Company pays fee. Number of placements per year: 0-50.

T-A-DAVIS & ASSOCIATES, INC.
500 Davis Center, Suite 1000
Evanston IL 60201
Contact Thomas G. Davis, President. 708/475-8900. Executive search firm. Appointment requested; no phone calls accepted; unsolicited resumes accepted. Founded 1979. Specializes in the area of: Food Industry. Contingency; noncontingency. Number of searches conducted per year: 26-50.

WESTCOTT ASSOCIATES INC.
One Prudential Plaza
Chicago IL 60601
Contact Robert F. Westcott, President. 312/856-1700. Executive search firm. Appointment required; unsolicited resumes accepted. Founded 1966. Independent management consulting firm which concentrates on organization planning, executive search, recruiting and appraisals. Specializes in the areas of: Administration, MIS/EDP; Advertising; Affirmative Action; Architechture; Banking and Finance; Broadcasting; Chemicals and Pharmaceuticals; Communications; Computer Hardware and Software;

Construction; Electrical; Engineering; Food Industry; General Management; Health and Medical; Human Resources; Industrial and Interior Design; Insurance; Legal; Manufacturing; Nonprofit; Operations Management; Printing and Publishing; Procurement; Real Estate; Retailing; Sales and Marketing; Technical and Scientific; Textiles; Transportation; Women. Noncontingency. Number of searches conducted per year: 51-100.

PHILIP WIELAND & ASSOCIATES
1150 Wilmette Avenue, Suite G
Wilmette IL 60091
Contact Philip J. Wieland, President. 708/256-8666. Executive search firm. Specializes in the area of: Legal.

Professional and Trade Associations

Anyone who has conducted a job search has heard the dictum, "It's not what you know, it's who you know." While the validity of this comment has just as often been exaggerated, it does contain more than a grain of truth. Connections can never replace good old hard work as the best method of finding employment, but they can't hurt.

If you don't have an uncle in high places who can set up some interviews for you with a few of his friends, don't worry. Most people don't. The important thing to remember is that in most instances, connections do not materialize out of thin air -- they are created. That means that anyone who works at it can make them.

One of the best ways to meet people in your area of interest is through professional trade associations. Trade associations exist so that professionals in an industry can meet, share information about trends in the field, and arrange new business. Many of them regularly publish newsletters and magazines that will help you stay abreast of the current state of your industry. In addition, many associations hold regular meetings, and these meetings may present you the opportunity not only to learn more about the field you hope to enter, but also to establish connections.

With this in mind, we have included this directory of professional associations. Many of the addresses listed are for headquarters offices only. Inquire about local chapters in your area.

ACCOUNTING

THE EDP AUDITORS ASSOCIATION
455 Kehoe Boulevard
Suite 106
Carol Stream IL 60188
708/682-1200

INDEPENDENT ACCOUNTANTS ASSOCIATION OF ILLINOIS
Carol Tarantur
1776 Ash Street
Northfield IL 60093
708/441-7800

INSTITUTE OF INTERNAL AUDITORS/CHICAGO CHAPTER
P.O. Box 973
Park Ridge IL 60068

For more information, contact:

**AMERICAN INSTITUTE OF
CERTIFIED PUBLIC ACCOUNTANTS**
1211 Avenue of the Americas
New York NY 10036
212/575-6200

NATIONAL SOCIETY OF PUBLIC ACCOUNTANTS
1010 North Fairfax Street
Alexandria VA 22314
703/549-6400

ADVERTISING, MARKETING, PUBLIC RELATIONS

AMERICAN MARKETING ASSOCIATION
250 South Wacker Drive
Suite 200
Chicago IL 60606
312/648-0536

FINANCIAL RELATIONS BOARD INC.
875 North Michigan Avenue
Suite 2250
Chicago IL 60611

TELEVISION BUREAU OF ADVERTISING/CHICAGO
400 North Michigan Avenue
Suite 616
Chicago IL 60611
312/527-3373

For more information, contact:

AMERICAN ADVERTISING FEDERATION
1400 K Street NW
Suite 1000
Washington DC 20005

AMERICAN ASSOCIATION OF ADVERTISING AGENCIES
666 Third Avenue, 13th Floor
New York NY 10017
212/682-2500

BUSINESS-PROFESSIONAL ADVERTISING ASSOCIATION
Metroplex Corporate Center
100 Metroplex Drive
Edison NJ 08817
201/985-4441

PUBLIC RELATIONS SOCIETY OF AMERICA
33 Irving Place
New York NY 10003
212/995-2230

TELEVISION BUREAU OF ADVERTISING
477 Madison Avenue
New York NY 10022
212/486-1111

APPAREL AND TEXTILES

AMERICAN APPAREL MANUFACTURERS ASSOCIATION
2500 Wilson Boulevard
Suite 301
Arlington VA 22201
703/524-1864

AMERICAN TEXTILE MANUFACTURERS INSTITUTE
1801 K Street NW
Suite 900
Washington DC 20006
202/862-0500

NORTHERN TEXTILE ASSOCIATION
230 Congress Street
Boston MA 02110
617/542-8220

TEXTILE RESEARCH INSTITUTE
Box 625
Princeton NJ 08542
609/924-3150

ARTS AND ENTERTAINMENT/LEISURE

AMERICAN FEDERATION OF MUSICIANS/CHICAGO
Local 10-208
175 West Washington Street
Chicago IL 60602
312/782-0063

NATIONAL ENDOWMENT FOR THE ARTS/CHICAGO
Lois Rubin
P.O. Box 597661
Chicago IL 60659-7661
708/965-6670

NATIONAL RECREATION AND PARKS ASSOCIATION/CHICAGO
Walter Johnson
c/o Great Lakes Service Center
650 West Higgins Road
Hoffman Estate IL 60195
708/843-7529

For more information, contact:

AMERICAN ASSOCIATION OF ZOOLOGICAL PARKS & AQUARIUMS
Oglebay Park
Wheeling WV 26003
304/242-2160

AMERICAN FEDERATION OF MUSICIANS
1501 Broadway, Suite 600
New York NY 10036
212/869-1330

AMERICAN FEDERATION OF TELEVISION AND RADIO ARTISTS
260 Madison Avenue
New York NY 10016
212/532-0800

NATIONAL ENDOWMENT FOR THE ARTS
1100 Pennsylvania Avenue NW
Washington DC 20506
202/682-5400

THEATRE COMMUNICATIONS GROUP
355 Lexington Avenue
New York NY 10017
212/697-5230

BANKING/SAVINGS AND LOAN

BANK ADMINISTRATION INSTITUTE
2550 Golf Road
Rolling Meadows IL 60008
800/323-8552

COMMUNITY BANKERS ASSOCIATION OF ILLINOIS
Robert J. Wingert, Executive Director
300 West Edwards Street
Suite 200
Springfield IL 62704
217/753-4331

ILLINOIS BANKERS ASSOCIATION
Suite 1111
111 North Canal Street
Chicago IL 60606-7204
312/876-9900

INSTITUTE OF FINANCIAL EDUCATION
111 East Wacker Drive
24th Floor
Chicago IL 60601
312/644-3100

For more information, contact:

AMERICAN BANKERS ASSOCIATION
1120 Connecticut Avenue NW
Washington DC 20036
202/663-5221

BANK ADMINISTRATION INSTITUTE
Plaza 1000, Suite 202
Voorhees NJ 08043
609/424-3233

INDEPENDENT BANKERS ASSOCIATION OF AMERICA
One Thomas Circle NW
Suite 950
Washington DC 20005
202/659-8111

NATIONAL COUNCIL OF SAVINGS INSTITUTIONS
1101 15th Street NW
Suite 400
Washington DC 20005
202/857-3100

BOOK AND MAGAZINE PUBLISHING

AMERICAN BOOKSELLERS ASSOCIATION
137 West 25th Street, 11th Floor
New York NY 10001
212/463-8450

ASSOCIATION OF AMERICAN PUBLISHERS
220 East 23rd Street
New York NY 10010
212/689-8920

MAGAZINE PUBLISHERS ASSOCIATION
575 Lexington Avenue, Suite 540
New York NY 10022
212/752-0055

WRITERS GUILD OF AMERICA EAST, INC.
555 West 57th Street, Suite 1230
New York NY 10019
212/245-6180

WRITERS GUILD OF AMERICA WEST, INC.
8955 Beverly Boulevard
Los Angeles CA 90048
213/550-1000

BROADCASTING

FEDERAL COMMUNICATIONS COMMISSION
Park Ridge Office, Room 306
1550 Northwest Highway
Park Ridge IL 60068
312/353-0196

ILLINOIS CABLE TELEVISION ASSOCIATION
c/o Richard J. Prendergast
111 West Washington Street
Suite 1100
Chicago IL 60602
312/641-0881

NATIONAL ASSOCIATION OF BROADCASTERS/ILLINOIS
2126 MacArthur Boulevard South
Springfield IL 62704
217/753-2636

TELEVISION BUREAU OF ADVERTISING/CHICAGO
400 North Michigan Avenue
Suite 616
Chicago IL 60611
312/527-3373

For more information, contact:

BROADCAST EDUCATION ASSOCIATION
1771 N Street NW
Washington DC 20036
202/424-5355

CABLE TELEVISION ASSOCIATION
1724 Massachusetts Avenue NW
Washington DC 20036
202/775-3550

INTERNATIONAL RADIO AND TV SOCIETY
420 Lexington Avenue
Suite 531
New York NY 10170
212/867-6650

NATIONAL ASSOCIATION OF BROADCASTERS
1771 N Street NW
Washington DC 20036
202/429-5300

**NATIONAL ASSOCIATION OF BUSINESS
AND EDUCATIONAL RADIO**
1501 Duke Street
Suite 200
Alexandria VA 22314
703/739-0300

TELEVISION BUREAU OF ADVERTISING
477 Madison Avenue
New York NY 10022
212/486-1111

WOMEN IN RADIO AND TV, INC.
1101 Connecticut Avenue NW
Suite 700
Washington DC 20036
202/429-5102

CHARITABLE, NON-PROFIT, HUMANITARIAN

**NATIONAL ORGANIZATION FOR HUMAN
SERVICE EDUCATION**
National College of Education
2840 Sheridan Road
Evanston IL 60201
708/256-5150

For more information, contact:

NATIONAL ASSOCIATION OF SOCIAL WORKERS
7981 Eastern Avenue
Silver Spring MD 20910
301/565-0333

CHEMICALS & RELATED: PROCESSING, PRODUCTION, DISPOSAL

AMERICAN INSTITUTE OF CHEMICAL ENGINEERING/CHICAGO
c/o Paul Rom
957 Highland Avenue
Glen Ellen IL 60137
312/693-1030

AMERICAN INSTITUTE OF CHEMISTS/CHICAGO
Marcus Bornfleth
1919 Swift Drive
Oak Brook IL 60521

For more information, contact:

AMERICAN CHEMICAL SOCIETY
Career Services
1155 16th Street NW
Washington DC 20036
202/872-4600

AMERICAN INSTITUTE OF CHEMICAL ENGINEERING
345 East 47th Street
New York NY 10017
212/705-7338

AMERICAN INSTITUTE OF CHEMISTS
7315 Wisconsin Avenue, Suite 525 E
Bethesda MD 20814
301/652-2447

ASSOCIATION OF STATE & INTERSTATE
 WATER POLLUTION CONTROL ADMINISTRATORS
444 North Capital Street NW
Suite #330 N
Washington DC 20001
202/624-7782

WATER POLLUTION CONTROL FEDERATION
601 Wythe Street Avenue NW
Alexandria VA 22314
703/684-2400

COLLEGES AND UNIVERSITIES/EDUCATION

AMERICAN ASSOCIATION OF SCHOOL ADMINISTRATORS
1801 North Moore Street
Arlington VA 22209
703/528-0700

ASSOCIATION OF AMERICAN UNIVERSITIES
One Dupont Circle NW
Suite 730
Washington DC 20036
202/466-5030

COMMUNICATIONS

COMMUNICATIONS WORKERS OF AMERICA/CHICAGO
650 East Devon Avenue
Suite 154
Itasca IL 60143
708/773-4570

For more information, contact:

COMMUNICATIONS WORKERS OF AMERICA
1925 K Street NW
Washington DC 20006
202/728-2300

UNITED STATES TELEPHONE ASSOCIATION
900 19th Street NW, Suite 800
Washington DC 20006
202/835-3100

COMPUTERS: HARDWARE, SOFTWARE AND SERVICES

ADAPSO/THE COMPUTER SOFTWARE AND SERVICES INDUSTRY ASSOCIATION
1300 North 17th Street, Suite 300
Arlington VA 22209
703/522-5055

ASSOCIATION FOR COMPUTER SCIENCE
P.O. Box 19027
Sacramento CA 95819
916/421-9149

ASSOCIATION FOR COMPUTING MACHINERY
11 West 42nd Street, 3rd Floor
New York NY 10036
212/869-7440

IEEE COMPUTER SOCIETY
1730 Massachusetts Avenue NW
Washington DC 20036-1903

SEMICONDUCTOR INDUSTRY ASSOCIATION
4300 Stevens Clark Boulevard, Suite 271
San Jose CA 95129
408/246-2711

CONSTRUCTION

BUILDING OFFICIALS AND CODE ADMINISTRATORS INTERNATIONAL, INC
4051 West Flossmoor Road
Country Club Hills IL 60478
708/799-2300

HOME BUILDERS ASSOCIATION OF GREATER CHICAGO
1010 Jorie Boulevard
Oak Brook IL 60521
708/990-7575

For more information, contact:

CONSTRUCTION INDUSTRY MANUFACTURERS ASSOCIATION
111 East Wisconsin Avenue, Suite 940
Milwaukee WI 53202
414/272-0943

INTERNATIONAL CONFERENCE OF BUILDING OFFICIALS
5360 South Workman Road
Whittier CA 90601
213/699-0541

NATIONAL ASSOCIATION OF HOME BUILDERS
15th & M Streets NW
Washington DC 20005
202/822-0200

ELECTRICAL AND ELECTRONICS

AMERICAN ELECTROPLATERS AND SURFACE
 FINISHERS SOCIETY/CHICAGO BRANCH
Frank Altmayer
c/o Scientific Control Labs
3158 South Kolin Avenue
Chicago IL 60623
312/254-2406

INSTITUTE OF ELECTRICAL AND ELECTRONICS
 ENGINEERS/CHICAGO
Robert Schrage
c/o Commonwealth Edison
P.O. Box 767, Seed 836
Chicago IL 60690
312/649-2800

For more information, contact:

AMERICAN ELECTROPLATERS AND SURFACE FINISHERS SOCIETY
12644 Research Parkway
Orlando FL 32826
407/281-6441

ELECTROCHEMICAL SOCIETY
10 South Main Street
Pennington NJ 08534-2896
609/737-1902

ELECTRONIC INDUSTRIES ASSOCIATION
2001 Pennsylvania Ave NW
Washington DC 20006
202/457-4900

ELECTRONICS TECHNICIANS ASSOCIATION
602 N. Jackson Street
Greencastle IN 46135
317/653-8262

INSTITUTE OF ELECTRICAL AND ELECTRONICS ENGINEERS
345 East 47th Street
New York NY 10017
212/705-7900

INTERNATIONAL BROTHERHOOD OF ELECTRICAL WORKERS
1125 15th Street NW
Washington DC 20005
202/833-7000

INTERNATIONAL SOCIETY OF CERTIFIED ELECTRONICS TECHNICIANS
2708 West Berry
Ft. Worth TX 76109
817/921-9101

NATIONAL ELECTRICAL MANUFACTURERS ASSOCIATION
2101 L Street NW, Suite 300
Washington DC 20037
202/457-8400

NATIONAL ELECTRONICS SALES AND SERVICES ASSOCIATION
2708 West Berry
Ft. Worth TX 76109
817/921-9061

ENGINEERING AND ARCHITECTURE

AMERICAN SOCIETY OF HEATING, REFRIGERATING AND AIR CONDITIONING ENGINEERS/CHICAGO
Paul Schwarz
c/o Henry Valve
3215 North Avenue
Melrose Park IL 60160
708/344-1100

AMERICAN SOCIETY OF LANDSCAPE ARCHITECTS/CHICAGO
c/o Theresa Sudges
501 Hill Avenue
Glen Ellen IL 60137
708/858-2462

AMERICAN SOCIETY OF SAFETY ENGINEERS
1800 East Oakton Street
Des Plaines IL 60018-2187
708/692-4121

ILLINOIS SOCIETY OF PROFESSIONAL ENGINEERS
1304 South Lowell
Springfield IL 62704
217/544-7424

INSTITUTE OF INDUSTRIAL ENGINEERS/CHICAGO
c/o Sarosh Khambatta
14200 Yorktown Drive
Orland Park IL 60462-2127
708/534-3400

SOCIETY OF FIRE PROTECTION ENGINEERS/CHICAGO
Barbara Filvis
8749 Summerdale
Chicago IL 60656

For more information, contact:

AMERICAN INSTITUTE OF ARCHITECTS
1735 New York Ave NW
Washington DC 20006
202/626-7300

AMERICAN SOCIETY OF CIVIL ENGINEERS
345 East 47th Street
New York NY 10017
212/705-7496

AMERICAN SOCIETY FOR ENGINEERING EDUCATION
11 Dupont Circle NW
Suite 200
Washington DC 20036
202/293-7080

AMERICAN SOCIETY OF HEATING, REFRIGERATING AND AIR CONDITIONING ENGINEERS
1791 Tullie Circle NE
Atlanta GA 30329
404/636-8400

AMERICAN SOCIETY OF NAVAL ENGINEERS
1452 Duke Street
Alexandria VA 22314
703/836-6727

AMERICAN SOCIETY OF PLUMBING ENGINEERS
3617 Thousand Oaks Boulevard
Suite #210
Westlake CA 91362
805/495-7120

ILLUMINATING ENGINEERING SOCIETY OF NORTH AMERICA
345 East 47th Street
New York NY 10017
212/705-7926

INSTITUTE OF INDUSTRIAL ENGINEERS
25 Technology Park
Norcross GA 30092
404/449-0460

NATIONAL ACADEMY OF ENGINEERING
2101 Constitution Avenue NW
Washington DC 20418
202/334-3200

NATIONAL SOCIETY OF PROFESSIONAL ENGINEERS
1420 King Street
Alexandria VA 22314
703/684-2800

SOCIETY OF FIRE PROTECTION ENGINEERS
60 Batterymarch Street
Boston MA 02110
617/482-0686

UNITED ENGINEERING TRUSTEES
345 East 47th Street
New York NY 10017
212/705-7000

FABRICATED METAL PRODUCTS/PRIMARY METALS

AMERICAN CASTE METALS ASSOCIATION
455 State Street
Des Plaines IL 60016
708/299-9156

NATIONAL ASSOCIATION OF METAL FINISHERS
111 East Wacker Drive, Suite 600
Chicago IL 60601
312/644-6610

For more information, contact:

AMERICAN POWDER METALLURGY INSTITUTE
105 College Road East
Princeton NJ 08540
609/452-7700

ASSOCIATION OF IRON AND STEEL ENGINEERS
Three Gateway Center
Suite 2350
Pittsburgh PA 15222
412/281-6323

FINANCIAL SERVICES/MANAGEMENT CONSULTING

AMERICAN SOCIETY OF APPRAISERS/CHICAGO
Charles Oeler
c/o Household International
2700 Sanders Road
Mt. Prospect IL 60070
708/564-6055

CHICAGO ASSOCIATION OF BUSINESS ECONOMISTS
John Sylvia
c/o Kemper Financial Services
120 South LaSalle
Chicago IL 60603
312/845-1755

CHICAGO ASSOCIATION OF CREDIT MANAGEMENT
315 South Northwest Highway
Park Ridge IL 60068
708/696-3000

FINANCIAL ANALYSTS FEDERATION/CHICAGO
600 South Federal Street, Suite 400
Chicago IL 60605
312/922-6222

FINANCIAL EXECUTIVES INSTITUTE/CHICAGO
Kent Lampkin
c/o Ameritech
30 South Wacker
Chicago IL 60606
312/750-5168

INSTITUTE OF FINANCIAL EDUČATION
111 East Wacker Drive, 24th Floor
Chicago IL 60601
312/644-3100

**INSTITUTE OF MANAGMENT CONSULTANTS/
GREATER CHICAGO CHAPTER**
John Chapin
c/o Coopers & Lybrand
203 North LaSalle Street
Chicago IL 60601
312/701-5500

For more information, contact:

AMERICAN FINANCIAL SERVICES ASSOCIATION
Fourth Floor, 1101 14th Street NW
Washington DC 20005
202/289-0400

AMERICAN SOCIETY OF APPRAISERS
P.O. Box 17265
Washington DC 20041
202/478-2228

ASSOCIATION OF MANAGEMENT CONSULTING FIRMS
230 Park Avenue, Suite 544
New York NY 10169
212/697-9693

COUNCIL OF CONSULTANT ORGANIZATIONS
230 Park Avenue
Suite 544
New York NY 10169
212/697-8262

FEDERATION OF TAX ADMINISTRATORS
444 North Capital Street NW
Washington DC 20001
202/624-5890

FINANCIAL ANALYSTS FEDERATION
1633 Broadway
Room 1602
New York NY 10019
212/957-2860

FINANCIAL EXECUTIVES INSTITUTE
10 Madison Avenue
P.O. Box 1938
Morristown NJ 07962-1938
201/898-4600

NATIONAL ASSOCIATION OF CREDIT MANAGEMENT
8815 Centre Park Drive
Suite 200
Columbia MD 21045-2117
301/740-5560

NATIONAL ASSOCIATION OF REAL ESTATE INVESTMENT TRUSTS
1129 20th Street NW
Suite 705
Washington DC 20036
202/785-8717

NATIONAL CORPORATE CASH
 MANAGEMENT ASSOCIATION
52 Church Hill Road
Newtown CT 06470
203/426-3007

SECURITIES INDUSTRY ASSOCIATION
120 Broadway
New York NY 10271
212/608-1500

FOOD: PROCESSING, PRODUCTION, AND DISTRIBUTION

ILLINOIS ASSOCIATION OF CEREAL CHEMISTS
Ronald Deis
c/o Nutra Sweet Co.
601 Kensington Road
Mt. Prospect IL 60056
708/506-4239

NATIONAL DAIRY COUNCIL
6300 North River Road
Rosemont IL 60018
708/696-1020

For more information, contact:

AMERICAN ASSOCIATION OF CEREAL CHEMISTS
3340 Pilot Knob Road
St. Paul MN 55121
612/454-7250

AMERICAN SOCIETY OF AGRICULTURAL ENGINEERS
2950 Niles Road
St. Joseph MI 49085
616/429-0300

AMERICAN SOCIETY OF BREWING CHEMISTS
3340 Pilot Knob Road
St. Paul MN 55121
612/454-7250

DAIRY AND FOOD INDUSTRIES SUPPLY ASSOCIATION
6245 Executive Boulevard
Rockville MD 20852
301/984-1444

NATIONAL AGRICULTURAL CHEMICALS ASSOCIATION
1155 15th Street NW
Suite 900
Washington DC 20005
202/296-1585

UNITED FOOD AND COMMERCIAL WORKERS INTERNATIONAL UNION
1775 K Street NW
Washington DC 20006
202/223-3111

GENERAL MERCHANDISE: RETAIL AND WHOLESALE

NATIONAL RETAIL MERCHANTS ASSOCIATION
100 West 31st Street
New York NY 10001
212/244-8780

HEALTH CARE AND PHARMACEUTICALS/HOSPITALS

AMERICAN COLLEGE OF HEALTHCARE EXECUTIVES
840 North Lake Shore Drive
Chicago IL 60611
312/943-0544

AMERICAN DENTAL ASSOCIATION
211 East Chicago Avenue
Chicago IL 60611
312/440-2500

AMERICAN MEDICAL ASSOCIATION
515 North State Street
Chicago IL 60610
312/645-5000

AMERICAN VETERINARY MEDICAL ASSOCIATION
930 North Meacham Road
Schaumburg IL 60196
708/605-8070

CHICAGO PHYSICAL THERAPY ASSOCIATION
Susan Suria
c/o NTS
3071 South Wolf Road
Westchester IL 60154
312/562-0999

ILLINOIS ACADEMY OF PHYSICIAN ASSISTANTS
20 North Michigan Avenue, Suite 700
Chicago IL 60602
312/263-7150

ILLINOIS SOCIETY OF HOSPITAL PHARMACISTS
c/o PAS
P.O. Box 6565
Athens GA 30604
404/613-0100

MEDICAL GROUP MANAGEMENT ASSOCIATION/ SPRINGFIELD BRANCH
Jan Garmong
c/o Moline Radiology Associates
1505 7th Street
Moline IL 61265-2992
309/762-1072

For more information, contact:

AMERICAN ACADEMY OF PHYSICIAN ASSISTANTS
950 North Washington Street
Alexandria VA 22314
703/836-2272

AMERICAN HEALTH CARE ASSOCIATION
1201 L Street NW
Washington DC 20005
202/842-4444

AMERICAN OCCUPATIONAL THERAPY ASSOCIATION
1383 Piccard Drive
Rockville MD 20850
301/948-9626

AMERICAN PHARMACEUTICAL ASSOCIATION
2215 Constitution Avenue NW
Washington DC 20037
202/628-4410

AMERICAN PHYSICAL THERAPY ASSOCIATION
1111 North Fairfax Street
Alexandria VA 22314
703/684-2782

AMERICAN SOCIETY FOR BIOCHEMISTRY AND MOLECULAR BIOLOGY
9650 Rockville Pike
Bethesda MD 20814
301/530-7145

AMERICAN SOCIETY OF HOSPITAL PHARMACISTS
4630 Montgomery Avenue
Bethesda MD 20814
301/657-3000

CARDIOVASCULAR CREDENTIALING INTERNATIONAL
P.O. Box 611
Dayton OH 45419
513/294-5225

MEDICAL GROUP MANAGEMENT ASSOCIATION
1355 South Colorado Boulevard
Suite 900
Denver CO 80222
303/753-1111

NATIONAL HEALTH COUNCIL
350 5th Avenue, Suite 1118
New York NY 10018
212/268-8900

NATIONAL MEDICAL ASSOCIATION
1012 Tenth Street NW
Washington DC 20001
202/347-1895

HOTEL AND RESTAURANT RELATED

**THE EDUCATION FOUNDATION OF
THE NATIONAL RESTAURANT ASSOCIATION**
250 South Wacker Drive
14th Floor
Chicago IL 60606
312/715-1010

For more information, contact:

THE AMERICAN HOTEL AND MOTEL ASSOCIATION
295 Lafayette Street, 7th Floor
New York NY 10012
212/941-5858

**COUNCIL ON HOTEL, RESTAURANT
AND INSTITUTIONAL EDUCATION**
1200 17th Street NW
Washington DC 20036
202/331-5990

INSURANCE

ALLIANCE OF AMERICAN INSURERS
1501 Woodfield Road
Suite 400 West
Schaumburg IL 60173-4980
708/330-8500

INSURANCE INFORMATION INSTITUTE OF CHICAGO
John Maes
10 South Riverside Plaza, Suite 1620
Chicago IL 60606

SOCIETY OF ACTUARIES
475 North Martingale Road
Suite 800
Schaumburg IL 60173-2226
708/706-3500

For more information, contact:

AMERICAN COUNCIL OF LIFE INSURANCE
1001 Pennsylvania Avenue NW
Washington DC 20004-2599
202/624-2000

AMERICAN INSURANCE ASSOCIATION
1130 Connecticut Avenue NW
Suite 1000
Washington DC 20036
202/828-7100

INSURANCE INFORMATION INSTITUTE
110 William Street
New York NY 10038
212/669-9200

NATIONAL ASSOCIATION OF LIFE UNDERWRITERS
1922 F Street NW
Washington DC 20006
202/331-6000

LEGAL SERVICES

AMERICAN BAR ASSOCIATION
750 North Lake Shore Drive
Chicago IL 60611
312/988-5000

FEDERAL BAR ASSOCIATION/CHICAGO CHAPTER
Lou Hegeman
c/o Gould & Ratner
222 North LaSalle
Chicago IL 60601
312/236-3003

NATIONAL FEDERATION OF PARALEGAL ASSOCIATIONS
Suite 201
104 Wilmot Road
Deerfield IL 60015
708/940-8800

For more information, contact:

FEDERAL BAR ASSOCIATION
1815 H Street NW, Suite 408
Washington DC 20006
202/638-0252

NATIONAL ASSOCIATION FOR LAW PLACEMENT
1666 Connecticut Avenue, Suite 450
Washington DC 20009
202/667-1666

NATIONAL ASSOCIATION OF LEGAL ASSISTANTS
1601 South Main Street, Suite 300
Tulsa OK 74119
918/587-6828

NATIONAL PARALEGAL ASSOCIATION
P.O. Box 629
Doylestown PA 18901
215/297-8333

MISCELLANEOUS ASSOCIATIONS

AMERICAN FEDERATION OF SMALL BUSINESS
407 South Dearborn Street, Suite 500
Chicago IL 60605
312/427-0206

For more information, contact:

NATIONAL COOPERATIVE BUSINESS ASSOCIATION
1401 New York Avenue NW
Suite #1100
Washington DC 20005
202/638-6222

NATIONAL SMALL BUSINESS UNITED
1155 15th Street NW
Suite 710
Washington DC 20005
202/293-8830

MISCELLANEOUS MANUFACTURING

NATIONAL ASSOCIATION OF MANUFACTURERS/
PARK RIDGE BRANCH
315 South Northwest Highway
Park Ridge IL 60068
708/698-3838

NATIONAL TOOLING AND MACHINING ASSOCIATION/
CHICAGO CHAPTER
Egon Jaeggin
c/o Numerical Precision Inc.
2200 Foster Avenue
Wheeling IL 60090
708/394-3610

NATIONAL SCREW MACHINE PRODUCTS ASSOCIATION/
NORTHERN ILLINOIS CHAPTER
Robert Kepler
c/o Commercial Tool Works, Inc.
3738 North River Road
Schiller Park IL 60176
708/678-9000

For more information, contact:

NATIONAL ASSOCIATION OF MANUFACTURERS
1331 Pennsylvania Avenue, NW
Suite 1500
Washington DC 20004
202/637-3000

NATIONAL MACHINE TOOL BUILDERS
7901 Westpark Drive
McLean VA 22102-4269
703/893-2900

NATIONAL SCREW MACHINE PRODUCTS ASSOCIATION
6700 West Snowville Road
Breckville OH 44141
216/526-0300

NATIONAL TOOLING AND MACHINING ASSOCIATION
9300 Livingston Road
Fort Washington MD 20744
301/248-1250

NEWSPAPER PUBLISHING

THE NEWSPAPER GUILD/CHICAGO LOCAL
230 North Michigan Avenue
Suite 1525
Chicago IL 60601
312/236-4924

For more information, contact:

AMERICAN NEWSPAPER PUBLISHERS ASSOCIATION
Box 17407
Dulles International Airport
Washington DC 20041
703/648-1000

AMERICAN SOCIETY OF NEWSPAPER EDITORS
P.O. Box 17004
Washington DC 20041
202/648-1144

THE DOW JONES NEWSPAPER FUND
P.O. Box 300
Princeton NJ 08543-0300
609/520-4000

INTERNATIONAL CIRCULATION MANAGERS ASSOCIATION
P.O. Box 17420
Washington DC 20041
703/620-9555

NATIONAL NEWSPAPER ASSOCIATION
1627 K Street NW
Suite 400
Washington DC 20006
202/466-7200

NATIONAL PRESS CLUB
529 14th St. NW
Washington DC 20045
202/662-7500

THE NEWSPAPER GUILD
133 West 44th Street
New York NY 10036
212/575-1580

PAPER PRODUCTS AND PACKAGING/CONTAINERS

PAPER INDUSTRY MANAGEMENT ASSOCIATION
2400 East Oakton Street
Arlington Heights IL 60005
708/956-0250

For more information, contact:

AMERICAN PAPER INSTITUTE
260 Madison Avenue
New York NY 10016
212/340-0600

TECHNICAL ASSOCIATION OF THE PULP AND PAPER INDUSTRY
P.O. Box 105113
Atlanta GA 30348
404/446-1400

PETROLEUM AND ENERGY RELATED/MINING AND DRILLING

AMERICAN INSTITUTE OF MINING, METALLURGICAL
AND PETROLEUM/CHICAGO
Douglas Hambley
1051 North Oakley Drive West
Westmont IL 60559
708/972-6478

AMERICAN NUCLEAR SOCIETY
555 North Kensington Avenue
La Grange Park IL 60525
708/352-6611

SOCIETY OF TRIBOLOGISTS
AND LUBRICATION ENGINEERS
838 Busse Highway
Park Ridge IL 60068
708/825-5536

For more information, contact:

AMERICAN ASSOCIATION OF PETROLEUM GEOLOGISTS
P.O. Box 979
Tulsa OK 74101
918/584-2555

AMERICAN GAS ASSOCIATION
1515 Wilson Boulevard
Arlington VA 22209
703/841-8400

AMERICAN GEOLOGICAL INSTITUTE
4220 King Street
Alexandria VA 22302
703/379-2480

AMERICAN INSTITUTE OF MINING,
METALLURGICAL AND PETROLEUM
345 East 47th Street
New York NY 10017
212/705-7695

AMERICAN PETROLEUM INSTITUTE
1220 L Street NW
Washington DC 20005
202/682-8000

CLEAN ENERGY RESEARCH INSTITUTE
P.O. Box 248294
Coral Gables FL 33124
305/284-4666

GEOLOGICAL SOCIETY OF AMERICA
3300 Penrose Place
P.O. Box 9140
Boulder CO 80301
303/447-2020

SOCIETY OF EXPLORATION GEOPHYSICISTS
P.O. Box 702740
Tulsa OK 74170-2740
918/493-3516

PRINTING

BINDING INDUSTRIES OF AMERICA
70 East Lake Street
Chicago IL 60601-5905
312/372-7606

For more information, contact:

ASSOCIATION OF GRAPHIC ARTS
5 Penn Plaza
New York NY 10001
212/279-2100

NATIONAL ASSOCIATION OF PRINTERS AND LITHOGRAPHERS
780 Pallisade Avenue
Teaneck NJ 07666
201/342-0700

PRINTING INDUSTRIES OF AMERICA
1730 North Lynn Street
Arlington VA 22209
703/841-8100

TECHNICAL ASSOCIATION OF THE GRAPHIC ARTS
Box 9887
Rochester NY 14614
716/272-0557

REAL ESTATE

**BUILDING OWNERS AND MANAGERS ASSOCIATION/
SUBURBAN CHICAGO**
3158 River Road, Suite123
Des Plaines IL 60018
708/635-6709

INSTITUTE OF REAL ESTATE MANAGEMENT
430 North Michigan Avenue
Chicago IL 60611
312/661-1930

**INTERNATIONAL ASSOCIATION OF CORPORATE
REAL ESTATE EXECUTIVES/CHICAGO CHAPTER**
Ed O'Donohue
c/o Illinois Bell
225 West Randolph, Room 25A
Chicago IL 60606
312/727-3905

NATIONAL ASSOCIATION OF REALTORS
430 North Michigan Avenue
Chicago IL 60611
312/329-8200

For more information, contact:

APARTMENT OWNERS AND MANAGERS ASSOCIATION
65 Cherry Plaza
Watertown CT 06795
203/274-2589

BUILDING OWNERS AND MANAGERS ASSOCIATION
1521 Ritchie Highway, P.O. Box 9709
Arnold MD 21012
301/261-2882

**INTERNATIONAL ASSOCIATION OF CORPORATE
 REAL ESTATE EXECUTIVES**
440 Columbia Drive, Suite 100
West Palm Beach FL 33409
407/683-8111

INTERNATIONAL REAL ESTATE INSTITUTE
8383 East Evans Road
Scottsdale AZ 85260
602/998-8267

NATIONAL ASSOCIATION OF REAL ESTATE INVESTMENT TRUSTS
1129 20th Street NW
Suite 705
Washington DC 20036
202/785-8717

RUBBER AND PLASTICS

SOCIETY OF PLASTICS INDUSTRY/DES PLAINES
2400 East Devon Avenue, Suite 301
Des Plaines IL 60018
708/297-6150

For more information, contact:

SOCIETY OF PLASTIC ENGINEERS
14 Fairfield Drive
Brookfield Centre CT 06804
203/775-0471

SOCIETY OF PLASTICS INDUSTRY
355 Lexington Avenue
New York NY 10017
212/370-7340

TRANSPORTATION/SHIPPING/AUTOMOTIVE

AIR LINE EMPLOYEES ASSOCIATION
5600 South Central Avenue
Chicago IL 60638
312/767-3333

AIR TRANSPORT ASSOCIATION OF CHICAGO
2128 South Road
Des Plaines IL 60018
708/299-7690

ASSOCIATION OF AMERICAN RAILROADS/CHICAGO
3140 South Federal Street
Chicago IL 60616
312/567-3606

AUTOMOTIVE SERVICE ASSOCIATION/CHICAGO
Mike Lane
c/o PAMS Inc.
625 South 2nd Street
Springfield IL 62704
217/528-5230

AUTOMOTIVE SERVICE INDUSTRY ASSOCIATION
444 North Michigan Avenue
Chicago IL 60611
312/836-1300

ILLINOIS TRUCKING ASSOCIATION
2000 5th Avenue
River Grove IL 60171
708/452-3500

NATIONAL MARINE MANUFACTURERS ASSOCIATION
401 North Michigan Avenue
Suite 1150
Chicago IL 60611
312/836-4747

NATIONAL MARINE MANUFACTURERS ASSOCIATION
401 North Michigan Avenue
Suite 1150
Chicago IL 60611
312/836-4747

For more information, contact:

AIR TRANSPORT ASSOCIATION OF AMERICA
1709 New York Ave NW
Washington DC 20006
202/626-4000

AMERICAN INSTITUTE OF AERONAUTICS AND ASTRONAUTICS
555 West 57th Street
New York NY 10019
212/247-6500

AMERICAN TRUCKING ASSOCIATION
2200 Mill Road
Alexandria VA 22314-4677
703/838-1700

ASSOCIATION OF AMERICAN RAILROADS
50 F Street NW
Washington DC 20001
202/639-2100

AUTOMOTIVE SERVICE ASSOCIATION
1901 Airport Freeway, Suite 100
Bedford TX 76021
817/283-6205

AVIATION MAINTENANCE FOUNDATION
P.O. Box 2826
Redmond WA 98073
206/828-3917

INSTITUTE OF TRANSPORTATION ENGINEERS
Suite 410
525 School Street SW, Suite 410
Washington DC 20024
202/554-8050

MARINE TECHNOLOGY SOCIETY
1825 K Street NW
Suite 218
Washington DC 20006
202/775-5966

MOTOR VEHICLE MANUFACTURERS ASSOCIATION
7430 2nd Avenue
Suite 300
Detroit MI 48202
313/872-4311

NATIONAL AERONAUTIC ASSOCIATION OF USA
1815 North Fort Meyer Drive
Arlington VA 22209
202/265-8720

NATIONAL AUTOMOTIVE DEALERS ASSOCIATION
8400 Westpark Drive
McLean VA 22102
703/821-7000

NATIONAL INSTITUTE FOR AUTOMOTIVE SERVICE EXCELLENCE
13505 Dulles Technology Drive
Herndon VA 22071
703/742-3800

PROFESSIONAL AVIATION MAINTENANCE ASSOCIATION
500 NW Plaza, Suite 809
St. Ann MO 63074
314/739-2580

SHIPBUILDERS COUNCIL OF AMERICA
1110 Vermont Ave. NW, Suite 1250
Washington DC 20005
202/775-9060

UTILITIES

AMERICAN WATER WORKS FOUNDATION/CHICAGO
William Plautz
c/o Consoer, Townsend & Associates
303 East Wacker Drive, Suite 600
Chicago IL 60601
312/938-0300

For more information, contact:

AMERICAN WATER WORKS ASSOCIATION
6666 West Quincy Avenue
Denver CO 80235
303/794-7711

Index

INDEX TO EMPLOYERS

ABB RAYMOND COMBUSTION ENGINEERING INC., 152
ABBOTT LABORATORIES, 181
ABF, 245
ACCO INTERNATIONAL, 208
ACE HARDWARE CORPORATION, 198
ADVANCE TRANSFORMER CO., 143
ADVANCED SYSTEM APPLICATIONS INC, 136
ADVERTISING METAL DISPLAY, 113
AIRCO, INC., 209
AIRCRAFT GEAR CORPORATION, 246
ALBERTO-CULVER CO., 198
ALDEN PRESS, INC., 239
ALLEN INDUSTRIES, 246
ALLIED CHEMICAL CORPORATON, 129
ALLIED PRODUCTS CORPORATION, 209
ALLIED TUBE AND CONDUIT, 155
ALLIED VAN LINES, 246
ALLSTATE INSURANCE CO., 191
ALLSTEEL INC., 209
ALTON AND SOUTHERN RAILWAY COMPANY, 246
ALTON MEMORIAL HOSPITAL, 181
ALTON MENTAL HEALTH CENTER, 181
ALTON TELEGRAPH PRINTING COMPANY, 226
AM INTERNATIONAL, 239
AMAX ZINC CO., 156
AMERICAN BAR ASSOCIATION, 196
AMERICAN DENTAL ASSOCIATION, 181
AMERICAN HOSPITAL ASSOCIATION, 182
AMERICAN NATIONAL BANK AND TRUST, 119
AMERICAN NATIONAL RED CROSS, 127
AMERICAN PRINTERS AND LITHOGRAPHERS, 239
AMERICAN SPRING AND WIRE SPECIALTY CO., 156
AMERICAN STEEL FOUNDRIES, 156
AMERICAN WARRANTY CORPORATION, 246
AMERITECH SERVICES, 134
AMES CORPORATION, 176
AMMCO TOOLS INC., 247
AMOCO CORPORATION, 236
AMOCO PETROLEUM ADDITIVES COMPANY, 236
AMSTED INDUSTRIES, 209
ANDREW CORPORATION, 135
ANIXTER BROTHERS, INC., 135
ANNING-JOHNSON CO., 139

AON CORPORATION, 191
APPLETON ELECTRIC CO., 143
APPLIED INFORMATION DEVELOPMENT, 136
APPLIED LEARNING, 137
ARA SERVICES, 187
ARATEX SERVICES, INC., 117
ARCHER DANIEL MIDLAND CO., 168
ARMSTRONG-BLUM MANUFACTURING CO., 209
ARNSTEIN AND LEHR, 197
ARROW GROUP INDUSTRIES, 209
ARTEX INTERNATIONAL INC., 117
ARTHUR YOUNG & COMPANY, 112
ARVEY CORPORATION, 228
ATCHISON TOPEKA & SANTA FE RAILWAY, 247
AUSTIN COMPANY, 153
AUTOMATIC DATA PROCESSING, 137
AYER INC, 113
B-LINE SYSTEMS INC., 156
BAGCRAFT OF AMERICA, 228
BAIRD & WARNER, 241
BAKER & McKENZIE, 197
BALL, INC., 168
BALLY MANUFACTURING, 116
BALLY MANUFACTURING/GAMING DIVISION, 199
BANKERS LIFE AND CASUALTY, 191
BARBER-GREENE CO., 139
BARCO CORPORATION, 210
BASF/COATING AND INKS DIVISION, 239
BASLER ELECTRIC COMPANY, 144
BAXTER HEALTHCARE, 182
BBDO CHICAGO INC., 113
BEALL MANUFACTURING DIVISION, 210
BEE CHEMICAL CO., 129
BELDING CORPORATION, 210
BELL & HOWELL COMPANY, 123
BELLEVILLE AREA COLLEGE, 133
BELLEVILLE SHOE MANUFACTURING COMPANY, 118
BELT RAILWAY CO. OF CHICAGO, 247
BENEFIT TRUST LIFE INSURANCE CO., 191
BENNETT INDUSTRIES, 228
BERKELEY-DAVIS, INC., 210
BEVERLY FARM FOUNDATION INC., 182
BINKS MANUFACTURING CO., 210
BLACKSTONE MANUFACTURING COMPANY, 237
BLUE M ELECTRIC COMPANY, 144
BOATMEN'S NATIONAL BANK OF BELLEVILLE, 120
BODINE ELECTRIC COMPANY, 144
BOISE CASCADE CORPORATION, 228

BORG-WARNER CORPORATION, 210
BOULEVARD BANK NATIONAL ASSOCIATION, 120
BOZELL, 113
BP CHEMICAL, 129
BRINK'S, INC., 247
BRUSH FUSES INC., 144
BURNS INTERNATIONAL SECURITY SERVICES, 225
BURTON SPRING, 247
CALSTAR CORPORATION, 199
CAMPBELL SOUP COMPANY, 168
CARSON PIRIE SCOTT, 187
CASTLE & COMPANY, 156
CATERPILLAR TRACTOR COMPANY, 247
CBI INDUSTRIES INC., 156
CECO CORPORATION, 139
CENTRAL CAN COMPANY, 228
CENTRAL ILLINOIS LIGHT COMPANY, 253
CENTRAL ILLINOIS PUBLIC SERVICE, 253
CENTRAL STEEL AND WIRE COMPANY, 157
CENTREVILLE TOWNSHIP HOSPITAL, 182
CF INDUSTRIES, 130
CHAPMAN AND CUTLER, 197
CHEMICAL WASTE MANAGEMENT, 130
CHICAGO BLOWER CORPORATION, 211
CHICAGO BOARD OF OPTIONS EXCHANGE, 164
CHICAGO BOARD OF TRADE, 164
CHICAGO DISPLAY COMPANY, 114
CHICAGO EXTRUDED METALS COMPANY, 211
CHICAGO FAUCET COMPANY, 211
CHICAGO LOCK COMPANY, 199
CHICAGO MERCANTILE EXCHANGE, 164
CHICAGO METROPOLITAN MUTUAL ASSURANCE COMPANY, 164
CHICAGO MILWAUKEE CORPORATION, 164
CHICAGO RAWHIDE MANUFACTURING COMPANY, 211
CHICAGO RIVET & MACHINE COMPANY, 211
CHICAGO TITLE & TRUST COMPANY, 241
CHICAGO TRIBUNE, 226
CHILDRENS PRESS, 124
CHRISTIANITY TODAY, INC., 124
CINCH CONNECTORS, 211
CITICORP SAVINGS OF ILLINOIS, 120
CLARK OIL & REFINING, 237
CLARK OIL AND REFINING CORPORATION, 237
CLIFTON GUNDERSON & COMPANY, 111
CNA INSURANCE COMPANIES, 191
CNW, 248
COLLINSVILLE HOLIDAY INN, 188
COLLINSVILLE MAC INC., 188

COLUMBIA QUARRY COMPANY, 237
COMBINED INSURANCE COMPANY, 192
COMDISCO, 137
COMMERCE CLEARING HOUSE, INC., 124
COMMERCIAL LIGHT COMPANY, 144
COMMERCIAL STAMPING & FORGING, INC., 212
COMMONWEALTH EDISON COMPANY, 253
CONAGRA FLOUR MILLING COMPANY, 169
CONSOER, TOWNSEND, & ASSOCIATES, INC., 153
CONTINENTAL AIR TRANSPORT, 248
CONTINENTAL CORPORATION, 165
CONTINENTAL GRAIN COMPANY, 169
CONTINENTAL ILLINOIS NATIONAL BANK, 120
CONTRACTING & MATERIAL COMPANY, 139
CONTROL DATA INSTITUTE, 135
COOK PUBLISHING COMPANY, 124
COTTER COMPANY, 199
COUNSELOR COMPANY, 199
COUNTRY COMPANIES, 192
CPC INTERNATIONAL/BEST FOODS DIVISION, 169
CRANE, INC., 228
CULINARY FOODS, INC., 169
CULLIGAN INTERNATIONAL, 212
CUMMINS ALLISON CORPORATION, 200
CURTIS INDUSTRIES, INC., 182
DAILY HERALD-PADDOCK PUBLICATIONS, 226
DAMON LABS, 183
DANA CORPORATION, 212
DANLY MACHINE DIVISION, 212
DANVILLE METAL STAMPING COMPANY, INC., 157
DAVY McKEE CORPORATION, 153
DDB NEEDHAM WORLDWIDE, 114
DEERE & COMPANY, 213
DELOITTE & TOUCHE, 111
DESOTO, INC., 200
DEXTER CORPORATION, 213
DICK COMPANY, 213
DO-ALL COMPANY, 214
DOMINICK'S FINER FOODS, 169
DONNELLEY DIRECTORY, 125
DRAKE HOTEL, 188
DRESSER FINANCE CORPORATION, 165
DRON ELECTRICAL COMPANY INC., 145
DUCHOSSOIS INDUSTRIES, INC,, 145
DUDEK & BOCK SPRING MANUFACTURING, 214
DUO-FAST CORPORATION, 214
DURO METAL PRODUCTS COMPANY, 214
DYNASCAN CORPORATION, 145

EAGLE BANCORPORATION INC., 120
EATON CONTROLS DIVISION, 145
EATON CORPORATION, 214
ECHLIN MANUFACTURING COMPANY, 248
ECONOMY MECHANICAL INDUSTRIES, 139
EDWARD DON & COMPANY, 170
ELECTRO-MOTIVE DIVISION, 248
ELGIN, JOLIET & EASTERN RAILWAY COMPANY, 248
ELGIN NATIONAL INDUSTRIES, 214
EMPIRE STOVE COMPANY, 200
ENCYCLOPEDIA BRITANNICA, 125
ENVIRODYNE INDUSTRIES, INC., 170
EQUIFAX INC., 165
EQUIPTO, 215
EUREKA COMPANY, 200
EVANS, INC., 176
EXCHANGE NATIONAL BANK OF CHICAGO, 120
EXECUTIVE HOUSE HOTEL, 188
F&B MANUFACTURING CO., 248
FABER ENTERPRISES, 188
FAIRMONT RACE TRACK, 116
FARLEY INDUSTRIES, 186
FEDERAL KEMPER INSURANCE COMPANY, 192
FEDERAL RESERVE BANK OF CHICAGO, 121
FEDERAL SIGNAL CORPORATION, 215
FERMI NATIONAL ACCELERATOR LABORATORY, 242
FIATALLIS NORTH AMERICA, INC., 215
FIELD MUSEUM OF NATURAL HISTORY, 116
FINKL & SONS, 157
FIRESTONE TIRE, 176
FIRESTONE TIRE AND RUBBER COMPANY, 249
FIRST CHICAGO CORPORATION, 165
FIRST NATIONAL BANK OF BELLEVILLE, 121
FISCHER'S RESTAURANT, 189
FLEX-O-GLASS, 243
FLORSHEIM SHOE COMPANY, 118
FLOUR DANIEL, 153
FLOUR MILLS DIVISION, 170
FLUID POWER SYSTEMS, 215
FMC CORPORATION, 130
FOLLETT CORPORATION, 125
FOOTE CONE AND BELDING COMMUNICATIONS, 113
FOOTE JONES, 215
FORT HOWARD CUP CORP., 170
FOUR FOUNTAINS CONVALESCENT, 183
FOURTH DEARBORN/BLUE CROSS, 192
FURNAS ELECTRIC COMPANY, 145
G&W ELECTRIC COMPANY, 145

G.R. GROUP, INC., 249
GARDEN CITY ENVELOPE COMPANY, 229
GARDNER, CARTON, & DOUGLAS, 197
GARRETT GENERAL AVIATION, 249
GATELY'S PEOPLE STORE, 176
GATX CORPORATION, 249
GBC, 216
GE RAILCAR SERVICES CORPORATION, 250
GEE COMPANY, 229
GENERAL BISCUIT BRANDS, INC., 170
GENERAL FIRE EXTINGUISHER CORPORATION, 130
GEORGIA PACIFIC, 229
GEORGIA-PACIFIC, 229
GERMANIA FEDERAL SAVINGS AND LOAN ASSOCIATION, 121
GLOBE INDUSTRIES, 139
GOLD BOND BUILDING PRODUCTS, 140
GOLDEN GRAIN, 170
GONNELLA BAKING COMPANY, 171
GOODMAN EQUIPMENT CORPORATION, 237
GOODYEAR TIRE AND RUBBER COMPANY, 250
GRACE, 130
GRAINGER, INC., 216
GRANITE CITY STEEL DIVISION, 157
GRAY CORPORATION, 140
GREAT LAKES MAINTENENCE & SECURITY CORPORATION, 225
GREELEY AND HANSEN, 153
GREIF BROTHERS CORPORATION, 229
GROEN COMPANY, 183
GUARDIAN ELECTRIC MANUFACTURING CO., 146
GUNDLACH MACHINE COMPANY, 237
HAEGER POTTERIES, 200
HALL CONSTRUCTION COMPANY, 140
HANDY BUTTON MACHINE, 157
HARCROS PIGMENTS INC., 130
HARRIS TRUST AND SAVINGS BANK, 121
HARRIS-HUB/DRESHER, 157
HARTMARX CORPORATION, 118
HEILEMAN BREWING CO., 171
HELLER FINANCIAL, 166
HENDRICKSON INTERNATIONAL, 250
HIGHLAND SUPPLY CORPORATION, 230
HODES ADVERTISING, 114
HOEFFKEN BROS. INC., 140
HOFFER PLASTICS CORPORATION, 243
HOLIDAY INNS, INC., 189
HOLLYMATIC CORPORATION, 216
HOME NURSERY GREENHOUSES INC., 177
HONEYWELL INC., 137

HOUSEHOLD INTERNATIONAL, 166
HYATT REGENCY CHICAGO, 189
HYRE ELECTRIC COMPANY, 146
HYSAN CORPORATION, 130
IBM, 137
IDEAL ROLLER COMPANY, 216
ILLINI FEDERAL SAVINGS AND LOAN ASSOCIATION, 121
ILLINOIS BELL, 135
ILLINOIS CENTRAL GULF RAILROAD COMPANY, 250
ILLINOIS FARM BUREAU, 171
ILLINOIS FARMERS INSURANCE COMPANY, 192
ILLINOIS GEAR, 216
ILLINOIS POWER, 253
ILLINOIS POWER COMPANY, 254
ILLINOIS TOOL WORKS, 217
INFORMATION RESOURCES, INC., 114
INGRID DIVISION OF SEVKO, INC., 243
INLAND STEEL INDUSTRIES, 157
INLANDER-STEINDLER PAPER COMPANY, 230
INTERMATIC, INC., 146
INTERNATIONAL ASSOCIATION OF LIONS CLUBS, 128
INTERNATIONAL HOUGH DIVISION/DRESSER INDUSTRIES, 217
INTERNATIONAL MINERALS & CHEMICAL CORPORATION, 131
INTERNATIONAL PAPER COMPANY, 230
INTERNATIONAL PAPER COMPANY/PEORIA, 240
INTERSTATE BRANDS CORPORATION, 171
ITEL, 186
ITEL/PULLMAN, 250
ITT McDONNELL & MILLER, 217
ITT/FLUID HANDLING DIVISION, 217
IVEX CORPORATION, 230
JAKEL INCORPORATED, 146
JAYS FOODS, INC., 171
JEFFERSON SMURFIT CORPORATION, 231
JEFFERSON-SMURFIT, 230
JOHNSON CONTROLS, 146
JOHNSON PRODUCTS COMPANY, 183
K'S MERCHANDISE, 177
K-MART CORPORATION, 177
KALMUS & ASSOCIATES, INC., 146
KEARNEY, INC., 166
KECK, MAHIN, & CATE, 197
KEEBLER COMPANY, 171
KEMPER GROUP, 166
KENNY CONSTRUCTION COMPANY, 140
KERR GLASS MANUFACTURING CORPORATION, 231
KETCHUM COMMUNICATIONS, INC., 115
KITCHENS OF SARA LEE, 172

KLEIN TOOLS, INC., 200
KNIGHT & ASSOCIATES, INC., 166
KNOWLES ELECTRONICS, INC., 146
KNOX COUNTY COUNCIL/DEVELOPMENTAL DISABILITIES, 128
KPMG/PEAT MARWICK, 111
KRAFT HOLLEB, 172
KRAFT, INC., 172
KROCH'S & BRENTANO'S, INC., 177
KROPP FORGE DIVISION, 158
LAKEWOOD ENGINEERING & MANUFACTURING COMPANY, 201
LANE BRYANT, INC., 118
LASALLE, 121
LASALLE BANK/LAKEVIEW BANK, 121
LAVENTHOL & HORWATH, 111
LAWSON PRODUCTS, 251
LEAF, INC., 172
LEEWARDS, 201
LERNER NEWSPAPERS, INC., 227
LERNER STORES CORPORATION, 118
LEVY CIRCULATING COMPANY, 125
LEWIS & CLARK COMMUNITY COLLEGE, 133
LIBERTY MUTUAL INSURANCE GROUP, 192
LIGHTOLIER, 201
LINDBERG CORPORATION, 158
LIQUID AIR CORPORATION, 238
LIQUID CARBONIC CORPORATION, 238
LLOYD'S ELECTRONICS, 201
LOCKE HOME PRODUCTS, 202
LORD, BISSELL, & BROOK, 197
MARSH COMPANY, 217
MAY & SPEH DATA PROCESSING, 166
McGRAW-EDISON COMPANY/MACOMB, 147
McKENDREE COLLEGE, 134
McMASTER-CARR SUPPLY COMPANY, 217
MEAD CONTAINER, 231
MEMORIAL HOSPITAL, 183
MERCHANDISE MART PROPERTIES, INC., 242
MERCHANDISE NATIONAL BANK, 122
MERRILL LYNCH, 167
METAL REMOVAL TOOLING, 158
METHODE ELECTRONICS INC., 147
MIDWEST RUBBER RECLAIMING COMPANY, 244
MIDWEST STOCK EXCHANGE INC., 167
MILLER FLUID POWER CORPORATION, 218
MILLER-DAVIS COMPANY, 140
MILLS-AMERICAN ENVELOPE, 231
MISSISSIPPI LIME COMPANY, 238
MITEK CORPORATION, 202

MODERN DROP FORGE COMPANY, 158
MOLEX INCORPORATED, 147
MONTGOMERY WARD & COMPANY, 177
MOORE BUSINESS FORMS & SYSTEMS DIVISION, 137
MORAN, 218
MOTOROLA INC., 148
MUSEUM OF SCIENCE & INDUSTRY, 117
NALCO CHEMICAL COMPANY, 131
NATIONAL BAKING COMPANY, 172
NATIONAL CASTINGS DIVISION, 158
NATIONAL METALWARES INC., 159
NATIONAL SAFETY COUNCIL, 128
NATIONAL STEEL CORPORATION, 159
NAVISTAR INTERNATIONAL CORPORATION, 218
NBC INC., 127
NCR CORPORATION, 138
NESCO STEEL BARREL COMPANY, 159
NESTLE FOODS CORPORATION, 173
NEWARK ELECTRONICS, 148
NEWELL, 186
NEWS DEMOCRAT, 227
NEWS-SUN, 227
NICOR, 254
NIELSEN, 127
NORTH AMERICAN COMPANY, 193
NORTHERN ILLINOIS GAS COMPANY, 254
NORTHERN TRUST COMPANY, 168
NORTHWEST NATIONAL BANK, 122
NORTHWESTERN STEEL AND WIRE COMPANY, 159
NUARC COMPANY INC., 202
NYSTROM COMPANY, 202
O'BRYAN BROTHERS, 118
O'NEIL CONSTRUCTION, 143
OAK SWITCH SYSTEMS INC.,, 148
OLD KENT BANK, 122
OLD REPUBLIC INTERNATIONAL, 193
OLIN CORPORATION, 131
OLIN CORPORATION, 219
OSCAR MAYER FOODS CORPORATION, 173
OTIS ELEVATOR COMPANY, 219
OUTBOARD MARINE CORPORATION, 203
OWENS AND COMPANY INC., 203
OWENS-ILLINOIS INC., 232
OXFORD CLOTHES, 119
OZITE CORPORATION, 119
PACKAGING CORPORATION OF AMERICA, 232
PACKARD INSTRUMENT COMPANY, 183
PANDUIT CORPORATION, 244

PARKER-HANNIFIN CORPORATION, 219
PARKVIEW METAL PRODUCTS, 160
PASCHEN CONTRACTORS INC., 141
PAYMASTER CORPORATION, 203
PEABODY MYERS CORPORATION, 219
PEERLESS OF AMERICA, 220
PENNEY COMPANY INC., 177
PEOPLES GAS COMPANY, 254
PETERSON, ROSS, SCHLOERB & SEIDEL, 198
PHEASANT RUN INC., 189
PHILLIPS, GETSCHOW COMPANY, 141
PINKERTON'S, INC., 225
PIONEER SCREW & NUT COMPANY, 220
PITMAN-MOORE, INC., 131
PITTWAY CORPORATION, 220
PLASTOFILM INDUSTRIES, INC., 233
POLK BROTHERS, 178
PRAIRIE FARMS DAIRY INC., 174
PREMARK INTERNATIONAL, 244
PRICE WATERHOUSE, 112
PRINCIPIA COLLEGE, 134
QUAKER OATS COMPANY, 174
QUASAR COMPANY, 203
R&D THIEL INC., 141
R.A. BRIGGS & COMPANY, 118
RAM GOLF CORPORATION, 204
RAMADA HOTEL O'HARE, 189
RAND McNALLY & COMPANY, 125
RAULAND-BORG CORPORATION, 149
RELIABLE ELECTRIC COMPANY, 135
REPUBLIC MOLDING CORPORATION, 244
RESPIRATORY CARE INC. (RCI), 184
REVCOR, INC., 221
REYNOLDS METALS COMPANY, 160
RHEEM MANUFACTURING COMPANY, 161
RHONE-POULENC BASIC CHEMICAL COMPANY, 132
RICHARDS BRICK COMPANY, 141
RICHARDSON ELECTRONICS, LTD., 149
RITZ CARLTON HOTEL, 190
ROADMASTER CORPORATION, 204
ROCK-OLA MANUFACTURING CORPORATION, 204
ROCKWELL GRAPHIC SYSTEMS, 251
ROCKWELL INTERNATIONAL, 135
ROESCH INC., 161
ROTARY INTERNATIONAL, 193
RUDNICK & WOLFE, 198
RUST-OLEUM CORPORATION, 204
SAATCHI SAATCHI DFS, 115

SAFECO INSURANCE COMPANIES, 194
SAFETY-KLEEN, 226
SAKS FIFTH AVENUE, 178
SALEM TECHNICAL SERVICES, 154
SALISBURY & COMPANY, 244
SANTA FE SOUTHERN PACIFIC CORPORATION, 251
SARA LEE, 174
SARGENT & LUNDY, 154
SARGENT-WELCH SCIENTIFIC COMPANY, 242
SAXON PAINT & HOME CARE CENTERS, 178
SCHAWK GRAPHICS INC., 240
SCHMIDT, GARDEN & ERIKSON, INC., 154
SCHOLLE CORPORATION, 233
SCHUMACHER ELECTRIC CORPORATION, 149
SCHWINN BICYCLE COMPANY, 205
SCIAKY BROTHERS INC, 221
SCOTT, FORESMAN AND COMPANY, 125
SCRIPTURE PRESS PUBLICATIONS, 126
SCULLY-JONES CORPORATION, 221
SEARLE & COMPANY, 178
SEARS, ROEBUCK & COMPANY, 179
SENTRY INSURANCE COMPANY, 194
SHEFFIELD STEEL CORPORATION, 141
SHELL OIL COMPANY, 238
SHELL OIL COMPANY/WOOD RIVER, 238
SHERWIN-WILLIAMS COMPANY, 179
SHURE BROTHERS INC., 149
SIGNAL PLASTICS, 245
SIGNODE INDUSTRIES INC., 234
SKIDMORE, OWINGS & MERILL, 155
SKIL CORPORATION, 205
SLOAN VALVE COMPANY, 161
SMITH DIVISION, 234
SMYTH'S HOMEMAKERS, 179
SOLA ELECTRIC, 150
SOLLITT CONSTRUCTION COMPANY, 142
SOLO CUP COMPANY, 234
SOUTHERN ILLINOIS UNIVERSITY AT EDWARDSVILLE, 134
SOUTHTOWN ECONOMIST, INC., 227
SPACEMASTER, 205
SPIEGEL INC., 206
SPOTNAILS INC., 222
SQUARE D COMPANY, 150
ST. CHARLES MANUFACTURING, 206
ST. CLEMENT HOSPITAL, 184
ST. ELIZABETH'S HOSPITAL, 184
ST. JOSEPH HOSPITAL, 184, 185
ST. LOUIS NATIONAL STOCK YARDS COMPANY, 186

ST. PAUL FEDERAL BANK FOR SAVINGS, 122
ST. PAUL'S HOMES FOR THE AGED, 185
STANDARD RATE & DATA, 126
STEIN ROE & FARNHAM, 167
STEPAN COMPANY, 132
STEPHENS-ADAMSON, INC., 222
STONE CONTAINER CORPORATION, 234
SUN CHEMICAL CORPORATION, 132
SUN ELECTRIC COMPANY, 150
SUNSTRAND, 251
SUPERIOR COFFEE COMPANY, 174
SWITCHCRAFT, INC., 151
SYMONS CORPORATION, 142
SYSCO FOOD SERVICES, 174
TAD TECHNICAL SERVICES CORPORATION, 155
TALMAN HOME FEDERAL SAVINGS AND LOAN, 123
TARACORP INDUSTRIES, 161
TC INDUSTRIES, 222
TELEPHONE & DATA SYSTEMS INC., 136
TEMPEL STEEL COMPANY, 162
TEMPLETON, KENLY & CO. INC., 222
TERMINAL RAILROAD ASSOCIATION/ST. LOUIS, 251
THOMPSON STEEL COMPANY, 162
THOMPSON USA INC., 115
THRALL CAR MANUFACTURING COMPANY, 252
TICOR TITLE INSURANCE, 194
TOPCO ASSOCIATES, INC., 174
TRAVELERS INSURANCE COMPANY, 195
TRI-CITY ELECTRIC COMPANY, 151
TRI-R VENDING SERVICE, 190
TUTHILL PUMP DIVISION, 223
UARCO INC., 240
UDDEHOLM CORPORATION, 162
UNION CARBIDE CORPORATION, 223
UNITED AIR CLEANER COMPANY, 223
UNITED AIRLINES, 252
UNITED EQUITABLE INSURANCE GROUP, 195
UNITED STATES TOBACCO MANUFACTURING COMPANY, 206
UNITED STATIONERS SUPPLY COMPANY, 206
UNR INDUSTRIES, INC., 186
UPPCO, INC., 223
USG COPORATION, 142
USS/A DIVISION OF USX CORPORATION, 162
VAPOR CORPORATION, 252
VEDDER, PRICE, KAUFMAN, & KAMMHOLZ, 198
VENTURE STORES, 180
VERSON, 162
VIENNA BEEF LTD., 175

VULCAN MATERIALS COMPANY, 224
WALDORF CORPORATION, 235
WALLACE COMPUTER SERVICES INC., 138
WASHINGTON NATIONAL CORPORATION, 195
WAUSAU INSURANCE COMPANIES, 196
WEBER MARKING SYSTEMS, INC., 151
WELDED TUBE COMPANY OF AMERICA, 163
WELLS MANUFACTURING COMPANY, 163
WELLS-GARDNER ELECTRONICS CORPORATION, 151
WEN PRODUCTS, INC., 207
WESLEY-JESSEN CORP., 185
WESTERN KRAFT PAPER GROUP, 235
WESTIN HOTEL, 190
WESTINGHOUSE ELECTRIC, 151
WEYERHAEUSER PAPER COMPANY, 235
WHITING CORPORATION, 224
WICKS ORGAN COMPANY, 117
WILCOX MANUFACTURING, 207
WILSON JONES COMPANY, 240
WILSON SPORTING GOODS CO., 207
WITCO CORPORATION, 133
WOOD RIVER TOWNSHIP HOSPITAL, 185
WOODLAWN ORGANIZATION, 128
WOODSTOCK DIE CASTING, 224
WOODWORK CORPORATION OF AMERICA, 236
WOOLWORTH COMPANY, 180
WORLD'S FINEST CHOCOLATE, 175
WRIGLEY, JR. COMPANY, 175
YEOMANS CHICAGO, 225
YOUNG & RUBICAM/CHICAGO, 115
ZENITH ELECTRONICS CORPORATION, 208
ZURICH-AMERICAN INSURANCE COMPANIES, 196

INDEX TO EMPLOYMENT SERVICES

ACCORD INC., 257, 277
ADVANTAGE PERSONNEL, 257
AMERICAN ASSOCIATION OF RETIRED PERSONS SENIOR
    COMMUNITY SERVICE EMPLOYMENT PROGRAM, 257
APT (ABLE'S POOL OF TEMPORARIES), 258
ASHTON & ASSOCIATES, LTD, 258
ASHTON & ASSOCIATES, LTD., 277
AVAILABILITY, INC., 258
B-W AND ASSOC., INC., 259
BRITT ASSOCIATES, INC., 259
CAREER MANAGEMENT ASSOCIATES, 259
CASEY FOR ACCOUNTANTS, 259
CATALYST SEARCH, INC., 277
CEMCO SYSTEMS, 260
CHICAGO FINANCIAL SEARCH, 278
COMPUSEARCH OF BARRINGTON HILLS, 278
COMPUSEARCH OF CHAMPAIGN, 278
COMPUSEARCH OF DES PLAINES, 279
CORPORATE ENVIRONMENT, LTD., 279
CORRUGATED BOX CONSULTANTS, 260
CPU ASSOCIATES, 260
CREATIVE OPTIONS, INC., 260
CREATIVE STAFFING ENTERPRISES, INC., 279
DAVID ASSOCIATES, INC., 264
DICKEY & ASSOCIATES, INC., 261
DUNHILL OF CHICAGO, 261
DUNHILL OF NORTHSIDE CHICAGO, 261
DUNHILL PERSONNEL SYSTEM OF ILLINOIS, 279
DYNAMIC SEARCH SYSTEMS, INC., 261
EDP TEMPS AND CONTRACT SERVICES, 261
ELITE PERSONNEL SERVICE, INC., 262
ELSKO EXECUTIVE SEARCH, 280
ESQUIRE PERSONNEL SERVICES, INC., 262
FARDIG ASSOCIATES, 262
FIRST SEARCH, INC., 280
FORESIGHT, 280
GEER, GRICE & HOLDENER, 280
GENERAL EMPLOYMENT ENTERPRISES INC., 263
GODFREY PERSONNEL INC., 263
GRAHAM ROBERTS ASSOCIATES, 280
GROVE PERSONNEL SERVICES, 263
HEALTH STAFFERS, 281
HILTON RESEARCH ASSOCIATES-MID WEST, 263
HIRTZ & ASSOCIATES, 281

J.C.G. LIMITED, INC., 264
JACOBSON ASSOCIATES, 281
KINGSLEY EMPLOYMENT, 264
MACINTYRE EMPLOYMENT SERVICES, LTD., 264
MANAGEMENT RECRUITERS OF ALBION, 281
MANAGEMENT RECRUITERS OF ARLINGTON HEIGHTS, 282
MANAGEMENT RECRUITERS OF BANNOCKBURN, 282
MANAGEMENT RECRUITERS OF BARRINGTON HILLS, 282
MANAGEMENT RECRUITERS OF CHAMPAIGN, 283
MANAGEMENT RECRUITERS OF CHERRY VALLEY, 283
MANAGEMENT RECRUITERS OF CHICAGO (DOWNTOWN), 284
MANAGEMENT RECRUITERS OF CHICAGO-SOUTHWEST, 284
MANAGEMENT RECRUITERS OF DES PLAINES, 284
MANAGEMENT RECRUITERS OF ELGIN, 285
MANAGEMENT RECRUITERS OF ST. CHARLES, 285
MANAGEMENT RECRUITERS OF WHEELING, 286
MANAGEMENT WORLD, 286
MURPHY GROUP, 265
OFFICEMATES5 OF BANNOCKBURN, 286
OFFICEMATES5 OF DES PLAINES, 287
OFFICEMATES5 OF NILES, 287
OFFICEMATES5 OF NORTHFIELD, 287
OFFICEMATES5 OF WHEELING, 288
OFFICEMATES5 OF WOODFIELD, 288
OPERATION ABLE, 266
OPPORTUNITY PERSONNEL SERVICE, 267
PAIGE PERSONNEL/PAIGE TEMPORARY, 267
PERMANENT PEOPLE, INC., 267
PINKERTON AND ASSOCIATES, INC., 289
POLLAK AND SKAN, INC., 267
PRESTIGE PERSONNEL, 268
PRESTIGE TEMPORARIES-CALUMET DIVISION, 268
PRESTIGE TEMPORARIES-HOMEWOOD DIVISION, 268
PROFILE FINANCIAL SEARCH, 289
PROFILE PERSONNEL, INC., 269
PROFILE TEMPORARY SERVICE, INC., 269
RAYMOND JAMES SMITH & CLINICAL LEGAL SEARCH, 293
RECRUITING RESOURCES GROUP, 289
RICHARD ALLEN WINTER ASSOC. INC., 269
RITT - RITT AND ASSOCIATES, 270
ROMAC AND ASSOCIATES OF CHICAGO, INC., 289
SALEM TECHNICAL SERVICES OF OAK BROOK, 270
SALES CONSULTANTS OF BARRINGTON HILLS, INC., 290
SALES CONSULTANTS OF CHICAGO (DOWNTOWN), 290
SALES CONSULTANTS OF CHICAGO (SOUTHWEST), 290
SALES CONSULTANTS OF FOX VALLEY, 291
SALES CONSULTANTS OF LINCOLNSHIRE, 291
SALES CONSULTANTS OF OAK BROOK, 292

SALES CONSULTANTS OF SCHAUMBURG, 292
SAMUELSON ASSOCIATES, 292
SEARCH DYNAMICS INC., 271
SELECTABILITY PERSONNEL, 271
SEVILLE TEMPORARY SERVICES, 271
SHEETS EMPLOYMENT SERVICE, INC., 271
SNELLING AND SNELLING OF DES PLAINES, 272
SNELLING AND SNELLING OF ROLLING MEADOWS, 272
SRS DATA SEARCH, 293
STAFF BUILDERS INC. OF ILLINOIS, 272
STIVERS TEMPORARY PERSONNEL, INC., 272
STONE ENTERPRISES, LTD, 273
SYNERGISTICS ASSOCIATES, 293
SYSTEMS RESEARCH INC., 273
T-A-DAVIS & ASSOCIATES, INC., 293
TALENT TREE OF ILLINOIS, 273
TALMAN & ASSOCIATES, 290
TEMP FORCE OF ILLINOIS, 274
TEMPSTATT, INC., 275
TRI-ASSOCIATES, INC., 275
VICTOR INTERIM, 275
VICTOR INTERIM SERVICES OF EVANSTON, 275
VICTOR INTERIM SERVICES OF OAK BROOK, 276
VICTOR PERSONNEL STAFFING, 276
WESTCOTT ASSOCIATES INC., 293
WIELAND & ASSOCIATES, 294
WORD PROCESSORS PERSONNEL SERVICE, 276
WORKING WORLD TEMPORARY PERSONNEL, 277

INDEX TO ASSOCIATIONS

ADAPSO/THE COMPUTER SOFTWARE AND SERVICES, 307
AIR LINE EMPLOYEES ASSOCIATION, 329
AIR TRANSPORT ASSOCIATION OF AMERICA, 330
AIR TRANSPORT ASSOCIATION OF CHICAGO, 329
ALLIANCE OF AMERICAN INSURERS, 319
AMERICAN ACADEMY OF PHYSICIAN ASSISTANTS, 317
AMERICAN ADVERTISING FEDERATION, 298
AMERICAN APPAREL MANUFACTURERS ASSOCIATION, 299
AMERICAN ASSOC. OF ZOOLOGICAL PARKS & AQUARIUMS, 300
AMERICAN ASSOCIATION OF ADVERTISING AGENCIES, 299
AMERICAN ASSOCIATION OF CEREAL CHEMISTS, 315
AMERICAN ASSOCIATION OF PETROLEUM GEOLOGISTS, 325
AMERICAN ASSOCIATION OF SCHOOL ADMINISTRATORS, 306
AMERICAN BANKERS ASSOCIATION, 301
AMERICAN BAR ASSOCIATION, 320
AMERICAN BOOKSELLERS ASSOCIATION, 302
AMERICAN CASTE METALS ASSOCIATION, 312
AMERICAN CHEMICAL SOCIETY, 305
AMERICAN COLLEGE OF HEALTHCARE EXECUTIVES, 316
AMERICAN COUNCIL OF LIFE INSURANCE, 320
AMERICAN DENTAL ASSOCIATION, 316
AMERICAN ELECTROPLATERS & SURFACE FINISHERS, 308
AMERICAN ELECTROPLATERS AND SURFACE, 308
AMERICAN FEDERATION OF MUSICIANS, 300
AMERICAN FEDERATION OF MUSICIANS/CHICAGO, 300
AMERICAN FEDERATION OF SMALL BUSINESS, 321
AMERICAN FEDERATION OF TELEVISION & RADIO ARTISTS, 300
AMERICAN FINANCIAL SERVICES ASSOCIATION, 314
AMERICAN GAS ASSOCIATION, 325
AMERICAN GEOLOGICAL INSTITUTE, 325
AMERICAN HEALTH CARE ASSOCIATION, 317
AMERICAN HOTEL AND MOTEL ASSOCIATION, 319
AMERICAN INSTITUTE OF AERONAUTICS & ASTRONAUTICS, 330
AMERICAN INSTITUTE OF ARCHITECTS, 310
AMERICAN INSTITUTE OF CHEMICAL ENGINEERING, 305
AMERICAN INSTITUTE OF CHEM. ENGINEERING/CHICAGO, 305
AMERICAN INSTITUTE OF CHEMISTS, 305
AMERICAN INSTITUTE OF CHEMISTS/CHICAGO, 305
AMERICAN INSTITUTE OF MINING,, 325
AMERICAN INSURANCE ASSOCIATION, 320
AMERICAN MARKETING ASSOCIATION, 298
AMERICAN MEDICAL ASSOCIATION, 317
AMERICAN NEWSPAPER PUBLISHERS ASSOCIATION, 323
AMERICAN NUCLEAR SOCIETY, 325

AMERICAN OCCUPATIONAL THERAPY ASSOCIATION, 318
AMERICAN PAPER INSTITUTE, 324
AMERICAN PETROLEUM INSTITUTE, 326
AMERICAN PHARMACEUTICAL ASSOCIATION, 318
AMERICAN PHYSICAL THERAPY ASSOCIATION, 318
AMERICAN POWDER METALLURGY INSTITUTE, 312
AMERICAN SOCIETY FOR BIOCHEMISTRY, 318
AMERICAN SOCIETY FOR ENGINEERING EDUCATION, 311
AMERICAN SOCIETY OF AGRICULTURAL ENGINEERS, 315
AMERICAN SOCIETY OF APPRAISERS, 314
AMERICAN SOCIETY OF APPRAISERS/CHICAGO, 313
AMERICAN SOCIETY OF BREWING CHEMISTS, 316
AMERICAN SOCIETY OF CIVIL ENGINEERS, 311
AMERICAN SOCIETY OF HEATING, REFRIGERATING, 311
AMERICAN SOCIETY OF HEATING, REFRIGERATING AND, 310
AMERICAN SOCIETY OF HOSPITAL PHARMACISTS, 318
AMERICAN SOCIETY OF LANDSCAPE ARCHITECTS, 310
AMERICAN SOCIETY OF NAVAL ENGINEERS, 311
AMERICAN SOCIETY OF NEWSPAPER EDITORS, 323
AMERICAN SOCIETY OF PLUMBING ENGINEERS, 311
AMERICAN SOCIETY OF SAFETY ENGINEERS, 310
AMERICAN TEXTILE MANUFACTURERS INSTITUTE, 299
AMERICAN TRUCKING ASSOCIATION, 330
AMERICAN VETERINARY MEDICAL ASSOCIATION, 317
AMERICAN WATER WORKS ASSOCIATION, 332
AMERICAN WATER WORKS FOUNDATION/CHICAGO, 331
APARTMENT OWNERS AND MANAGERS ASSOCIATION, 327
ASSOCIATION FOR COMPUTER SCIENCE, 307
ASSOCIATION FOR COMPUTING MACHINERY, 307
ASSOCIATION OF AMERICAN PUBLISHERS, 302
ASSOCIATION OF AMERICAN RAILROADS, 330
ASSOCIATION OF AMERICAN RAILROADS/CHICAGO, 329
ASSOCIATION OF AMERICAN UNIVERSITIES, 306
ASSOCIATION OF GRAPHIC ARTS, 326
ASSOCIATION OF IRON AND STEEL ENGINEERS, 312
ASSOCIATION OF MANAGEMENT CONSULTING FIRMS, 314
ASSOCIATION OF STATE & INTERSTATE, 305
AUTOMOTIVE SERVICE ASSOCIATION, 330
AUTOMOTIVE SERVICE ASSOCIATION/CHICAGO, 329
AUTOMOTIVE SERVICE INDUSTRY ASSOCIATION, 329
AVIATION MAINTENANCE FOUNDATION, 330
BANK ADMINISTRATION INSTITUTE, 301, 302
BINDING INDUSTRIES OF AMERICA, 326
BROADCAST EDUCATION ASSOCIATION, 303
BUILDING OFFICIALS AND CODE, 307
BUILDING OWNERS AND MANAGERS ASSOCIATION, 328
BUILDING OWNERS AND MANAGERS ASSOCIATION, 327
BUSINESS-PROFESSIONAL ADVERTISING ASSOCIATION, 299

CABLE TELEVISION ASSOCIATION, 303
CARDIOVASCULAR CREDENTIALING INTERNATIONAL, 318
CHICAGO ASSOCIATION OF BUSINESS ECONOMISTS, 313
CHICAGO ASSOCIATION OF CREDIT MANAGEMENT, 313
CHICAGO PHYSICAL THERAPY ASSOCIATION, 317
CLEAN ENERGY RESEARCH INSTITUTE, 326
COMMUNICATIONS WORKERS OF AMERICA, 306
COMMUNICATIONS WORKERS OF AMERICA/CHICAGO, 306
COMMUNITY BANKERS ASSOCIATION OF ILLINOIS, 301
CONSTRUCTION INDUSTRY MANUFACT. ASSOCIATION, 308
COUNCIL OF CONSULTANT ORGANIZATIONS, 314
COUNCIL ON HOTEL, RESTAURANT, 319
DAIRY AND FOOD INDUSTRIES SUPPLY ASSOCIATION, 316
DOW JONES NEWSPAPER FUND, 323
EDP AUDITORS ASSOCIATION, 297
EDUCATION FOUNDATION OF, 319
ELECTROCHEMICAL SOCIETY, 309
ELECTRONIC INDUSTRIES ASSOCIATION, 309
ELECTRONICS TECHNICIANS ASSOCIATION, 309
FEDERAL BAR ASSOCIATION, 321
FEDERAL BAR ASSOCIATION/CHICAGO CHAPTER, 320
FEDERAL COMMUNICATIONS COMMISSION, 303
FEDERATION OF TAX ADMINISTRATORS, 314
FINANCIAL ANALYSTS FEDERATION, 314
FINANCIAL ANALYSTS FEDERATION/CHICAGO, 313
FINANCIAL EXECUTIVES INSTITUTE, 314
FINANCIAL EXECUTIVES INSTITUTE/CHICAGO, 313
FINANCIAL RELATIONS BOARD INC., 298
GEOLOGICAL SOCIETY OF AMERICA, 326
HOME BUILDERS ASSOCIATION OF GREATER CHICAGO, 307
IEEE COMPUTER SOCIETY, 307
ILLINOIS ACADEMY OF PHYSICIAN ASSISTANTS, 317
ILLINOIS ASSOCIATION OF CEREAL CHEMISTS, 315
ILLINOIS BANKERS ASSOCIATION, 301
ILLINOIS CABLE TELEVISION ASSOCIATION, 303
ILLINOIS SOCIETY OF HOSPITAL PHARMACISTS, 317
ILLINOIS SOCIETY OF PROFESSIONAL ENGINEERS, 310
ILLINOIS TRUCKING ASSOCIATION, 329
ILLUMINATING ENGINEERING SOCIETY OF N. AMERICA, 311
INDEPENDENT ACCOUNTANTS ASSOCIATION OF ILLINOIS, 297
INDEPENDENT BANKERS ASSOCIATION OF AMERICA, 302
INSTITUTE OF ELECTRICAL AND ELECTRONICS, 308
INSTITUTE OF ELECTRICAL AND ELECTRONICS ENGINEERS, 309
INSTITUTE OF FINANCIAL EDUCATION, 301, 313
INSTITUTE OF INDUSTRIAL ENGINEERS, 311
INSTITUTE OF INDUSTRIAL ENGINEERS/CHICAGO, 310
INSTITUTE OF INTERNAL AUDITORS/CHICAGO CHAPTER, 298
INSTITUTE OF MANAGMENT CONSULTANTS, 313

INSTITUTE OF REAL ESTATE MANAGEMENT, 327
INSTITUTE OF TRANSPORTATION ENGINEERS, 330
INSURANCE INFORMATION INSTITUTE, 320
INSURANCE INFORMATION INSTITUTE OF CHICAGO, 319
INTERNATIONAL ASSOCIATION OF CORPORATE, 327
INT'L BROTHERHOOD OF ELECTRICAL WORKERS, 309
INTERNATIONAL CIRCULATION MANAGERS ASSOCIATION, 323
INTERNATIONAL CONFERENCE OF BUILDING OFFICIALS, 308
INTERNATIONAL RADIO AND TV SOCIETY, 303
INTERNATIONAL REAL ESTATE INSTITUTE, 328
INTERNATIONAL SOCIETY OF CERTIFIED, 309
MAGAZINE PUBLISHERS ASSOCIATION, 302
MARINE TECHNOLOGY SOCIETY, 330
MEDICAL GROUP MANAGEMENT ASSOCIATION, 318
MEDICAL GROUP MANAGEMENT ASSOCIATION, 317
MOTOR VEHICLE MANUFACTURERS ASSOCIATION, 331
NATIONAL ACADEMY OF ENGINEERING, 311
NATIONAL AERONAUTIC ASSOCIATION OF USA, 331
NATIONAL AGRICULTURAL CHEMICALS ASSOCIATION, 316
NATIONAL ASSOCIATION FOR LAW PLACEMENT, 321
NATIONAL ASSOCIATION OF BROADCASTERS, 304
NATIONAL ASSOCIATION OF BROADCASTERS/ILLINOIS, 303
NATIONAL ASSOCIATION OF BUSINESS, 304
NATIONAL ASSOCIATION OF CREDIT MANAGEMENT, 314
NATIONAL ASSOCIATION OF HOME BUILDERS, 308
NATIONAL ASSOCIATION OF LEGAL ASSISTANTS, 321
NATIONAL ASSOCIATION OF LIFE UNDERWRITERS, 320
NATIONAL ASSOCIATION OF MANUFACTURERS, 322
NATIONAL ASSOCIATION OF MANUFACTURERS, 322
NATIONAL ASSOCIATION OF METAL FINISHERS, 312
NATIONAL ASSOCIATION OF PRINTERS & LITHOGRAPHERS, 326
NATIONAL ASSOC. OF R.E. INVESTMENT TRUSTS, 315, 328
NATIONAL ASSOCIATION OF REALTORS, 327
NATIONAL ASSOCIATION OF SOCIAL WORKERS, 304
NATIONAL AUTOMOTIVE DEALERS ASSOCIATION, 331
NATIONAL COOPERATIVE BUSINESS ASSOCIATION, 321
NATIONAL COUNCIL OF SAVINGS INSTITUTIONS, 302
NATIONAL DAIRY COUNCIL, 315
NATIONAL ELECTRICAL MANUFACTURERS ASSOCIATION, 309
NATIONAL ELECTRONICS SALES & SERVICES ASSOCIATION, 309
NATIONAL ENDOWMENT FOR THE ARTS, 301
NATIONAL ENDOWMENT FOR THE ARTS/CHICAGO, 300
NATIONAL FEDERATION OF PARALEGAL ASSOCIATIONS, 320
NATIONAL HEALTH COUNCIL, 318
NATIONAL INSTITUTE FOR AUTOMOTIVE SERVICE, 331
NATIONAL MACHINE TOOL BUILDERS, 322
NATIONAL MARINE MANUFACTURERS ASSOCIATION, 329
NATIONAL MEDICAL ASSOCIATION, 318

NATIONAL NEWSPAPER ASSOCIATION, 324
NATIONAL PARALEGAL ASSOCIATION, 321
NATIONAL PRESS CLUB, 324
NATIONAL RECREATION & PARKS ASSOCIATION/CHICAGO, 300
NATIONAL RETAIL MERCHANTS ASSOCIATION, 316
NATIONAL SCREW MACHINE PRODUCTS ASSOCIATION, 323
NATIONAL SCREW MACHINE PRODUCTS ASSOCIATION, 322
NATIONAL SMALL BUSINESS UNITED, 322
NATIONAL SOCIETY OF PROFESSIONAL ENGINEERS, 311
NATIONAL SOCIETY OF PUBLIC ACCOUNTANTS, 298
NATIONAL TOOLING AND MACHINING ASSOCIATION, 323
NATIONAL TOOLING AND MACHINING ASSOCIATION, 322
NEWSPAPER GUILD, 324
NEWSPAPER GUILD/CHICAGO LOCAL, 323
NORTHERN TEXTILE ASSOCIATION, 299
PAPER INDUSTRY MANAGEMENT ASSOCIATION, 324
PRINTING INDUSTRIES OF AMERICA, 327
PROFESSIONAL AVIATION MAINTENANCE ASSOCIATION, 331
PUBLIC RELATIONS SOCIETY OF AMERICA, 299
SECURITIES INDUSTRY ASSOCIATION, 315
SEMICONDUCTOR INDUSTRY ASSOCIATION, 307
SHIPBUILDERS COUNCIL OF AMERICA, 331
SOCIETY OF ACTUARIES, 319
SOCIETY OF EXPLORATION GEOPHYSICISTS, 326
SOCIETY OF FIRE PROTECTION ENGINEERS, 312
SOCIETY OF FIRE PROTECTION ENGINEERS/CHICAGO, 310
SOCIETY OF PLASTIC ENGINEERS, 328
SOCIETY OF PLASTICS INDUSTRY, 328
SOCIETY OF PLASTICS INDUSTRY/DES PLAINES, 328
SOCIETY OF TRIBOLOGISTS, 325
TECHNICAL ASSOCIATION OF THE GRAPHIC ARTS, 327
TECHNICAL ASSOC. OF THE PULP & PAPER INDUSTRY, 324
TELEVISION BUREAU OF ADVERTISING, 299, 304
TELEVISION BUREAU OF ADVERTISING/CHICAGO, 298, 303
TEXTILE RESEARCH INSTITUTE, 300
THEATRE COMMUNICATIONS GROUP, 301
UNITED ENGINEERING TRUSTEES, 312
UNITED STATES TELEPHONE ASSOCIATION, 306
WATER POLLUTION CONTROL FEDERATION, 305
WOMEN IN RADIO AND TV, INC., 304
WRITERS GUILD OF AMERICA EAST, INC., 302
WRITERS GUILD OF AMERICA WEST, INC., 302

AVAILABLE AT YOUR LOCAL BOOKSTORE

Knock 'em Dead With Great Answers to Tough Interview Questions
Will you have the answers when the recruiter asks: Why do you want to work here? What can you do for us that someone else cannot? How much money do you want? Why do you want to change jobs? In Knock 'em Dead, Martin John Yate gives you not only the best answers to these and scores of more difficult questions, but also the best way to answer — so that you'll be able to field any tough question, and get the job and salary that you deserve. Don't leave your success to chance! Get Martin John Yate's best-seller book, Knock 'em Dead with Great Answers to Tough Interview Questions, 4th edition, 6x9 inches, 204 pages, paperback, just published, $6.95.

Hiring The Best
Contrary to popular belief, not all managers are mystically endowed with the ability to hire the right people. Interviewing is a skill that must be developed, and Martin Yate shows just how to identify the person who provides the best "fit" for any given position. Includes sections on interviewing within the law and hiring clerical help, as well as prewritten interview outlines. 6 x 9 inches, 204 pages, paperback, $9.95.

ALSO OF INTEREST . . .
The Job Bank Series
There are now 18 *Job Bank* books, each providing extensive, up-to-date employment information on hundreds of the largest employers in each job market. Information includes contact person, address to send resumes to, phone number and company description. Most listings include common professional positions, educational backgrounds sought and even fringe benefits offered. Recommended as an excellent place to begin your job search by *The New York Times, The Los Angeles Times, The Boston Globe, The Chicago Tribune,* and may other publications, *Job Bank* books have been used by hundreds of thousands of people to find jobs.

Books available: *The Atlanta Job Bank —The Boston Job Bank —The Chicago Job Bank —The Dallas Job Bank —The Denver Job Bank —The Detroit Job Bank —The Florida Job Bank — The Houston Job Bank — The Los Angeles Job Bank — The Minneapolis Job Bank —The New York Job Bank —The Ohio Job Bank — The Philadelphia Job Bank —The Phoenix Job Bank — The St. Louis Job Bank —The San Francisco Job Bank —The Seattle Job Bank —The Washington DC Job Bank.* Each book is 6 x 9 inches, over 250 pages, paperback, $12.95.

If you cannot find a book at your local bookstore, you may order it directly from the publisher. Please send payment including $2.75 for shipping and handling (for the entire order) to: Bob Adams, Inc., 260 Center Street, Holbrook, MA 02343. Credit card holders may call 1-800-USA-JOBS (in Massachusetts 617-767-8100). Please first check at your local bookstore.